GUIDE TO WESTERN ARCHITECTURE

FLORENCE: THE CRADLE OF THE RENAISSANCE

S. Maria del Fiore, 1296–1462, designed by Arnolfo di Cambio, with the Campanile, 1334–1387, designed by Giotto. The dome of the cathedral was added by Brunelleschi, 1420–1437, and crowned by the lantern in 1462. (*Photograph by Richard C. Grierson.*)

GUIDE TO WESTERN ARCHITECTURE

FLORENCE: THE CRADLE OF THE RENAISSANCE

S. Maria del Fiore, 1296–1462, designed by Arnolfo di Cambio, with the Campanile, 1334–1387, designed by Giotto. The dome of the cathedral was added by Brunelleschi, 1420–1437, and crowned by the lantern in 1462. (*Photograph by Richard C. Grierson.*)

GUIDE TO
WESTERN ARCHITECTURE

BY

JOHN GLOAG

With more than 400 illustrations
of which 161 were drawn by

HILTON WRIGHT

A.R.I.B.A.

GROVE PRESS INC.   NEW YORK

This edition is published by arrangement with THE MACMILLAN CO., NEW YORK. The original edition was published by GEORGE ALLEN & UNWIN LTD., LONDON, 1958.

Grove Press Books and Evergreen Books are published by Barney Rosset at Grove Press Inc. 795 Broadway   New York 3, N. Y.

Dedicated to
HUBERT DE CRONIN HASTINGS

CONTENTS

ILLUSTRATIONS IN THE TEXT

LIST OF PLATES

Florence: the cradle of the Renaissance   *Frontispiece*

The Plates

The Plates

ACKNOWLEDGMENTS

I should like to thank both Mr. Christian Barman and Mr. Hilton Wright for reading the typescript of this book, and I must acknowledge my debt to the late Professor Lionel Budden for his advice and encouragement when I was planning and writing it. I am grateful for the help I have received from the Librarian of the Royal Institute of British Architects, and to Dora Ware for her work on Appendix II, and for making the Index.

Of the illustrations in the text, 161 were drawn by Mr. Hilton Wright, and the maps and many of the diagrams were drawn by Miss Marcelle Barton. The names of the artists, and the sources of illustrations (other than those drawn by Mr. Hilton Wright) are acknowledged in the captions. I am indebted to Mr. Roy M. Hyslop for letting me reproduce the illustrations on pages 328–331 from his copy of *A Balloon View of London*.

J. G.

April
1957.

REFERENCES

References to authorities, sources of quotations and so forth, are numbered consecutively from 1 to 217, and are listed at the end of Section X, beginning on page 347.

I

THE UNWRITTEN RECORD

HISTORY comes alive in architecture. It has been well named "The Mistress Art," for it creates the opportunity for the other visual arts to flourish. It is also a veracious record of the ways and beliefs of all manner of men, of their habits, tastes and circumstances of life, and of the racial aspirations and abilities—artistic, military, or commercial—of whole peoples. It reveals more fully than other arts the degree of skill attained by a civilisation, and, by the nature of its ruins, marks the varied fortunes of a nation, the quality of its government and rulers, and the wisdom or ignorance of its conquerors. Music, poetry, and dramatic art may in a benign climate be independent of architecture, but they are sustained and encouraged by larger audiences when shelter transcends the cave and the hut.

The study and occasionally the writing of history have been inspired by the contemplation of buildings. Gibbon conceived the idea of writing *The Decline and Fall of the Roman Empire* amid the ruins of the Capitol at Rome. Buildings, whether in ruins or in use, give an account of social, religious and economic history. They reveal progressive or retrogressive phases of a nation's life, and are marked by the influences that elevate or degrade national character: thus the study of Western architecture becomes a study of visible history, disclosing a comprehensive three-dimensional view of Western civilisation, but with buildings to read instead of words.

A practical builder, a mason or a joiner, a man who habitually thinks with his hands and has the craftsman's intuitive appreciation of good work and the why and wherefore of its execution, is able to read far more *from* an actual building than a tourist could read *about* it in a guide-book: the building speaks intimately to the builder: to the layman it often remains a mute, impassive monument. This need not be so, for it is not necessary to be apprenticed to the building trade in order to interpret the language of architecture. Any observant person can do so in time; but the significance of architecture cannot be learnt or understood properly from words and pictures alone; it must be supplemented and expanded by the constant study of buildings, anywhere and everywhere. The Law Courts in London can tell you as much about the pretentious blindness of mid-nineteenth century taste, and the warped, earnest piety of the Gothic revival, as, say, the glazed roundels in the arched windows of the little Byzantine church at Daphni on the Sacred Way from Athens to Eleusis can tell you about the transition of the Christian Church from a dark, mysterious cave, to what it ultimately became in the fifteenth century, a framework of stone enclosing great expanses of coloured glass, which flooded the interior with tinted light. The English Victorian example tells a story of uninspired imitation; the Greek, of living and growing architectural genius. Even as a ruin, the Law Courts would reveal the cultural flabbiness of a period when architects, blind to the possibilities of their own age with its industrial techniques and materials, resorted to copying the external characteristics of mediaeval building.

The Convent at Daphni was built late in the ninth century A.D., on the site of a temple of Apollo, which dates from the fourth or fifth century B.C. The church incorporates some of the material from the older building. It is a particularly interesting Byzantine structure, and the triple arched narrow windows, with a central arch rising above the level of the others, are filled with thin marble slabs, pierced with circular holes which are glazed. This is a very simple form of plate tracery—decorative without and dazzling within. The church has a shallow dome, and inside are the remains of mosaics, which were partly destroyed by the Turks, who, after the fall of Constantinople in 1453, gradually penetrated Greece, reaching Daphni two years later. The Moslem soldiery amused themselves by shooting arrows at the saints and other holy figures and succeeded in doing almost as much damage as some modern temporary soldiers do when they are billeted in a country mansion. Destruction by carelessness is preferable to deliberate destruction, encouraged by religious zeal. The Moslems defaced most of the mosaics in this church in the name of the Prophet; some centuries earlier the Christians had destroyed a building of classical beauty in the name of Christ, for they pulled down the temple of Apollo and replaced it with a church. There are a few traces of the temple; part of a great Ionic column is built into the north wall, the delicate volutes of its capital suggesting the elegant splendour of the original building. The materials were broken up and used for the church.

The way buildings are adapted and their materials re-used may disclose the needs imposed by some religious faith which has supplanted an older belief, or show how an orderly civilisation has broken down and been replaced by small, aggressive, independent states, which, beginning as brigand bands, developed into stable military tyrannies. In our own day the adaptation of buildings often illustrates the changing demands of industrial techniques.

The triple-arched window at the Convent of Daphni, ninth century A.D. These narrow windows are filled with thin marble slabs, pierced with circular holes, which are glazed—a very simple form of plate tracery. See example of mediaeval plate tracery on page 19.

3

In Ankara, the modern capital of Turkey, architecture records the transition from the Roman city of Ancyra, which was the capital of the province of Galatia, to the isolated mediaeval town of Angora, that sank almost to the level of a large village, and rose finally to be the capital of a modernised state. All the changes of religious beliefs and social customs which have occurred in over twenty centuries are shown by the buildings that survive. There is the temple of Augustus, a fine stone structure, roofless and in ruins, with storks nesting on the top of the high walls, and within the temple are the remains of a Byzantine church. The Christian builders did not demolish the pagan edifice. Perhaps it was too much trouble; perhaps it was too solidly built; or, as Ankara is scorchingly hot in summer, those high temple walls may have afforded irresistibly welcome shade.

The city itself is built on three hills and ringed by the sand-coloured mountains of Anatolia. To-day, Ankara is cooled by tree-lined boulevards, parks and gardens, and has more water flowing into it than even the Romans, those specialists in competent plumbing, secured for Ancyra, its forerunner. The water is supplied by the Çubuk dam, a few miles from the city; in the intervening country apricot orchards flourish, with vines and a few olives, and the dusty roads run between cypress hedges. The city is approached by dual carriageways, separated by a row of pines and bordered with acacias. Never before in its long and varied history has the place commanded such spacious planning and varied amenities. This new capital, largely the creation of Kemal Attaturk, is distinguished by many modern buildings, which owe something to the classical tradition and something to the modern movement in architectural design. But the old city is unmistakably Oriental, and apart from a few Roman remains, like the temple of Augustus, the huddled, casual conglomeration of buildings is characteristic of the architecture that so often grew up under Moslem rule.

A city such as Ankara may tell a comprehensive story of change and decay, neglect and revival, but it does not exhibit, like Rome, an array of adapted buildings, mutilated, or destructively enlarged or strengthened to suit religious or military needs. The Christians let the temple of Augustus fall into decay, appropriating part of its area for building their church, and the Ottoman Turks, ignoring both temple and church, built a mosque, Haci Bayram, beside the temple, without attempting to use its shell. Rome, when Edward Gibbon visited it, was full of examples of makeshift adaptation. He noted that "some of the noblest monuments which had braved the injuries of time were left in a desert, far remote from the habitations of mankind. The palaces of the senators were no longer adapted to the manners or fortunes of their indigent successors; the use of baths and porticos was forgotten; in the sixth century, the games of the theatre, amphitheatre, and circus, had been interrupted: some temples were devoted to the prevailing worship. . . . But if the forms of ancient architecture were disregarded by a people insensible of their use and beauty, the

The Convent of Daphni, built late in the ninth century A.D., on the site of a
temple of Apollo. This church incorporates some of the material from the older
building. See page 3 for a detailed drawing of one of the triple-arched windows,
and compare the design of the church with St. Saviour in the Chora, Constantinople, shown on page 97 and plate 12, and St. Luke of Stiris, near Delphi, on
the same plate.

plentiful materials were applied to every call of necessity or superstition; till the fairest columns of the Ionic and Corinthian orders, the richest marbles of Paros and Numidia, were degraded, perhaps, to the support of a convent or a stable. The daily havoc which is perpetrated by the Turks in the cities of Greece and Asia, may afford a melancholy example; and in the gradual destruction of the monuments of Rome, Sixtus the fifth may alone be excused for employing the stones of the Septizonium in the glorious edifice of St. Peter's. A fragment, a ruin, howsoever mangled or profaned, may be viewed with pleasure and regret; but the greater part of the marble was deprived of substance, as well as of place and proportion; it was burnt to lime for the purpose of cement."[1]

For the "mischievous purpose" of civil war and military necessity, "the remains of antiquity were most readily adapted: the temples and arches afforded a broad and solid basis for the new structures of brick and stone; and we can name the modern turrets that were raised on the triumphal monuments of Julius Caesar, Titus, and the Antonines. With some slight alterations, a theatre, an amphitheatre, a mausoleum, was transformed into a strong and spacious citadel. I need not repeat, that the mole of Adrian has assumed the title and form of the castle of St. Angelo; the Septizonium of Severus was capable of standing against a royal army; the sepulchre of Metella has sunk under its outworks; the theatres of Pompey and Marcellus were occupied by the Savelli and Ursini families; and the rough fortress had been gradually softened to the splendour and elegance of an Italian palace. Even the churches were encompassed with arms and bulwarks, and the military engines on the roof of St. Peter's were the terror of the Vatican and the scandal of the Christian world. Whatever is fortified will be attacked; and whatever is attacked may be destroyed."[2]

The penetrating wisdom of that last sentence is abundantly and regrettably demonstrated by ruins all over the former provinces of the Roman Empire, from the far western cities of Viroconium (Wroxeter) and Calleva Atrebatum (Silchester) in England to Palmyra on the eastern extremities of Syria. Gibbon referred to the havoc "perpetrated by the Turks in the cities of Greece and Asia," and the history of the Parthenon at Athens is a record of destruction deliberately carried out in the name of religion or casually ordained by military necessity. In the fifth century A.D., the temple was despoiled and turned into a Christian church, and a thousand years later when Greece was occupied by the Turks after the fall of Constantinople, all evidence of Christian worship was removed, and it became a mosque. Finally, it was used as a powder magazine, when the Venetians were besieging Athens in 1687, and was blown up as a result of a new technique of plunging fire invented by a German artillery officer.

Priests and soldiers, for entirely different and equally bad reasons, have been consistent pioneers of destruction—neglect following depopulation and desertion

Remains of one of the public buildings of the Romano–British city of Viroconium, near Wroxeter by the Severn, in Shropshire. Courses of tiles are used between six or more of the brick courses, and this technique is similar to that used on the city walls of Roman London. (See page 10, also compare with example of Roman masonry on plate 6.) From Corbet Anderson's *Roman City of Uriconium*, published in 1867. The site of Viroconium has since been carefully excavated, but until the nineteenth century, this mass of pink-tinted masonry was the chief indication of the city that lay buried below the surrounding fields.

has done far less to denude Europe, Asia Minor and North Africa of architectural treasures than the combined effect of forcible conversions, crusades, and wars of defence or aggression. Sometimes the religious fanatic and the warrior were one and the same person, and then the results were disastrous indeed. In the early eighth century, when the Arabs poured over the whole of North Africa and up through Spain to the plains of France, they converted not only lukewarm Christians to the new faith of Islam, but they converted buildings too, and their early architectural misdemeanours occurred all over the North African littoral. Lisle March Phillipps, in one of his early books, *In the Desert*, pointed out that an Arab building was a "signally graphic presentment of Arab life and history." He particularises as follows: "Look at this masonry, with its blocks of stone, probably filched from some earlier classic building, and fitted hastily and feebly together with wide joints of inferior mortar. Look at these irregular, nodding arcades, with their air of insecurity, their lack of symmetry and precision. Note the eccentric forms of arch used, the horseshoe, the stilted, the ogive, the foliated. Commonly enough the arch-ribs, intersecting at the apex, expand, then meet, then expand again, and so go wobbling up the wall with something of the fluctuating motion of tongues of flame. Naturally most of these buildings are falling into decay. They were not built to endure. The columns are generally old fragments stuck together. The Roman capitals, of all shapes and sizes, are often put on upside-down and heightened, where necessary, by rude fragments of stone, or even by billets of wood. Even where some care was taken and more regard for symmetry observed, the fantastical nature of the forms employed was an element of inherent weakness. Simplicity is the essential of strength, an essential in which the whimsical structures of the Arabs were wholly wanting."[3]

A little earlier the author had said: "The interpretative quality in architecture is its main fascination. There is no form of art which so faithfully portrays the character of its creators as this does." Possibly that reflection prompted him to admit that the value of Arab architecture lay in its very obvious drawbacks. "As architecture it is indeed worthless," he wrote. It was its significance as a record that mattered, for "as a human document it is among the most interesting, and it is in its very deficiencies that its interest is embodied. All this furious speed and zeal, this straw-fire energy and whimsical extravagance, are a humorously exact personification of the very qualities we meet in Arab history. They have the Arab expression. They have his look and way. In them the evolution of Arab civilisation, a civilisation defying the ordinary constructive rules, fanciful and feeble, is reproduced to the life. The heat, the haste, the luxuriant imagination, the lack of all common sense and sound judgment, are all there. Neither civilisation nor architecture was made to cope with time. The fatal instability that is the root of Arab character possessed them."[4]

If the Moslem army had not been defeated by Charles Martel in 732, at Moussais-la-Bataille, between Tours and Poitiers, the ethical, social, and architectural history of Europe would have been wholly different, though not inevitably Arabian in character. Sir Mark Sykes, in *The Caliph's Last Heritage*, reminds us that "In Spain the followers of the Prophet had swept beyond the Pyrenees; but as the Arabian leaven in their hosts wore thin and weak they lost that strange power of assimilating the people whose lands they over-ran, degenerating from colonists of Morocco to the conquerors of Spain, from conquerors to the marauders of France, and as marauders breaking before the hosts of Charles Martel, retiring into the Iberian Peninsula never to emerge again save as enemies or freebooters."[5] In Spain the Western Caliphate was established; the Moslem power was consolidated, and a new, luxuriant civilisation arose which became a great light of learning and culture during one of the darkest periods of European history. The influence and achievements of Arab civilisation in Spain are either neglected or minimised by European historians, possibly because they are conscious or unconscious partisans and express a conventional Christian point of view about the works of the infidel— but the influence of the so-called infidel civilisation is still apparent. The architecture of Spain has, to this day, perceptible Oriental affinities although the last Moslem state, Granada, was conquered by the Christians as long ago as 1492, and the Moriscoes were finally expelled in 1610. Comparatively few buildings survive from the days of the Western Caliphate: the great mosque at Cordova, the Alcazar and the Giralda at Seville, and, magnificently proclaiming its dedication to pleasure, the Alhambra at Granada. (See page 236 and plate 16.) They still stand, the architectural witnesses of the claim made by Sir William Flinders Petrie that "the fullest histories, the strongest literature, the largest life, were all south of the Pyrenees throughout the Dark Ages."[6] Had no other records remained, such structures would have suggested the existence of a civilisation with cultural and artistic traditions of a high order.

Almost any building, whether it is ruinous or well preserved, or has been adapted or enlarged to suit some use other than that for which it was originally designed, has an individual story to tell, which may be related by its plan, structure, and the way its materials have been selected and used. No building is altogether inarticulate. Materials alone are a persistent reminder of the past, and if we trace back the ancestry of nearly any technique of building, we are confronted with historical events and associations, long forgotten, obscured by the passage of centuries, but momentarily recovered by our observation of the method used for building a wall, piercing a window, or supporting a roof. We obtain a glimpse of a far-away period, remote but clear, like a view seen through the wrong end of binoculars. For instance, in England every brick wall built in the mid-twentieth century is linked with a time when the country was governed by accomplished and highly efficient Italians. If we start enquiring into this most ordinary affair of bricks and mortar, we find ourselves travelling back eighteen centuries, for the technique of laying bricks and tiles and blocks of stone in mortar has been practised by builders, with few interruptions, since the Romans introduced cement. Those alien technicians and soldiers and administrators made their exile tolerable by teaching the natives a little about the refinements of life and a lot about the building crafts, for when they annexed Britain and made it a province of the Roman Empire, the only permanent buildings in the country were a few primitive temples, groups of trilithons, constructed from rudely dressed blocks of stone—two uprights supporting a cross-piece, like an empty doorway—arranged in circles, and a few dome-shaped huts built of loose stones, like the walls that separate the fields in Yorkshire, Derbyshire and the Cotswolds. This form of dry construction, as it is called, was still in a crude stage in Britain: elsewhere in Europe and the ancient world it had been developed and perfected, and six centuries before Britain became a Roman province the walls of Greek temples were built of blocks of marble, so finely jointed that in course of time those joints often grew together and the wall became a solid mass. The Romans made their walls into a solid mass as they built them. Instead of leaving blocks of stone or courses of bricks to be kept in place by their own weight, they bedded them in mortar; and in the iron grip of Roman cement those walls endured for centuries. All that those efficient Roman rulers of Britain left to posterity were roads and "remains." Many of their roads are still in use; while everywhere in England there are Roman "remains," recalling the almost forgotten period of history

The wall of Roman London at Trinity Place, from a drawing by F. W. Fairholt, made in
1852, and reproduced from Roach Smith's *Illustrations of Roman London* (1859). The Roman
work survives for several courses, and consists, above the plinth, of four courses of squared
rag-stone, a triple bonding of thin bricks, the courses diminishing above that until the
Roman masonry merges with mediaeval work. (See page 12, and plate 6.)

when, for nearly four hundred years, British towns were miniatures of the opulent cities that basked in sunlight round the shores of the Mediterranean.

Londinium, as London was then called, was once described by Lethaby as "a little Rome in the West"[7]; in Herefordshire there was "a third century Birmingham," a big industrial centre, devoted to ironfounding, which now lies beneath some fields south-west of the village of Brownsash near Ross-on-Wye; while up and down the country were great estates with luxurious, centrally heated villa houses, and cities with public baths and temples and amphitheatres: all built with masterly skill, and largely by the use of bricks, laid in courses with very wide joints and bound into an age-defying mass by Roman cement. Within a century of the final collapse of Roman rule in Britain, when the country was being parcelled out into petty kingdoms by the barbarians that overran it, those cities and fine country houses were almost all deserted; and just over two hundred years later, early in the eighth century, a learned and pious man writing history in a monastery at Jarrow recorded, as Gildas had before him in the sixth century, that "the island was formerly embellished with twenty-eight noble cities, besides innumerable castles, all strongly secured with walls, towers, gates, and locks." (See page 122.) This monk, whom we know as the Venerable Bede, lived in a land of mournful ruins, and although the building arts were slowly reviving, those who practised them were incapable of achieving anything comparable with the Roman work that still remained above ground—huge masses of masonry that were regarded with superstitious dread by countrymen and with envy by builders. Barely affected by the weather, those roofless ruins slowly disintegrated as, generation after generation, their materials were used for building churches and monasteries and castles. The only Roman work that continued to serve its original purpose was the city wall, for a wall was a condition of survival for any city in the Dark Ages. Even so, cities were sacked and rebuilt and London, although it retained its Roman walls, did not escape occasional disasters. (The city has had eleven great fires since it was first burnt down by Boadicea in A.D. 61, the second occurring in 961, and eight between that year and 1264: the last two were in 1666 and 1940.)

Some of the deserted Romano-British cities stood for a long time. Four and a half centuries after Bede wrote his history, another scholarly churchman, Gerald de Barri, described the ruins of Caerleon-on-Usk in Monmouthshire, which, he said, was "handsomely built of masonry, with courses of bricks, by the Romans." He wrote of "immense palaces, formerly ornamented with gilded roofs," also "a tower of prodigious size, remarkable hot baths, relics of temples, and theatres, all inclosed within fine walls, parts of which remain standing." There were other ruins: Calleva, at Silchester in north Hampshire, still retains its walls, which encircle the ploughed land where that small town stood, and the earliest known Christian church in Britain was built. In some fields near the Severn, close to the little village of Wroxeter in Shropshire, a wall of pink-tinted masonry is all that is left of one of the public buildings of

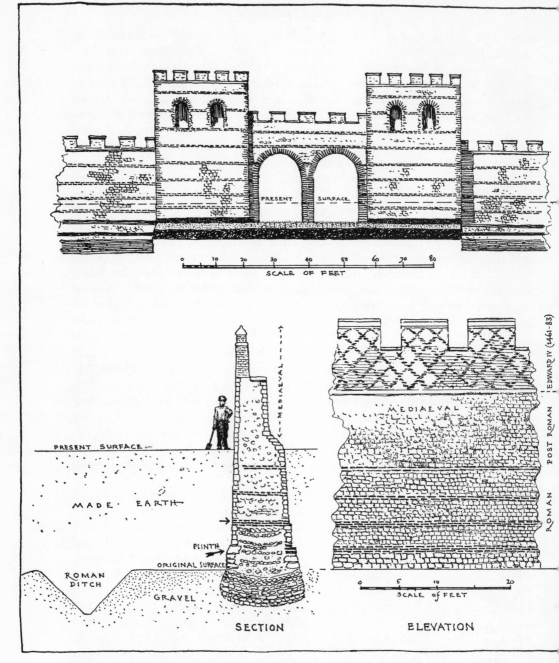

The town wall of Roman London. This shows the method of construction to the average height of 15 feet. Compare this with the drawing of London Wall at Trinity Place, on page 10. The illustration at the top suggests the probable appearance of Roman Newgate, based on the dimensions and level of its foundations. This type of double gateway, flanked by towers, was common to cities all over the Roman Empire. From a drawing by Mr. Gordon Home, F.S.A.(Scot.), and reproduced from the 1948 edition of his book, *Roman London*, with his permission and by courtesy of the publishers, Eyre & Spottiswoode.

The Roman gateway at Lincoln. (From *An Introduction to the Study of Gothic Architecture*, by J. H. Parker.) The quality of the masonry used in a remote province of the Empire, like Britain, would be far inferior to that in buildings like the temples and triumphal arches of Italy. Compare this Romano–British example with the section of wall of the temple of Augustus at Ancyra (Ankara) in the province of Galatia, shown on the lower part of plate 6. The Lincoln gateway is faced with large stones, without the layers of tiles that were often laid in horizontal bands at regular intervals. (See page 10.)

the Roman city of Viroconium: a similar mass of masonry stands in front of the Norman church of St. Nicholas at Leicester, a ruin that has been known for centuries as the Jewry Wall, but is really a part of the old Roman basilica. The pink hue of so many of these fragments of Roman building is imparted to the masonry by the cement, which was made from clean, coarse gravel, finely divided lime, and pounded tiles. The Romans did not invent this mixture; the use of crushed pottery in cement was known in Crete, fourteen centuries before Christ; but Roman builders used it for their best work, and often made the proportion of crushed tiles so great that the mortar became red.

To the Saxon and early Norman builders, the way the Romans built and the materials they used were lost, almost magical arts. For a long time brick-making was certainly a lost art, though the use of baked bricks continued during the Middle Ages. At first bricks were taken from Roman ruins; but the formula for Roman cement eluded the mediaeval builders. In the thirteenth century Villard de Honnecourt gave this recipe: "Take lime and pounded pagan tile in equal quantities until its colour predominates; moisten this with oil and with it you can make a tank hold water."[8] Some of the mediaeval recipes for cement included wax, pitch, sulphur and eggs: this particular mixture was used for work in lining a well at Silverstone in 1279—pitch being the chief ingredient.[9]

Early examples of English brickwork, such as Little Wenham Hall in Suffolk, date from the thirteenth century; and in the following century the town of Hull was built largely of bricks that were made locally, for records of the corporation brickyards exist from 1303 onwards. The term brick, or "brike,"

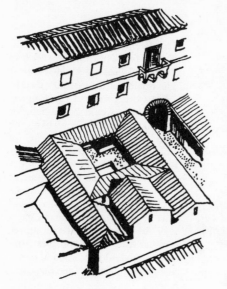

Conjectural reconstruction, by Hilton Wright, of a second century house at Ostia, built behind one of the earlier multi-storey blocks which lined the important streets. The house was approached through a porch penetrating the higher block. The ground plan only of the house remains.

does not seem to have been used earlier than the fifteenth century. Mediaeval bricks resembled tiles in shape, and were called *tegulae*, or wall tiles; and the bricklayer was a *tegulator*, or tiler. Although the contemporary brick-built house owes a lot to the technique developed two thousand years ago by the Romans, it owes far more to the English builders of the late fifteenth and early sixteenth centuries, who turned brickwork into a beautiful and decorative method of building. The Romans, always utilitarian, and sometimes rather grimly so, used cement to bind a wall of small units, individually of no great strength, into a weather-resisting and time-defying structure: and as their cement was the strongest part of the wall they used a large mortar joint. In England, builders decreased the size of the mortar joint as they improved the quality of their cement; so that from the early sixteenth century to the Victorian period, English brickwork exhibits a progressive neatness as well as a structural staunchness comparable with its Roman forerunner. The art of "pointing" or smoothing the cement joints between the bricks, the light colour of those joints and the variety of texture and tone of the bricks, made the walls of Tudor, Stuart and Georgian England vastly superior in appearance to any Roman brickwork. The Romans had used their cement and bricks and tiles as structural conveniences. They never appreciated the decorative quality or the fine finish of brickwork, and only in Ostia, the seaport of Rome, did they recognise, as English, Dutch and German builders recognised long after, that brick walls were decorative "in their own right." Sun-dried bricks in Greece and Italy had needed a rainproof covering, and were usually faced with plaster or marble; but even when baked bricks were introduced which required no such protection,

Roman builders persisted in hiding their superb brickwork behind a veneer of some other material.[10]

Brick walls in England had nothing to hide until, in the early nineteenth century, it became fashionable to plaster and paint wall surfaces. The English building craftsman's frank and sympathetic understanding of materials, whether he was working with wood, metal, stone, or brick, is revealed by the development and perfection of brickwork since the late fifteenth century. Cement was the senior partner in Roman masonry and brickwork: in England, as in Holland and Germany, it became the junior partner, at least on the surface. After the Middle Ages it ceased to be a mystery material, and it helped to encourage the development of fine domestic and civic architecture in Europe, particularly in Germany and the Low Countries and England.

This brief examination of the origins of such an ordinary thing as a brick wall has taken us a long way into the past—not so far as it could have taken us, for we have gone back only to the introduction of bricks and mortar into Britain in the first century A.D., and bricks were in use in the civilisations that existed in Asia Minor at least twenty centuries before the founding of Rome, and earlier still in Egypt. From almost any stretch of brick or stone walling we can learn if it was built in a spirit of uncompromising utility, inspired perhaps by fear, or whether the bleakness of utility was tempered by the human affection for ornament, or whether decorative effects seemed so important that they obliterated every other consideration, even structural soundness.

The walls of nearly all buildings are composed of voids and solids, with the latter usually predominating. The treatment of voids, of windows and doorways, discloses the fluctuating standards of security, prosperity, comfort, and health. In Knossos, in ancient Crete, there were spacious windows in the upper storeys of town houses; in Egyptian houses, two thousand five hundred years before Christ, windows were pierced in the first and second storeys of houses, and on the top floors light was admitted by openings formed by rows of small columns. In Crete and Egypt secure and settled civilisations were established; so the window passed from the peep-hole in a watch-tower to a generous aperture for admitting daylight; and in the Graeco-Roman world it transcended the utilitarian stage of development and became an artistic amenity: cultivated and wealthy people could enjoy a room with a view. Gardens, parks and groves, rivers, lakes and fountains, were more intimately related to the dwelling; and the distant scene, the prospect of mountains, forests, and the sea, was carefully considered when a house was planned. This literal interpretation of the point of view is exemplified in a sentence from Pliny's letter to Gallus, describing his Laurentine villa: "A little set back on the left is a roomy bedroom, then a smaller one, with one window to let in the dawn, another to hold the sunset; with a view too of the sea below—farther off, certainly, but safer."[11] This is quoted by Atkinson and Bagenal in their *Theory and Elements of Architecture*, and they make the significant comment that the "sentence is interesting as also illustrating in the last two words some of that early apprehension—a last breath of primeval terror of the elements which we have forgotten to-day but from which we were first emancipated by the great Greeks and Romans."(12)

In Western urban civilisation we have, it is true, forgotten those ancient fears, though they still linger in some parts of the countryside in Europe and Britain, their presence fitfully attested by the survival of rites and superstitions of pre-Christian origin; but we have been compensated for the loss of mystery and terror in nature by the military by-products of our scientific fecundity. Windows react to fear in terms of design more readily than any other feature in architecture. They were the first victims of air warfare, and reverted to the narrow slits of the Middle Ages in order to shield the inmates of buildings from splinters and bomb-blast, when they were not masked by heavy shutters or blocked up altogether. After the shrinking of the Graeco-Roman world, windows shrank too, and all over Western Europe the history of window design is at first the history of fear, reimposed by the barbarian conquests, then of the gradual emancipation from fear and insecurity, beginning in the towns and cities, cowering behind the walls that compressed their growth, till at last, as mediaeval civilisation grew splendidly out of the chaos and savagery of the Dark Ages, the buildings in the countryside were gradually released from the tyranny of fortification.

Windows are to our minds so closely associated with glass that we are apt to forget the long interval between the accomplished industrial organisations of the Western Roman Empire and the establishment of the craft industries of the Middle Ages. In many European countries, and in Britain, glass-making was a lost art, and the very name window emphasises this technical deficiency, for it is derived from the old Norse word *vindauga*, which means "wind-eye." In English houses it remained for several centuries the "wind-eye" or "wind-hole," its proportions being determined by the need for excluding weather and missiles. Until the fifteenth century the use of glass for domestic building was rare in England, and even then the panes were small, and irregularly transparent.

The ability to make large panes was denied alike to the Roman and mediaeval glass workers. Roman window-glass was developed very slowly, and even when its use was fairly common, it did not entirely displace mica, thin-ground alabaster and shells.(13) The persistence of this preference for translucent materials is understandable in the Mediterranean civilisation, where relief from the intense brightness of daylight is welcome; and in the sixteenth and seventeenth centuries Portuguese architects used mother-of-pearl instead of glass in the churches of Goa, "which suffused a soft yellowish under-sea light," a restful contrast with the glare of the Indian sky.(14) The largest size of Roman window-pane of which we have any record was only 3 feet 8 inches by 2 feet 8 inches, and that was used in the public baths at Pompeii.(15) Those made and used in a remote

The house of Loreius Tiburtinus, at Pompeii, seen from the garden. Only the ground floor exists, and this has been partly reconstructed with new timber beams to form the pergola, which is covered with vines. (The conjectural restoration of the first floor is by Hilton Wright.) Designed for the gracious use of leisure, such houses were built all over the Roman Empire. "Gardens, parks and groves, rivers, lakes and fountains, were . . . intimately related to the dwelling," so that "cultivated and wealthy people could enjoy a room with a view." (See page 15.)

province like Britain were much smaller, and an almost complete pane, 1 foot square, has been found and is preserved in Rochester Museum. This pane, according to Lethaby, had been cemented into its frame.[16] Romano-British window-glass was a clumsy material, seldom less than $\frac{1}{8}$ inch in thickness, and made in various shades of green, which sometimes deepened into bluish-green. Daylight passing through that translucent green or blue-tinted glass would have seemed cold and gloomy. The remains of Roman glassworks have been found in Lancashire, at Wilderspool, near Warrington, a short distance from the great glass manufacturing industry that has grown up at St. Helens since the late eighteenth century. The glazing technique used by Romano-British builders is difficult to reconstruct, but they certainly used putty, and traces of cement have been found not only on the Rochester pane but on window-glass excavated at Silchester. It seems likely that a wooden framework was used, with glazing bars grooved to receive the panes. The appearance of the windows can only be guessed at, but they were probably rather small.

During Britain's four centuries as a Roman province, building practice was static, as indeed it was all over the Roman Empire. This petrification of technique applied not only to building but to the manufacture and design of armour, weapons, vehicles, and ships—progress was arrested by standardisation and discouraged by bureaucracy. In Britain buildings changed only when skilled labour became scarce and craftsmanship declined, and during the fifth and sixth centuries architecture and the building crafts were in eclipse. As domestic building dropped to the primitive level of wattle-and-daub huts and wooden halls and watch-towers, the window degenerated to a mere hole for letting in daylight and letting out smoke, for the fireplace was not yet invented and Roman central heating was a thing of the past. The peaceful enjoyment of a room with a view was unknown to the white savages who ultimately overran Britain and founded England. By the seventh century, glass-making, like brick-making, had been forgotten in the island. Bede records that in A.D. 675, Benedict Biscop, Abbot of Wearmouth, sent to France "to fetch makers of glass (more properly artificers), who were at this time unknown in Britain, that they might glaze the windows of his church, with the cloisters and dining-rooms. This was done, and they came, and not only finished the work required, but taught the English nation their handicraft, which was well adapted for enclosing the lanterns of the church, and for the vessels required for various uses."

This reintroduction of glass as a rare foreign commodity did not affect domestic building. There is no evidence that the knowledge of glass manufacture, imparted by the French workers to the builders at Wearmouth, survived. Eighty-three years later, in 758, the Abbot of Jarrow wrote to the Bishop of Mainz asking him to send artisans who could manufacture glass for windows and vessels. Meanwhile the problem of window design was a simple one. A hole had to be filled with some substance that would admit light and keep out bad weather. In Saxon and Norman England windows were small apertures, set high in the wall, shielded by wooden shutters. In walled towns, where the need for protection was not so pressing, windows were larger than in the castles and fortified manor-houses of the countryside. Oiled linen, parchment and other fragile substances came into use. How they were fastened to the window is unknown; but they must have been constantly renewed. The technique of glazing probably began with the use of thin-ground panes of horn, framed in channelled strips of lead. The lead worker was responsible for glazing, and this association remains, for to-day plumbers are also glaziers.

When glass was again introduced to England, its rarity and fragility confined its use almost exclusively to the only buildings that were immune from the intermittent private warfare of nobles and the punitive expeditions of the Plantagenet kings. The great religious houses, the abbeys and priories, that began to adorn the country during the eleventh and twelfth centuries, may have had their small, round-headed windows glazed with material imported from France. Glass began to perform a function of immense significance in a sacred edifice. Lethaby reminds us that stained glass was used for the choir of Durham Cathedral by Bishop Pudsey, Hugh de Puiset (1125–1195) and also refers to the Guthlac roll in the British Museum, a twelfth century set of

Left: Plate tracery in a window of the Great Hall of Winchester Castle.

Right: Example of bar tracery with the stone members built up separately. (Reproduced from *Building for Daylight*, by Richard Sheppard and Hilton Wright.)

designs for stained-glass windows. "If technical designs for stained glass of a high quality like these were made in England," he wrote, "there must at the same time have been a school of glass workers here; and much of our thirteenth and fourteenth century glass is obviously not French."[17] The development of stained and painted glass greatly influenced the design of churches; for the windows had a task to perform and builders strove to enlarge the scope and glorify the nature of that task. Unhampered by the needs of fortification, church builders could progressively reduce the area of wall, until the church became in Lethaby's phrase "a cage of stone"; a building where voids dominated over solids. And in those voids were pictures, animated by daylight, a translucent panorama, which conveyed to the illiterate congregations of a bookless age the precepts of their faith, the stories of saints, martyrs, miracles, the hopes of celestial reward and the warnings of eternal punishment.

The great church window might ascend in tall, narrow and continuous apertures filled by a translucent mosaic of coloured glass set in lead cames, like the Five Sisters window at York Minster; or, like the choir at Gloucester Cathedral, the whole east end of the church might become a vast window with the slenderness of the stone framework accentuated by the luminous character of the glass. The lancet-shaped Five Sisters window is Early English, a period when the "cage of stone" was foreshadowed although there was no marked

Exterior view of the Five Sisters window at York Minster. Mid-thirteenth century. (Reproduced from *Building for Daylight*, by Richard Sheppard and Hilton Wright.)

The great east window at Gloucester Cathedral, marking the predominance of voids over solids in English perpendicular Gothic, when a church became a vast stone lantern. (From *Building for Daylight*, by Richard Sheppard and Hilton Wright.)

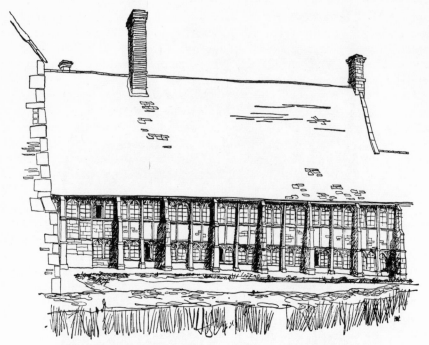

An example of continuous horizontal window development in the late
fifteenth century. Much Wenlock Priory, Shropshire.

ascendancy of voids over solids. The east window at Gloucester shows how the
tendency was later carried to its logical conclusion. (See pages 20 and 21.)

It was only in church building that mediaeval architects were encouraged
to make experiments from which new techniques of construction could arise.
Their capacity for experiment was demonstrated by the development of the
window between the twelfth century and the beginning of the sixteenth.
Norman windows were small round-arched apertures, with deeply splayed
internal jambs. Sometimes a double window with a central shaft would be
used, and occasionally groups of three, the middle window being the largest.
In the early English period, the lancet window was introduced, and stone
tracery was used. This tracery was first made by piercing apertures in a slab
or plate of stone and was known as "plate" tracery. Then it became "bar"
tracery with its vertical and horizontal members built up separately. (See page
19.) It was the progenitor of the mullioned window used by the early Tudor
and Elizabethan builders, which survived in ordinary building practice well
into the eighteenth century. In the decorated period of English Gothic architecture, the window grew larger; mullions divided it into two or more lights,
those vertical stone members melting into a geometrical maze of tracery at
the springing point of the arched head. Stained glass lost its early, crude

character, and began to perform its evangelising task. In the final phase of English Gothic architecture, the Perpendicular, mullions became tenuous ligatures of stone, binding masses of pictorial glass. Secular subjects were introduced in windows, and heraldic devices reminded worshippers of the power and splendour of the great ruling families and of the loyalty due to the monarch.

All these experiments and achievements in church window design were reflected on a much smaller scale in domestic building after the twelfth century. Law and order were gradually established, and although England was far from enjoying the peace and security of the Roman province, at least the fear of war and destruction departed from large areas of the land. Between the Scottish border and Yorkshire and in the Welsh Marches, fortification was an ever-present necessity, and long remained so; but in the south and south-west, in the south Midlands and in East Anglia, country houses and town houses began to lose the grimness that was imposed by the need to keep out enemies. The fortified manor-house, century by century, became more of a home and less a place to be defended. Windows instead of being slits, or ragged holes high up in the wall, gradually expanded in size. The output of glass was limited; its cost was high and it was made only in small sizes. Although the dimensions of individual panes were restricted, as production increased glass became cheaper. Even in the late fourteenth century, houses like Penshurst Place in Kent had tall, spacious windows; but it was not until after the Wars of the Roses in the late fifteenth century that there was a general release from the tyranny of fortification. At last houses could be built for the full enjoyment of daylight. The room with a view was restored to its place among the pleasures of life.

Comparable developments took place throughout Western Europe. The bay window was invented, and an early English example is furnished by the stone house of William Grevel, the wool merchant who died in 1401 at Chipping Campden in the Cotswolds. In peaceful, secluded valleys, all manner of subsequent developments in window design were foreshadowed, and when at last gardens took the place of moats, and windows were allowed to expand, they began to eat away the walls of manor-houses and palaces, as they had eaten away the walls of churches. Bay windows were thrust out, they ascended through two or more storeys; oriel windows projected from upper floors; mullions both of stone and wood were thinner; the technique of glazing improved. The lead glazing bars clasped a regular geometric pattern of small, diamond-shaped panes, occasionally diversified by decorative roundels of coloured glass, or shields with heraldic emblems. The bay window in the great hall at Hampton Court Palace and the first-floor windows of Ockwells Manor, at Bray, Berkshire, are fine examples of the use of coloured glass, examples too of the type of window that was developing in the native domestic architecture of the late fifteenth and early sixteenth centuries, before that development was obscured and finally arrested by the Italianate fashions of the early English Renaissance.

Only the mullion outlived the architectural changes introduced in the latter

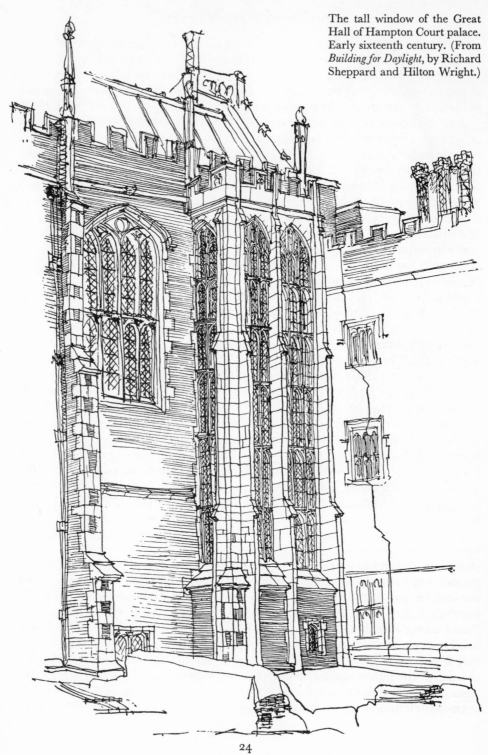

The tall window of the Great Hall of Hampton Court palace. Early sixteenth century. (From *Building for Daylight*, by Richard Sheppard and Hilton Wright.)

Detail of the bay window
from the house of Sir
William Grevel at Chip-
ping Campden. Its place
in the façade is shown in
the general view of the
house on page 26. (Re-
produced from *Building
for Daylight*, by Richard
Sheppard and Hilton
Wright.)

part of the sixteenth century. Glass-making improved steadily, sustained and
periodically invigorated by fresh injections of foreign skill. It is likely that from
the twelfth and certainly from the thirteenth century English glass furnaces
drew their fuel from the forests of Sussex and Surrey, which were the chief
glass-making localities until Tudor times. During the reign of Elizabeth I, the
English glass industry expanded; new centres of manufacture were established,
and fresh foreign talent introduced. With the improvement of window-glass,
the size of the panes was increased; but not before various decorative elabora-
tions of the diamond pattern, formed by a grille of diagonal glazing bars, had
been invented. By the early seventeenth century, such glazing patterns were

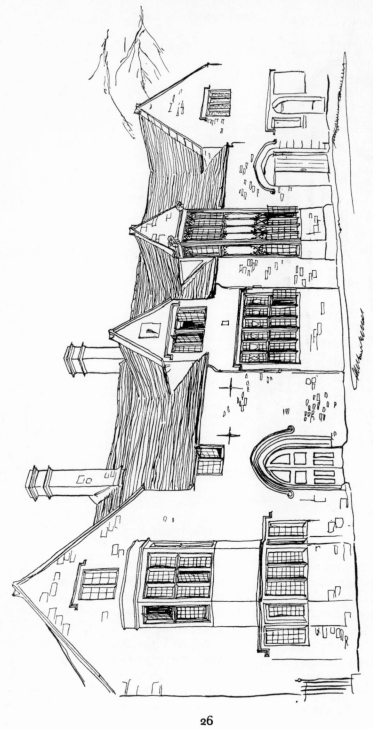

The house of Sir William Grevel, Chipping Campden, Gloucestershire, built in the late fourteenth century. The tall bay window ascends through two storeys. (See page 25 for detail of bay.)

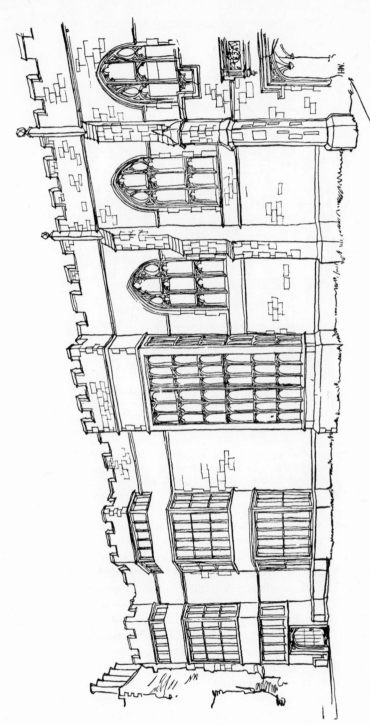

Windows in Cowdray House, Midhurst. The tall bay window and the pointed windows light the great hall, and these date from the early and middle years of the sixteenth century. The two other bay windows on the left of the building were built at the end of the sixteenth and the beginning of the seventeenth century.

27

Casement windows, with very small glass panes, formed a
continuous horizontal band across the front of a building. The
Bear and Billet Inn, Chester, a typical example of timber-
framed domestic architecture of the early sixteenth century.

giving way to small rectangular panes, which filled window openings whose
proportions were often based on two squares, one above the other, thus antici-
pating a form of opening that represented common building practice a hundred
years later. This double square opening would be divided by four horizontal
and three vertical lead glazing bars. A wrought-iron frame bordered this area of
twenty panes and was often hinged, to allow the window to swing open. These
casement windows allowed some control over the temperature of a room and the
freshness of its air. (There are mediaeval records of glass windows being repaired
so that they would open and shut: at Sherborne Castle in 1250, for example.)

The English liking for open windows and fresh air may have originated in
the latter part of the sixteenth century, though it did not become a national
passion until the twentieth. Architects used daylight abundantly, even to the
extent of using the frieze on the external walls of a room as a continuous window

above the panelling. Fresh air was admitted with caution; possibly too much of it had entered the mediaeval house involuntarily for it to be regarded as an advantage; so the early glazed windows of town and country houses were generally air-tight, save for one or two small panes, hinged to open. The vertical and horizontal elements, the mullions and transoms that were used as stiffeners in tall windows, were characteristic of the transitional period from early Tudor times until English Renaissance architecture was brought to effective maturity by the work of Sir Christopher Wren.

McGrath and Frost, in *Glass in Architecture and Decoration*, suggest that sash windows in some form were known early in the sixteenth century, and quote a contemporary reference, dated 1519, to windows that slid up and down.[18] The sash window was probably introduced from Holland. The word "sash" is derived from the Dutch *sas*, a sluice, and the French *chassis*, a frame.[19] The first recorded use of the balanced sliding sash in England is in 1685 in the windows of the Banqueting House at Whitehall. The panes used were 13 inches by 10 inches, the glazing bars were of wood, rebated to receive the panes, which were fixed with putty. The general introduction of the sash coincided with fresh improvements in the manufacture of English glass; again, largely as a result of skill transplanted from abroad. In 1697 a window tax was imposed on houses with more than six windows and worth over £5 per annum. This tax checked the use of windows, without altering their form, and it remained until 1851—a severe and unhealthy limitation on house design. The great period of freedom for using as much daylight as possible had lasted for just over two centuries. Over two more centuries were to pass before architects again had both the liberty and the desire to use daylight fully. The window tax was increased six times between 1747 and 1808, and although it hardly affected the nobility and gentry, who as educated patrons of architecture set the fashions which ultimately permeated society, the size of windows certainly increased during the eighteenth century. The tax was assessed on the number of windows; not on their area.

The history of sash window design in England during the long Georgian period shows a progressive refinement of the glazing bar. The thick, flat sections of the late seventeenth century, like those in the windows of Wren's part of Hampton Court, with the external surface of the glass almost level with the woodwork that framed the small, rectangular panes, were ponderous compared with the attenuated glazing bars used in the spacious windows of houses designed by Soane or Nash. Wren was limited by the material available; his work was done at the beginning of a period of evolution in window design, which was to attain an elegant perfection in that gracious phase of domestic architecture which distinguished the opening decades of the nineteenth century.

Architects in England and the American Colonies had devised many pleasant variations upon the double hung sash, sometimes grouping the sashes, occasionally crowning the central window with an arched head, and using the delicate glazing bars of the sashes to reflect the disposition of the horizontal and vertical elements in their façades. There were progressive improvements in the production of glass throughout the eighteenth century. As early as 1693 plate glass had been made in France; the process, according to Professor W. E. S. Turner, originated there in 1688, and was invented by Lucas Nehou; but crown glass was the principal material used in the windows of better class town and country houses throughout the middle and late Georgian period.[20] Polished plate glass was available in the latter part of the eighteenth century in England, but it was very costly, and was used almost wholly for mirrors and for the windows of private vehicles.

The character of glass manufacture changed during the Industrial Revolution; and nineteenth century improvements in the production of sheet and plate glass allowed the sizes of panes to be increased, so that the glazing bar was no longer necessary and the two sashes of a window could be glazed completely by sheets which filled the sash frame without any divisions. This technical achievement allowed an entirely new approach to be made to window design; but Victorian architects continued to think of windows as a pattern of apertures in an elevation; they were obsessed by the conventional idea of fenestration, interpreting that term in a purely drawing-board sense, rejecting the possibilities contemporary industry disclosed, and, as we have seen earlier in referring to the design of the Law Courts in London, resurrecting many of the mediaeval limitations which architects since the days of Henry VIII had successfully outgrown.[21]

This glance at the history of the window and its development in England has suggested how the mutations of spiritual and social life and the changes of taste and fashion are recorded by variations in design. In the great period of English civilisation, that lasted from the late seventeenth century to the eighteen-thirties, the increasing refinements of design in architecture, in furniture and interior decoration, in silver, glass and pottery, were impressed upon the moulded detail of window glazing bars. The slender section of those wooden bars in the sash windows of the latter part of the eighteenth century corresponded with the greater delicacy in the shape of chairs and other articles of furniture, and of the elegantly formed classical ornament used by architects like the brothers Adam and their contemporaries.

Occasionally some event, some chance happening in the life of a building, enables us vividly to reconstruct the past. During the Second World War the mediaeval stained glass was removed from the hundred and thirty windows of Chartres Cathedral, and stored to preserve it from possible bomb damage. Those who visited the cathedral when it was thus denuded were conscious of an alteration in its scale: within, it seemed to have shrunk to a small stone shell, clearly but depressingly delineated in pallid monotone, its loftiness reduced, its mystery diminished. Some people had the good fortune to see the glass being restored to the windows; and they witnessed a scene that re-enacted the sort of collective effort that the service of religion inspired in the Middle Ages. Under the direction of the priests and skilled specialists, the citizens supplied the labour; and on ladders and scaffolding, men, women, and the older children worked for days and weeks to give back to their church its resplendent beauty. Those who were old, frail or crippled helped with the unpacking and assembling of the glass. The cathedral was thronged with workers. The task itself imparted to such happily devoted people the semblance of another age: those who saw them at work could forget the drab garments worn by modern men and women in a small French city, could ignore the external evidence of their daily life in the twentieth century—what they were looking at was a crowd transfigured by the nature of their work, for a time spiritually identical with those who dwelt in Chartres in the twelfth and thirteenth centuries when the glass was made.

The scrutiny of such components of architecture as walls and windows reveals their competitive relationship, which in turn reveals innumerable facts about the structural history of building. Walls, windows, doorways, and colonnades are the components that usually survive; and though they may survive only in a fragmentary form, they can generally provide the evidence needed for reconstruction. There are enough ruins and buildings still in use throughout Europe to make the study of the successive waves of architectural achievement relatively easy. Although architectural development has been periodically arrested, and liberty to experiment checked by the adoption and universal imposition of some system of design throughout a state or group of states, a tendency to change is inseparable from the practice of architecture in a living and growing civilisation. It may be dormant for a few centuries: it may be abruptly awakened by disaster, when fortification becomes a sudden and pressing need; but it may, with the discovery of new materials or structural methods, become urgently creative. Again, it may be a by-product of some new way of life, some social or economic revolution that accidentally fosters fresh architectural experiments. An example of this has occurred during the last hundred and fifty years in Europe, Britain, and the United States, where the demands of organised industry have been variously accommodated. There has been an architectural ebb and flow, so to speak, caused by the needs of industrial building. Early industrial architecture in Britain was traditional in character, and only when industrial processes became more complicated and industry expanded were characteristic forms evolved, notably in connection with railway development. Throughout the nineteenth century industrial building was constantly changing. All kinds of structures were altered and adapted, sometimes beyond recognition. The process continues. For instance, in West London there is a disused railway line that once ran from Hammersmith to Shepherd's Bush and was carried for most of the way on a brick-built viaduct. This line has long been abandoned, the land sold, the arches filled in, and fresh buildings straddled over them. From the air this lost branch line is still discernible, broken here and there in places where the viaduct has been pulled down. Two or three thousand years hence such remains may intrigue excavating archaeologists, who may lavish upon the industrial accretions of the twentieth century an interest comparable with that which we now devote to the remains of sacred and civic edifices, bequeathed to us by former ages.

Enough has been said to suggest the variety and extent of the unwritten records that architecture everywhere puts before our eyes. We have deliberately roved here and there within the boundaries of the Graeco-Roman world, to which our civilisation is still spiritually and artistically attached; and we have roved back and forth through time, for one of the objects of this book is to enable the reader to act as his or her own guide to Western architecture, and to observe and compare the achievements of the past and relate them to the new western architecture that is arising to-day.

II

ORIGINS

THE character of architecture has been formed by three structural inventions and the periodic discovery and use of new materials and techniques. Events may have determined the purpose of buildings but the imaginative use of structural methods and materials has often allowed architects to rise above the purely practical demands of their patrons, and to give, even in periods of fear, frugality, or spiritual destitution, some hint of latent powers, some token achievement to suggest splendours that might come after liberation from repressive military needs or economic stringency. The first and second of those structural inventions are now as obvious, familiar, and traditional as bread and butter or chairs and tables: the third, still visually strange, is often discreetly concealed, its potential majesty swaddled by some shock-absorbing disguise, for although it has been established and in use during and since the late nineteenth century, only in the mid-twentieth has it been openly and widely acknowledged.

The first structural invention was made when men found that two upright posts could support a horizontal member, and from this arose what is called post-and-lintel, post-and-beam, or trabeated construction. To this day it remains the basic constructional principle of the majority of buildings; for walls act as posts that uphold the horizontal members which bear floors and roofs. The application of this structural principle inspired other inventions, such as the column and the colonnade, both originated by the Egyptians of the old kingdom, some two thousand five hundred years before Christ.[22]

The second invention was the arch, which led to arcuated construction. In both structural methods buildings were upheld by walls, piers or columns—all conspicuously visible means of support which encouraged experiments in form and ornamentation. When the arch was used as a structural principle and not as a structural convenience, as the Romans generally used it, large

33

spaces could be spanned without intervening supports, so that great masses of stone could be borne aloft, and their weight distributed and dispersed, carried along the curves of arches downwards to piers and walls. Columns could now attain a new elegance by supporting a row of arches, and the arcade was thus created.

The third invention is based on the cantilever principle, and has been made effective by the use of steel and concrete, so that buildings are supported by an internal skeleton, and walls have become thin skins, hanging like curtains from the steelwork. (The contemporary term is curtain walling.) This represents a structural revolution, but one that is not always frankly proclaimed in contemporary architecture. In the mid-twentieth century, steel and reinforced concrete are still largely used as structural conveniences, as the Romans used arches. Loyalty to the forms evolved in Greece and Rome, which since the Renaissance represented a living tradition in design, has for half a century hampered the growth of what is called the modern movement in architecture. That movement is nourished, sustained, and expanded by the diffusion of scientific knowledge, which has spread through western civilisation, as the so-called "heliolithic" culture once spread over the world during and after the Neolithic Age. The resources of modern industry, the materials it produces, the light, strong alloys and plastics, the improved cements and ranges of glasses with new properties, are available to the architect, whose trained imagination is no longer circumscribed by the first two structural inventions. There was a limit to the space that could be spanned by a wooden beam—even with the arch, which enormously enlarged that space, there would come a moment when the builder had perforce to say: thus far and no farther. Justinian's architects created the supreme expression of arcuated construction when they built Santa Sophia at Constantinople in the sixth century. No other dome had floated so airily over so large an area of unobstructed space. The form of the arch itself had to be changed before it could again offer a new adventure in building, and tempt mediaeval architects to rear their towers and spires to the skies, as the advent of steel and concrete tempted American architects to build up and up—as though both were inspired like the descendants of Noah in the land of Shinar who had said "let us build us a city and a tower, whose top may reach unto heaven. . . . "(23)

All three structural inventions have been restricted or amplified by the materials available to builders. Trabeated construction could be used with timber as the sole material, or with undressed blocks of stone. The trilithons of Stonehenge represent an elementary expression of post-and-lintel architecture—the skeletal outline, as it were, of something that could be as ambitiously massive as an Egyptian temple; while the primitive log cabin could foreshadow the stone or brick-built houses of later ages, and be revived as the most suitable form of dwelling for pioneers in new lands where timber was abundant.

The dome-shaped stone huts of neolithic tribes in Europe unconsciously

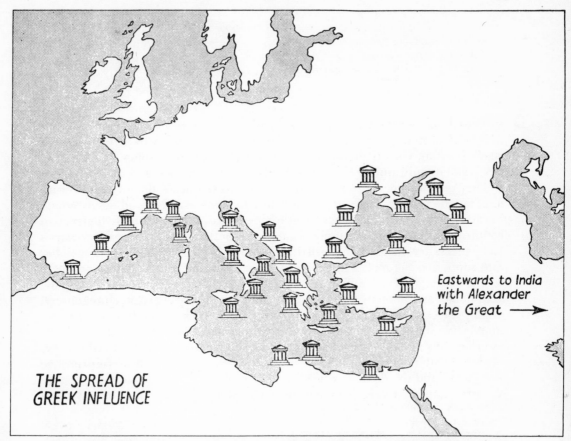

Eastwards to India
with Alexander
the Great ➔

THE SPREAD OF
GREEK INFLUENCE

Greek colonies were established in Italy, Sicily, in that part of Asia Minor that is now called
Anatolia, round the shores of the Black Sea, and as far west as Spain and the south of France.
There were colonies too in North Africa, Cyrene in Libya, and in Egypt the great Greek
city of Alexandria (see plan on page 50), which became as cosmopolitan as modern New York.
In France, their colony and port of Massalia, founded about 600 B.C., is now Marseilles;
Syracuse, the chief Greek city of ancient Sicily, was founded earlier, in the eighth century B.C.
The arts and architecture of Greece were spread by colonists and traders; their influence
pervaded the Mediterranean world, and left a mark upon the eastern empire of Alexander
the Great, from Syria to the Punjab. Compare this with the map on page 60, which shows
the Roman Empire at its greatest extent, five hundred years after Alexander made his great
eastern raid, an area in which the classic orders represented the only form of architectural
expression. The barbarian successor states to the Western Roman Empire are shown on page
104. *Drawn by Marcelle Barton.*

A restoration of Stonehenge in Wiltshire. This represents an elementary expression of post-and-lintel architecture.

expressed the arch principle, though their builders never developed it; nor did the Egyptians, who certainly knew of the arch as early as the thirtieth century before Christ. Breasted has recorded its use in masonry in a tomb at Bet Khallâf, built during the Third Dynasty between 2980 and 2900 B.C.[24]

The Assyrians made arches of kiln-burnt bricks during the seventh century B.C., for the vaulted drains that ran below the palace at Nimrud.[25] Although the arch was known it did not come into general use in the eastern Mediterranean countries until the timber supply began to fail in the seventh and sixth centuries B.C.; thereafter builders discarded the bearer beam, the horizontal member that supported the roof, and began to use instead domed or vaulted roofs.[26]

The shortage of a familiar and easily worked material thus compelled the adoption of another structural principle; but the history of architecture, though greatly affected by the character of building materials, depends upon so many impalpable influences that to interpret it in terms of materials alone would be as misleading as a purely economic interpretation of social and national history. Such elementary essays in building as the wattle-and-daub huts of the primitive Europeans and the domed or beehive houses of stone already mentioned, were shelters—nothing more. They had no architectural pretensions: they supplied

Vaulted drain beneath the south-east palace at Nimrud: an example of the Assyrian use of the arch principle in the seventh century B.C. (From Layard's *Discoveries in the Ruins of Nineveh and Babylon*.)

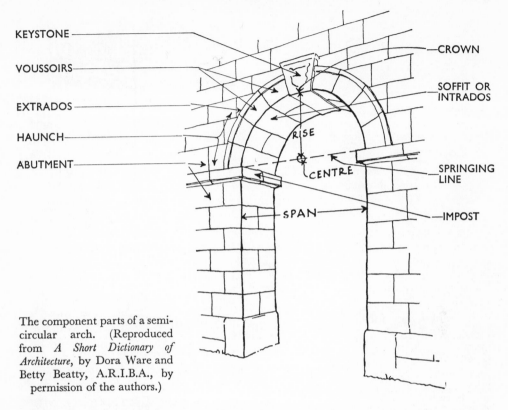

KEYSTONE

VOUSSOIRS

EXTRADOS

HAUNCH

ABUTMENT

CROWN

SOFFIT OR INTRADOS

RISE

CENTRE

SPRINGING LINE

IMPOST

SPAN

The component parts of a semi-circular arch. (Reproduced from *A Short Dictionary of Architecture*, by Dora Ware and Betty Beatty, A.R.I.B.A., by permission of the authors.)

a need and satisfied it over a long period, for in some localities, notably the west of Scotland and the Outer Hebrides, beehive houses were still being built and used in the early nineteenth century.[27] Buildings that transcended the simple requirements of shelter were conceived for reasons more recondite: and in ancient Egypt, where the architectural forms originated that have been impressed upon subsequent civilisations, architecture was evoked by the nature of religious belief and that integral part of it, the practice of mummification. Dr. Elliott Smith has pointed out that "No student of the evidence provided by the earliest civilisation of Egypt can fail to realise that the crafts of the carpenter, the brickmaker, the potter, and the stonemason, developed out of the attempt to preserve the bodies of the dead. The artificial preservation of the corpse by embalming provided a tremendous stimulus to these practices. It was mainly responsible for the evolution of the art of architecture and the belief that the dead king, whose corpse was made incorruptible, had thereby secured a prolongation of existence and had attained divine powers."[28]

The tomb and the temple provided the opportunity for architectural invention. The column, the colonnade, the grand approach, the pylon—that monu-

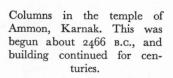
Columns in the temple of Ammon, Karnak. This was begun about 2466 B.C., and building continued for centuries.

mental entrance to the temple—and the partnership between sculptor and builder, all originated from the autocratic patronage of the Pharaohs and the priesthood of Egypt; and once created and established those forms were perpetuated, not for five or six centuries like the standardised architectural forms of the Roman Empire, but for nearly thirty. The healthy tendency to change was deliberately repressed: architecture never developed beyond a stage when it attained a massive stability: inspiration either died or was deliberately killed, and like the royal and noble dead was embalmed. Only once during the period of nearly three thousand years that elapsed between the First Dynasty and the Twenty-sixth, when Egypt became a Persian province, was art released from "the narrow proficiency of perpetual iteration."[29] That release occurred during the Eighteenth Dynasty, in the reign of Ikhnaton (1375–1358 B.C.), a Pharaoh whose innovations in religion and art were short-lived, and did not survive his death. For a few years sculptors and artists were liberated from the rigid conventions that had governed their work: Breasted has observed that "the modelling of the human figure at this time was so plastic that at the first glance one is sometimes in doubt whether he has before him a product of the Greek age,"[30] but after that brief interval of freedom and experiment the arts reverted to their former rigidity.

When Egyptian architectural ideas were transplanted to other civilisations, fresh forms were evolved, as the process of growth was resumed, uninhibited by a sacred regard for precedent. This happened in Crete, the European island that is nearest to Egypt, where the Minoan civilisation, based on sea-power, flourished for sixteen centuries (3000–1450 B.C.), and was known in Hellenic tradition as "the thalassocracy of Minos." Crete as the base of a maritime empire that qualified for Toynbee's description of "a universal state"[31] drank up the wealth and controlled the commerce of the eastern Mediterranean, Minoan builders became as technically accomplished as the Romans, and as attentive to luxurious plumbing. Their architects owed much of their initial inspiration to Egypt; they created their own styles, but retained some of the less admirable characteristics of Egyptian design.

Although architecture in Egypt became static, it had made a permanent contribution to design; the genius that had invented the column and the colonnade had freed buildings from their previous dependence upon walls to enclose space. By those inventions, architecture had opened out, and though the shape of the Egyptian column was such that it often appeared merely as an upright ornamental device, it did initiate a new form that was used by architects for thousands of years. The Egyptian column was a gigantic replica of the lotus plant: the shaft often tapered at the base, and budded out at the top, forming a capital that was either a bell-shaped representation of an expanding flower or a tightly closed bud. This tapering at the base, and the ponderous bulk of the column itself, denied its structural significance as a support; the treatment of the base suggested weakness, the proportions, determined by ornamental considerations, seldom acknowledged the functional fact that the column was carrying the weight of a horizontal member. It was strange that Minoan designers should have adopted and perpetuated a comparable form, which, although considerably refined, still exhibited the weakness of a column that tapered from the capital to the base.

In writing of the origins of Western architecture, Egypt cannot be ignored— we have inherited so many architectural conceptions from that civilisation. For instance, the long avenues by which the temples of Karnak were approached, were lined with sphinxes, and to-day architects who design spectacular monuments recall, perhaps unconsciously, the grandeur of those sculptured guardians. In Ankara, the immensely broad avenue that leads to the mausoleum of Kemal Attaturk is guarded by stone lions, crouching in pairs, at intervals throughout

Pylons at the temple of Khons, Karnak. *Circa* 1200 B.C.

Two examples of capitals used on Egyptian columns.
Left, the lotus bell; *right*, the lotus bud.

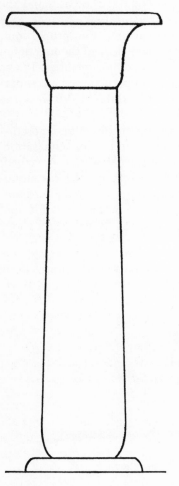

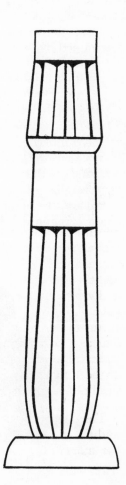

The Egyptian column was often a gigantic replica of the lotus plant: the form simple, but, in the words of Lisle March Phillipps, "Egyptian simplicity is really not of the intellectual but of the primitive order." The shaft often tapered at the base, which suggested weakness, and denied its structural significance as a support. The vast bulk of the column was reassuring; but the note of weakness had been implied by that inward curving base. The capitals reinforced the debt to a natural prototype: the lotus was symbolised, as a bud or a bell. (See details of lotus capitals above.) *Drawn by Marcelle Barton.*

Columns in the grand staircase in the palace at Knossos, *circa* 3000 B.C. This shows the diminishing of the columns towards the base. Compare these with the column shown on the Gate of the Lions, Mycenae, on page 44 and plate 4.

its length. In Eastern Berlin, the Russian War Memorial is approached by a long path through a garden, flanked by massive stone blocks, with vigorous bas-reliefs carved on the sides. The staircase that ascends to the huge rotunda of the Memorial is at the far end of this broad, impressive pathway. Karnak was the progenitor of these two examples of mid-twentieth century monumental design.

Egypt initiated the basic forms, but the refinement of those forms and their development as "orders" of architecture began in Greece as early as the eighth century B.C., perhaps earlier. The term classical architecture denotes the orders that were perfected and used by the Greeks and the Romans, and the individual character of each order depends upon the relative proportions of the column and the horizontal member that it supports which is called the entablature and is divided into architrave, frieze and cornice. The classical architecture that gave such bland distinction to the buildings of the Graeco-Roman world was matured in Greece: it was copied, adapted and slightly vulgarised by the Romans, degenerating and falling into disuse after the collapse of the Western Roman Empire, reviving after an interval of nearly a thousand years, and then, at the Renaissance, restoring to Western Europe the great system of architectural design represented by the orders.

The three orders of Greek architecture are Doric, Ionic, and Corinthian; and the prototype of the Doric may have evolved in the colonies founded on the mainland of Greece by the Minoans. There are conflicting views about the origin, extent and locality of these colonies; but at Mycenae there are remains where some of the characteristics of Minoan architecture are perceptible. Mycenae is in eastern Peloponnese, on the edge of the Argive Plain, and is built on a hill from which Argos is visible, with a glimpse of the sea beyond. It has been in ruins for two thousand five hundred years, and Pausanias, who toured the Peloponnese in the second century A.D., described what was then visible. He recorded that "there are still some remains of the precincts and the gate, and there are some lions on it: which were they say executed by the Cyclopes, who built the wall at Tiryns for Proetus."[32] Subsequent excavation has revealed far more than Pausanias saw. The gate of the lions has survived. Despite the erosion of centuries those lions are still a strenuous pair, bluntly but vigorously carved, standing taut as if ready to spring upwards, their forepaws resting on two symbolic altars, and between them a column, slightly tapering towards the base. The shape of the gateway, the carved pediment above, with that column between the headless lions, have an undeniable affinity with Minoan architecture. This archaic example may represent the prototype of later Greek architecture; the tapering column and its base and capital may be an early stage in the development of the Doric order, but it is also a link with the older civilisation of Crete, long dead before Mycenae was built. Although according to some schools of thought the theory that Mycenae was a Minoan colony is discredited, the connection between the builders of Mycenae and the architects of Crete is veraciously recorded in terms of design. The palace within the citadel may well be the forerunner of later Greek buildings. Something may be read from the ruins: it is possible to follow the plan of the palace, but the details of the architectural treatment are blurred and fragmentary. The bases of columns are visible as worn stone discs rising above floor level; you can see the walls, largely of dry construction, though some courses—rather crudely laid—are bound with cement. Here and there traces of plaster appear, and from these it is conjectured that the interior walls were smooth and painted. Some evidence of floor painting is apparent, now carefully covered with cloths kept in place by loose soil. Exploring the ruins of Mycenae you gain the impression that architectural inspiration was still young and fertile; that although the scope of builders was curbed by the need to ensure security, their ideas were not conditioned by established conventions; and if the place had not been destroyed by the Argives, growth would have continued, inventively, perhaps graciously. Pausanias mentions that the Argives destroyed Mycenae through jealousy. "For though they took no part against the Medes, the people of Mycenae sent to Thermopylae eighty men, who shared in the glory of the famous three hundred. This public spirit brought about their destruction, by provoking the Argives to jealousy."[33] In the end the skill of the Mycenaean builders was unavailing: military aggression, touched off by a contemptible passion, all but obliterated their work, but left enough of it for us to learn something about the pre-Hellenic period.

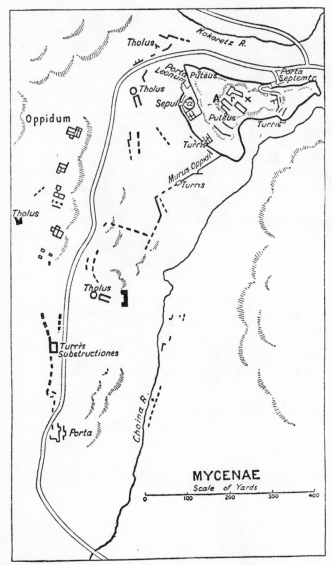

MYCENAE

Scale of Yards

Mycenae, situated on the north-eastern extremity of the Argive plain in eastern Peloponnese. The city was built on a hill, from which Argos and the sea are visible. The city consisted of an Acropolis and a lower town, both walled, and the Acropolis which was the site of the Royal palace, occupied the summit of a steep hill, which was a spur of a high mountain behind it. (See page 44 and plate 4 for illustrations of the Gate of the Lions and examples of masonry.) The city has been in ruins for two thousand five hundred years. (Reproduced from the *Atlas of Ancient and Classical Geography*, by permission of J. M. Dent & Sons Ltd., the publishers, and John Bartholomew & Son Ltd., the Geographical Institute, Edinburgh, the owners of the copyright.)

This period, if Minoan architecture is included, extended from 3000 to 700 B.C., though after 1450 B.C., when civilisation in Crete was submerged by some disaster from which it never recovered, there was a bleak, barbaric interlude, comparable to the Dark Ages that followed the collapse of the Roman Empire, when building reverted to crude and simple methods of providing shelter and safety. On the mainland of Greece the memory of Minoan achievements was still potent—an active memory rather than a languishing tradition, for it could

The Gate of the Lions, Mycenae, *circa* 1200 B.C. The column between the
lions certainly has Minoan affinities and should be compared with those
on page 41, in the grand staircase of the palace at Knossos. A close-up
view of the masonry at the back of this gate is given on plate 4. A comparable
device, interpreted by Assyrian sculptors, is shown opposite.

invigorate tentative architectural experiments, and by 1200 B.C. the Gate of
the Lions at Mycenae had been built. This has been described as the oldest
piece of European sculpture, but there were sculptors in the Aurignacian Age,
and such accomplished works as the bisons in the cavern of the Tuc d'Audoubert
—that picture gallery of Palaeolithic designs—are, according to Dr. Sollas,
about twenty thousand years old.[34] The Gate of the Lions is perhaps the oldest
example in Europe of sculpture in association with an architectural feature,
and may well be the progenitor of those carved groups of figures that embellish

the tympanum on the pediment of a Doric temple, and of the horsemen, centaurs and animals that are so often the subjects of the metopes that enrich the frieze. (A tympanum is the triangular space enclosed by the inclined cornice and the horizontal base of a pediment, and a metope is the space between two triglyphs on a frieze in the Doric order. See detailed diagram on page 47.)

The promise of Mycenae was richly fulfilled in the Hellenic period, which began about 700 B.C. and lasted until 146 B.C., when Greece became a Roman dependency. In the pre-Hellenic period, about the ninth century B.C., the Doric order had taken shape, passing through an archaic phase before acquiring the matchless perfection of form that it exhibits in such buildings as the Parthenon. Two or three centuries later it was followed by the Ionic and Corinthian orders. Those three orders, by their proportions and disposition, could supply the profound visual satisfaction that the Greeks demanded from architecture. As a nation, they exalted the sense of sight, and the builders of the Doric temples of Greece and Sicily, and colonies like Paestum in southern Italy, devoted their mathematical and artistic skill to correcting the optical distortions that occurred in the vertical and horizontal elements of their structures. Each column gradually diminished in diameter upwards from the base, this progressive diminishing following a gentle convex curve along the outline of the shaft, which counteracted the illusion of inward curving lines that a straight shaft would create. This carefully calculated convex curve was called an entasis.

An Assyrian fountain at Bavian, with lions carved in low relief. (From Layard's *Discoveries in the Ruins of Nineveh and Babylon.*)

Diagram illustrating the entasis on a column. The convex curve is deliberately exaggerated. (From *A Short Dictionary of Architecture*, by Dora Ware and Betty Beatty, reproduced by permission of the authors.)

The real shape of masses—of columns and colonnades—was less important than their apparent shape. The defects of human vision were recognised, measured and adjusted by careful calculation and infinite labour, so that a level surface was made unlevel in order to appear level; the long horizontal line of a stylobate, the sub-structure upon which a colonnade stands, that to the eye appears to become concave in the middle, although it is perfectly straight, would be given convexity to remove the ostensible concavity, and vertical lines that seemed to slant would be made to slant in order to appear strictly vertical. Every stone of the Doric temple was in some slight and imperceptible degree deliberately irregular—deflected from mechanical regularity because it was taking part in a major readjustment of ascending and lateral lines so that the whole design became fit for the critical eyes of a people for whom the sense of sight had acquired a significance it had never before attained in human history, and has certainly never approached since. The beauty of the Parthenon, even in its ruined state, is fabulous: built of Pentelic marble, which in the distance is the colour of honey and seems to exude radiance but is dazzlingly white when seen close to, it discloses with every shift of shadow some fresh felicity of form. The delicate inflections which modify the vertical and horizontal lines of the temple would never be suspected, nor is it apparent that the Parthenon, like other Doric temples, is really a minute part of the base of a stupendous pyramid, which would rise to the height of a mile if the inwardly inclined lines of the columns and other vertical features were projected upwards until they met.[35] The Parthenon dominates the Acropolis of Athens, and was built in the time of Pericles (490–429 B.C.) by the architects, Ictinus and Callicrates, with Pheidias as the master sculptor. This temple, dedicated to Athena Parthenos, was one of the works on which Pericles spent the war chest of the allies of Athens when he rebuilt and greatly beautified the city. There are other temples, such as the Theseion at Athens, and the temple of Poseidon at Paestum, which are in a better state of preservation, but in the Parthenon the Doric order attained an unequalled perfection. (See plates 1, 2 and 3.)

The Ionic and Corinthian orders, like the Doric, consisted of upright columns supporting an entablature divided into architrave, frieze and cornice, differentiated by their proportions and embellishment. A plain, moulded capital appears on the Doric column; the Ionic capital has ornamental scrolls called volutes; and the Corinthian a band of formalised acanthus leaves, surmounted by small volutes. The Ionic order, with its volute or scroll capital, gave an impression of greater delicacy than the Doric, though this was due more to its ornamental characteristics than to any additional refinement of line. The Corinthian order introduced a conventionalised natural form that has probably appeared more frequently in the works of man than any other: the acanthus leaf. The origin of the Corinthian capital is described by the Roman architect, Vitruvius, who wrote his ten books on architecture during the reign of Augustus. He admitted that the story was probably apocryphal, but gave it as follows:

"A Corinthian virgin, of marriageable age, fell a victim to a violent disorder. After her interment, her nurse, collecting in a basket those articles to which she had shown a partiality when alive, carried them to her tomb, and placed

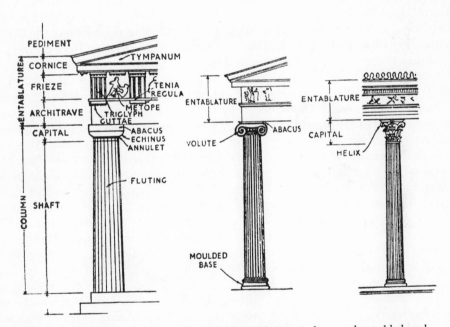

The Greek orders of architecture, with the various members and moulded and ornamental details named. Reading from left to right the orders are: Doric, Ionic, and Corinthian. These are intentionally simplified diagrams: larger and fuller illustrations of the three Greek orders appear on pages 62, 65, and 66. (Reproduced from *A Short Dictionary of Architecture*, by Dora Ware and Betty Beatty, A.R.I.B.A., by permission of the authors.)

a tile on the basket for the longer preservation of its contents. The basket was accidentally placed on the root of an acanthus plant, which, pressed by the weight, shot forth, towards spring, its stems and large foliage, and in the course of its growth reached the angles of the tile, and thus formed volutes at the extremities. Callimachus, who, for his great ingenuity and taste was called by the Athenians, Catatechnos, happening at this time to pass by the tomb, observed the basket, and the delicacy of the foliage which surrounded it. Pleased with the form and novelty of the combination, he constructed from the hint thus afforded, columns of this species in the country about Corinth, and arranged its proportions, determining their proper measures by perfect rules."(36)

Buildings in nearly every country that is included in Western civilisation may trace their architectural lineage back to those three Greek orders, Doric, Ionic, and Corinthian. Their influence has been exerted almost continuously upon architectural thought for over twenty-five centuries; and after being interpreted and added to by Roman architects, the ghosts of the orders haunted European building throughout the Middle Ages, until at the Renaissance they were resurrected. The Romans produced their own versions of Doric, Ionic, and Corinthian and to these they added the Tuscan, which was a simplified form of the Doric, and the Composite, a voluptuously luxurious rendering of the Corinthian. The Roman orders lacked the subtlety and grace of their Greek prototypes; and they became part of a standardised system of architectural design which was imposed upon the whole Roman Empire. The orders, Greek and Roman, were basic influences that determined the character of architecture throughout the Graeco-Roman world. In Greece, they provided inspired guidance—in Rome, inexorable rules. Perhaps the way they were used reflected the stiffly dignified demeanour of the Roman gentleman—the famous Roman *gravitas*. Although a high degree of *gravitas* was incompatible with vulgarity, Roman architecture occasionally overbalanced into that deplorable condition. Clive Bell, in his essay *Civilisation*, has reminded us that "The Athenians wished to live richly rather than to be rich; which is why we reckon them the most highly civilised people in history." The Romans were not averse to the enjoyment and display of material wealth, and their buildings betray their inclinations. Respect for *gravitas* helped to counterbalance the love of ostentation, but it also gave to the Roman mind a certain inflexibility, and this too is apparent in the buildings and the layout of cities in the Roman Empire.

Both architecture and town planning are the responsibility of the architect, and in those activities the same problems and needs arise in every civilisation, although the scale changes. The Greeks had a deep sense of civic responsibility, which pervaded society, and promoted the happy social conditions when architects and artists, and all those who are creatively responsible for the environment of their fellow-men, were encouraged by the sympathy and understanding of the public for whom they worked. In Greek civilisation, art and life were

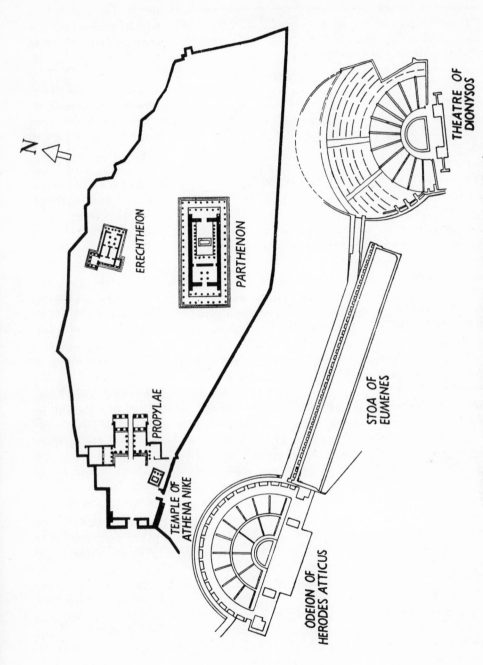

The Acropolis at Athens, showing the relative positions of the Parthenon, Erechtheion, and Propylae. The Odeion of Herodes Atticus and the Theatre of Dionysos are on a much lower level, and the cliffs of the Acropolis tower above them. *Drawn by Marcelle Barton.*

Ancient Alexandria, showing the grid street plan, and the limitations of its site, on a narrow strip of land between the harbour and Lake Mareotis. (Reproduced from the *Atlas of Ancient and Classical Geography*, by permission of J. M. Dent & Sons Ltd., the publishers, and John Bartholomew & Son Ltd., the Geographical Institute, Edinburgh, the owners of the copyright.)

inseparable. The artist was respected, not suspected; the state was small enough for its citizens to enjoy this partnership between art and life—there were no large pockets of unhappy, insensitive people, incapable of appreciating the work of creative minds in architecture, sculpture, or dramatic art. This partnership was demonstrated, not only by the public buildings of Greek cities, but also by the manner in which their architects used the grid plan for their streets. This grid plan may or may not have been a conscious invention, and in Greece it may have originated from a desire to tidy up the buildings that lined some main street or processional way, being adopted casually at first, until its advantages became manifest, though the Greek mind was too lucid and alert to allow it to become a rigid net. Haverfield has suggested that Greek town planning was inspired by Eastern examples, and he accepted the view, on Aristotle's authority, that the first town planner to use straight, wide streets, was Hippodamus of Miletus.[37] Hippodamus, who worked for Pericles in the fifth century B.C., planned Piraeus, the harbour town of Athens, where he showed how convenient the grid plan could be. Greek architects never allowed themselves to be mastered by that plan because of its convenience; they used it as a framework for bringing orderliness to their city thoroughfares and processional ways, and for providing clear sites for buildings and monuments.

The most uncharacteristic of all the cities of Greek origin, Alexandria, was the most luxurious and cosmopolitan. Its grid street plan, its eminence as a port, its situation upon a narrow strip of land, was akin, more nearly than any other city of the Graeco-Roman world, to modern New York. Both cities were enormously wealthy and luxurious. Like New York, Alexandria had a polyglot population, and there are other common characteristics. The street plan of Alexandria, squeezed in between the harbour and Lake Mareotis, suggests

Manhattan in miniature. Both cities, in vastly different fashions, overcame the limitations of the grid plan, through the imposing size, variety, and brilliancy of the buildings that occupied the lozenge-shaped sites between the streets. Alexandria was designed for Alexander the Great by Dinocrates, and was built largely of dazzling white marble. The streets were colonnaded, and below their level was a labyrinth of cisterns, descending to the depth of four or five storeys, each supported by thousands of columns. It was said, by an Arab writer, that even by night "the moonlight reflected from the white marble, made the city so bright that a tailor could see to thread his needle without a lamp."[38] Another Arab observer, who wrote in the tenth century A.D., said that "awnings of green silk were hung over the streets to relieve the dazzling glare of the marble."[39]

In town planning, the Greeks never lost the spirit of adventure. Many of the ancient Greek cities were built on hills. The citadel that crowned the hill was known as the Acropolis. The treasury and the principal temples of the city were on the Acropolis, overlooking the residential areas. The site of Alexandria demanded a different conception of town planning. It was the work of one man, who, like Alexander the Great, was a Macedonian. Dinocrates would have attracted attention in any age, and his approach to architecture and town planning was unusual, indeed almost eccentric, and his first meeting with Alexander, which has been described by Vitruvius in the second of his ten books on architecture, was dramatically contrived. Dinocrates, a tall, handsome man, became bored with waiting for his letters of introduction to be presented to Alexander, so he removed his usual clothes, anointed himself with oil, put a wreath of poplar on his head, slung a lion's skin from his left shoulder, and carrying a large club, visited the Royal Tribunal, where Alexander sat in judgment. Such a flamboyant figure was impossible to ignore, and when Alexander caught sight of him, he became as curious as the crowd attending the Tribunal. The people were ordered to make way, and the stranger was questioned personally by the king. Dinocrates introduced himself as a Macedonian architect, and immediately propounded a scheme for carving Mount Athos into a colossal statue of a man, whose left hand would hold a spacious city, and his right a vast cup, into which all the mountain streams would flow, and from thence be poured into the sea. Such a proposal would not have sounded as fantastic in the ancient world as it does to-day, and Dinocrates, a born salesman, had no hesitation in submitting it to a man who had the power to commission it, and might become an indulgent and adventurous patron. Alexander had too much practical sense to build a city at the end of a bleak peninsula, where the soil could not grow enough food for the inhabitants, who would have had to depend upon sea-borne supplies, but he was impressed by Dinocrates, and made him his consulting architect. This appointment brought him the commission to design a city that, after Rome, became the most famous in the ancient world.

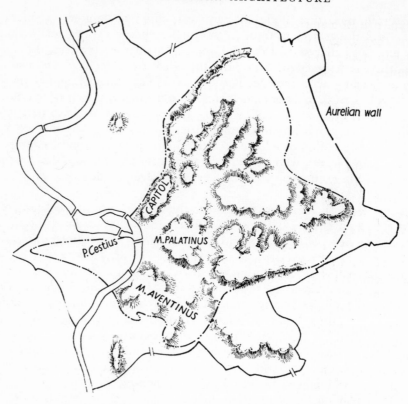

The physical features and the area of ancient Rome enclosed within the walls. The walls of Aurelian were more than twelve miles in circuit, and they surrounded the fourteen *regiones* into which Augustus divided the city. Like mediaeval and twentieth century London, ancient Rome spread far beyond its walls into the countryside, and when the Emperor Aurelian restored and enlarged the city walls late in the third century A.D., he protected an area far larger than the original city covered in the days of the Republic. The earlier wall, built by Servius Tullius is shown in an broken and dotted line: its date as well as its origin are conjectural, for Servius Tullius is a shadowy figure—a legendary king of Rome who is supposed to have lived in the sixth century B.C. *Drawn by Marcelle Barton from Notes by Hilton Wright.*

Roman town planning in the provinces of the Empire was rather shadowed by military needs, and often arose from the type of grid plan that was convenient in a military encampment. In Germany, near Bad Homburg, a few miles from Frankfort-on-Main, a Roman camp has been reconstructed at the Saalburg, on the site of the very considerable remains that were excavated in the late nineteenth century. This reconstruction was carried out between 1898 and 1907, and shows clearly how the form of a military encampment could become the prototype of a Roman city. This fortified camp was a frontier post on the Limes, the line that formed the northern boundary of the Empire, which was held by Roman troops until about A.D. 260, when the Germanic tribes reoccupied the country up to the Rhine.

The wall of a Roman city was usually a limiting factor. In contrasting the comparatively minor part played by walls in a Greek city with their significance in Egyptian, Oriental and Italian cities, Professor Wycherley has pointed out that "Italian town planning had strong military and religious associations; the town was related to the camp, in which a regular *vallum* with its gates placed in the axis of the two main streets defined the whole plan and fixed the type."[40] In Greek cities of the Hellenic period, the wall had generally been a late addition, not an essential part, and often it was confined to the encirclement of the citadel. Roman town planning was devoid of daring or imagination: all material considerations were honoured—safety, comfort, health, water supply, drainage, and general utility. Vitruvius set forth his ideas for a city in the first book of his work on architecture. Cautious and practical, he produced a utilitarian specification, which occupied the last four chapters. For military reasons he recommended a polygonal plan; and within the eight-sided walls the streets formed a web, corresponding to the eight facets, those running parallel with the facets being crossed by eight streets which led inwards from the walls to the open space in the centre where the forum stood. The area was thus divided into eight wedge-shaped blocks. The plan made no provision for processional ways or grand approaches to the open centre; it was exactly the sort of rigid net of streets which the Greeks consistently avoided.

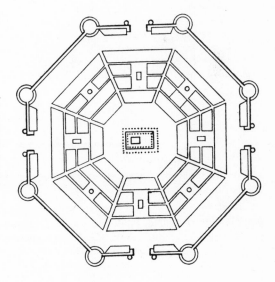

A town planned to the directions of Vitruvius, with eight-sided walls, enclosing a web of streets, with a central open space for the forum. The plan was tight, rigid, and utilitarian—the sort of plan the Greeks had consistently avoided. *Drawn by Marcelle Barton.*

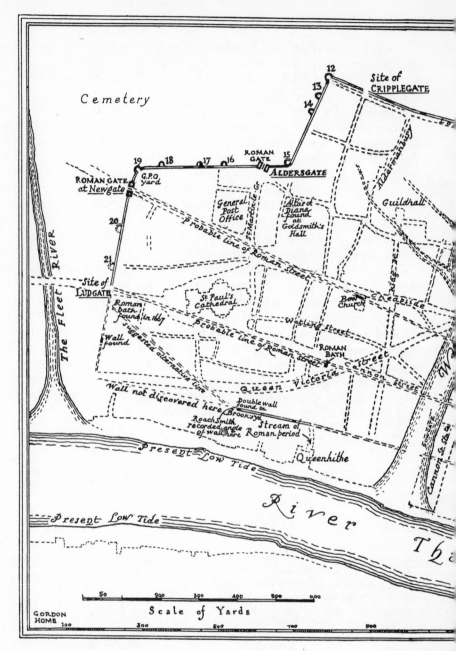

Cemetery

Site of
CRIPPLEGATE

Guildhall

ROMAN
GATE
ALDERSGATE

ROMAN GATE
at Newgate

G.P.O.
yard

General
Post
Office

Altar of
Diana
found
at
Goldsmith's
Hall

Probable line of Roman street

Site of
LUDGATE

Roman
bath
found in 1667

St Paul's
Cathedral

Bow
Church

CHEAPSIDE

Wall
found

suggested alternative line

Probable line of Roman street

Watling street

ROMAN
BATH

Cannon Street

Queen Victoria Street

Wall not discovered here

Double wall
found on
Brook's yd

Roach Smith
recorded angle
of wall here

Stream of
Roman period

Queenhithe

Present Low Tide

Present Low Tide

River

Thames

The Fleet River

Scale of Yards

50   200   300   400   500   600

100   300   500   700   900

GORDON
HOME

A PLAN O

The landward wall that surrounded the city is shown with double lines from Ludgate to the Tower: where it still exists the space between the lines is shown in solid black. The Walbrook, then a stream of some size, divided the area of 326 acres into two unequal parts. The Walbrook and its tributaries, like the Fleet River, have since become sewers. (See page 56.)

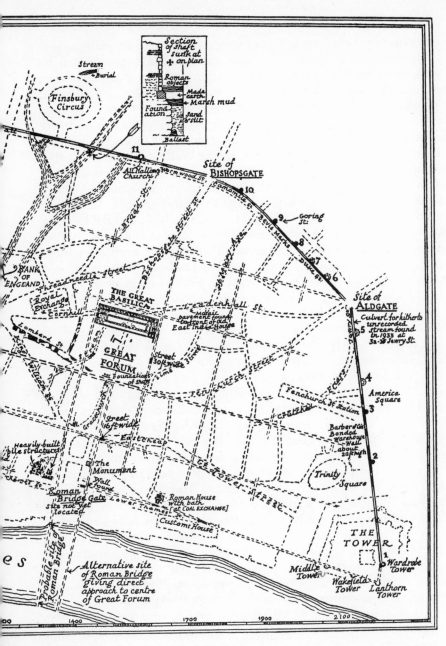

ROMAN LONDON

The eastern part of the city contained the Basilica, the Forum and probably most of the temples and public buildings. This conjectural plan, shown on these two pages, is by Mr. Gordon Home, F.S.A.(Scot.), and is reproduced from the 1948 edition of his book, *Roman London*, with his permission and by courtesy of the publishers, Eyre & Spottiswoode.

Roman cities that grew up from camps or strong points were generally square or rectangular, the axial lines of their main streets initially determined by military needs, and the grid or chessboard pattern of streets coming later. The areas of Roman towns were small, seldom more than three hundred acres, often very much less; and the rectangular form and grid plan though favoured were not universally imposed. Roman London, *Londinium Augusta*, covered three hundred and twenty-six acres, and was roughly semicircular in shape, bounded on the south side by the Thames, and bisected by the Walbrook, then a considerable and navigable stream. Some fifty yards away from the western wall, the Fleet flowed into the Thames. Paris, the Roman *Lutetia*, was originally confined to the small island in the Seine on which the cathedral of Notre Dame now stands on a site formerly occupied by a great temple to Jupiter. Like London, Paris spread beyond its original boundaries even in Roman times, and spilled over into suburbs on either side of the Seine after Gaul became a settled province of the Empire. The street plan of Roman London has been partly recovered, but it does not correspond with the mediaeval or modern street plan. London has probably, Paris certainly, been continuously inhabited without a break since Roman days, and many Italian cities too, but there is abundant evidence to show that the Roman town plans have seldom, if ever, endured. Even in Rome to-day there is barely one street that was in use in the ancient city. Such detailed knowledge as we have of Roman town planning is recovered chiefly from cities that have been long deserted, and in England the little country town of Calleva, adjacent to the village of Silchester, has supplied highly detailed information of the layout of a small, under-developed provincial town. Calleva is still surrounded by walls, but the walls were an after-thought, added long after the town had been laid out on a grid plan, and those walls are eight-sided, with irregular facets—not a tidy eight-sided town like that devised by Vitruvius, for the walls chop off the grid plan here and there without any reference to it. Silchester was an attempt, so Haverfield has suggested, "to insert urban features into a country-side." [41] The plan was probably conceived and laid out all at once, but the town was never fully developed; it was built up only here and there; by modern standards, a tiny place, though nearly a third of the size of Londinium, for the walls enclosed one hundred and two acres. Excavations were carried out there between 1890 and 1909, and have furnished us with fuller knowledge of a provincial Roman town than of any other site in the western provinces of the Empire. [42] It contained a forum and basilica, public baths, four small temples, and a very small Christian church, the earliest known in Britain, which was built about the middle of the fourth century—certainly not later. W. R. Lethaby considered that it was a Bishop's church, because of the important position it had in the city, close to the forum. [43] Although there were many private houses in the town, and it was full of gardens, the houses did not form continuous streets, and it seems like a tentative approach to the twentieth century garden city, though it was nothing of the kind, merely a country town, and probably the seat of local government for quite a large region.

The white bones of dead Roman cities are scattered over the sands of North Africa, and the excavations of recent years have revealed many facts about their character and appearance. Some were magnificent, like Leptis Magna, the birthplace of the Emperor Septimius Severus (A.D. 146–211), who lavished money on beautifying the place. In south-eastern France, the towns of Arles and Vaison are rich in Roman remains: both have amphitheatres, and that at Arles is one of the most impressive monuments in Europe. (See plate 9.)

All over the provinces of the Empire there were small, competently planned towns, some of which survived in mediaeval times. These Roman towns with their orderly plans were comfortable places to live in, even when they were hurriedly surrounded by walls, as many of them were in Britain and Gaul, and other provinces that were subjected to barbarian raids in the third and fourth centuries. Their plans were lost in the Dark Ages, for straight, broad streets were less easy to defend than the tangle of narrow lanes and crooked ways which replaced them in the mediaeval city. Narrow, twisting streets can be very easily defended—a fact that was discovered by revolutionary mobs some centuries after the Roman Empire had disappeared, a fact that Napoleon III recognised when he encouraged the replanning of Paris by Baron Haussmann in the sixties of the nineteenth century, so that its broad, radiating boulevards would afford no opportunity for mobs to erect barricades for defying the carefully constructed tyranny of the Second French Empire.

Like the ghost of the classical orders of architecture, the ghost of the Roman city plan haunted the Middle Ages; like the classical orders which were resurrected at the Renaissance, a modified version of the rectangular grid plan was revived in the thirteenth century. In England, Edward I replanned Winchelsea, one of the Cinque Ports in Sussex, which was laid out with rectangular streets intersecting at right angles: the Emperor Frederick II (1194–1250) built Terra Nova, in Sicily, on a grid plan, and in 1231 Barcelonette in south-east France was also built on a chessboard pattern.[44]

Orderly planning was reintroduced to Europe, and with it came back an understanding of the importance of clear, open spaces within a city, other than those occupied by cathedrals or markets. It was not until the Renaissance that the architectural significance of the street was rediscovered, so that once more the street itself, like the processional ways of the Greek cities, invited great architectural compositions. Nearly all these developments which occurred in the late Middle Ages and at the Renaissance had their origin in the Graeco-Roman world. It was in the cities and towns of that world that classical architecture grew into a variety of recognisable styles, and town planning became coherent, lucid, and occasionally inspired.

Seats in the Theatre of Dionysos, Athens (340 B.C.), which have exerted an influence upon the design of furniture, particularly during the Greek and neo-Greek revivals which began in England about 1795, and developed as a style during the opening decades of the nineteenth century, affecting taste not only in England but in the United States. "Many ornamental and structural forms that were ultimately carved in stone were probably tried out first in other materials; but sometimes a shape may have been brought to its final perfection in stone. In Greece the chair form may have evolved from a stone prototype. The elegant concave curve below some of the solid stone seats in the Theatre of Dionysos at Athens is reproduced in the legs of the chairs that are shown in detail on many Greek vases. The free-standing chair in ancient Greece may have developed from the marble seat, set against a wall, or carved complete from one solid block of stone." (*A Short Dictionary of Furniture*, Section I, page 42.)

III

CLASSICAL ARCHITECTURE

THE Greek and Roman orders have already been described briefly, and in this section they are illustrated in detail, so their individual characteristics may easily be recognised. Familiarity with their forms may be acquired from drawings, but the significance of their proportions is apparent only in actual examples. The ruins of Greece, Asia Minor, Sicily and Italy provide numerous examples of the Greek orders, and some remains are almost complete, like the three Doric temples at Paestum, south of Naples. In Athens, the Parthenon is the great example of the Doric order. (Plates 1 and 3.) Although many temples and other buildings in Greece are in a ruinous state, enough survives for many of them to be restored on paper and in the mind's eye. A detailed water-colour drawing of the probable appearance of the Parthenon, made during the last century by Charles Robert Cockerell (1788–1863), is reproduced on plate 2; an excellent scale model may be seen in the British Museum; and a model of the Acropolis by Mr. Gorham Phillips Stevens, as it appeared at the end of the first century B.C., is in the Museum of the Agora at Athens. Such conjectural restorations, though excellent, are obviously less satisfying than visits to actual ruins, with the imagination fortified by some knowledge of the character, proportions, and embellishment of the various orders.

It is not suggested that the modern equivalent of the Grand Tour is necessary before architecture may be appreciated, but to-day travel is far simpler for more people than ever before in the history of civilisation, and the monuments of the ancient world are reached far more easily than they were a couple of hundred years ago, when only adventurous and wealthy people were prepared to risk trouble and danger and fatigue in order to see for themselves what had survived in Greece and Asia Minor after centuries of barbarian occupation. In England, bodies like the Society of Dilettanti financed expeditions and commissioned architects and artists to make measured drawings and write detailed accounts of Athens as it was under Turkish rule. Compare Cockerell's restoration of the Parthenon with the drawing made under the direction of Stuart and Revett as they saw it in the mid-eighteenth century. (Both appear on plate 2.) To-day the temples are cleared of the Turkish houses which then sprawled over the Acropolis, and everywhere Greek and Roman ruins are treated with respect and care by governments and watchful private societies.

Although the orders had established proportions and characteristic forms of ornamentation, there were occasional departures from those forms. On the

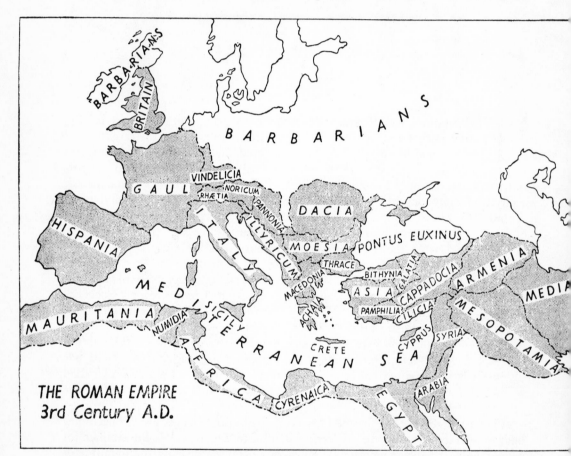

THE ROMAN EMPIRE
3rd Century A.D.

Throughout this vast territory, the classic orders stamped an unvarying style upon architecture. The triumphal arches and temples, the palaces, official and private buildings, everywhere exhibited the same proportions, the same standardised forms of ornamentation, whether they were erected in Londinium in Britain, Leptis Magna in Africa, or Ancyra in Asia Minor. Compare this map with that on page 104, which shows the barbarian successor states, after the Western Roman Empire had collapsed at the end of the fifth century. *Drawn by Marcelle Barton.*

The temple of Demeter, one of the three Doric temples at Paestum, South Italy. *Circa* 550 B.C.

Right: Detail of Greek Doric column and capital from the temple of Poseidon, Paestum. This is earlier than the temple of Demeter, and dates from 500 B.C. (See page 62 for details of Greek Doric order.)

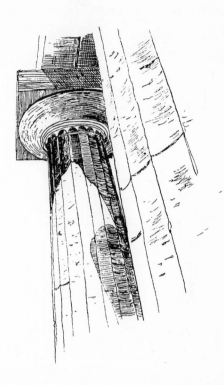

Acropolis at Athens, the south portico of the Erechtheion, an Ionic temple built between 420 and 393 B.C., has six female figures instead of columns, upholding an entablature, rather inelegantly, upon their heads. These caryatids, as they are called, are nearly 8 feet high and stand on a marble wall or base. They are in a poor state of preservation; the second one from the west is in the British Museum, though it is to be hoped that it will eventually be restored to its rightful place, and the terra-cotta replica, now used to fill the gap, removed. The word caryatid is derived from Caryatis, a woman of Caryae, a city in Laconia that sided with the Persians at Thermopylae, and was punished for that action by the Greeks, who destroyed the place, killed the men, and enslaved the women. It is possible that the disgrace of that enslavement was symbolised by the figures; though the term caryatids (or karyatides) was not used before Roman times. Similar figures support the entablature of the Treasury of Cnidus, at Delphi, a small building in the Ionic style. Whatever their origin they illustrate a rare lapse in the faultless taste and judgment of Greek architects. (See page 67 and plate 4.) Another departure from established

Doric

The Greek Doric order. The column has no base, and stands directly on a stylobate, usually of three steps. (See plate 5, for examples from the Parthenon, Sunium, and the temple of Apollo, Corinth.) The circular shaft of the column gradually diminishes from bottom to top, and is generally divided into twenty shallow flutes, though the number varies. There are twenty-four flutes on the columns of the temple of Poseidon at Paestum. (See detail on page 61.) The entasis is slightly convex, which corrects the slightly hollow appearance straight columns would otherwise have. The capital consists of annulets, or horizontal fillets, the echinus above them curving outwards and supporting the plain square slab of the abacus.

The columns support an entablature, consisting of three members: the architrave, the frieze—which is vertically divided into triglyphs with three upright channels, alternating with metopes, which are square open spaces—and the upper member, the cornice. The Roman variation of Doric is shown on page 72. *After Nicholson.*

This small Greek Doric building is the Treasury of the Athenians at Delphi, which has been extensively restored. The shaft of the right-hand column has been replaced, but the middle section of the left-hand column, and the capitals of both are original; so, too, are the entablature and pediment.

forms is a type of capital related to the Corinthian order, but with only one band of acanthus leaves round the lower part, and thin, blade-shaped leaves, resembling palm leaves, curving out above. These capitals appear on the Corinthian columns of the Tower of the Winds at Athens, and the writer has photographed a similar capital among the ruins of Corinth. (See plate 5.)

The capital of the Greek Ionic order had a few variations. Occasionally, the column would terminate in a band enriched with honeysuckle ornament below the volutes. Ionic columns of this type appear in the Erechtheion. (See page 66.) Sometimes the upper part of the capital is curved, bending round sharply to form the volute, as in the Temple of Apollo Epicurius at Bassae, whose ruins lie south of Andritsaina in the Peloponnese. Generally a simple, moulded band terminates the Ionic column, with an enriched moulding, carved

The Temple of Nikè Apteros (Athena Nikè) at Athens, built in 438 B.C., and
designed by Callicrates. It stands on the south-western spur of the Acropolis,
with the Propylae to the north. The plan of the Acropolis on page 49 shows the
relative positions, and another view of the temple is given on plate 5. It is a
delicate example of the Ionic order, and has been restored with great skill, for it
was demolished by the Turks in A.D. 1687, but the materials were recovered and
the temple rebuilt in 1836. *Drawn by Hilton Wright from a photograph by Alan Deller.*

with the egg-and-dart or egg-and-tongue ornament, appearing between the
volutes.

The type of acanthus leaf used on the Greek Corinthian order was more
delicately defined than the Roman acanthus, and on the capitals of the Roman
order, conventional clusters of olive leaves were often used, as on the capitals
of the Temple of Castor and Pollux at Rome. The acanthus appeared not only
on the Corinthian capital in Roman architecture, it coiled and flowed over
surfaces and mouldings, effectively and even urgently decorative, though Greek
sculptors used it with moderation to accentuate some beauty of line or subtlety
of proportion. Given the bones of the orders, and their proportions, Greek
architects could use a variety of ornamental forms without ever overloading
any building. The Romans were not always so happily capable.

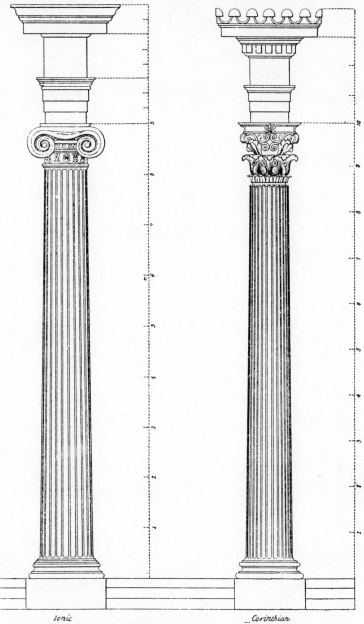

Ionic   *Corinthian*

The Greek Ionic and Corinthian orders. In both these orders the
capitals are highly decorative, the Ionic having large spiral ornaments
called volutes, while smaller volutes and formalised acanthus leaves
characterise the Corinthian capital. The entasis on the columns is less
marked than in the Doric order. Compare these with the Roman
variations shown on pages 74, 75, 77 and 78. *After Nicholson.*

Two examples of the Grecian Ionic capital, showing variations in the use of the anthemion ornament on the neckings. The upper capital is the type that appears on the Erechtheion on the Acropolis at Athens. Simpler types of Ionic capital are shown on pages 65 and 68. *After Nicholson.*

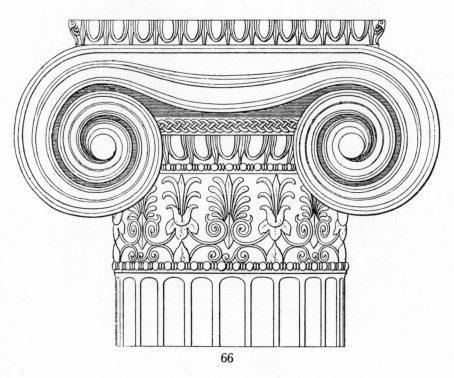

The south portico of the Erechtheion at Athens, showing the six caryatids supporting the entablature. (Detail of masonry on plate 4.) The Erechtheion was designed by Mnesicles, and built between 420 and 393 B.C.

Right: Detail of enriched moulding on the base of one of the Ionic columns on the east portico of the Erechtheion. (Detail of capital at top of page 66.)

In Greek architecture and ornament, the quality of design gave deep **and** sustained satisfaction to the eye. The ornamental forms were drawn from many sources, largely natural. Those derived from plants and flowers and the anatomy of animals are almost as old as civilisation, and nearly all the ornament associated with the orders, Greek and Roman, was drawn from organic sources: the labyrinth or Greek fret, and the bead and reel, being among the few devices unconnected with any natural prototype. The Ionic volute, a very ancient device, appears in a rudimentary form on the capitals of some Egyptian columns,

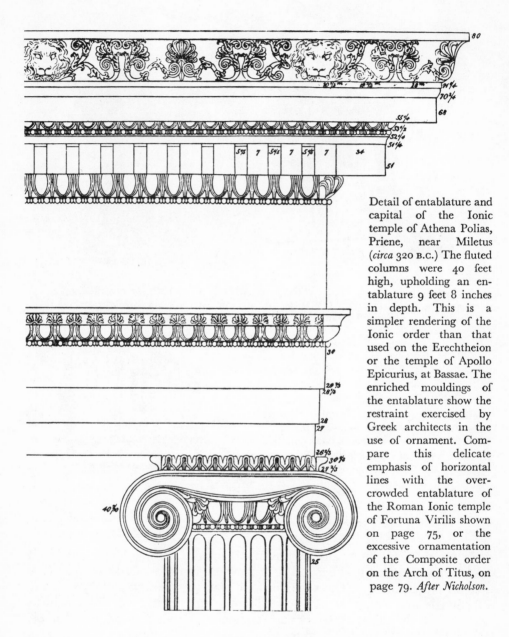

Detail of entablature and capital of the Ionic temple of Athena Polias, Priene, near Miletus (*circa* 320 B.C.) The fluted columns were 40 feet high, upholding an entablature 9 feet 8 inches in depth. This is a simpler rendering of the Ionic order than that used on the Erechtheion or the temple of Apollo Epicurius, at Bassae. The enriched mouldings of the entablature show the restraint exercised by Greek architects in the use of ornament. Compare this delicate emphasis of horizontal lines with the overcrowded entablature of the Roman Ionic temple of Fortuna Virilis shown on page 75, or the excessive ornamentation of the Composite order on the Arch of Titus, on page 79. *After Nicholson.*

Left: Capital used on a Corinthian column, from the Tower of the Winds, Athens (100–35 B.C.). This has one band of acanthus leaves, with a form of palm leaf above. *Drawn by Hilton Wright.* Capitals of this type are comparatively rare: another example, from the ruins of Corinth, is shown on plate 5.

Right: Greek Corinthian capital from the Monument of Lysicrates, Athens (335 B.C.). The lower band of the foliage is formed from lotus leaves, with a single band of very delicate acanthus leaves above. Compare this with the Roman examples on pages 77 and 78. *After Nicholson.*

and the nautilus shell provides an obvious model. Vines and bunches of grapes and honeysuckle were formalised and used, as well as the acanthus, but for some reason the acanthus plant appeared to satisfy the decorative needs of carvers and designers: in their hands it became so fluid and flexible that it is impossible to think of classical architecture without calling to mind some rendering, restrained or ornate, of this ubiquitous plant. The animal kingdom made a great contribution, and goats and lions were particularly favoured, the hooves and legs of the former, and the paws and masks of the latter appearing as supports and embellishments for furniture, altars and a variety of objects. The horse, with or without riders, was always galloping across Greek buildings, usually on the frieze, occasionally on the pediment, and in addition there was the fabulous fauna of mythology—satyrs, centaurs, and the griffin, chimera and sphinx. The type of frieze thronged with animals as well as human figures, was sometimes known as zoophorus.

The basic simplicity and clarity of the three Greek orders may be seen on pages 62 and 65. They should be compared with the Roman orders which

Anthemion ornament, from the temple of Apollo Epicurius, Bassae, *circa* 430 B.C.

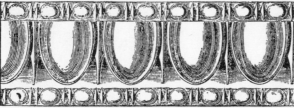

Echinus and astragal enrichment, from the Erectheion, Athens.

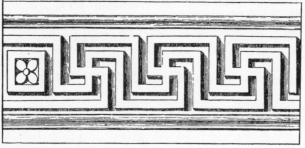

Greek fret or labyrinth.

Guilloche ornament.

Reproduced from Wornum's *Analysis of Ornament*.

Two variations of the formalised acanthus leaf: Greek on the left: Roman on the right. *Drawn by Hilton Wright.*

appear on pages 72, 74 and 79. They provided the bones. The manner in which they were arranged depended upon the architect. Some were men of genius, others were just competent; but in the Greek world there was nourishment for the genius, in the Roman there was discouragement—at least strong pressure would be exerted upon eccentric and unusual designers, so that they would feel it was politic to conform, and certainly far more comfortable. Criticism was unwelcome. Although cultivated Romans admired Greek philosophy and Greek art, in the staid, commercial atmosphere of Rome the Greek mind would have been hideously circumscribed. When Rome had become an elaborate tyranny, operating through an efficient bureaucracy, imaginative flights of fancy and critical comments were not encouraged, as Apollodorus of Damascus discovered when he made an amusing and perfectly true remark about the Emperor Hadrian's plans for a temple. As an architect, Apollodorus realised that if the statues of the goddesses seated in the temple could stand erect, their heads would go through the roof; and he was tactless enough to mention this to the Emperor, thus losing his client, and, a little later, his life.

Although the Roman approach to architecture was wholly different from that of the Greeks, the achievements of Roman architects should not be minimised, nor should their great gifts as engineers and town planners be ignored. The Greeks attained one of those great peaks of civilisation that sometimes occur—possibly the highest that has yet occurred. Their civilisation, centred upon Athens in the fifth century B.C., unlocked something in the human mind that has never since been wholly lost. The Greek deification of the sense of sight was not the only reason for their buildings having such lucent beauty; in serving their sense of sight they were mobilising not only the skill of master builders but the skill of master mathematicians, who employed mathematics to serve an aesthetic end and to express a belief in reason and beauty; so it is the intellectual clarity of the Greek mind that shines forth from the great Greek

The five Roman orders. Reading from left to right, they are: Tuscan, Doric, Ionic, Composite, and Corinthian. These orders spread over the whole of the Western Empire, and adorned buildings in every province, from Britain to Syria, from North Africa to the borders of Germany. *After Rickman.*

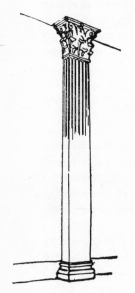

Left: A Corinthian pilaster, or rectangular column, attached to a wall surface. Pilasters conformed with the design of the various Roman orders. (From *A Short Dictionary of Architecture*, by Dora Ware and Betty Beatty.)

The temple of Fortuna Virilis at Rome, 100 B.C. An example of a simple, rectangular Roman Ionic temple. (See details of column and entablature on pages 74 and 75.)

temples. There have been other ages of reason, and the last was in the eighteenth century, when in Western Europe architecture again reached a high and lucid level of accomplishment, particularly in France and England.

The Romans and their buildings and engineering feats gave to Europe, and to the whole of subsequent Western civilisation, a respect for orderliness, a reverence for law, and an admiration for technical achievement which, though periodically submerged, still persists. The impact of Rome upon the Greek world was not unlike the impact of the United States of America upon the Old World of Europe and Asia. This is suggested by some Greek ruins, like those on the site of Delphi, which lies on the slopes of Mount Parnassus, looking as if it had been carved from the mountain-side, with grey, orange-streaked cliffs rising above the ruins. The area is covered by the remains of temples, and some days would be needed thoroughly to explore what has been carefully excavated. The great temple of Apollo, where the Oracle spoke, was of the Greek Doric order, a tall and relatively simple structure that probably had some of the stupendous calm and dignity of the Parthenon. There have been various attempts to reconstruct some of the temples, but the ruins tell an easily read story of how the Romans came along in rather a bustling, business-like way, to regularise the commercial possibilities of the place, and to see that it paid dividends, though there is no reason to suppose that the Greeks had failed to exploit it commercially. Large areas were covered with shops, there was a *bureau de change*, where visitors had to convert their money into currency that was acceptable to the servants of the Oracle, and then reconvert it, while the money-changers took their immemorial commission. Similar scenes probably took place in the forecourt of the Temple at Jerusalem.

The Oracle had an international reputation. Delphi attracted thousands of people yearly, although most people knew that the Oracle was discreet to the point of bewildering ambiguity. You had to interpret yourself what she said,

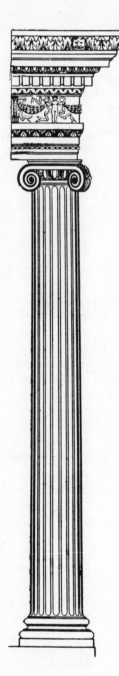

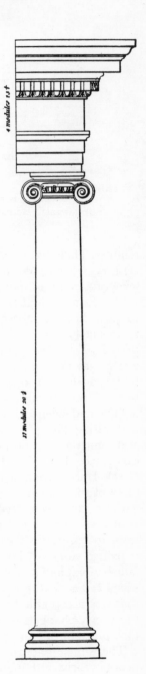

The Roman Ionic order had less grace than its Greek prototype: like the other Roman orders, it was often used in conjunction with the pier and arch, to the detriment of its structural significance, so that it became a decorative addition to a façade. The example on the left is from the temple of Fortuna Virilis at Rome, which is illustrated on page 73. Angular capitals are used so the scrolls of the volutes show on all four sides. (See detail of the capital and entablature on page 75.) On the right is an unfluted Ionic column from the Theatre of Marcellus, at Rome (23–13 B.C.). The Ionic order was used for the upper tier of arcading, superimposed on the Doric of the lower tier. *After Nicholson.*

Detail of the capital and entablature of the Ionic temple of Fortuna Virilis at Rome (100 B.C.). The three members of the entablature, cornice, frieze, and architrave, are encrusted with carved ornament: the volutes on the angular capitals are enriched on the side with a formalised acanthus leaf, and the scrolls terminate in rosettes. When compared with the scrolls on the Greek Ionic capitals shown on pages 66 and 68, the Roman version has less elegance. The Greek scrolls have a greater subtlety of line.
After Nicholson.

The Pantheon at Rome, which was
built between 27 B.C. and A.D. 14. The
best preserved of all the ancient
buildings of Rome. (Detail of the type
of Corinthian capital used on the
Pantheon is shown opposite, below on
the right.)

and history records that many people made the wrong interpretation. King
Croesus certainly did, and after following what he thought was the Oracle's
advice, and then losing his kingdom and most of his fortune, he presented a
large silver bowl to the temple, inscribed with a testimonial to the Oracle, with
a frank confession of his own misinterpretation of what she had said. The place
where the bowl was accommodated is still visible—at least, it is alleged to be
the place. But the story suggests that the temple and its precincts were loaded
with offerings of all kinds, and the wealth that poured into the place must
have been enormous. It was a strange mixture of reverence and graft. The
buildings were finely sited, and interspersed with statues, memorials to victories,
and all the odds and ends of pious junk that accumulate at holy places.
Christianity finally ended the prosperity of Delphi. The attempt of Julian, the
Apostate Emperor, to revive it, after it had fallen into disuse, failed. There
is a tradition that the last pronouncement made by the Oracle was "The gods
are dead."

The Romans did not inherit or copy all their architectural ideas from Greece.

These examples of Roman Corinthian capitals are from the temples of Mars
Ultor (*left*) and the Jupiter Tonans (*right*), built by Augustus on the Capitoline
hill. They lack the refinement of the Greek capitals of this order (see page 69), but
have not yet become too florid; the modest proportions of the volutes below the
abacus are retained.

These two examples are from the temple of Vesta at Tivoli (*left*) and the Pantheon
(*right*). The four capitals on this page are all from buildings erected during the
reign of Augustus, 27 B.C.–A.D.14. (See page 76 for illustration of the Pantheon.)
After Nicholson.

As Mycenaen architecture preceded Doric, so did Etruscan architecture precede
Roman. The Etruscans inhabited central Italy, and some of their architecture
dating from the middle of the eighth century B.C. employed arch forms that
were adopted by the Romans who, as we have mentioned earlier, used the
arch extensively, but did not allow it to inspire architectural composition; it

Later examples of the Roman Corinthian capital display greater elaboration than those shown opposite. Here are two, dating from the second and third centuries. *Left:* From the temple of Antoninus and Faustina at Rome, A.D. 141. *Right:* From the temple of Vesta at Rome, A.D. 205. *After Nicholson.*

was immensely useful to them, particularly in the construction of the great aqueducts that strode across the Campagna to carry water into Rome, and, as arrow-straight as their roads, crossed valleys and plains in every province.

What did the Romans bequeath to Europe, apart from the respect for law, order, town planning and technical ability? A road system, which still forms the basis of many road systems in European countries, and particularly in England; though that, to be sure, was just a part of Roman order. They worked out with admirable precision the sorts and types of houses suited to different degrees of citizens, to different ranks and standards of wealth. They also evolved for use in some of the bleaker provinces, as well as for their own baths, the most admirable heating system—a system of central heating that has never been bettered, and enabled Roman colonists, officials and army officers to settle comfortably with their families, even in the tricky and unpredictably trying British climate. Vitruvius wrote extensively about all the admirable regulations for domestic buildings, and to this branch of architecture the Romans made a far greater contribution than the Greeks. In Greece, there is every encouragement to live out of doors. The ancient Greeks did, so do the modern Greeks. Houses are mere shelters for the night. In the Athens of Pericles, they were of the simplest kind. In the Rome of the Antonines they were most luxuriously appointed, and even the artisans' dwellings had accommodation and convenience of a kind unknown in Athens.

The whole development and spread of classical architecture throughout the ancient world was based upon the use of the post-and-beam structural principle.

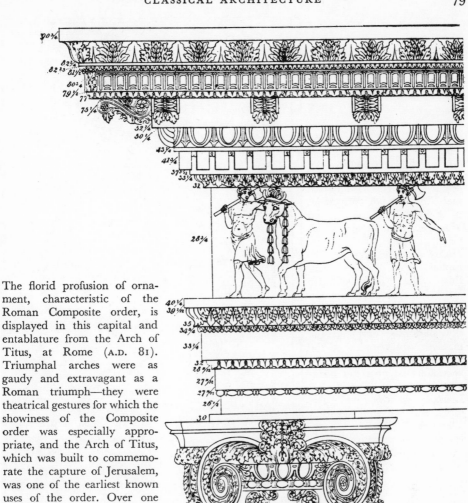

The florid profusion of ornament, characteristic of the
Roman Composite order, is
displayed in this capital and
entablature from the Arch of
Titus, at Rome (A.D. 81).
Triumphal arches were as
gaudy and extravagant as a
Roman triumph—they were
theatrical gestures for which the
showiness of the Composite
order was especially appropriate, and the Arch of Titus,
which was built to commemorate the capture of Jerusalem,
was one of the earliest known
uses of the order. Over one
hundred and twenty years later
it figured on an even more
extravagant design: the Arch of
Septimius Severus (see page
84). *After Nicholson.*

An example of the use of the scroll and the acanthus, from a fragment of pilaster, second century A.D. This is a typical piece of Roman ornament, using the *Acanthus mollis*, or soft acanthus. The Greeks used, very sparingly, the narrow, prickly *Acanthus spinosus*. For capitals on the Roman Corinthian order, clusters of olive leaves are often used, a modification which arose, according to Wornum "out of the necessity for strong effect in the massive lofty temples of the Romans: but this peculiar conventional leaf does not occur otherwise than on the capitals." (*Analysis of Ornament.*) The scroll, enriched with acanthus foliations, is characteristically Roman. (See pages 71, 75, 79, and 81.)

It encouraged the invention of harmonious relationships between horizontal and vertical elements, with the arch used as an incidental convenience in Roman building, and not at all in Greek. The materials employed were stone and brick and timber; and the fineness of Greek and Roman masonry is one of the reasons why so many of their buildings have survived. By the time Greece

Ornamental treatment of the frieze on the Forum of Trajan (A.D. 98–117). This was probably the work of the Greek architect, Apollodorus of Damascus, who also designed the Trajan column (A.D. 114). In his *Analysis of Ornament*, Wornum said that the Roman style was "simply an enlargement or enrichment of the florid Greek. It did not add a single important element to the Greek, but elaborated the established elements with every possible variety of effect, and with all the exuberance and richness of which they are capable, developing some into comparatively colossal proportions. It was, therefore, original only in its treatment of the Greek materials. Roman art is accordingly still Greek art; and it is more than probable that nearly all the great artists employed by the Romans were Greeks. . . ." He added that though it was not original, Roman ornament had its peculiar characteristics. "The chief of these is its uniform magnificence. The most simple Greek ornament becomes, under Roman treatment, if not a magnificent, at least an elaborate decoration." (See page 70.)

was incorporated in the Roman Empire, the lively architectural inspiration of the Greeks had been expended, and no longer gave an impetus to great building. Having established and perfected a system for the design of practically everything, Roman architects, though personally ambitious, lost the spirit of adventure, and their inventive powers were atrophied. By the second century of the Christian era, architecture was static, dully repetitive, and gave the impression that not only architects but their patrons had already sunk far into the state of fatuous complacency that leads to apathy. Some new movement, some fresh stimulant was needed, and it came, at first in a tentative, experimental fashion, from an underground religion, a slave religion, that was intermittently persecuted, and consistently frowned upon by the best people. After Christianity became the official religion of the Roman Empire, and churches could be built openly, a new form of architecture arose, and one that almost from the outset adopted the arch as an integral part of structure and design. One of the earliest examples of Christian architecture at Rome is the basilican church of St. Paul's-outside-the-Walls, which was built about A.D. 380. It was destroyed in 1823, but was rebuilt to the original design. Such early Christian

The Colosseum at Rome, sometimes known as the Flavian Amphitheatre, was built between A.D. 70 and A.D. 82. The structural use of the arch, though apparent, has no significant influence upon the exterior: it is deliberately "played down" in the decorative interests of the superimposed orders, Tuscan, Ionic, and Corinthian, represented by half-columns on the first three tiers of the façade, with Corinthian pilasters used on the upper tier. A comparable technique, subordinating the structural arches to the non-structural orders, is shown in the detail of one of the tiers of the Amphitheatre at Arles on plate 9. Vitruvius regarded the arch chiefly as a device that could relieve pressure on beams, for he thought— as Roman architects generally thought—in terms of the orders and post-and-lintel construction.

The arch was known in pre-Roman Italy, though it was invented long before it was employed by the architects of ancient Etruria. (See page 36.) This is an example of an Etruscan archway, which forms part of the Arch of Augustus at Perugia. Roman additions have been made above the line of the frieze.

Roman engineers consistently used arches when building the great aqueducts that strode across the valleys and plains of Italy and the provinces of the Empire. The Pont du Gard, at Nîmes, France, constructed by Agrippa in 19 B.C. Masonry arches for aqueducts and bridges remained in use for hundreds of years, and even in the late nineteenth century when new materials such as cast iron and steel were available, immense masses of brickwork were still used for aqueducts and viaducts.

The Arch of Septimius Severus at Rome, erected in A.D. 204 and dedicated to the Emperor and his two sons. The triple arches have not been allowed to become structurally significant: they are, first and last, apertures with semicircular heads, pierced in the great white marble mass of masonry, their function mini-mised in the general composition, and their lines unrelated to the detached columns of the Composite order, which rise from pedestals to support the entablature. Originally this large, pretentious triumphal arch was surmounted by statues of the Emperor and his sons, in a four-horse chariot, while at each end, vertically aligned with the end columns, were figures of soldiers.

churches were modelled on the Roman basilica, and they incorporated the traditional characteristics of classical architecture; but it was in the Eastern rather than the Western Empire that this architecture developed its characteris-tic form. After the Western Roman Empire lost its political independence in A.D. 476, when the barbarian king Odoacer informed Constantinople that there was no longer an Emperor in the West, architectural growth was vigorously resumed, and the second great principle of construction, the arch, openly and intelligently employed.

IV

TRANSITIONAL: BYZANTINE

C LASSICAL architecture had imposed standardised forms throughout the Western Empire; the five orders and their regulated ornamentation, variously employed in public and private buildings, had effectively repressed local expression in architectural design. Very rarely there was a hint that independent inspiration existed, though it could find an outlet only in sculpture. For example, in Britain, far from the central government and the artistic fashions of the imperial city, native sculptors occasionally indulged an unconventional individualism. At Bath, the hot springs were under the patronage of a goddess called Sul, who was identified by the Romans with Minerva,(45) and on the tympanum of a pediment of a temple of this goddess, there is a bearded Gorgon head, quite unclassical in vigour of execution and intensity of expression. The temple itself, so far as may be judged from its remains, followed the conventional architectural pattern. (The Roman name for Bath was Aquae Sulis.)

Another piece of Romano-British sculpture found at Corbridge (the Roman Corstopitum, a little south of Hadrian's Wall), representing a lion devouring a stag, is a virile piece of barbarian art. It was part of the decoration of a fountain, a subject common enough as a classical motif, but the lion might have come out of a mediaeval bestiary. These are isolated instances of native artists momentarily escaping from accepted conventions. They suggest that in the western provinces of the Empire, submerged native talent could still break through to the surface of life, if given opportunity. That opportunity was presently to be supplied by church-building.

It has already been said that the early Christian churches were modelled on the Roman basilica—the large hall, used for public administration, with a semicircular apse at the end—but there were other influences which formed the character of early Christian architecture. Although Christianity was officially

85

recognised and adopted as the state religion of the Empire, throughout the fourth century and for many centuries after it was competing with other religions. In the early days of its freedom, its most formidable rival was the cult of Mithras, by far the most important and widely established religion, which in many ways resembled Christianity. The Mithraic cult was very popular with soldiers, and wherever there were garrisons, some evidence of Mithraism usually occurs. The form of its sanctuaries and chapels may indeed have suggested some of the characteristics of the early Christian churches. The worshippers of Mithras were many and varied, and like Christianity it was a classless religion, patrician and slave, officer and legionary, worshipping side by side in the Mithraeum. It was for men only, women were rigidly excluded; but Mithraism, because of its excellence as a religion, was the most serious competitor of Christianity, and was, as Phythian-Adams has pointed out, "a constant peril to the Church. It failed at last, not because it was entirely bad, but because it was so nearly good."(46)

The resemblance of the Mithraeum to the form of the Christian church is significant. The temple or cave where the rites were celebrated was intended to suggest a rock-hewn vaulted chamber, and was often built underground. If this was not possible, then the level of the adjoining chambers was artificially raised so that a short descent could indicate the subterranean character of the rites. A full and detailed description of Mithraic monuments has been given

Interior view of St. Clemente, Rome, a basilican church, built in its present form between 1084–1108, but based on the remains of a fifth century church which occupied the site. The proportions of the orders are still preserved, which suggests that the character of the original basilican church was closely followed by the architect who rebuilt the structure.

An early Christian basilican church. The interior of St. Paul's-outside-the-Walls, Rome, founded about A.D. 380, destroyed in 1823, and
completely rebuilt to the original design. The architects of many of
the early Christian churches adopted the arch principle, and used the
the orders in relation to arches, as part of a structural pattern, not merely
as surface decoration.

by Phythian-Adams. "The main design of the *Mithraeum* itself seems hardly
ever to have varied," he wrote. "Once seen, even in a state of dilapidation,
it is easily and quickly recognised. The eye is immediately caught by the
Benches or platforms which run from end to end of the chapel on either side
of the central *Aisle*. In width about 4 feet, they stand 2 feet high in the centre
of the spelaeum, but slope gradually backwards to its lateral walls. Sometimes
they are on a level with the door; sometimes they rise above it, and are ascended
by a few steps from the floor of the 'nave.' Not infrequently a ledge was left
along the whole of their length to support lamps and statues, and thus free the
central aisle of any encumbrance."[47]

The Mithraic chapels were usually very small, providing room for barely
fifty worshippers, while even the largest could barely accommodate twice that
number. The cave, the underground sanctuary, had a profound effect upon
the early Christian communities, who had performed their rites in catacombs

St Maria in Cosmedin, Rome, a church with a Romanesque tower, which was a comparatively late addition, as the basilica was built in the sixth century, and the church was enlarged at the end of the eighth century by Adrian I, who was Pope from 772 to 795. Alterations and restorations were made in the twelfth century, also in the eighteen-nineties. It is basically an Early Christian church.

and other secret places. These influences may have generated the desire for a dim, half-lit mysterious place of worship.

Christianity's conflict with paganism continued for centuries, for in all the provinces of the Empire both native and Roman cults survived, at first, openly, and then, as the Church grew stronger, they became what Christianity had once been—secret and hunted down. Their priests and priestesses were identified with wizards and witches, who unlawfully practised "the old religion," which the early Christians had condemned as heathenism and the mediaeval churchmen as witchcraft. That "old religion" survived in Europe until far into the seventeenth century, and even appeared in the English colonies of North America, which led to the witch hunts of New England. In most of the provinces, heathenism was still firmly entrenched throughout the fourth, fifth and sixth centuries, and in some provinces, like Britain and Gaul, it was reinforced by pagan invaders and settlers. In what remained of the Empire after the fourth century, the various pagan cults were deliberately despoiled, their temples desecrated, or adapted as Christian churches, and few, if any, new buildings arose in honour of the old gods. Perhaps one of the last to be built in the Western Empire was in Britain, when, about A.D. 365, a great temple was erected at Lydney, in the Forest of Dean, in honour of Nodens, or Nudens, a native British god, who has been identified with Nud, or Ludd, the Nuada of Celtic mythology.[48] This sacred edifice at Lydney was a most ambitious undertaking, with a hostelry and baths, and probably owed its existence to the encouragement given by the Emperor Julian (331–363) to the pagan cults.

St. Apollinare-in-Classe, Ravenna (A.D. 534–539). This was built on the
site of a temple to Apollo, by Justinian, and shows very strong Byzantine
influence. The campanile, which is the same date as the church, is probably
one of the earliest of these bell towers.

Christianity as a state religion supplied patronage for building on a scale
and of a kind that soon surpassed the humble places of worship to which the
faithful had formerly resorted. The official recognition of the Church by the
Roman state was indicated by the adoption of the basilical form for churches,
thus simulating the specific features of a Roman hall of justice, with its apsidal
end which, in the secular edifice, accommodated the tribunal for the judges
and assessors. The Roman basilica was rectangular in plan, twice as long as its
width, with two or four rows of columns running the whole length, thus forming
three or five aisles. This type of plan was probably derived from the Greek
temple, so that, through Rome, the early Christian churches had a tenuous
connection with Greece in the conception of a sacred building, apart from the
more obvious affinity that sprang from the use of the orders.

The removal of the seat of empire from Rome to Byzantium led ultimately
to the development of a new style of church; for Byzantium was a Greek city,
and its transformation into an Imperial capital gave Greek architects and
craftsmen an opportunity for discarding the arid conventions of Roman
architecture. A new city was laid out and built, named Constantinople in
honour of the Christian Emperor, and dedicated in the year 330 to the Blessed
Virgin. Despite this dedication, there were many things in the city calculated
to wound the pious and infuriate the fanatic. Zosimus, who lived there and
wrote his history of the Roman emperors in the latter part of the fifth century,
states that after enlarging the city, Constantine "built a palace little inferior
to that of Rome, and very much embellished the hippodrome, or horse-course,

Exterior view of St. Vitale, Ravenna (A.D. 526–547). The interior dome is not visible from the outside, and is covered with a tiled, octagonal roof, rising in a gentle slope to the cross. This is a comparatively simple design, with an octagonal plan. The church was founded by Justinian.

taking into it the temple of Castor and Pollux, whose statues are still standing in the porticoes of the hippodrome. He placed on one side of it the tripod that belonged to the Delphian Apollo, on which stood an image of the deity. As there was at Byzantium a very large market-place, consisting of four porticoes, at the end of one of them, to which a numerous flight of steps ascends, he erected two temples; in one of which was placed the statue of Rhea, the mother of the gods. In the other temple he placed the statue of the Fortune of Rome."(49)

It was at Constantinople that architects began to use the arch as a structural principle as it had never been used before, and created the Byzantine church, with its vaulted roof and central dome. The basilican churches had arches, springing from rows of columns, as exemplified by the interior of St. Paul's-outside-the-Walls at Rome; but those arches made no structural contribution to the roof, which remained flat or pitched. By floating a dome over the square or polygonal plans of their churches and tombs, Byzantine architects re-animated architectural design, and their adventures in building from the fourth to the seventh centuries represent the last original manifestation of classical architecture in the Graeco-Roman world. Through their adroit use of the arch and the dome, they restored to architecture an intellectual power which approached, though it could not equal, that exhibited by the Greek Doric temples. They were handicapped by an obligation to venerate a faith that had established the reign of intolerance on earth, had suppressed independent thought, and was hostile to intellectual values. The lucidity that marked this late and final flowering of Greek architectural genius could not be wholly masked, even though the interiors of Byzantine churches were clothed with the burning jewellery of mosaics, superbly executed though often indifferently conceived. By the time of Justinian, when Santa Sophia was built at Constantinople, the age of reason was over. The passing of that bright period of human enlightenment and intellectual adventure was proclaimed to what was left of Western civilisation when Justinian closed the schools of Athens.

The Byzantines used concrete and brickwork in the construction of their

Left: Detail of capital from the basilica of St. Vitale at Ravenna (A.D. 526–547). In form and ornament, the capital has lost its classical likeness: the acanthus leaf is handled quite differently from the upright formal appearance it has on a Roman Corinthian capital, and is enclosed within an intricate framework.

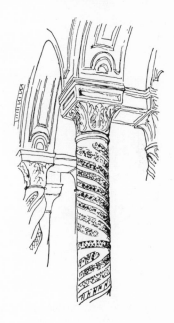

Right: In this example, from the cloisters of St. Paul's-outside-the-Walls, Rome, the relationship of the capital with the Corinthian order is still perceptible, but the likeness is blurred, and the the detail of the abacus—the flat, upper part of the capital from which the arches spring—and the decoration of the columns show how far architects have departed from the rules governing the use of the orders. The next stage in the flight from classic discipline may be seen in the cloisters of St. John, Lateran, Rome, on page 139.

buildings, which supplied internally an admirable surface for applying marble and mosaics. An almost Oriental lusciousness in the use of colour characterised the interiors of churches, large and small, while columns and their bases and capitals underwent exotic changes. Those churches with their domes, building up out of each other, their arches springing from marble columns, and the opulent decoration of their walls, glowing with golds and rubies and blues, had a sensuous atmosphere; the clarity of form which had distinguished Greek and Roman buildings was subordinated to an emotional appeal, that might be holy in intention but was often voluptuous in effect.

Greek architects had already made a supreme contribution to the education of the Western world by idealising form in the fifth and fourth centuries B.C.— a thousand years later, through Byzantine architecture, they were to idealise colour. Arches and domes provided the curved surfaces which gave depth to rich, dark, gleaming compositions in mosaics: irresistibly potent in their assault upon the senses: indisputably Greek in the thoroughness of that calculated impingement. Santa Sophia, though it has not been a church since 1453, and

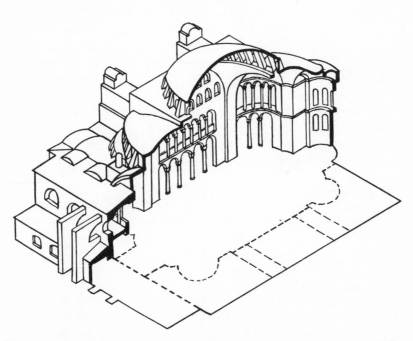

West to east section through Santa Sophia, showing the dome and semi-domes supported on pendentives. (See diagram of interior on page 95, also plate 11.) The dotted lines complete the plan of the interior. Examples of two types of columns used in Santa Sophia are shown on page 96. *Drawn by Marcelle Barton.*

is no longer a mosque, only a rather forlorn state museum, makes an impact upon the emotions comparable with the impact of the Parthenon upon the mind. Only the interior of Santa Sophia makes this impression: outside it is disappointing, and it is difficult to get a comprehensive view of the exterior. Seen from a distance, it is surrounded by lesser and rather muddled buildings, the dome appearing to rise from amid a froth of red roofs. Like the older mosques of the Turkish city, it is elephant grey in colour, and resembles them superficially in form, a resemblance that is accentuated by the four minarets that surround it, as abruptly vertical as exclamation marks.

Istanbul to-day is a larger and far more congested city than Roman Constantinople. Viewed from the high ground above Eyub, the industrial quarter at the far end of the Golden Horn, it has a skyline spiked with minarets, their thin pencil point towers contrasting sharply with the seven great domes that are visible, of which Santa Sophia is one. Beneath that dome there is an air of spaciousness, calm, vast, and mystical—you can forget momentarily that the odour of sanctity has departed, that the great building is mourning its lost worshippers, Christian and Moslem, that it is now only a museum, chilled by the uninspired breath of the modern state that owns and preserves it for the benefit of tourists. The great dome appears to hover over the central area, which is 107 feet square—free, open space, uninterrupted by columns, for at each corner are massive stone piers, upholding four semicircular arches upon which the dome rests. On the huge pendentives, curved in contiguity with those supporting arches, the figures of Cherubim with six wings seem to bear aloft the dome on their pale green and brown pinions. (A pendentive is a curved, triangular, overhanging surface, which, springing from the corner of a square, hexagonal or decagonal compartment, supports a circular dome. See diagram on page 95.) The dome resting on pendentives was probably invented and perfected in the East, and the adoption of this structural technique enabled Byzantine architects to create those untroubled interiors over which domes swim with the lightness of bubbles.

East and west of the central area in Santa Sophia are great semicircular spaces, with half-domes above, flanked by tall alcoves also rising to half-domes, and at the far eastern end is an apse. The central dome and the half-domes thus cover an oval nave, 107 feet wide and 225 feet long. The dome is lit by forty small arched windows, pierced in the lower part. (Some authorities suggest that those windows were not part of the design but were apertures made to accommodate scaffolding when the dome was built.) Arches, pendentives and domes appear to flow into each other; there is an illusion of movement, as though the semi-domes and the dome itself were gently oscillating—an effect that may be due partly to daylight shimmering on the dull gold of the mosaics above the line of the upper arcade. North and south of the square beneath the dome are two arcades, one above the other, and the great piers at the corners of the central area are pierced by arches to allow the aisles and galleries to pass through them. The walls on either side of the lower arcade are faced with marbles of white, blue, green and black. The Turkish additions to the interior are inconspicuous, apart from eight circular panels which are hung round the walls, inscribed in gold with appropriate quotations from the Koran. When the church was transformed into a mosque, after Constantinople was captured by Mahomet II, the walls were whitewashed, the mosaics covered, and all symbols of Christianity removed. Since the interior has been restored almost to its original state, and the building has ceased to be a mosque, the Turkish authorities have contented themselves with a little modest cancellation, so where crosses appear, they are partly obliterated.

The interior of the church shows how the builders had breathed fresh life into traditional ideas, for they did not wholly renounce tradition. Justinian's architects, Anthemius of Tralles and Isodorus of Miletus, had, according to Gibbon, "discreetly confessed how much their laborious meditations were surpassed by the intuitive knowledge or celestial inspiration of an emperor, whose views were always directed to the benefit of his people, the glory of his reign, and the salvation of his soul."[50] Whatever may have been the source of the architects' inspiration, they gave an almost magical property to the materials they used. Lethaby and Swainson, in their study of Santa Sophia, pointed out that "After more than a thousand years of working marble through one complete development, Greek builders, by considering afresh the prime necessities of material, and a rational system of craftsmanship, opened the great quarry of ideas in constructive art which is inexhaustible. In a hundred years architecture became truly *organic*, features that had become mere 'vestiges' dropped away, and a new style was completed; one, not perhaps so completely winning as some forms of Gothic, but the supremely logical building art that has been. If anywhere this vitalising had not been completed, it would have been in the more decorative forms; but here we find no mere exercise in applying architectural orders, everything is as real and fresh as in the structure. Having the Corinthian and Ionic capitals before their eyes and without forgetting or rejecting them, the Byzantine builders invented and developed an entirely fresh group of capitals fitted in the most perfect way for arched brick construction."[51]

Those builders invented what was virtually a new order, by "shaping the block of marble which formed the capital so that a simple transition from the square block to the circle of the column was formed. When they were sculptured, and most of them are most elaborately sculptured, the general form is not altered but the carving enriches the surface only."[52] Four principal variations of this new capital appear in Santa Sophia. Those who admired the purity of the classic orders might feel as outraged as Gibbon did, when in the course of his description of the columns in the interior, he praised their size and beauty, but added "every order of architecture disclaims their fantastic capitals."[53]

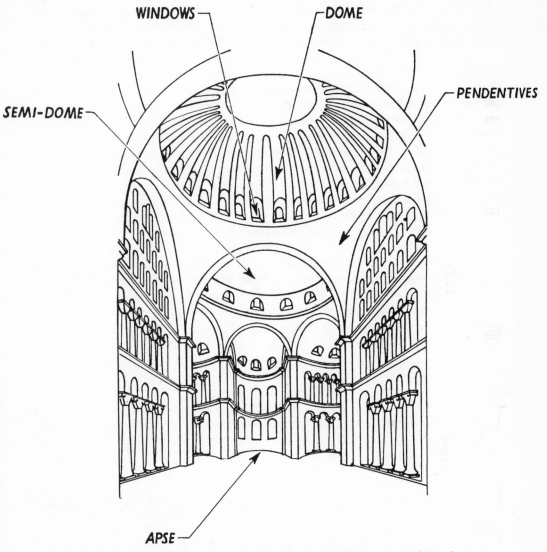

WINDOWS

DOME

SEMI-DOME

PENDENTIVES

APSE

Diagram of interior of Santa Sophia, looking east towards the apse, and showing the pendentives which support the dome. The structural significance of the pendentives is shown in the west to east section through the church on page 92. (See plate 11.) Details of columns and capitals, showing the great order, are on page 96. *Drawn by Marcelle Barton.*

Santa Sophia is a unique example of Byzantine architecture; although the use of a principal dome and various minor domes distinguishes the churches that were built throughout the Eastern Empire, the actual form of Justinian's masterpiece was never repeated, even on a smaller scale. St. Mark's at Venice, built five hundred years later, owed its inspiration less to Santa Sophia than to the Church of the Apostles at Constantinople, which was destroyed in 1463 to provide a site for the mosque of Sultan Mahomet II.

One of the smaller churches in Constantinople that still survives is St. Saviour in the Chora. There was probably a church on the site before the fifth century, but about 413 one was built, and repaired over a century later by Justinian. During the Fourth Crusade it was sacked when the Crusaders were looting the Christian capital of the Eastern Empire. It was restored during the fourteenth century, and the mosaics date from that time, though they are probably based on much earlier designs. It is a typical example of the darkly rich, coloured interior which Byzantine architects perfected. The dome rests on a tall drum, pierced with windows; smaller domes cluster around the central dome, while outside a wholly inappropriate minaret has been attached. Because of the richness of the mosaics, it was formerly known as the Mosaic Mosque. The introduction of black and white gives exceptional definition to some of the designs; the whole interior appears to be covered with cloth of gold; and the rugged crudity of the figures portrayed is easy to ignore because they are brought together in a masterly pattern. A few details have refinement, notably

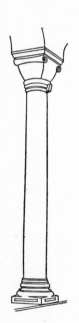

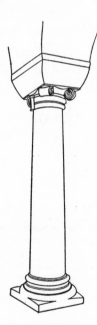

What was virtually a new order of architecture was invented by the designers of Santa Sophia, with capitals shaped to simplify the transition from the circle of the column to the square block of marble it supported. These capitals were intricately carved, and their richness had been anticipated in other parts of the Roman Empire—at St. Vitale at Ravenna, for example. (See page 91.) Here are two types of columns, with the capitals shown in outline only: that on the left is of the great order, from the interior of Santa Sophia—one of the slender columns that support the gallery—and on the right is one of the gallery columns. *Drawn by Marcelle Barton.*

The church of St. Saviour in the Chora, Constantinople, showing one of the smaller domes, and the surface variation of the masonry. Drawn by Hilton Wright from a photograph of the south-western end of the church by the author. (See plate 12.)

the hands of some of the figures. The church has a placid air, and the dome, like Santa Sophia, seems to be floating above the space beneath, which is unimpeded by supporting columns.

The dome had been used by the Romans, whose invention of a remarkable cement called pozzolana enabled them to use both the dome and vault structurally. This use of pozzolana, inherited from Rome, and the domical tradition from the East were associated at Constantinople.[54] Through Byzantine architecture the use of the dome spread over the Eastern Empire and those provinces of the West which Justinian re-conquered. Domes and vaults were visible externally in Byzantine churches and tombs; the relationship between interior and exterior is consistently obvious, arising from the structural frankness of design that followed the uninhibited use of the arch. In Roman buildings, like the Colosseum, the structural use of the arch though apparent is not significant; it has no moulding influence upon the form of the building, though it is an integral part of the composition. Those three tiers of arches create an agreeable contrast with the attic storey, with its rectangular window spaces and Corinthian pilasters; but their part in the façade is deliberately played down, as it were, by the half-columns of the Tuscan, Ionic, and Corinthian orders. The repetition of arches and the columnar treatment are part of a decorative façade. (See page 82.) Vitruvius wrote of the arch only as a device that could relieve pressure on beams; for he thought in terms of the orders and post-and-lintel construction. His advice was "to discharge the weight of walls by arches consisting of wedges concentrically arranged; for if these are turned over beams or lintels, the beam, being relieved from the weight, will not sag; and when afterwards it is decayed through age, it may be easily replaced without the necessity of shores."[55]

The arch and all its gifts and promise was buried by the Romans in the wall, brought into the open only in triumphal monuments, or when it bridged a stream or bore an aqueduct; and when Byzantine architects rescued it from its menial status, buildings recovered the structural and aesthetic unity that had been partly lost during the rise and decline of the Western Roman Empire. The interior of a building no longer resembled an excavation, tunnelled out of a mass of masonry—instead it corresponded with the exterior: the shape of the space enclosed was not only admitted but boldly proclaimed. Nothing was disguised, and with few exceptions the central dome was the dominant feature, solitary and impressive like that of the church at Daphni near Athens (page 5); surrounded by small domes, like St. Saviour in the Chora at Constantinople; or protected by a tiled timber roof that does not correspond with the curve of the dome for a good structural reason, as exemplified by St. Vitale at Ravenna. (See page 90.) In the latter church the dome is formed by earthenware pots that fit into each other—a light and unusual form of construction which demanded the protection of a detached roof. St. Vitale, though founded by Justinian, was modelled on a much earlier building, the Minerva Medica at Rome, erected in the latter part of the third century, which anticipated the Byzantine use of pendentives. Early in the fourth century, the design of the vaulted basilica of Constantine at Rome (known also as the basilica of Maxentius), created an impression of immense space which again foreshadowed the achievements of Byzantine architects. This is a rare example of the Roman use of arcuated construction, and, even in its ruined state, demonstrates clearly that some architects in the Western Empire had the courage and opportunity to build inventively. The basilica was a form that continued to appeal to architects, and was used concurrently with the characteristic Byzantine structures whose airy domes hovered over great square or octagonal spaces. St. Apollinare-in-Classe, a basilican church, built by Justinian in Ravenna on the site of a temple to Apollo, was almost certainly the work of Byzantine architects. Erected between A.D. 534 and 539, it has one of the earliest examples of a circular bell tower. (See page 89.)

Such features of Byzantine architecture as the use of domes and semi-domes on pendentives and penetrating vaults and the spanning of great spaces without intervening supports and the introduction of arcades and columns with ornately carved capitals and bases, gradually spread north-westwards into Russia, west to Italy, and east and south to Asia Minor and North Africa. By the efforts of Justinian, who died in A.D. 565, the Byzantine Empire had recovered the whole of Italy and Dalmatia from the Ostrogoths; North Africa, west of Egypt, from the Vandals; and the south-east provinces of Spain from the Visi-Goths. Egypt had not been invaded by barbarians; nor had Syria and Anatolia; their mercantile prosperity was undisturbed, their cultural and architectural continuity with the great Roman Empire unbroken. In these provinces the impact of Byzantine influence was at first comparatively slight, though it had some effect upon Coptic churches in Egypt and churches in Syria. It was destined at a later date to exert a significantly formative power on Moslem architects when they built their great domed mosques. Until they were conquered by the Arabs, the Asian and African provinces retained their architectural independence, and in the "greasy, voluptuous, busy world" of Syria the classical conventions of design sank to a level of vulgarity that reflected a condition of moral and intellectual bankruptcy. Sir Mark Sykes, whose trenchant phrase has just been quoted, described the rise and establishment of this vicious commercial society.

"The rich corn lands," he wrote, "produced immeasurable wealth, which was increased by the profitable traffic of the caravans from Arabia and the East. Out of these riches rose large and populous cities inhabited by a race of cosmopolitan merchants and traders and their satellites, among whom there was no ideal higher than gain and self-indulgence. The Empire did not concern them, their politics were municipal, their art imported; patriotism had been killed by Empire; and luxury and money were the only objects of serious consideration. There were no traditions of ancient virtue to check excess; and consequently the cultured vice of the decadent Greek, the frenzied beastliness of the frantic superstitions of the East, the soft effeminacy of Egypt and the gross lewdness of Rome flourished and mingled together on this congenial soil. Huge temples, florid and debased, were built in honour of gods, too foul to name, whose priests, the self-gelt eunuch and the honoured prostitute, leered invitation from the steps on the passers-by to enter and adore. Theatres, baths and taverns stood in every street, thronged with their attendant ministers of vice, who scientifically plundered the large floating population of legionaries, muleteers, merchants, caravan masters and officials."(56)

As usual, the unwritten records are candid. Unenlightened self-interest, ruthlessly operating a slave system, is revealed. "The arts of Greece, imported long before, had been developed into magnificence that bordered on vulgarity. The richness of ornamentation, the lavish expense, the flaunting wealth, all tell that the tastes of the voluptuous and artistic Semites were then as now. I have stood in the colonnades at Palmyra and I have dined in the Hotel Cecil, and save that the latter is built of iron, daubed with sham wood, sham stucco, sham gold, sham velvet, and sham stone, the effect is identical. In Syria there were slaves in sufficient quantity to make real buildings, but the artistic spirit is as debased as anything made by machinery."[57] Sir Mark Sykes wrote that in the second decade of the present century (his book, *The Caliph's Last Heritage*, was published in 1915), when mechanical processes were habitually used to imitate work formerly done by hand, and before industrial design, and the industrial designer, had gained the recognition they now enjoy.

The commercial civilisations of the ancient world had little to commend them. In one of Kipling's Stalky stories, King described Carthage as "a sort of God-forsaken nigger Manchester."[58] The description is probably apt enough; but unfortunately the scanty remains of Carthage do not allow us even to attempt to reconstruct the life of the place. But Syria "is still so rich in ruins and remains . . . that it is not difficult to picture to oneself the nature of its civilisation."[59] The picture is depressing, as it must inevitably be when the creative gifts of architects and the skill of builders are employed in the service of greed and lust.

The picture of Byzantine civilisation is equally depressing, and Gibbon's comparison of the quality of life in Constantinople with that of Athens in the Periclean Age is reinforced by architectural evidence. "In the last moments of her decay," he wrote, "Constantinople was doubtless more opulent and populous than Athens at her most flourishing aera, when a scanty sum of six thousand talents, or twelve hundred thousand pounds sterling, was possessed by twenty-one thousand male citizens of an adult age. But each of these citizens was a freeman who dared to assert the liberty of his thoughts, words, and actions; whose person and property were guarded by equal law; and who exercised his independent vote in the government of the republic. Their numbers seem to be multiplied by the strong and various discriminations of character: under the shield of freedom, on the wings of emulation and vanity, each Athenian aspired to the level of the national dignity: from this commanding eminence, some chosen spirits soared beyond the reach of a vulgar eye; and the chances of superior merit in a great and populous kingdom, as they are proved by experience, would excuse the computation of imaginary millions."[60] Contrasted with the Athenians "the subjects of the Byzantine Empire, who assume and dishonour the names both of Greeks and Romans, present a dead uniformity of abject vices, which are neither softened by the weakness of humanity, nor animated by the vigour of memorable crimes."[61]

The later phases of Byzantine architecture certainly disclose the intellectual subjection of the architect. After the masterly demonstration of arcuated construction in Santa Sophia, the intellectual rejuvenation of architecture had seemed assured: who could forget or ignore that splendid example of candour and clarity, where form, unshackled from traditional stylistic obligations, asserted a basic principle of design? In that open interior, so flooded with daylight that some of the mosaics seem pallid, the crisply delineated curves assume a significance that might well have encouraged further valorous structural experiments, comparable with those made much later by mediaeval architects. But in the corrupt atmosphere of the Byzantine Empire innovations could not mature: intellect was compelled to hide beneath the trappings of faith; and structural form, the palpable expression of logic and reason and mental lucidity, was subordinated to colour, the vehicle of emotion. Vast pictures flowed over walls, domes, semi-domes, and pendentives, so that the interior of a church became, as it were, a three-dimensional frame for compositions in deep reds and blues, sombre browns and warm gold, built up from minute particles of glass embedded in cement. Those mosaics either obliterated structural lines or minimised their purport, for they demanded the elimination of angular features, and an increase in curved and rounded surfaces for the better display of Christian symbols and the ever-growing army of saints. Light, always the foe of mystery, was deliberately subdued; the gloom of those furtive, cavernous meeting-places of the first Christian communities was reproduced, and some memory of the perpetual dusk of the Mithraeum may well have been preserved, for as mentioned at the opening of this section, Christianity had borrowed selectively from its rivals and forerunners. Only the choir of the Mithraeum was brilliantly illuminated, by contrast with the obscure body of the chapel—another point of resemblance with Christian churches, where lights blazed about the altar in contrast with the intentional dimness of the interior. Only in Santa Sophia was the mystical character of the interior enhanced by daylight, which, far from diminishing emotional appeal, gave it such potency that the Crusaders who sacked Constantinople in the thirteenth century, unable to believe that the great dome could have been reared by human hands, attributed its design to magic. Fortified by this belief, they may have felt fully justified when they destroyed the altar and systematically looted the gold and silver adornments of the church.

There was an immutable quality about Byzantine architecture that was dispelled only when it was transplanted, and could thrive in a mental and social climate less enervating than that of the East Roman Empire. For example, in St. Mark's at Venice, which was built between A.D. 1042 and 1071, some of the structural frankness that distinguishes Santa Sophia was recovered; for the architects used and acknowledged the arch principle, and the five domes float up from arches and pendentives. The plan is that of a Greek cross, with a central dome 42 feet in diameter, and slightly smaller domes over the four arms of the cross. Those semicircular domes do not correspond with the external structures, which were added in the thirteenth century, and are of timber,

The west façade of St. Mark's, Venice (1042–1071). The five domes may have been copied from the Church of the Apostles at Constantinople, which was founded by Constantine, and rebuilt by Justinian. Coloured mosaics are used on the exterior and within.

rising high above the façade. The interior has a grave and darkly resplendent magnificence, and, despite the rich gold mosaics which clothe them, the buoyant lines of arches and domes are unblurred.

St. Mark's stands on the site of a basilican church that was founded about A.D. 864, and the present structure, which faces the great Piazza, has a complex but impressive façade, with five arched portals, and a multiplicity of features—mosaic panels, trophies, columns of alabaster and porphyry from Constantinople and Alexandria—brought into coherent relationship by the bold framework of tall arches, for those on the portals are repeated on a smaller scale above. The domes echo the contours of those arches, and their immense and stable air of calm corrects the restless elements that might otherwise suggest unending conflict; for canopied niches and crocketed pinnacles were added in the fifteenth century, intended no doubt to supply the contrast of delicate stonework with gleaming mosaics; but contrast can generate competition. Without the later Gothic additions, the original façade must have presented one of those rare, harmonious alliances of form and colour so seldom achieved by design, though often created by the effects of age and weathering on buildings. As such it reflected some characteristics of the adventurous, commercial civilisation of Venice, its capacity for independent experiment, its familiarity with the colour and erratic variety of the East, and its own orderly life, guided by wise laws, and throbbing with enterprise. Byzantine architecture exerted a potent influence on the buildings of Venice, and St. Mark's was the last great example of Greek genius finding expression through arcuated structure.

Apart from Santa Sophia and St. Mark's, there is justification for Sir Harold Nicolson's admission that he "never came to see that the Byzantines had ever built very differently, or carved and painted very differently, in the course of the eleven hundred years that stretch between May 11th, 330, and May 30th, 1453."[62]

The five domes of St. Mark's, at Venice. The central dome is 42 feet in diameter, and there is a smaller dome over the arm of each cross.

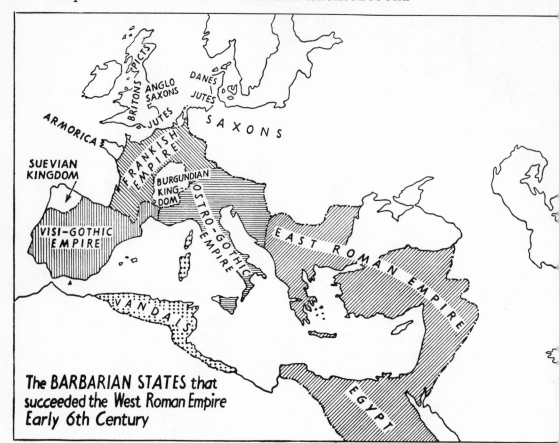

The BARBARIAN STATES that
succeeded the West Roman Empire
Early 6th Century

The architectural evidence of Rome's former power in the West remained, but architecture
was temporarily in the makeshift, adaptive phase. Buildings were patched up when they
needed repair; private building continued in a few regions, notably in the former Roman
province of Gaul; but the skill of builders was required mainly for two activities: fortification
and church-building. Compare this map with that showing the Roman Empire at its greatest
extent, on page 60. *Drawn by Marcelle Barton.*

V

TRANSITIONAL: ROMANESQUE

BYZANTINE architecture had developed within the established and largely secure framework of a civilisation in going order. While the Western Empire was tottering, the Eastern Empire was still a strong-hold, reasonably immune from barbarians, capably administered though intermittently oppressed by tyrants or unsupervised bureaucrats on the make. Property was in general protected; the rich, with nothing to lose but their lives if they drew too much attention to themselves, were satisfied with comfortable obscurity, and provided consistent patronage for architects, which was amplified when the Church began to build for the glory of God. Such conditions allowed continuity between classical, early Christian and Byzantine architecture; but outside the Eastern Empire, in the former provinces of Rome, civilisation had either broken down—as in large areas of Britain—or was adjusting itself to barbarian occupation, and the overlordship of warrior chieftains, who presently began to call themselves kings. The machinery of Roman government still existed; magistrates and officials performed their duties and worked out compromises with the tribal customs of their conquerors, government became local, and the dim outlines of future European nations were presently apparent.

In Gaul during the fifth century the life of the wealthy nobles continued, undisturbed by the proximity of their barbarian neighbours. Roads were maintained, buildings were erected, including churches of ambitious design, and an air of settled luxury, almost of tranquillity, is revealed by the literature of the time. The letters and poems of Apollinaris Sidonius contain descriptions of great country houses, and a new church built by Patiens, Bishop of Lugdunum (Lyons); and they portray also a society that was dedicated largely to pleasure, Christian in name but pagan in training and outlook, and concerned with the literary trivialities of a culture from which all vitality had long departed. The

great landlords lived in splendid houses on their self-contained estates, cultivat-
ing their fields and orchards and vineyards. In the immediate neighbourhood
of the large house were villages occupied by slaves, freedmen, or free tenants,
and the accommodation of these dependants on an estate of any magnitude
approached the dimensions of a small town. The landlord's surplus wealth
could be invested only in loans on mortgage, the purchase of additional
property, or by indulging the Roman aristocrat's insatiable passion for
building.[63]

Caius Sollius Apollinaris Sidonius was born, probably at Lyons, about 430,
and belonged to one of the oldest and most influential families in Gaul. He
was raised to the post of prefect of Rome in 467, and later to the dignity of
a patrician and senator; and in 472 he became Bishop of Arverna (Clermont).
His nine books of letters and poems are pervaded by a belief in the eternal
quality of the Roman way of life; the incursions of barbarians, the recurrent
strife caused by their war bands, are regarded as inconveniences, probably
of a temporary nature; there is a blind worldliness about his letters that took
no account of the inexorable changes that were contracting the shape and
upsetting the economic stability of the Roman Empire. He was preoccupied
with literary style, with entertaining observations and gossip, and his letters
are as conversational in tone as those of Horace Walpole, but unlike that
sensitive and perceptive Georgian Englishman, he seemed to be unaware of the
political structure of the world he lived in, and was incurious about the future.

"The aim of all true Romans," wrote Sir Samuel Dill, in his classic study
of the end of Roman society, "was to reproduce in successive generations the
forms and ideas of the great past, undisturbed by any hope or ambition of
ever excelling it. To such a condition of death-like repose or immobility had
the imperial system reduced the most intelligent class in the Roman world.
Faith in Rome had killed all faith in a wider future for humanity. Society
had been elaborately and deliberately stereotyped."[64] There was little hope
of any new architectural inspiration arising in that complacent atmosphere.
Sidonius, as a typical Roman aristocrat, exhibits a consistent interest in buildings, and gives a detailed account of the site and architectural character and
abundant luxury of his own house at Avitacum, the name of the farm which
came to him with his wife. He describes the hot room, with its semicircular
end and ample bath, the excellent plumbing and constant hot water, the
anointing room and the cold room adjoining, conceived on a scale that challenged comparison with the great public baths. The architect had covered it
with a peaked roof of conical shape—which Sidonius compared favourably
with a similar feature at Baiae, when he eulogised the baths at Avitacum in
his poem, De Balneis Villae Svae. The bath-chamber could accommodate chairs
for as many bathers as the semicircular bath could comfortably hold. The
wall, where it was joined by the vaulting, was pierced by a pair of windows,
opposite each other, "so as to disclose to the view of guests as they look up

This house, drawn by a ninth century artist, may have been copied from a Romano-British structure, though it is possible that the original may not have been in Anglo-Saxon England. The drawing reproduced above was made from the Harleian Manuscript, No. 603, by F. W. Fairholt, and is included in Thomas Wright's books, *A History of Domestic Manners and Sentiments in England*, and *The Homes of Other Days* (London, 1862).

the cunningly-wrought coffered ceiling." The walls of plain smooth white concrete were undefiled by the carnal posturing of sleek nudes, illustrating some lascivious pagan legend, so often the subject of mural decorations. Attached to the main hall of the bath was a swimming pool, into which water flowed from six pipes ending in lions' masks. They were, he pointed out, particularly realistic wild-eyed lions. Leaving the swimming pool, you passed across the front of the ladies' dining-room, with the household store-room and the weaving-room adjoining. On the east a portico, supported on round composite pillars, overlooked the lake. There was a room for female dependants and slaves; a winter dining-room with a vaulted fireplace, and a living-room or small dining-room open to the portico, with the semicircular dining couch placed to command a view of the lake. The rooms were chosen carefully for their aspect—the summer room faced north, to provide a cool retreat on sun-baked days. Sidonius lingered over each detail, affectionately, not boastfully, but making it clear how he rejoiced in the efficient comfort of the house and the orderly charm of its environment.[65]

The church built by Bishop Patiens at Lyons, and dedicated to St. Justus, was the subject of a short poem by Sidonius which was included in a letter to his friend Hesperius. The church replaced an older building, and survived until the sixteenth century, when it was destroyed by the Hugenots in 1562. It was a basilican church, and there was obviously no dimness in an interior where, as Sidonius wrote: "the light flashes and the sunshine is so tempted to the gilded ceiling that it travels over the tawny metal, matching its hue." Coloured marbles enriched the vaulting, the floor, and the windows, "forming designs of diverse colour, a verdant grass-green encrustation brings winding lines of sapphire-hued stones over the leek-green glass."[66] The church had a triple colonnade of marble columns.

Technical skill was preserved throughout the fifth and sixth centuries; church-building continued, and in the sixth century the restoration of ancient shrines was a feature of Church life, and was encouraged and practised by such famous churchmen as Gregory of Tours.[67] In addition to the great churches, landed proprietors built chapels and oratories for their households. "As the modern French village is the descendant of the group of dwellings around the great house of the ancient Gallo-Roman villa, so an immense proportion of the parish churches of France spring from these ancient oratories."[68]

Gradually the church was becoming the recognised repository of art. "European culture, which had been moulded by the penetrating intellectual influence of classical civilisation, had been long declining and was soon to reach its nadir. Such education as there was, was of a rudimentary type, giving only a scrappy, imperfect knowledge of a few Roman poets, with only faint glimpses of Greek thought and science. Great nobles, and even men destined to high places in the Church, in the essentials of education, were hardly on the level of our humble villagers."[69] Throughout the sixth century the civilising influence of the Gallo-Roman aristocracy diminished. In the days of Sidonius, the landed proprietors, preoccupied with their luxuriously furnished houses, their letter-writing and decadent poetry, their dancing girls and flute players, could maintain an air of amused condescension towards their barbarian neighbours, occasionally inviting some rugged chieftains to dinner, in a hopeful attempt to educate such children of the forest. They could still indulge their architectural foibles; but if they added, say, a new portico to a country house, they would repeat the traditional features, so that Corinthian or Tuscan columns upheld a correctly moulded entablature and nicely proportioned pediment—a dead pattern, as dead as the imitative literary exercises of the nobleman who had commissioned it. In a few generations the elegantly appointed houses and the life they sheltered fell into decay; the luxury and comfort that depend upon good plumbing, constant hot water, and efficient drainage became memories. Something akin to Puritanism accompanied the growing power of the barbarian nobles. Their interpretation of Christianity encouraged a far simpler and more austere way of life than that of the Gallo-Roman aristocrats, whose spiritual beliefs were diluted by an urbane materialism. Sidonius unconsciously expressed this divided allegiance when he wrote to Donidius, "as I am now approaching you in person and intend with Christ's help to visit you immediately, the dinners of my friends will be more expeditiously related when you and I are dining together."[70] This followed an exhaustive account of the hospitality he had received when "visiting two charming properties and two most sympathetic hosts. . . . "

Although that sort of life, with its round of social duties, its enervating pleasures and busy idleness, passed away, the skills that had ministered to it remained in France and Italy. Throughout the Dark Ages, a new architecture was evolving, linked with classical traditions, but infused with a new, soaring spirit that was to find an outlet in fresh conceptions of form. It was dedicated to the service of the Church, and it changed the dependence of a sacred edifice upon colour and decoration and the pictorial representation of holy legends to a new, awe-inspiring loftiness, so that the interior of a church, like its towers, predicted the striving, upward thrust heavenwards that ultimately created Gothic architecture. From the sixth to the eighth centuries church-building began to acquire characteristics indicative of the nascent nationalism that was imposing a new pattern on European civilisation. Affinities with Rome were always apparent in this tentative, experimental architecture; and it developed into the Romanesque, which lasted from the eighth to the twelfth century. In parts of Italy, particularly in Venice, it met and blended with Byzantine influences; in France, it had unbroken continuity with the classic orders; in Germany it lasted until the thirteenth century, and derived some of its features from classic Roman prototypes.

The interiors of the early Romanesque churches were wholly different from the richly embellished Byzantine interiors. Like the Byzantine churches, they appealed to the emotions, but the appeal was more austere, for they were built by men who had known suffering and insecurity. The Western understanding and respect for form re-emerged, and dominated the long and stately naves and aisles. This was particularly noticeable in England, where Romanesque architecture developed late in the eleventh century, after the Norman conquest, and was preceded by some centuries of adaptive, almost makeshift architecture, for the old Roman province of Britain, unlike Gaul, had lost its heritage of technical skill in building during the fifth and sixth centuries.

Technical ability had not been extinguished in Europe during the Dark Ages; it had been diminished, but only in very few places were established crafts and industries deliberately disturbed by barbarian conquerors, and then not as a result of ignorance or stupidity, but because of Christian zeal. For example, since the beginning of the second century glass-making had been carried out in northern Gaul, in the area that lies between the Seine and the Rhine. For over five hundred years this local industry had been conducted by Syrians, who were the pioneers of glass-blowing—a process that had probably been invented at Sidon about the time of Alexander.[71] This Seine–Rhine glass industry survived the barbarian conquests, and it was only in the late sixth and early seventh centuries that the persecution of its Syrian operators proclaimed the anti-Semitic policy of the Church. It has been suggested by some authorities that this instance of anti-Semitism was racial rather than religious,[72] but the Church had inflicted so many disabilities on the Jews in Gaul that the disruption of the Syrian glass industry by earnest Christians was almost inevitable.[73] It was not only in Gaul that anti-Jewish enactments were made; in the Visigothic kingdom established during the sixth and seventh centuries in the former Roman province of Spain, Church and State collaborated in the planned persecution of the Jewish community with a thoroughness and ferocity that anticipated the excesses of Hitlerite Germany.[74]

Industrial and commercial interests die hard, and although in Gaul the Syrian managers and workmen in the glass-houses might be proscribed, the industry persisted. The importation of French glass-makers in 675 by the Abbot of Wearmouth to teach their craft to English workers, and the letter sent by the Abbot of Jarrow in 758 to the Bishop of Mainz asking for artisans who could make glass for windows and vessels, suggest that the Seine–Rhine industrial establishments were still famous and flourishing. (See page 18.) There had been a change in the activities of the glass-houses, for during the sixth, seventh and eighth centuries "the bias of production shifted from domestic and fancy to broad glass," in response to the demands of the Church for window-glass, according to Mr. W. A. Thorpe's admirable study of this branch of industrial history.[75] Churchmen had thus interfered with the management and staffing of an industry, and architects, employed by those churchmen, had increased the demand for one of its products. Bishop Patiens' church at Lyons, which Sidonius described, showed how pre-Romanesque structures were already depending upon the decorative properties of coloured glass; and the latent possibilities of the window were recognised by Romanesque builders.

Such refinements as window-glass were, by the seventh century, confined almost wholly to sacred buildings. Even in Gaul, where the Gallo-Roman ruling class had come to terms with their barbarian conquerors, the technical abilities of builders were no longer enlisted in the service of luxury. Life in the town and country-side was, for the rulers and the well-to-do, simpler, less agreeable, and ostensibly cleaner in the purely moral sense, though human nature remained unchanged. Many things had gone out of life altogether, including voluptuous pleasures, mechanical efficiency, art for art's sake, literary dalliance, and respect for intellectual activities. Christian ethics supplied a bleak substitute; and as standards of material comfort were lowered, the characteristic carelessness of a primitive community about washing, drains, and the disposal of refuse encouraged epidemics and other afflictions, which were officially recognised by the Church as divine chastisements for spiritual shortcomings.

All over Europe, builders had to take account of the comparatively unsettled state of large areas of country. The Church required the services of the most highly skilled craftsmen, and the rulers of the various kingdoms generally accommodated the needs of the Church, and were earnestly pious, though often, as Sidonius had observed when describing the character of Theodoric II, the King of the Goths, their devotion was "a matter of routine rather than of conviction."[76] Those rulers and their followers were apt to be corrupted by the urban civilisation of the Graeco-Roman world; many of them rejected it, and because they did so, urban civilisation decayed in various parts of Europe, and died out almost completely in Britain. Towns were walled, and became self-contained, squalid, architecturally static and culturally sterile. Commercial intercourse continued in the lost provinces of the Empire, but was often local and limited. The influence of the Church minimised the importance of material things, while approving of such material accomplishments as architecture and the ancillary arts and crafts, so long as they were lavished upon church-building and adornment. The Church thus became the trustee of the arts and of all learning, and in the non-Christian lands north and east of the former boundaries of the Empire, military, agricultural and seafaring peoples lived and practised their own distinctive arts and crafts, which were similar to those practised by the barbarian successors of the Roman Empire, who were often their kinsmen.

Secular architecture in both Christian and non-Christian Europe had some common characteristics, resulting partly from the rejection of urban life and partly from the use of an abundant and tractable material. Nearly all domestic building in the country-side and in the towns was of timber, which has perished, so that the appearance of this architecture of wood, of the sixth, seventh and eighth centuries, is conjectural. The chieftain's house was usually a great hall, surrounded by a stockade or curtain wall, and the forerunner of the mediaeval castle appeared in the form of a single square tower of wood or stone, built on high ground and surrounded by a turf wall, strengthened with wooden stakes.

The arch was not forgotten, and a new form of it was employed as a result of building with timber. A type of wooden framing arose from a fortuitous partnership between the forester, the builder, and the shipwright. The influence of shipbuilding on timber architecture was considerable, and the sea-going savages who poured out of Scandinavia and Jutland, and settled in Britain and raided the coasts of Europe, were expert shipwrights. When they settled down in lands they had seized, they preferred to build their own halls rather than to inhabit the deserted country houses of some devastated Roman province. In Britain, for example, there were vast forests, which afforded such a variety of trees that it was a comparatively easy task to select timber bent naturally, which could be used to form one half of a pointed arch. The selection of these pieces enabled large spaces to be roofed without central supports, the two bent members joining at the top to form an arched roof. The framework of such a

Two views of a walled town, depicted by an artist in the ninth century. The lower illustration shows an amphitheatre, in which games are taking place. Both illustrations are from drawings, copied by F. W. Fairholt from an Anglo-Saxon manuscript of the Psalms (MS. Harl., No. 603), and included in Thomas Wright's books, *The Homes of Other Days*, and *A History of Domestic Manners and Sentiments in England* (London: 1862). Compare the walls and towers with those shown in the view of the mediaeval city of Canterbury on page 174.

house looked rather like a boat turned upside-down, the keel forming the ridge of the roof, and the ribs the uprights and roof supports. (The word "keel" is still used for the type of pointed arch known as ogee.) These naturally curved parts of the framework were called crucks, a word used in Germany to describe the ribs of a boat. Large country houses and halls, and some of the larger houses in villages, would be built on this pointed arch system of timber construction. Thus an architecture of wood evolved that led to the making of many beautiful roofs, and grew to perfection in Scandinavia. The invention of this cruck system of building was significant, because it freed large areas from the need of wooden uprights to support the roof, which enabled the living space of a house to extend, so that a hall gradually became the great hall of the Middle Ages, when stone largely replaced timber. Few of the commodious and well-equipped Roman houses that still existed in the sixth and seventh centuries were occupied by barbarian invaders, and in Britain there is no evidence of a single Roman villa-house underlying a Saxon dwelling, or yielding any evidence of occupation during the Saxon period.

Britain had ceased to be a Roman province during the first half of the fifth century, though long before that its towns had lost their vitality; the will or desire to build was lacking, and may have expired after the initial planning of a city had been approved by Roman officials. Silchester, the Roman town of Calleva mentioned in Section II, was planned but never fully developed, nor was Verulamium, the city near St. Albans, which was founded at the end of the first century B.C., Romanised after the conquest of A.D. 43, and re-planned for development in the second quarter of the second century. In a report on the excavations of Verulamium, prepared for the Society of Antiquaries, it is stated that "The plan of the new site allowed optimistically for a further expansion which never wholly materialised."[77] During the third century the city decayed, and was largely rebuilt after 296, but "a century later this renewed attempt to naturalise Roman urban life in Britain had failed in turn, and the city was once more languishing into decay. All material evidence ceases at Verulamium by the end of the fourth century; and, when in 429 Germanus visited the city, he found, as his biographer indicates, a tradition of Roman citizenship but, as archaeology equally indicates, very little of the actuality of Roman culture."[78] Viroconium, the Roman city on the Severn in Shropshire, affords another example of the failure of civic ambition and responsibility. Shortly after A.D. 155 the forum and basilica of the city were burnt down, and rebuilt on much the same plan; 120 years later, at some time between A.D. 275 and 300, they were again destroyed by fire, together with a part of the public baths, and the forum and basilica were never rebuilt.[79]

Christianity was established in Britain in Roman times, and British Christians ceased to be persecuted early in the fourth century. According to Bede, those who "during the time of danger, had hidden themselves in woods and deserts, and secret caves" reappeared in public and "rebuilt the churches which had

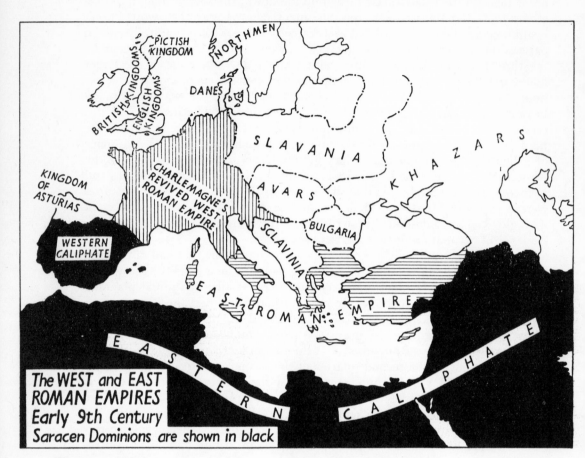

The WEST and EAST ROMAN EMPIRES Early 9th Century Saracen Dominions are shown in black

The extent of Moslem territory, and the corresponding shrinkage of the East Roman Empire, which had lost Egypt and its Syrian provinces, shows how Western civilisation was threatened from the east and south and in Spain. The contracted Eastern Empire is separated from the west in the Balkans by a wedge of Barbarian states, though it still has contact in Italy with Charlemagne's revived Western Empire. The establishment of that new Empire of the West in A.D. 800 has seemed to many historians to be "the culmination of centuries of endeavour, the achievement of the conscious strivings of Western intellects like Alcuin and of the movement of blind forces binding together the peoples of the West under the rule of the Frankish kings. For many it was a conscious revival of ancient Roman glory, symbolised in the erection at Aachen [Aix-la-Chapelle] of a cathedral—originally the chapel of Charlemagne's own palace—the architectural inspiration of which was the Emperor Justinian's foundation, San Vitale in Ravenna. These two churches, the one completed in 547, the other consecrated in 805, seem to reveal graphically and symbolically the bonds uniting the last great emperor of Rome and the first great emperor of the west." (*The Origins of Modern Germany*, by Geoffrey Barraclough. Chapter I, page 3.) *Drawn by Marcelle Barton.*

been levelled with the ground; founded, erected, and finished the temples of the holy martyrs, and, as it were, displayed their conquering ensigns in all places. . . . " The martyrdom of St. Alban took place in A.D. 305, "near the city of Verulam," Bede states, "which is now by the English nation called Verlamacestir, or Varlingacestir, where afterwards, when peaceable Christian times were restored, a church of wonderful workmanship, and suitable to his martyrdom, was erected. In which place, there ceases not to this day the cure of sick persons, and the frequent working of wonders."(80)

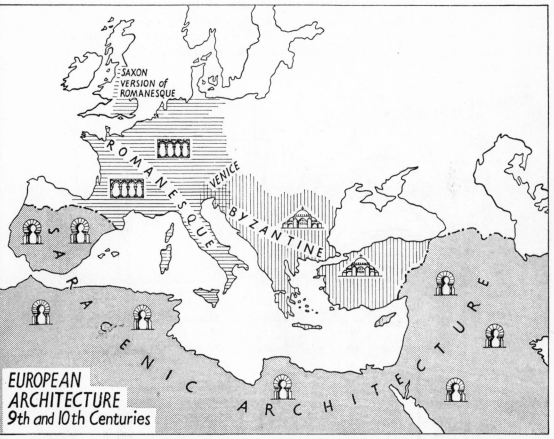

EUROPEAN ARCHITECTURE 9th and 10th Centuries

Romanesque architecture spread over the area of Charlemagne's revived Roman empire, and beyond to the Saxon states of England. The political relationship of the Rhineland with Lombardy was recorded by a visible kinship between German and Lombardic versions of the Romanesque style. South of the Pyrennees the style was halted by Moslem rule, for in Spain, which was the Western Caliphate, characteristically Oriental forms of building were established, which subsequently exerted a potent influence upon Spanish mediaeval architecture. In the East, Romanesque and Byzantine influences met and mingled in Venice. (See map on opposite page, and those on pages 35, 60 and 104.) *Drawn by Marcelle Barton.*

Three British bishops attended the Council of Arles in A.D. 314, and their names are known: Eborius of York (Roman York was called Eboracum), Restitutus of London, and Adelphius of either Lincoln or Caerleon. They were accompanied by Sacerdos, a priest, and Arminius, a deacon.[81] Apart from the names of a few martyrs, like St. Alban, and those five representatives who attended the Council of Arles, hardly anything is known of the early history of the British Church, though it certainly demanded, inspired, and obtained architectural expression. Bede's reference to the building of a church at Verulamium to commemorate St. Alban's martyrdom "when peaceable Christian times were restored," is vague, and no date can be ascribed to the first structure on the site of what ultimately became the abbey church of St. Albans. Mr. Walter Johnson in a critical examination of continuity in the

The nave of Durham Cathedral, a fine example of Norman architecture in England (1096–1133). The massive columns in the nave are carved with zigzag ornament, spirals and flutes. An exterior view of the cathedral is shown on plate 14.

The Norman interior of St. Bartholomew the Great, Smithfield, London.
(See opposite, also pages 119, 123,
and 127.)

use of sacred sites has said that although Bede stated that a church was built
over the grave of St. Alban "and it is possible that the spot is now covered by
the cathedral . . . we cannot wisely go beyond this, especially when we remember
how plentiful were the Roman materials close at hand. The fact remains: from
the time of the erection of the memorial church to the founding of the monastery
in A.D. 793, we have an interval which is unbridged by trustworthy testimony."[82]

Dr. William Bright, in his *Chapters of Early English Church History*, mentions
Canterbury and Caerleon, as well as Verulamium, as places where British
churches were known to exist, and these, like the church at Calleva, which has
been mentioned earlier, were probably built about the middle of the fourth
century. Dr. Bright adds Glastonbury to his list, where the abbey church was
built in place of a much older edifice "made of twisted wands, the earliest
sanctuary on that venerable ground of which Christianity has held uninterrupted possession."[83] This is a tradition, and Mr. Walter Johnson has pointed
out that while "St. Joseph's Chapel at Glastonbury Abbey, presents us with
an interesting case of probable retention of site, though not necessarily of
continuous buildings," he discredits the tale "told by the imaginative William
of Malmesbury, a millennium after the alleged event, that, so early as the first

The tower and crossing of Tewkesbury Abbey, seen from the north-west. The Abbey Church is a cruciform building, consisting of nave and side aisles, with transepts and an arcaded central tower. An interior view is shown opposite.

century of the Christian era, a chapel constructed of osiers existed at this spot. That some kind of primitive church or oratory, with walls of wattle, and a roof of reeds, was set up during the Roman occupation is, however, very probable, and it may fairly be supposed, though it cannot be proved, that no break had occurred when the Saxon abbey was founded."[84]

The churches built for British Christians have perished; apart from the church at Calleva, nothing now exists that can with certainty be identified as a Romano-British Christian church. There is evidence that some of the wealthier Christian converts allowed their houses to be consecrated, and Mr. Walter Johnson examines this when describing churches that occupy or are adjacent to the sites of Roman villa-houses. He assumes that "from a small reception-room, arranged like an ordinary church, there might be developed a Christian building, with chancel, nave, and aisles complete." He supports this by "a

The nave of Tewkesbury Abbey, looking east. The Abbey church was consecrated in 1125, and is a fine example of Early Norman, bold, massive and stately. (See opposite page.)

Few examples exist of Norman domestic building, and the stone-built Jew's House at Lincoln retains only a few of its original features, notably the arched door and window openings, showing characteristic restraint in the embellishment of moulded detail. *Right:* The west door and part of the wall aracade of Waltham Abbey, a late example of English Romanesque. The bases of the columns are probably Early English; the main arch above the arcading is only partly Norman; and the enrichment of the mouldings shows a fresh and lively interest in ornament.

scrap of testimony, slight though it may be," namely "the discovery, on a mosaic, among the ruins of a Roman villa at Frampton, Dorsetshire, and again on a tile from the villa at Chedworth, Gloucestershire, of examples of the Chi-Rho monogram. This sacred monogram has also been met with on such objects as bowls, seals, and rings. Seeing that the symbol was not used in Rome before A.D. 312, its presence in Britain cannot date earlier."[85]

Bede described the "stately church" built by St. Ninian, which still existed when he wrote his history, as a stone structure "which was not usual among the Britons."[86] This stone church, dedicated to St. Martin, was built in 397 by St. Ninian in north Britain, beyond Hadrian's Wall, in what is now Galloway, on the western side of Wigtown Bay, at Whithorn. Ninian called this place Leukopibia, his church was known as the White House (*Candida Casa*), and he is said to have visited St. Martin at Tours, when returning from his period of training at Rome, "and obtained from him masons for the purpose of building a church after the Roman manner. . . . "[87]

That it was necessary to bring skilled masons from Gaul, suggests a complete separation between north and south Britain, and possibly a partial breakdown of technical skill throughout the province. Building craftsmen were certainly available thirty-two years before Ninian built his church, when the pagan temple to Nodens had been erected at Lydney, some 230 miles south of Whithorn; but Ninian had deliberately chosen a locality that had never been effectually Romanised, and was inhabited by Picts. As the crow flies, it was nearly sixty miles from the western end of Hadrian's Wall, and although a few military stations have been traced in the area between that wall and the chain of forts which had formerly linked the Forth and the Clyde and was known as the Antonine Wall, it was a troublesome, savage place, abandoned by the Roman government over two centuries before Ninian's mission to the Picts. So it was beyond the northernmost frontier of Roman civilisation that Ninian founded the first British monastery, which "under the name of '*Magnus Monasterium*' or Monastery of Rosnat, became a great seminary of secular and religious instruction."[88] Bede states that Ninian was buried in the church, which was still standing in "the province of the Bernicians,"[89] when he wrote his history. (Bernicia was an English kingdom that was ultimately united with Northumbria.) Ninian's mission extended beyond Galloway, and St. Ninian's well and St. Martin's church, within the walls of the Roman fort at Brampton in Cumberland show that it reached the Irthing valley, westwards along the line of Hadrian's Wall. We are back in the age of adaptation in architecture, which in fifth-century Britain may have been the result of deliberate policy by British evangelists who chose Roman forts for the sites of their churches, "because they found British communities living there, or in order to emphasise the truth that Christianity was the spiritual heir of the Roman empire. . . . "[90]

The next phase of Christian architecture in Britain began after St. Augustine's mission in 597 to the pagan English kingdom of Kent. There was no continuity with any classical tradition of building, as in Gaul; no gradual evolution of the Romanesque style; the period of adaptation was prolonged, and supplemented by a few tentative experiments in building, often with impermanent materials. St. Augustine and his fellow missionaries encouraged the use of existing buildings, even though they had formerly been pagan temples. That there were many such structures still standing is suggested by a sentence in the writings of Gildas (circa A.D. 516–570), the earliest British historian, and the only native authority for the events of the fifth and sixth centuries. He refers contemptuously to the "diabolical idols of my country, which almost surpassed in number those of Egypt, and of which we still see some mouldering away within and without the deserted temples, with stiff and deformed features, as was customary."[91] There is evidence which suggests that St. Augustine used a Christian church that had been built at Canterbury in the Romano-British period, and Bede states that it lay on the east side of the city, and was "dedicated to the honour of St. Martin, built whilst the Romans were still in the island."[92] This church of St. Martin exists to-day in its mediaeval form, and incorporates Roman masonry and brick and tile in its structure. Technical skill was limited and scarce, and although new churches were built, masonry was rarely used, and the architecture of wood was still in the early stages of evolution. Bede describes a church built in 652 on the Isle of Lindisfarne, of oak walled with reeds, which suggests that some form of thatching was employed. This thatch was subsequently removed by Bishop Eadbert, who covered the walls and roof with lead plates. This experiment happens to be recorded, but there were probably other examples of invention in church-building, for, as in Christian Europe, the Church alone could provide patronage and encouragement for architecture.

After the Augustinian mission and the slow conversion of the pagan states of England throughout the seventh century, the history of English church-building really begins, and a remarkable but short-lived civilisation arose in Northumbria. It was in Northumbria "that Anglo-Saxon culture, and perhaps the whole culture of Western monasticism in the Dark Ages, achieved their climax at the beginning of the eighth century."[93] Not only in Northumbria, but throughout the Saxon states, abbeys and churches were built, though this first flowering of a vigorous native style did not endure, for its fruits were destroyed by the Danes in the ninth and tenth centuries. Even before that disaster, the surviving towns had ceased to provide opportunities for architecture, or for building work of any kind apart from the patching up of existing structures, and, most important of all, the maintenance of the town walls. Gildas wrote of twenty-eight walled cities in Britain, formerly flourishing, which, since the Saxon invasions of the fifth century, were depopulated, and, he said, "being forsaken and overthrown, still lie desolate; our foreign wars having ceased, but our civil troubles still remaining."[94] It is doubtful whether much life was left in any city when Gildas wrote his querulous condemnation

An example of French Romanesque architecture, showing the
barrel vault, and the tall
columns which support it.
Although this church, Notre
Dame la Grande, Poitiers,
dates from the eleventh century, the "ghost of the orders"
still haunts the nave. Those
elongated columns, despite the
Byzantine influence in the
capitals, have classical affinities.

of British morals during the sixth century. It was long before urban life revived,
though there is some reason for assuming that London, the Saxon Lundenwic,
had unbroken continuity with the Roman Londinium Augusta.

The city of London was included in the kingdom of Kent, and seems to have
been turbulently independent; for the citizens, early in the seventh century,
rejected Mellitus, the Christian bishop, against the wishes of their king, Eadbald
of Kent. Bede states that the Londoners refused to receive Bishop Mellitus,
"choosing rather to be under their idolatrous priests; for King Eadbald had
not so much authority in the kingdom as his father, nor was he able to restore
the Bishop to his church against the will and consent of the pagans."[95] Such
defiance of royal authority has characterised the history of London, and from
its early expressions of independence, some authorities have concluded that
it retained at this time "some of the attributes of the ancient city state. . . . "[96]
London must have relied, not only on walls in good repair, but on citizens
who were ready to defend them. Trade almost certainly supplied the means
and encouragement for their independence, and London, as an active trading

port, would have maintained warehouses and offices and market-places. We have no means of knowing what those buildings looked like, or what sort of houses merchants and artisans and slaves lived in, but Lethaby, who was both an architect and an archaeologist and whose views thus have a special significance, believed that even in the time of Alfred the Great (A.D. 848–?900) much of the original Roman city remained standing. "Here a Roman mansion with its mosaic floors would still be inhabited. There a portico would be patched with gathered bricks and covered with shingles, while by its side stood a house of wattle and daub. Here was a Roman basilican church, while in another place would be found one of timber and thatch. . . . Garden and tillage filled up wide interspaces."(97) This picture of a city in the transitional period before the building crafts and architecture were creatively re-established to serve urban life was probably true of many European towns.

Although we know nothing of the character of the town houses of Saxon England, we know that the country house, beginning as a single chamber, developed into the hall, which, as the cruck system of timber building was improved, became increasingly spacious. Those timber houses with their walls of wattle and daub and their thatched roofs were weather-proof, but always in danger of destruction by fire, and their vulnerability was increased by the unguarded open hearth, with its mound of hot wood ash on which logs crackled and spat sparks when the fire was made up. In appearance those houses probably resembled large thatched barns, with the roof pierced in one or more places to let out the smoke from the open fire, and the generous size of such crude chimneys is indicated by the story of the Burning of the Warlocks in the Saga of King Olaf Trygvesson. The king arranged for all men who were suspected of witchcraft to be invited to a feast, seated them in one room, made them drunk, and then had the house set on fire. They all perished, save one, "who contrived to escape by the smoke-hole in the roof."(98)

Evidence of the appearance of Saxon dwellings supplied by contemporary, or nearly contemporary, manuscripts is misleading. For example, the illustration on page 107, which is from a drawing by a ninth century artist, and appears in the Harleian Manuscript, No. 603, has been described as an Anglo-Saxon mansion by many writers who have reproduced it in their works; but it may be asked whether this muddled conglomeration of buildings is really characteristic of eighth and ninth century domestic architecture in England. It has a central hall, roofed with pantiles, approached through a triple arched porch, with the arches springing from Tuscan or Doric columns. This hall is flanked by other buildings, with walls of masonry, and at the back is a circular building with a cupola. The drawing illustrates the giving of alms to beggars by the just and righteous chieftain, and the house may have been copied from some existing Romano-British house, though the locality of the original may not have been Anglo-Saxon England. It was not for the production of such extravagantly uninspired domestic architecture that the Saxon builders are

St. Front, Périguex, in Aquitaine, viewed from the river. Built in 1120, on a Greek cross plan, this church exhibits strong Byzantine influence, and resembles St. Mark's at Venice. This is one of the farthest Western examples of Byzantine influence in French Romanesque architecture. The campanile attached to the church is 200 feet high, surmounted by a circular ring of columns bearing aloft a conical dome.

remembered; indeed, so little of their work remains unmutilated that the very memory of their accomplishments is endangered, and it is endangered too by the deliberate and effective anti-Saxon propaganda conducted by the Normans after their conquest of the country.

Although the creative impulse was denied the opportunity for full and varied expression in domestic architecture, it was during those pre-Norman centuries that the foundations of English craftsmanship were laid. Mediaeval masons and carpenters drew upon the cumulative skill of many generations of craftsmen when they built the naves and transepts and towers of abbeys and minsters, and the keeps and walls of castles. Before the Norman Conquest there were notable achievements, "the aesthetic sense and the craftsmanship of the Kentish Jutes had set standards for Continental imitation,"[99] and the Northumbrian civilisation also had a potent influence upon Europe. During the period between the arrival of Theodore, the seventh Archbishop of Canterbury, in A.D. 669, and the death of Bede in 735, "the remote province of England, happily aloof from a continent made miserable by barbarian wars and the Arab invasion, achieved a position that without exaggeration may be described as supreme in Western civilisation."[100] Alcuin, born in York in the year Bede died, and educated at the cathedral school there under Aelbert, became the friend and mentor of Charlemagne before the end of the eighth century, and his learning and example contributed to the Carolingian renaissance, and supplemented the political and military ambitions of the emperor with nobler aspirations. In one of his letters to Charlemagne, he said: "If your intentions are carried out it may be that a new Athens will arise in France, and an Athens fairer than of old, for our Athens, ennobled by the teaching of Christ, will surpass the wisdom of the Academy. The old Athens had only the teachings of Plato to instruct it, yet even so it flourished by the seven liberal arts. But our Athens will be enriched by the sevenfold gift of the Holy Spirit and will, therefore, surpass all the dignity of earthly wisdom." Commenting on this letter, which he quotes in *Religion and the Rise of Western Culture*, Dr. Christopher Dawson remarks upon the pathos and even the absurdity of "a monkish schoolmaster like Alcuin, and an illiterate barbarian like Charlemagne" dreaming of "building a new Athens in a world which possessed only the rudiments of civilisation and was about to be overwhelmed by a fresh tide of barbarism."[101] But he adds that "their ideal of a Christian culture which would restore and preserve the inheritance of ancient civilisation and classical literature was never lost and ultimately found its progressive realisation in the development of Western culture."[102]

Everywhere in Europe, and throughout the area included in the Graeco-Roman world, the architectural monuments of classical civilisation stood as reminders of ancient order and technical achievement which even unlettered barbarians could read. When traditional technical skills had been obliterated by wars and invasions, the example of the classic orders and all that they implied remained, tranquilly impressive amid civic and political chaos, inviting emulation, their stability and harmonious proportions rebuking the crudities of an uncreative age. The relationship of early Romanesque art and architecture to the familiar classical forms did not depend wholly upon continuity of technical skill. In England, that brief and brilliant civilisation of Northumbria was destroyed, but the preliminary glimpse it had afforded of a noble Romanesque art[103] was not forgotten, and despite the wars that disrupted the Anglo-Saxon states, and the Danish raids of the ninth century, a pre-Norman Romanesque architecture developed. Unfortunately few of those Saxon buildings survive apart from a few small exquisite churches like the examples at Escomb, Durham and St. Lawrence, Bradford-on-Avon; and the well-planned propaganda of the conquering Normans has done much to minimise the significance of such early English Romanesque architecture. Dr. Adamson has drawn attention to the enduring effectiveness of this Norman policy of decrying everything Saxon, and in his book, *The Illiterate Anglo-Saxon*, has pointed out that "the pre-Conquest English were not the nation of universally illiterate, sottish boors, as they are pictured by Norman monks and by the popular historians of a much later day. The process of belittling Anglo-Saxon England to justify Norman aggression began early and in a way which has become all too familiar to the present generation. Paul, the first Norman abbot of St. Albans (1077–1093), destroyed the tombs of his predecessors in office since, as

St. Trophîme, Arles, 1150. *Left:* An interior view, looking east down the nave. *Right:* The porch. Although the church is of the late period of French Romanesque, the porch has very obvious classical affinities, its form recalling that of a Roman triumphal arch. A row of sculptured figures adorns the entablature; behind the columns are stone figures of saints; and the carved tympanum has a representation of Christ as judge of the world. The sculptured detail has great delicacy, and a Byzantine richness of effect is created.

he alleged, they were rude and unlearned although, unlike himself, of royal or noble lineage. Their language was 'barbarous,' 'alien,' declared another ecclesiastic of Norman times, the Italian Faritius, abbot of Abingdon, who died in the year 1115."[104]

Great churches like St. Alban's Abbey suggested the power and promise of English builders. Much may be read from that building, although it was refashioned by the Normans and restored by the Victorians. Whether it had any architectural continuity with the church which Bede mentioned or not, it perpetuates the memory of the Roman city of Verulamium, and not only because Roman bricks and tiles are used in the walls. The square central tower, like the sturdy square towers of smaller Saxon churches, has something Roman about it—something that recalls the towers that so often flanked the gateways of Roman cities; the rounded arches and their moulded detail also have a faded familiarity; and inside the Abbey church, the nave, which is the longest in England, has six bays of original Norman work on the north flank, where arches are piled on arches, with vertical members, dimly reminiscent of pilasters, ascending the face of the piers, the general effect suggesting the façade of some Roman public building. The transepts, apart from the modern windows, are Norman, and the shafts of turned stone, upholding the triforium arches, are part of the original Saxon building.

Norman influence had penetrated Saxon England several decades before the Conquest, as Roman influence had seeped into Britain before the Claudian invasion, and when Norman civilisation was imposed, architecture almost immediately began to reflect the vigour and artistic vitality of those restless and efficient adventurers, who carved out kingdoms, principalities, and dukedoms and made fortunes for themselves all over Europe, and built like men inspired by angels, while fighting like men possessed by devils. The Anglo-Norman rendering of Romanesque architecture was different in character from French, German and Italian; it had a magnitude, spectacular in the impression it created of calm stability, comparable to the suggestion of mastery over materials, mass employed and weight sustained, that hitherto Egyptian temples had alone conveyed. This is apparent, not only in such great cathedrals as Durham, Ely and Peterborough, in churches like St. Bartholomew, Smithfield, but in hundreds of parish churches dating from the eleventh and twelfth centuries, and in the naves of abbeys, such as Tewkesbury, and others now in ruins, like Buildwas, which exhibit a stately procession of cylindrical columns, linked by rounded arches, sparingly embellished. (See page 119.)

This bold and massive architecture originated in Normandy, where the Northmen, establishing themselves early in the tenth century, had adopted the French language, and French social and legal systems. It marked the Norman conquests and settlements in Europe; and its severe beauty, enlivened by local variations, was an inspiration to master masons and their patrons, who built churches far beyond the sphere of Norman influence, in Scotland, for example, and as far north as Kirkwall in the Orkneys, where in 1137 the sandstone cathedral of St. Magnus was founded by Earl Rognvald.

In Norman churches, cylindrical or barrel vaulting forms a roof by means of a continuous rounded arch, which was the structural technique used in Roman building, and this gave way to the pointed arch in vaulting, of which Durham Cathedral (1096–1133) is one of the earliest examples. A French Romanesque example of the use of barrel vaulting is in Notre Dame la Grande, Poitiers, where the arches spring from the capitals of tall columns. This church, like so many French Romanesque buildings, is haunted by the ghost of the classic orders. French Romanesque work, particularly in Aquitaine and Anjou and throughout the Rhône valley, often bears a family likeness to Roman, for there were so many remains of the Imperial Age that they were imitated, perhaps unconsciously, certainly not slavishly. The nave of Notre Dame la Grande is obviously nearer a classical model than the nave of Durham or Ely;

and some of the French churches of this period display even closer links with Imperial Roman architectural design. The west porch of St. Trophîme at Arles is an instance of this, for it recalls the form of a Roman triumphal arch, and Arles was particularly rich in Roman buildings. The carved decoration of many French Romanesque churches displays Byzantine influence, though this seldom affected their form. A notable exception is St. Front, Périgeux, in Aquitaine, built in 1120, which resembles St. Mark's at Venice. It is one of the most westerly examples of Byzantine design, and, with its five cupolas, marking a Greek cross plan, its square bell tower, 200 feet high, crowned by a conical dome, St. Front was a prototype for other French churches with cupolas. (See illustrations on pages 123, 125 and 127.)

There was little Romanesque architecture in Spain, for that country was lost to Christendom after the Arab invasions, which left only the kingdom of Asturia, in the north-west, free from Moslem domination. South and east of that independent Christian kingdom, the Western Caliphate was established. (See Section I, page 8.) North-west of Moslem Spain lay the Frankish Empire that Charlemagne had created in imitation of Rome, which included, at the beginning of the ninth century, all the former Roman province of Gaul, central Germany, Lombardy, and central Italy. Charlemagne may have been an "illiterate barbarian," but his patronage of the arts was responsible for the development of Romanesque architecture, and for the employment of masons and other building craftsmen throughout a vast area of Europe. After the break up of the Empire which followed his death, the example of his patronage remained, the Romanesque style flourished and expanded despite the inter-mittent squabbling of his successors, and their destructive and often inconclusive military adventures.

In Germany the character of Romanesque architecture as an arcuated style was less emphatically expressed than in the Norman cathedrals; there was more refinement and less vitality; the arch was used not only as a structural form but as an internal and external decorative device, and there was visible kinship between German and Lombardic examples of the style. The use and treatment of the arch in buildings as far apart as St. Michele, Pavia, and the Church of the Apostles, Cologne, bear the impress of a common approach to design, indicative of a related culture, which had been fostered by the political unity which followed the revival of the Western Roman Empire by Otto the Great (A.D. 912–973). The Roman Empire had been struggling into some semblance of its former shape ever since Charlemagne had briefly and by conquest restored it at the beginning of the ninth century; for the memory of Roman prestige remained in men's minds as a supreme example of power and security and civilisation and, like the classic orders, encouraged imitation. The results, politically and architecturally, were not unalike: the political ideas were filtered and diluted by the centuries of barbarism that separated them from the great original, the architectural forms were blurred or distorted. "The Holy

The Church of the Apostles at Cologne (1220–1250). Compare the arcading of the external walls with the illustrations of St. Saviour in the Chora, on page 97, and on plate 12. Another view of this church is shown on the opposite page. (From Thomas Hope's *Essay on Architecture*.)

The Church of the Apostles at Cologne, seen from the eastern end, showing the triapsal choir. The surface of the apses and the curved bases of the twin towers is arcaded in two storeys, with arcaded eaves above. Another view is given on the opposite page. (From Thomas Hope's *Essay on Architecture*.)

Roman Empire, taking the name in the sense which it commonly bore in later centuries, as denoting the sovereignty of Germany and Italy vested in a Germanic prince, is the creation of Otto the Great."[105] The stylistic relationship between the Romanesque churches of Lombardy and the Rhineland reflects the political relationship.

In Germany there was a picturesque association of features, melted together; a flourish of turrets circular and octagonal, polygonal domes, and arcaded galleries below the eaves, as in the Church of the Apostles and St. Gereon at Cologne, and the cathedrals at Worms and Spires. A peculiarity of German Romanesque church plans is the duplication of the apse, which appears at the western as well as the eastern end of the church. There is a theory that this additional apse may have survived from the separate baptistry which was a feature of earlier churches, but however it originated, the addition of a western apse deprives German Romanesque churches of the distinctive feature of their French counterparts, the west porch. The Church of the Apostles at Cologne (1220–1250) has a triapsal choir, which gives to the eastern end five external semicircular features, flowing into and out of each other—the three apses, separated by the curved bases of the twin towers. The surface of apses and towers is arcaded in two storeys, with the eaves arcade above. There were Byzantine prototypes for the use of arcading on external walls, and the German examples illustrated on pages 130, 131 and 135, and the apsidal end of St. Michele at Pavia on page 137, should be compared with St. Saviour in the Chora at Constantinople on page 97.

German, French and English Romanesque buildings, while recognisably related and connected, obviously or tenuously, with Roman forerunners, developed characteristics of their own, variously emphasised in different localities, and suggesting the future emergence of a distinctive nationalism. In Italy the link with classical tradition was stronger than in any other part of Europe, and the arch as a structural form did not dominate and pervade the design of Italian Romanesque buildings, though it was used as a decorative feature, and ornamental arcades were piled one above the other, reaching up into the gables. Italian architects, like their Roman predecessors, used the arch as an occasional convenience in building, but made no bold use of it in the basic design of their churches. North, central and southern Italy and Sicily evolved their own styles. In the north the development of vaulting supported by constructional ribs, known as ribbed vaulting, led to fresh constructional techniques long before they were adopted in other parts of Italy; and builders were subjected to influences from Germany, where, as in France, vaulting was extensively used.

One of the distinctive features of Italian Romanesque churches is the campanile, or bell tower, a free-standing structure, separate from the church, though sometimes connected with it by cloisters. These bell towers had a secular function in northern Italy, for they served as watch-towers, and also as monu-

St. Gereon, Cologne, an example of German Romanesque that shows how various features were melted together. The arcaded galleries below the eaves are characteristic. They occur in many German churches of this period. (From Thomas Hope's *Essay on Architecture*.)

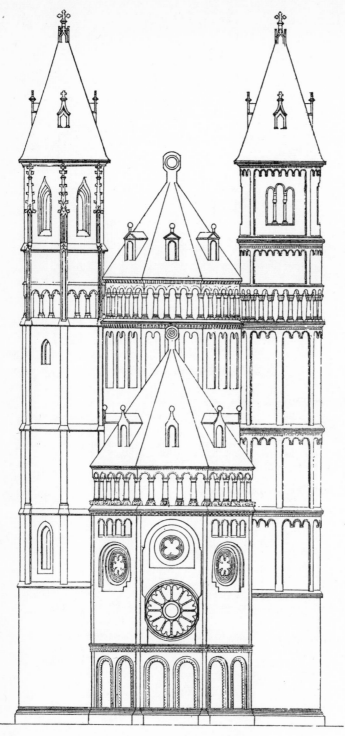

Worms Cathedral (1110–1200), showing the octagonal tower with its pointed roof. Twin circular towers flank the two apses, for the plan is apsidal at both ends. Arcading appears below the eaves of the apse. (From Thomas Hope's *Essay on Architecture*.) Compare with the cathedral of Spires opposite, and the Church of the Apostles at Cologne on pages 130 and 131.

The Cathedral of Spires (1030), an example of German Romanesque, with twin towers and an octagonal cupola. (From Thomas Hope's *Essay on Architecture*.)

135

The cathedral at Piacenza, an example of the Lombard Romanesque style, was built between
1122 and 1233 on the site of an earlier church which had been destroyed in 1117. The stylistic
relationship between the German and Lombardic Romanesque churches is perceptible, and
in this Italian example the characteristic arcading is far more delicate in treatment than the
German. The west front, shown here, has three doors, with columned porches of exceptionally
interesting design. A detailed sketch of the left-hand porch is given above, showing how the
bases of the columns rest upon crouching sculptured figures. The massive square campanile,
223 feet high, is built of brick.

The apsidal end of St. Michele, Pavia, 1188. Compare the exterior surface treatment of this example of Italian Romanesque with the exterior of the Byzantine church, St. Saviour in the Chora, at Constantinople (see page 97 and plate 12.) This church has a cruciform plan.

ments of civic pride. Civic architecture thrived in Italy, where urban civilisation had continued fitfully during the Dark Ages, though always sustained by the large respect of generations of Italians who saw in it a way of life that differentiated them from the inhabitants of the semi-barbaric successor states of the Western Empire. Also, they could protect that chosen way of life, for, in H. A. L. Fisher's memorable phrase, "long before the Roman Empire went down, its cities had adopted the mediaeval livery of fear."[106] Behind the walls of such cities as Milan, Florence, Pisa, Genoa and Verona, public buildings, palaces and great houses arose in competition with the splendours of church architecture, and in Venice, protected by the sea, the immensely wealthy republic erected buildings of dazzling beauty and fabulous richness. In the bitter centuries when Saxon England was gradually assimilating its Norman conquerors, and the countryside was the preserve of brigand barons, the free cities and independent commonwealths of Italy, enriched by organised industry and trade, were in a ferment of artistic activity; and architects, painters and sculptors had greater opportunities, and more varied and encouraging patronage than they had known since the days of Augustus.

The architects were absolved from the tyranny of a conventional system of design, and they had the zest that is generated by an appreciative audience, for the city state had been restored to Europe, that comparatively small unit of civilisation wherein men could be actively informed and interested in the social, political and artistic events of their own community. Like the Greek

city states, those of Italy quarrelled and fought with each other, and lavished
money and talent on military forays, monuments and buildings. Architects built
with a strong memory of the past, and of the guidance supplied by the classic
orders, and in central and southern Italy, removed from Germanic influences,
their version of the Romanesque style had a lightness and a lively originality
that created such masterpieces as the cathedral, campanile and baptistry at
Pisa, and St. Miniato at Florence, while in Sicily Byzantine and Saracenic
ornamental forms were handled with a sensitive understanding of their power
to relieve the severity of line in such impressive buildings as Monreale Cathedral,
which stands above Palermo. The growth of the Romanesque style had been
occasionally checked or diverted in central Italy by the use of columns, removed
from Roman ruins, and neatly incorporated in new buildings; but when this
labour-saving device was rejected, architects invented such delicate variations
of the classic type as the carved and twisted columns in the cloisters of St. John,
Lateran, in Rome. (See opposite page.)

Throughout Italy, the manifestations of the Romanesque style suggest a
mastery of design, and a new, intellectual appreciation of architectural composition. The churches were not built for the glory of faith alone; already the first
light of another age of reason glows. That superb group of buildings at Pisa,
the cathedral, baptistry and campanile demonstrates the new powers architects were acquiring, powers that transcended mere technical ability, and had
not been exercised since the Greeks built their temples. Externally, the cathedral,
baptistry and campanile at Pisa, have a quality of design, a lucidity of form,
that disclose not only the operation of intellect, but a wholly new sense of
elegance. Even the inept fourteenth century Gothic additions which surmount
the arcade of the baptistry cannot mask the refinement and power of the design,
while the campanile with its eight storeys of encircling arcades is a most
delicately adjusted harmony of horizontal and vertical elements. The purity
of its composition is apt to be ignored because of its unfortunate inclination,
which attracts attention to it as a freak instead of a work of genius. The cathedral
was built between 1063 and 1092, the campanile in 1174, and the baptistry,
which was designed by Dioti Salvi, between 1153 and 1278. (See pages 140
and 141.)

The cathedral, similar to other basilican churches in plan, has transepts with
a segmental apse at each end, and an elliptical dome over the crossing, which
was added at a later date. It exhibits no structural innovations, but its proportions, and the gracious fusion of the exterior arcades, particularly on the west
front, assert the independent judgment of the designer. This independence is
less apparent within the cathedral; there concessions have been made to the
needs and established form of a Christian church; only outside has the architect
allowed an heretical hint of intellectual adventure to appear. Elsewhere in
Europe the architecture of emotion triumphantly expressed the intent faith
of Christendom in the spiritual life, and a preoccupation with the world to

St. John, Lateran, at Rome, has been re-built and altered so often since its foundation in the fourth century, that its original character as an early Christian church is obliterated. The cloisters still retain a tenuous connection with the classic orders, though they exhibit many delicate variations of the basic forms such as slender, twisted columns. (From Thomas Hope's *Essay on Architecture*.)

come: in Italy alone an audacious flirtation with things of the mind was divulged in terms of architectural design. Sometimes a touch of levity is apparent, a light-hearted rationalism in the use of form and colour, as exemplified by the marble sheathing of the exterior and interior of St. Miniato in Florence, (1013), and the porch of Pistoia Cathedral (1150). The exterior of St. Miniato is shown on plate 13. Again, in Italy the reverence for Christian symbolism was diminished when the individual symbols, the monogram of Christ and the emblems of saints, were regarded as components in a decorative scheme, and were associated with actual fragments or copies of Roman ornament. Acanthus scrolls wound in and out on walls, and imitations of classic mouldings regulated the play of light and shade. There was still a ripple of pagan laughter, just below the surface of life in the Italian city states—the gods were not really

The Baptistry, Pisa, designed by Dioti Salvi, and built between 1153 and 1278. The purity of the design is marred, though not destroyed, by the Gothic additions which surmount the arcade and were made in the fourteenth century. It is obvious that Italian architects of the Romanesque period acknowledged their debt to classical architecture: in Italy it was never forgotten. The plan of the Baptistry is circular, and within the central space is 60 feet in diameter. With the Cathedral and the Campanile it forms part of a group of buildings that is world famous, and marks the break with that architecture of emotion which found expression in massive solemnity in other parts of Europe.

Pisa Cathedral (1063–1092) and the Campanile (1174), viewed from the south-
west. The ground storey is faced with wall arcading, and on the entrance façade
open arcades ascend into the gable. *Drawn by Hilton Wright.*

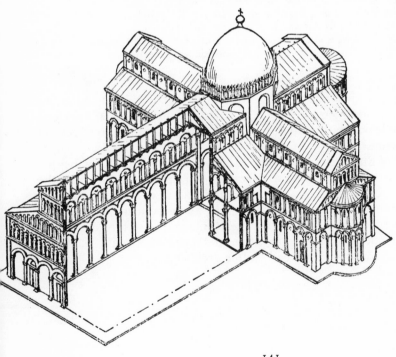

Diagram showing
section through the
nave, with its
columns connected
by arches. *Drawn
by Marcelle Barton.*

A thirteenth century example of the timber architecture which developed
in Scandinavia, Hitterdals Kirke is the largest of the mediaeval Nor-
wegian "stavekirker" or timber-built churches. The body of the church
is rectangular, with a square choir terminating in an apse at the eastern
end. Above the gabled roof of the nave there is a square, gabled tower
with a spire above. The carved enrichment of the gables is similar to
that used on the prow of a ship—another example of the link between
the Scandinavian shipwright and builder. The roof of the choir is lower
than that of the nave, and is decorated by a round turret. A distinctive
feature of the building is the single-storey arcade which encircles it.

dead, they only slept, and even in the eleventh century unconscious preparations
were being made by architects for their reception in new temples. In Italy,
the Romanesque style was less a prelude to Gothic than preliminary architectural
training for the Renaissance.

All over the rest of Europe, except in the Moslem part of Spain, Romanesque
church architecture had established a solemnity of form that spoke, like the
tolling of deep-toned bells, of hell, purgatory and paradise, and also of duty,
hope and redemption. Architecture was fashioning an instrument of instruction
and praise that was awaiting perfection. The Romanesque style was the first
phase of that stupendous adventure in stone and brick and glass, the glory
of mediaeval civilisation, which we call Gothic architecture.

VI

THE EMERGENCE OF GOTHIC

GOTHIC is the term generally used to describe European architecture of the thirteenth, fourteenth and fifteenth centuries, though it was misleading when it first became current in the seventeenth century, because it implied that the style had been invented by the barbarous Goths, who had established the Visi-Gothic Empire in Spain and the Ostro-Gothic Empire in Italy in the sixth century. Those warlike and uncreative barbarians were incapable of inventing an architectural style, but their name has been perpetuated because of its association with the use of the pointed arch, which gave to mediaeval buildings an elasticity and a fluidity of form that had been foreshadowed in some of the later Romanesque work, but had never occurred in Roman structures. The term was used first by Giorgio Vasari (1511–1571), the Italian art historian; and it became one of reprobation, partly because the very word *Goth* stood for something rude and savage, partly because it was attached to a style that had been superseded by the revival of the classic orders at the Renaissance. John Evelyn, in the mid-seventeenth century, described the Palazzo Farnese, in Rome, as "a magnificent square structure, of the three orders of columns after the ancient manner, and when architecture was but newly recovered from the Gotic barbarity."[107] Even as late as the eighteen-thirties, architectural purists like Thomas Hope could write of "the youngest branch of the art, that erroneously called Gothic,"[108] and the study of mediaeval architecture has suffered during the last three hundred years, at first from the initial contempt for a style which did not conform with the proportions of the five orders, and later because of its romantic appeal, which, in the eighteenth century, made Gothic design and ornament fashionable, and, in the following century, morally obligatory, for by then the style had acquired a spiritual significance, indubitably sincere, but essentially artificial. The rejection of Gothic forms in the late fifteenth century and during the sixteenth, was common throughout Europe; but, as we shall see in a later section, isolated pockets of the mediaeval styles survived here and there, just as pockets of the old pagan religions had survived as witch covens.

Gothic architecture grew out of Romanesque, and the different phases of the Gothic style were also the result of continuous growth, for throughout the Middle Ages, sacred and secular buildings were being put up in every European country; the cathedrals of France and England and Germany were always partly webbed with scaffolding as some new addition, some fresh ambitious recasting of the original structure, was carried out. The round arch, which had been in continuous use since Roman times, gave way to the pointed arch, and because of this characteristic structural form, Gothic architecture has some-times been called *Pointed* architecture; but such a term attributes, at least by implication, the invention and use of the pointed arch to mediaeval builders, whereas it had been known long before the Christian era in the Middle East, but like other architectural inventions it had been dormant—its latent possibili-ties unappreciated, until the new experimental spirit in architectural design, begotten during the Romanesque period, was nourished by an expanding civilisation, by the increasing power and immense wealth of the Church, and the security which the Church gave.

Europe by the thirteenth century had become Christianised; even the old fierce Scandinavian nations were incorporated in the general structure of Christendom; and the northern limits of the Faith went far beyond the borders of Germany, the influence of Rome meeting that of the Greek Church in the ill-defined, still half-barbaric countries that lay between Russia and the German states ruled by the Emperor. Raids from pagan pirates and Vikings, seldom threatened the property of the Church. The day when tall minsters and abbeys automatically went up in flames during times of war was over, and with this new security architects and builders were liberated for making experiments of increasing boldness. Not only did the Church provide opportunities for architectural design; within the walled towns of Europe the increasing prosperity of merchants and traders furnished fresh patronage for building, and a new sense of civic pride arose, supported by the personal interest of those who governed the towns. This was very different from the impersonal, cold, bureau-cratic ordering of cities under the Roman Empire, subjected as they were to the remote control of a central and unsympathetic authority. European towns were adorned with fine buildings, city and market halls and exchanges, and the rebuilding of churches went on continuously, so that the mediaeval city thrust into the air a forest of towers and spires, on which gilded crosses and weather vanes, with their swallow-tailed pennons, glittered beneath the unpolluted skies of the pre-industrial age.

Romanesque architects had given to their buildings an air of serene stability; there was something settled and calm and eternal about the stalwart columns and the rounded arches they supported—something both placid and inert. The

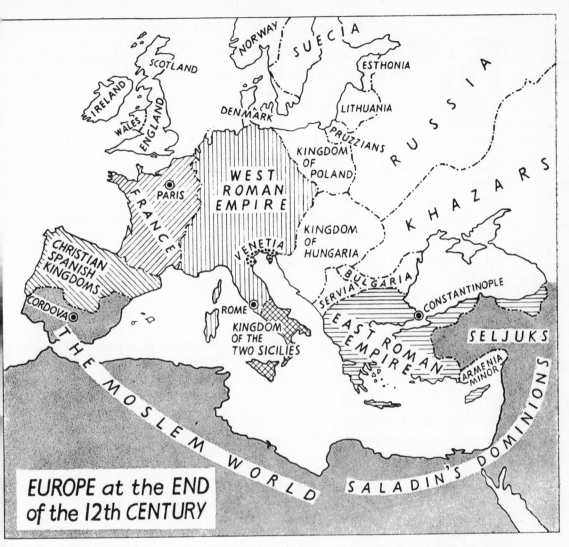

EUROPE at the END of the 12th CENTURY

Compare this map with Europe in the early ninth century, on page 114. The political environment of Western architecture has changed since Charlemagne's attempt to revive the West Roman Empire. The East Roman Empire has recovered some of its territory in the Balkans, but has lost its Italian provinces. The Moslem grip on Spain is relaxing, and the Christian Spanish kingdoms have advanced until they occupy the whole of the northern and much of central Spain. Cordova, with its university and flourishing arts and industries, was still a centre of culture that radiated Oriental influence, and attracted craftsmen and scholars from Europe. The University of Paris, founded by Philip Augustus in 1200, was the great Christian centre of culture; France was leading European civilisation in architecture and the arts of life by the opening of the thirteenth century; and Normandy was conquered in the early years of that century. A revival of the arts was beginning in Rome, as a result of the work of the family of Cosmati, which produced four generations of outstanding architects, sculptors, and workers in mosaic. (See page 367.) *Drawn by Marcelle Barton.*

girth of the columns in the nave of a Norman cathedral, like Ely or Durham, had undeniable impressiveness and dignity, but those columns suggested safety first; they said so clearly that the builders were taking no risks, that they associated bulk with strength, and had not yet tested the capacity of the material they were using; but within a century, at the beginning of the mediaeval period, this approach to structure changed. This change followed the introduction and general use of the pointed arch, and in conjunction with buttresses, and the impulsion to build higher and higher, a new conception of design arose which turned the ideas of builders towards vertical lines. Some Greek temples, as we saw in Section III, were really the bases of gigantic pyramids, which if they were carried to their logical height would rise hundreds of feet into the air. The great Gothic churches of the Middle Ages were nearly all designed to send towers striving upwards, not through any conscious desire to provide optical satisfaction, but to satisfy the innate craving for symbolism—almost as though hands were being held up in praise.

The initial inspiration for a sacred building did not come from the architect: it came from some commanding personality in the hierarchy of the Church. In the course of five centuries the status of the architect had changed. In the Graeco-Roman world he had been known by name and reputation and was recognised as a professional man. The mediaeval architect had no such standing. He was usually anonymous, and often a master mason himself; or if he was some great churchman who acted as an impresario for craftsmen, he would almost certainly have a close knowledge of, as well as a deep interest in, building technique. It was not until the Renaissance that the architect emerged from anonymity and again became identified with the buildings he created, and he was often an accomplished creative artist in one or more of the fine arts. Michelangelo is a conspicuous example of the sculptor and painter who was also an engineer and a great architect.

Church-building was in progress in every European country, ostensibly for the glory of God, though often to satiate the ambitions of some prelate. The air of every city was tremulous with the melody of bells, the country-side was punctuated with beckoning spires and towers. "In one hundred years the French put up eighty cathedrals and five hundred churches of the cathedral class. According to an estimate made in 1840, they would at that time, with the mechanical power then available, have cost £200,000,000 to build."[109] Christian Barman, who records this in his masterly essay on *Architecture* adds that it was far more than was ever achieved in Norman England. "The whole people lived for these giant enterprises," he wrote, "and thought of little else. They went on international begging expeditions to raise funds. They harnessed themselves to the carts that bore stone from the quarries. Their buildings are so well known that the names alone bring them vividly before the minds of most, Paris, Chartres, Amiens, Beauvais, and Bourges are a quincunx that no one will forget."[110] The emotional content of such buildings, erected by the

The cathedral of Notre Dame, Paris (1163–1235). One of the oldest of the French Gothic cathedrals. Above the central doorway of the triple arched west front is a great wheel window of exceptional beauty. This western façade, one of the finest in France, was the prototype for many later churches.

collective enthusiasm of the faithful, was stupendous, and survives to this day, awakening the reverence of the susceptible, or the distaste of the classically minded purist. As a corrective to the sentimental awe that is apt to swamp the critical faculties when a Gothic cathedral is contemplated, the views of Norman Douglas, one of the last great Europeans of the twentieth century, are worth recalling. On leaving Athens he wrote: "Let me have a last look at the Parthenon, for soon I may be seeing monuments of another school. It was my fate, during the war, to spend several days at Amiens, where I passed some hours in front of that cathedral, trying to decide whether this stuff was architecture or nightmare. I have not yet made up my mind."[111] Norman Douglas, whose antipathy to Christianity was almost pathological, was obviously disturbed and uneasy by the proselytising urgency of that intricate west front at Amiens, which gives out the message of the Faith, demanding adherence, breaking down the rational resistances of the unregenerate, as contemptuous of the world and the flesh as a saint, and as strongly armoured against them.

In the course of all this striving and adventurous experiment, structural discoveries were made which changed the whole conception of the wall as a supporting element in building. The Gothic masons used stone as it had never been used before; they approached architecture as engineers; they were unconscious of creating a style, they were not attempting to do anything of the kind, but they found that by the use of the vault and the pointed arch

Right:
The east end of Beauvais Cathedral (1225–1568) showing the tiers of flying buttresses which take the thrust of the vault.

Left:
Flying buttresses could, in late examples of French Gothic, become as intricate as these examples at Rodez. The cathedral of this southern French town was built between 1277 and 1535.

The east end of Albi Cathedral (1282–1512), which is a long vaulted church, with series of chapels on each side of the nave, separated by internal buttresses. The tall, narrow windows are devoid of ornament, apart from some simple tracery in the heads of the upper row. This cathedral of St. Cécile is a fortress-church, and an austere example of French Gothic.

they could refine stonework so that the weight and thrust of a building could be coaxed downwards. Structural lines that distributed thrust and bore weight, crossing voids, arching over voids, and floating down through buttresses, actually suggested ascent rather than descent; weight it is true was carried downwards, but those arches and vaults and buttresses gave the impression of lines ascending, sweeping up to the vaulted roofs and lofty naves and to towers and spires that were increasingly exalted. The columns that supported the pointed arches in naves and aisles diminished in girth, as they only partially supported the weight of the building, and the wall gradually began to melt away, its solid sections being replaced by voids, for as the new structural system developed, windows grew larger and larger, and eventually the church became a great stone lantern, with huge expanses of stained glass through which daylight gave animation to coloured pictures. The whole building was a composition of glass in brilliant hues, lightly clasped, so it appeared, by a slender framework of stone.

Inevitably there were a few set-backs: sometimes a tower would collapse, or the foundations of a nave give way, and this was not always a result of too much boldness and ambition in design—after 1200 some of the great cathedrals in France and England show signs of economy, and even carelessness and cheapness in construction.[112] Owing to faulty foundations the west tower of Gloucester fell about the end of the eleventh century, the central tower of Winchester collapsed in 1107, so did the west tower of Worcester in 1175.

The main entrance to the Palace of the Popes, Avignon. This building is more like a fortress than a palace, with high walls, and rather incongruous Gothic tourelles and pinnacles here and there relieving the military severity of the design. It was begun in 1316 by John XXII, and continued and added to by the popes who succeeded him, until its completion in 1370.

In 1284 the roof of Beauvais Cathedral fell. The central tower of Ely, which for some time had been in a shaky condition, came down in 1321, "a disaster which proved a blessing to posterity as it made way for the glorious octagonal lantern."[113]

Such occasional accidents did not deter mediaeval builders; they could learn something from the fall of a tower or a roof; they were always learning; and, generation after generation, they made fresh experiments, adding to the cathedral churches until they had perfected a technique that consisted of sections of wall, called buttresses, set at right angles to a building to take the accumulated pressure of the ribbed vaulting. The use of these buttresses represented a considerable structural invention, and when they took the form of an arch springing from a detached pier and abutting against a wall to allow pressures and thrusts to glide down them to the ground they were, appropriately enough, called flying buttresses. The section through the nave of Westminster Abbey, on the opposite page, illustrates the thrust and counter-thrust of the vaulting and buttresses. That nave, the highest Gothic vault in England, rising to 102 feet, is strutted by flying buttresses across the aisles and north cloister. At Rheims Cathedral, where the height of the nave is just over 124 feet, flying buttresses over the single aisles of the nave and the double aisles of the east end transmit the thrust of the vault to piers, stabilised and weighted with statuary and pinnacles; and at Beauvais Cathedral the thrust of the highest vault in Europe, 157 feet, is taken by flying buttresses of great strength.

Mediaeval architects, unhampered by any stylistic conflicts, were always improving their technique, not because of any conscious conversion to a new structural doctrine, but because the infiltration of new ideas affected and enlarged the general knowledge of one or more generations of building craftsmen, as, in the course of a century or more, some abbey or cathedral was completed, though not with any finality, for no mediaeval cathedral was ever really completed—it continued to grow in beauty, to acquire additions and embellishments, within and without. In England, particularly, this almost unceasing building activity has provided many examples which show the beginning and the end of Gothic architecture; all its phases associated in amity. A brief description of this process of continuous growth may be quoted, with Peterborough Cathedral as the example.

"Until 1541 it was the Abbey Church of St. Peter, the third church to stand upon the site, and it was founded in 1117 or 1118 by John de Sais after the destruction of an earlier building by fire in 1116. The work of the founder

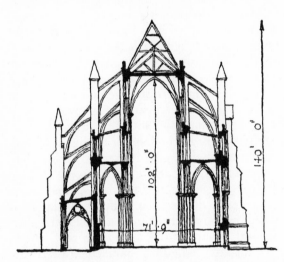

Section through the nave of Westminster Abbey, showing the thrust and counter-thrust of the vaulting and buttresses. The nave vault is the highest Gothic vault in England, and is strutted by flying buttresses across the aisles and north cloister. *Drawn by A. S. Cook.*

was confined to the choir, which terminates in an apse, and this was dedicated about 1140. Between 1149 and 1155 the aisles of both transepts and the south transept were completed by Martin of Bec. William de Waterville finished the work on the transepts and built the central tower between 1155 and 1175. The nave was built by Abbot Benedict, 1177–1193, and Abbot Andrew was responsible for the western transepts, which were erected by the beginning of the thirteenth century. Throughout that century work on the Abbey continued. The triple-arched west front was probably completed by 1250; the Lady chapel (which was demolished in the seventeenth century) was consecrated in 1290; some fifteen years earlier the bell-tower was built, and the pinnacles of the towers of the west front carried work on into the fourteenth century, when decorated windows were introduced. In the fifteenth century an eastern chapel was added in the Perpendicular style; this was begun in 1438 and finished ninety years later. For about two centuries after its foundation builders were at work almost continuously on the Abbey, and the Perpendicular addition—the 'new building,' as the eastern chapel is called—accounted for nearly another century. Not far short of three hundred years of mixed work, the skill and thought of nine generations of craftsmen, are embodied in this church.

"Such protracted instalments of architectural activity might be expected to produce an effect of conflict, especially when spread over centuries of change. But here again the purpose of the church dominated the minds of the builders; and the fulfilment of that purpose was recognised throughout the Middle Ages; every generation of craftsmen sought the same goal, although they improved on the methods their forerunners had known. The easy blending of all those years of work is at once apparent inside Peterborough Cathedral. If you stand below the central tower, the first suggestions of an unwonted slenderness in Norman building may be seen in the upward-streaming lines of the piers; and the transepts show that Norman solidity is melting. The arches of the transepts that shoulder the weight of the tower are rounded, with the lines of pointed relieving arches above them; those that carry the tower above the choir are pointed. The broken sweep of their curve gives a gentle hint of thrust spread widely; a mere concession to contemporary 'modernism'; remote as yet from that strident structural proclamation of weight driven earthwards by a score of sloping pathways that was to be one of the phases of Gothic building.

"Although there is an air of quiet discovery in the interior of this cathedral, arising from the discreet incorporation of new ideas as it grew to completion, the ultimate dominance of voids over solids is clearly foreshadowed. It is an early stage in the evolution of the 'cage of stone,' in Lethaby's phrase; soon such sturdy skeletons acquired refinements, devised too skilfully to mar their strength. Before that stage was reached builders had achieved a placid formality, as the nave of Peterborough Cathedral illustrates throughout its cool length. About it there is something faintly eastern, something Saracenic, awed into mildness, bereft of any flamboyant heathenish flavour, an oriental spirit chilled: possibly a dying murmur of Byzantium, only articulate since the church lost most of its glass and form gained an ascendancy over colour. The harmony in stone wrought by the builders of this church survives the withdrawal of that vivid element of its composition—colour."[114]

Very many English cathedrals were originally part of some monastic establishment, grouped with other buildings—cloisters, refectory, and the abbot's or prior's house—and as the work on them was spread over centuries, diversity of style naturally followed. Salisbury is the exception, for that cathedral, with its lofty spire, 404 feet, the highest in England, is almost entirely in the Early English style, and was erected between 1220 and 1258. (See page 154.)

As Gothic architecture developed, builders, confident of their capacity, exercised their talents in the service of God, and great churches in every European country, but especially in France and England, began to speak a language that was understood by Christians everywhere. They still have

The triple-arched west front of Peterborough Cathedral, completed about 1250.
Until 1541 it was the Abbey Church of St. Peter, and the third church to occupy
the site. It was founded in 1117 or 1118 by John de Sais, after an earlier building
had been destroyed by fire. Peterborough Cathedral illustrates, perhaps more
fully than any other sacred edifice in England, the process of continuous growth,
the almost unceasing building activity, which kept some part of every mediaeval
church webbed with scaffolding, century after century.

153

Salisbury Cathedral, built almost entirely in the Early English style, between
1220 and 1258. The spire is now the highest in England, but only since the spire
of old St. Paul's cathedral was destroyed by lightning in 1561. Salisbury's spire
is 404 feet high; old St. Paul's was 489 feet. The two upper storeys of the tower
and the spire are later than the rest of the church, and are early examples of
Decorated Gothic: the steeple was the work of the mason, Richard of Farleigh.
It dates from the first half of the fourteenth century.

something to say to men and women of our own century, and we have cited
the case of Amiens Cathedral which had something disconcerting to say to
a sceptical modern author; but, as we suggested in the first section, all buildings
have something to say. They may be as talkative, as obsessed by trivialities,
as some people, or as tongue-tied as others: some buildings chatter like starlings
or monkeys, others sing, cheerfully or solemnly, with grace or pomp, or out
of tune. The French and English cathedrals spoke not only with towers and

St. Mary's, Bloxham, Oxfordshire, an example of Decorated Gothic, with the octagonal spire rising 198 feet above ground level. The spire rises from an octagonal drum above the square tower, with angle pinnacles enriched with crockets.

spires, which shouted praises to the skies, or through their blazing windows and strenuous sculpture, but in a manner more massively and unforgettably impressive. It was a bookless age, and in his analysis of the motives of Gothic builders, Christian Barman has suggested that the idea of fabricating light into pictures accounts for the preponderance of windows in churches and cathedrals and for their ultimate vast size. Through coloured glass, a flaming message burned in the daylight hours; each window spoke to the responsive worshippers, and beyond them "lay a dark and fluid world in process of formation, its noises drowned by the glazier's fiery, enveloping speech."[115] In his essay, *Heaven and Hell*, Aldous Huxley has emphasised the significant part played by stained glass in inducing visionary experience, and how those jewelled windows could turn a whole building "into something magical and transporting."[116]

A mediaeval church without its original glass is empty indeed, a speechless shell, often maliciously despoiled by fanatics, sometimes blatantly looted by collectors. The glazier was a specialist in symbolism; so was the sculptor. "The upward rush of the stone mass was punctuated by figures. The saints stood as guardians to the fabric. The evils that assail mankind were shown: devils grinned; the fauna of magic and witchcraft crawled leering over mouldings, capitals and corbels; birds and beasts, sins and virtues, were shaped with fantastic zest, and humour was vigorously abundant. The sculptor was not merely a specialist in ornament, to be called in at the discretion of the architect: like the glazier, he created a voice; like the glazier, he was a fellow-craftsman with the masons. Like all the craftsmen who worked at church building, he enjoyed a measure of creative freedom that enabled him to be boldly experimental, florid, profuse, and grotesque as his fancy desired. It was the golden age for those who carved in wood and stone. Never again were they to enjoy such an unfettered partnership with architecture.

"Sculpture to-day has to stand on or cling to a few projections, casually left vacant in the architectural composition; it has no intimate relationship with building; and the sculptor himself has nothing in common with the men who erect with all the devices of machine-craft the building he embellishes. He belongs to the artist caste; and the setting of his work is the studio and not the scaffold. He is a stranger where once he was a fellow-craftsman. The architect is in undisputed control of his work; and as for many generations both sculptors and architects have thought of sculpture as an isolated art-form, the sculptor has lost the architectonic sense which in mediaeval times gave to his carven figures and ornamentation a decorative stability."[117]

In some churches a more permanent form of symbolism was apparently contrived by the nature of the plan, when the axes of nave and chancel were varied to give the building an angular twist. There are two main schools of thought about the significance of buildings constructed with this distortion: the rationalist school, which attributes it to the defects of the method used by mediaeval architects for setting out a church, and the romantics, or symbolists, who contend that many cathedrals and churches were distorted by deliberate calculation, so that the axes of nave and chancel did not correspond. The change of alignment between nave and chancel may well have been intentional when churches were built on the plan of a cross, to symbolise the figure of the crucified Christ, with His head inclined to the left, or south side; though in many European and some English churches with varied axes the inclination is towards the north. Lichfield Cathedral, one of the most famous English examples of deflected buildings, leans to the north, while Canterbury, Ely and York incline to the south.[118] Much has been written on this subject, and some

Gloucester Cathedral, showing the central tower, which is 225 feet high. Originally the Benedictine Abbey of St. Peter, when it was converted into a cathedral after the Dissolution, many of its buildings, large and small, were preserved. The tower is fifteenth century, a fine example of Perpendicular Gothic. (See page 21 for an illustration of the east window.)

authorities have suggested that in the course of building a cathedral, "the axis of the nave or the choir, whichever portion was already standing, would probably be hidden from the mason's view, through the temporary blocking up of the chancel arch. This might render harmonious alignment a task of some difficulty. It has been averred that every case of deflection occurs in a church that has been partially rebuilt; hence the lack of agreement."[119] It has also been asserted "that many cases of deflection were discovered only when, in modern times, the rood-screen was, for one reason or another, taken down. In such instance, it is argued, the mason would have his standard line concealed while setting out the new section of the building."[120] The symbolists, who believe that the whole vast bulk of the church was designed to impress, in perpetuity, the agony of the crucifixion, are not over-estimating either the creative powers or technical ability of mediaeval architects, and there is another view, less ardently held, that "the bend was designed to produce an artistic illusion—a perspective effect whereby a building appeared to be longer than it actually was. Thus, if one of the side walls of a church with a 'weeping chancel' be viewed from the western entrance, an impression of greater length and of undefined distance is received by the spectator. Again, where a rood screen exists, the bend in the wall, not a pleasing feature, considered separately, would be concealed, but a change in the direction in a lofty roof would still produce an illusion that the church is indefinitely extended. Moreover, as the beholder caught a glimpse of a portion of the sanctuary window, which was often richly ornamented, both in form and colour, the beauty of the vista was much enhanced."[121] Whether the Gothic architects possessed this Greek-like reverence for the sense of sight, or whether they carefully calculated the relative alignment of nave and choir for the glory of God, must remain a matter for conjecture; but it seems unlikely that such accomplished technicians were unable to build straight.

Despite wars, revolutions, intentional destruction or indolent neglect, there are still thousands of examples of sacred and secular buildings standing in Europe and the British Isles which attest the genius of mediaeval architects. From the Romanesque style with its classical connections, they had developed a new approach to architectural design, which checked all refluent tendencies, except in Italy where the memory of Roman structures persistently impinged upon the imagination of builders and artists. Gothic architecture was, as Thomas Hope said, "the youngest branch of the art," and remained so until the present century, when another new conception of architectural design, comparable with that revealed to and acted upon by the Gothic architects, has been adopted and practised in Western civilisation, and, for want of a better term, is called "the modern movement," or, less explicit still, "contemporary design," though it is really the new Western architecture.

Gothic architecture was young and vital and supple when it began its development in France about the middle of the twelfth century; in that country it lasted until the early years of the sixteenth, and spread throughout Europe, exhibiting, like the Romanesque style which preceded it, national and regional characteristics. In mediaeval Europe those local variations could not have been recognised as incipient indications of nationalism: the continent was certainly split up into kingdoms and principalities, and associations of states under one ruler, like the Holy Roman Empire, but the idea of nationhood, of nationality as we understand it to-day, was alien to the conception of a united Christendom; nevertheless the regional variations of Gothic architecture forecast the ultimate pattern of the European nations, long before peasants or princes were conscious of them or churchmen reluctantly acknowledged them. In *St. Joan* Shaw puts into the mouth of the Bishop of Beauvais a condemnation of the Maid's heresy in these words:

"To her the French-speaking people are what the Holy Scriptures describe as a nation. Call this side of her heresy Nationalism if you will: I can find you no better name for it. I can only tell you that it is essentially anti-Catholic and anti-Christian; for the Catholic Church knows only one realm, and that is the realm of Christ's kingdom."

An unceasing task of the Church was to override local and limiting patriotisms by demanding from all Christian men a broader and spiritual allegiance to that realm of Christ's kingdom; and the ideal of a united Christendom was sufficiently powerful to motivate the Crusades, and to inspire in every European country passionate and often popular support for building and decorating churches. But the increasing differences between the growth of Gothic architecture in one country and another, though partly attributable to the use of local

The original Gothic interior of the Storkykran, or Great Church, dedicated to
St. Nicholas; the oldest church in Stockholm. It was founded in the second half
of the thirteenth century by Birger Jarl, and almost entirely rebuilt about 1740.
The austere lines of what remains of the Gothic work are disrupted, and partly
obliterated, by the ornate additions, which display in pulpit and canopy, screen
and stalls, the ornamental fecundity of Renaissance carvers.

and convenient materials—wood in many parts of Scandinavia, brick in
Holland, stone in France and England—cast the warning shadows of a future
disunity.

In England the Gothic style developed, as Romanesque had developed, much
later than upon the Continent. Anglo-Norman architecture was followed by
the Early English period, when the first, tentative use of the pointed arch
occurs, and from the floreated capitals of tall clustered columns, those arches
spurted in smooth jets, curving to meet and form lofty vaults, while tall stained-
glass windows dyed the daylight that illuminated nave and aisles, transepts,
choir and sanctuary. The framework of the Gothic cathedrals and churches
of England is classified by three convenient terms: Early English, which began
late in the twelfth century and lasted until the early fourteenth, then giving
place to Decorated, when the austere lines evolved in the preceding period
were enriched with a splendour of carved ornament, a period which
lasted until the late fourteenth century when English Gothic entered upon its

final period, the Perpendicular, which ended in the first half of the sixteenth century. Those terms, Early English, Decorated, and Perpendicular, first used by Thomas Rickman in the early nineteenth century, do not represent rigid periods: they occasionally overlap, and the Perpendicular style began to appear in some localities, for example, in the mid-fourteenth century. But they do stand for three distinct phases of English Gothic, each revealing how accumulated structural experience tended to refine stone masses, to melt away walls, until the "cage of stone" was attained, and the slender vertical lines of the Perpendicular style represented the ultimate achievement of English mediaeval architects.

In France most of the great cathedrals had been built during the first half of the thirteenth century, and they did not originate like the English cathedrals as part of monastic establishments; they were an integral part of French town life, supplying an example of architectural splendour for the emulation of the civic authorities, and a constant reminder of the power and spiritual guardianship of the Church. Soissons Cathedral was one of the exceptions, for it was the church of a Royal Abbey, built between 1160 and 1212, an early example of French Gothic, or *Style Ogivale* as it is known in France. Like English Gothic, the style has been broadly classified in three main periods, following the Romanesque. The first, covering the twelfth century, *Gothique à Lancettes*, marks the transition from Romanesque and the use of pointed arches and windows filled with geometric tracery, corresponding to Early English Gothic, though beginning nearly a hundred years earlier. The second period follows in the thirteenth century, and is known as *Rayonnant*—literally a radiant and sparkling phase, for it was then that circular windows with wheel tracery were introduced, like those at Notre Dame, Paris, Rheims, Rouen and Amiens. The last period, *Flamboyant*, includes the fourteenth and fifteenth centuries, and the term is derived from "the flame-like wavings" of the tracery of windows and panels.[122] *Flamboyant* was the final contribution of French architects to the Gothic style: like Perpendicular in England it died out when the classic orders were re-introduced at the Renaissance.

One of the oldest of the French Gothic cathedrals is Notre Dame, Paris, built between 1163 and 1235, and having, like Rheims, Amiens, Laon and St. Vulfran, Abbeville, and many others, a bold, triple-arched west front. In Notre Dame the partnership between glass and stone gives a sombre richness to the interior; but it is at Chartres that the most impressive example of that partnership occurs. (Section I, page 30.) A characteristic feature of French cathedral architecture is the use of twin towers, flanking the western façade, usually, though not always, identical. At Amiens the towers of the west front, though symmetrically disposed, vary in height; and at Chartres the towers form a striking contrast, and were built at different periods, the spire of the north tower dating from 1506, the south being four hundred years earlier. (See plate 15.) Strassburg Cathedral has two western towers, one of them surmounted by an openwork spire, which was added in 1439, and upsets the balance of the design by giving the west front a lopsided appearance. The cathedral was built between 1250 and 1290. Where identical towers appear, they avoid the visual odium of the "unresolved duality," to use Mr. Trystan Edwards's descriptive phrase, because of the unifying influence of the triple arches of the doorways, and the rose window that appears above the central arch.

There is a marked difference between the Gothic architecture of northern and southern France. In the south the Roman traditions, transmitted from the Romanesque style, persisted, though they were progressively modified. In the north the fresh, urgent verticality of Gothic was marked by boldness of conception allied with great delicacy of detail. Within, the vivid quality of stained glass filled naves and aisles and transepts with moving carpets of colour; and it is inside the French cathedrals that the richness and variety of mediaeval stained glass may best be studied. France, which remained a Catholic country until the Revolution, did not suffer the systematic pillage and destruction to which English churches were subjected at the Reformation and by the God-fearing and art-hating Puritans of the Commonwealth. The Huguenots were occasionally destructive; their opportunities were more limited; though they were responsible for the destruction of the fifth century church built by Bishop Patiens at Lyons—an irreparable loss.

French civic buildings reflected many of the contemporary characteristics of Gothic architecture, to which was added a stately magnificence. The disposition of windows in the façade, the use of arcades, and the steepness of roofs, put an accent on vertical features, and there was respect too for symmetry, which is particularly marked in such buildings as the Palais de Justice, Rouen (1493–1508), the Hôtel de Ville at Dreux (mid-sixteenth century), and the Hôtel de Ville at Compiègne (fifteenth century). These buildings belong to a late period of Gothic architecture, and were neither cramped in dimensions nor cautious in design, for by the fifteenth century civic buildings were becoming important in France; and outside the towns large houses both in France and England were released from the needs of fortification. Even so, there were visible traces of former concessions to security: the tops of walls still had battlements, windows were still meagre in size, and it was not until the middle years of the fifteenth century that they generally enjoyed an enlargement comparable with those of the great churches.

At the end of the Romanesque period, civic buildings were humble and unambitious compared with churches; large-scale dwellings built outside the protection of city walls had to be fortified; and in every European country these strong-walled structures provided the material for the picturesque ruins that were to command the admiration of travellers in later ages.

Castles with curtain walls, moats, gateways, draw-bridges, towering walls with their battlements, and tall central keeps, were placed strategically throughout the European country-side. Such buildings were military machines, little different in conception from the military architecture of former ages, indeed borrowing something from the buildings erected a thousand years earlier by Roman legionaries. The towers of a castle were built for observation, for strength, and with the central tower, the keep, as the place where the last stand could be made when the castle was besieged, and the outer walls breached. Enclosed by the walls was a small and squalid residential area, into which cattle and peasants from the nearby villages were hustled in time of war. More spacious dwelling quarters were also provided: a great hall, sleeping-chambers, a chapel, and innumerable store-rooms.

Castles were usually built on high ground, dominating a valley, guarding a pass, a ford, or commanding some traffic route. These strong buildings would rise often to a considerable height, their thick walls presenting a hard, unbroken surface for thirty or more feet above the ground level, pierced only by very small apertures. Higher still, the battlements would give shelter for archers, and they were projected forwards, resting on corbels to provide an over-hang so that boiling water, molten lead and other defensive weapons could be used to the best advantage when the castle was attacked. This projection of the battlements made it extremely difficult to use scaling ladders.

Many of the large castles in France were transformed during the latter part of the Middle Ages, and became agreeable and conveniently appointed dwelling houses; additional storeys would rise above the level of the battlements, and more windows would be pierced in the walls, as the military quality of the building was subordinated to civilised usage. But that military quality left its mark on large houses, not only in France but in other parts of Europe, in England and Scotland. French mediaeval architecture greatly influenced Scottish builders, and the Gothic castles and mansions of Scotland derived some of their characteristic features from French sources; for on many occasions during the Middle Ages France and Scotland were allies against England, their common enemy, and this consistent friendliness between the two nations was impressed upon the architecture of the small, fiercely independent kingdom that occupied northern Britain.

North of France lay Flanders and Holland, remnants of the Empire that Charlemagne had created and which was still thought of as the Roman Empire, though large pieces of it were periodically detached by conquest or by revolution to secure independence. During the sixteenth century, what we now know as Belgium and much of Holland were called the Spanish Netherlands, and early in that century those countries had passed under the dominion of Charles V who became King of Spain in 1516, and Roman Emperor three years later. Before this introduction of Spanish influence, Belgium and Holland had developed a most distinctive secular architecture which was created under the patronage of rich and independent traders, a class that had escaped from the limitations imposed by other mediaeval states in Europe, and had used their liberty to create wealth on a large scale through trade and had used that wealth

The Doge's Palace at Venice reflects the fastidious taste of the commercial aristocracy that drew its wealth from international trade, and whose city was the meeting-place of Western and Eastern culture. The façades date from 1309–1424, and this sketch shows the turn of the arcades, and the lace-like tracery of the upper tier. The Palace is the finest example of mediaeval civic architecture in the city, and formed part of a great scheme of town planning. (See plate 17.)

to beautify and enrich their cities. The town halls and guild houses and such ambitious buildings as the Cloth Hall at Ypres had an importance, an architectural significance, often more impressive than the neighbouring ecclesiastical buildings.

Perhaps the most triumphant example of the architecture of a great commercial community is to be found in Venice, which, like Ghent and Ypres, was run by a commercial class, and was the capital of a magnificent and powerful mercantile republic. Venice was governed by an acute, fastidious aristocracy, and the city, built upon piles and occupying a group of small islands at the north-west end of the Adriatic, was the place where eastern and western influences met, where, as we have seen in Section IV, Byzantine influence inspired the design not only of a great church, St. Mark's, but the form and decoration of palaces and civic buildings. To-day Venice is a vast, well-organised tourist trap, and its fall from the days of commercial supremacy is reflected in the out-at-elbows magnificence of its buildings; its dilapidated architecture still suggesting the atmosphere of hopelessness and ruin and neglect, which descended on the independent republic when Napoleon I

The Pisani Palace, on the Grand Canal at Venice, is an example of fifteenth century Venetian Gothic. The traceried openings and balconies, rhythmically disposed, provide a tranquil reflection in the water below, for in Venice the surface of the canals was one of the elements of architectural composition.

casually tossed it into the political dustbin, without a thought for the brilliant civilisation he was destroying.

The buildings of Venice have a character of their own, partly derived from the Byzantine influences they have absorbed, but partly because the republic was governed by highly civilised business men, who as patrons of architecture had a completely different outlook from the ecclesiastics and noblemen who generally supplied the patronage for buildings in other parts of Europe. They displayed their wealth in terms of architecture and interior decoration with taste and judgment, and although ostentatious their buildings were never vulgar. Venice, on a group of islands, had much the same development problem as New York on Manhattan Island, so architects built upwards, and nearly all the buildings are tall, separated by dark alleys and shadowed slips of water. Consequently it is almost impossible to see any building in Venice unless it faces the Grand Canal or some big open space like St. Mark's Square, and viewed from the top of the campanile of St. Mark's, the city with its red pantile roofs does not lie out in plan like many European cities but is an agglomeration of rust-hued pantiles, crowding against each other, almost identical in appearance with other Italian towns or those of southern Spain, like Granada. Although many buildings in Venice are classified as Gothic, and come into the period, they are anything but Gothic in character. There is no striving note about them; instead they convey, with almost sensual emphasis, a luxurious and languorous reverence for beauty for its own sake; and this is apparent not only in the private palaces, but in the Doge's Palace, with its open arcades and columns and pointed arches, and the lace-like effect of long horizontal lines of open tracery (plate 17.) That Palace was completed between 1309 and 1424, though it was begun in the ninth century and rebuilt several times. Its Oriental and Byzantine affinities are obvious, and it was completely different from other examples of Italian Gothic, an independent development of that style, as independent as the wealthy republic itself, and can be classified only as Venetian Gothic. This fusing of Oriental, Byzantine, classical and Gothic influences produced an architecture that was unique in Europe, as indeed the civic, social and commercial structure of the Venetian Republic was unique. It was fantastic, gay, blazing with colour, both delicate and bold, adventurous and irreverent— irreverent in the sense that it arrogantly overshadowed all the sacred buildings, and even St. Mark's plays second fiddle to the Doge's Palace, which, shouldering up against it, permits only a peep of some of the crosses that crown the domes to be visible from the lagoon.

In a comparable but far more sombre way the secular architecture of Belgium and Holland dominated the rich, spaciously planned cities of those countries. The Halles and Belfry at Bruges, the town halls of Brussels, Louvain, Ghent, and the magnificent Cloth Hall at Ypres, are all proudly competitive with churches, sending up towers and spires to rival those of the cathedrals. By comparison such churches as St. Gudule at Brussels (1226–1280), and the Cathedral at Tournai (1066–1338), are modest and retiring: not so Antwerp Cathedral, which rears a lofty tower and spire 400 feet into the sky and is a rich—almost florid—example of late Gothic, for the towers on the west front were built between 1422 and 1518. (The lower part of a second tower exists in Antwerp Cathedral but it was never completed.) As for Dutch churches, they have a simplicity and plainness, derived partly from the use of brick, which as a material has controlled both form and decorative treatment. An

The Halles and Belfry at Bruges. The tower is 352 feet high, and the magnificence of the building shows the ascendancy of secular architecture in Belgium, for such towers were competitive with those of churches. It was built in 1280.

architecture based on the use of bricks arose in Holland and Germany, and the texture and colour of brick walls gave a characteristic quality to the churches, and civic and domestic buildings of that part of Europe.

German Gothic was derived from France; it was transplanted, and not adopted until the middle of the thirteenth century, and it was long before it supplanted the Romanesque style. Gothic was an import; Romanesque had been a native German growth, and there was no link between them. German Gothic churches were distinguished by fine towers and spires, and the use of twin towers on the west front frequently occurs. Examples of this feature are to be found at the cathedrals of Cologne and Ratisbon. Often large churches would be richly decorated, but their towers and spires have a certain element of clumsiness: both in Cologne and Ratisbon the junction of the spire and the tower is blurred with ornament, the spires are prickly with crockets, and there is no clean, vivid definition in these vertical features, which give an effect of woven stone work, that, in the case of Cologne Cathedral, has been unkindly compared with knitting.

One of the characteristic forms of German Gothic was the "hall" type of church, in which nave and aisles were of approximately the same height, and

The Town Hall, Middelburg, built by Anton Keldermans about 1512. The tal
square tower is 180 feet high, and the façade has pointed windows and is adorned
with statues of the counts and countesses of Zeeland and Holland, standing in
canopied niches. This is another example of the splendour of civic architecture
in a commercial community, competing in scale and richness with the churches
of a city.

the Frauenkirche at Nuremburg (1354–1361), St. Elizabeth at Marburg (1233–
1283), and St. Stephen in Vienna (1300–1510), are excellent examples. The
interior of a "hall" church was sober and orderly; columns and vaults fulfilling
their function with rather dull regularity; there were no upward-sweeping lines,
none of the tense feeling of ascent conveyed by French and English Gothic,
and, as no thrusts had to be taken up and sent gliding to the ground, there were
no flying buttresses or tall independent piers to receive them. Towers, spires
and tracery gave character to these grave and unambitious buildings, and the
tracery was often limited and clumsy because in north Germany brick was
chiefly used, even for the mullions of windows. Perhaps as a reaction from the
comparative austerity of most churches, a few German cathedrals were exces-
sively ornate, technical capacity for the execution of carved detail often exceeding
the ability to control the floreated convolutions of ornament, the branch-tracery,
which occasionally overloaded exterior and interior surfaces with a plethora of
ill-conceived naturalistic motifs.

In France and England, Gothic architecture had followed Romanesque,
budding out as it were from the sturdier and more solid style, and climbing

upwards, shedding weight without losing strength. France and England were parts of Christendom where the Church could pursue its architectural experiments uninterrupted by secular disturbances, peacefully developing arts and crafts, and not only through its teaching but through the visual example of beauty supplied by its great cathedrals, continue its civilising mission, for although France and England were ostensibly Christian lands, there were innumerable outcrops of paganism, and through all ranks of society there was a placid acceptance of cruelty and a tolerance of lust, against which the Church was forever fighting. The monastic establishments in England and the cathedral churches in France, were educational centres, and peasant, townsman, and aristocrat were alike sadly in need of Christian education.

The loss of Spain to Christendom has been mentioned in the previous section, and after the Arab conquest there was little opportunity for developing Romanesque architecture; but some Spanish kingdoms gradually won independence. The Oriental civilisation of Spain was concentrated in the south, and a transitional Romanesque style, of which there are some scanty remains, was followed by the Spanish interpretation of Gothic, which only superficially resembled the Gothic architecture of France and England, for it burst forth into a richly ornamental style that owed much to Moorish influence. The

Haarlem Cathedral, which derives from its rich-hued brick walls the characteristic quality of the Dutch style of Gothic. It dates from the fifteenth century.

The great church of St. Severus at Erfurt, a German city midway between Gotha and Weimar. This example of German Gothic dates from the fourteenth century, and is a particularly interesting design, with the steep roof and the tall, triple spires, showing how the urgent, upward sweep of Gothic architecture was interpreted by German builders. The church stands side by side with the cathedral on an eminence called the Domberg, and both churches are approached by a flight of forty-eight steps.

embellishment both of the interiors and exteriors of Spanish churches between the eleventh and sixteenth centuries had strong Oriental characteristics, and there is reason to suppose that some of the early Spanish churches were largely the work of Moorish craftsmen. Eastern influences were introduced to French and English Gothic architecture as a result of the Crusades; but the Spanish kingdoms had as their next door neighbour an Oriental state, a highly civilised Moslem country, which supported the great university of Cordova, one of the lights of learning in mediaeval Europe, and one, as we have mentioned in an earlier section, that is apt to be ignored by pro-Christian historians.

It was through the character of ornament that Moorish influence worked most vigorously in Spain, through the introduction of pierced stone tracery, intricate geometrical patterns, and the horse-shoe arch. The impact of Moorish architecture on the ideas of Christian craftsmen in Spain must have been considerable, but it is significant that they were content to adopt only the superficial gaiety of ornamental devices—the horse-shoe arch was used sparingly. It may be that masons, trained in a different structural tradition, rejected this device. To-day there are several surviving examples of Moorish architecture in Spain, which suggest that the effectiveness of much of such work depended

St. Francesco, Assisi (1228–1253), sited on a hill in a commanding position. It was a great pilgrimage church, and its place on the slope of a hill enabled an upper and a lower church to be built. The church rises from the surrounding monastic build-ings, which are on a vast masonry substructure.

upon the use of a white, gleaming material. For example, in Malaga there is a much admired Moorish gateway set in a market hall (the Mercado). It is a horse-shoe arch, weakly conceived, suggesting conflict and indecision—there is something irritatingly unstable about its form, but it is in sparkling white marble, and for many observers the richness of the material may perhaps redeem the poverty of design.

In Spanish Gothic the very early use of the pointed arch may be due to Moorish examples, though Spanish builders used this arch in a way that gave structural significance to it, and no weakness, no indecisiveness, is observable in the great cathedral churches that arose in the Spanish kingdoms of Leon, Castile and Aragon. The fantastic surface ornament used on walls acknowledged a debt to Moorish prototypes, but it was disciplined, not as luscious and overwhelmingly flamboyant as, say, the ornament in the Alhambra; also it was used to frame groups of sculptures, to provide settings for scenes that told some Christian story, or exalted the acts of some Christian saint. The interior of a Spanish church was often completely dominated by an immense reredos, which sometimes completely filled the east end, spanning the nave and rising high up to the vault. Many superb examples still exist, and demonstrate the ability of Spanish craftsmen to absorb Oriental ideas of rich ornament and to use them with a sense of design and purpose which Moorish craftsmen could seldom command.

Gothic architecture in Spain acquired a character that differs from manifestations of that style in other parts of Europe—the difference is marked by an almost excessive richness of ornament, that gives to the interiors of Spanish churches a dramatic quality which escapes vulgarity because the detail of the ornamental work is always refined, never loose, weak or sprawling. The designer is always the master of his theme. Until the Civil War of the mid-nineteen-thirties the interiors of Spanish churches had not been despoiled, and consequently presented a truer picture of the copious richness of mediaeval Christian churches than was to be found elsewhere in Europe. One of the characteristics both of ecclesiastical and secular architecture in Spain was the use of arcades, which provided shelter from the intense sunlight, and gave architects an opportunity for surrounding the courtyards of palaces with delicate arches, which often sprang from columns that had an obvious classical origin, arches that were pointed, enriched with cusps, and brilliant with carved decoration. The Spanish interpretation of the Gothic style is distinguished by an unusual gaiety—unusual because it seems to have caught the excitement and sparkle and lightheartedness of Oriental ornamentation, but without being overdone.

A very different interpretation of Gothic occurred in Italy, for there the Roman classical tradition survived and coloured everything that was built. The spires and towers that raced each other to the sky in France and Germany, the Low Countries and England, the vertical striving apparent in the naves of the tall Gothic cathedrals, were not to be found in Italy. There, a respect for classical stability, for preserving harmony between vertical and horizontal elements, remained undisturbed. In the country-side buildings changed very

A street in San Gimigano, near Florence, a small town that once boasted over seventy towers: there are now only thirteen. In the fourteenth century the skyline "must have presented a silhouette not unlike that of lower Manhattan to-day," as G. E. Kidder Smith has suggested in *Italy Builds*. The towers were residential, and at one time it is supposed that the wealthy merchants competed with one another as to who could afford to build the highest tower—perhaps the most permanent and wasteful form of "keeping up with the Joneses" ever devised. Two of the remaining towers are shown at the end of the street.

little, and to-day, in the mid-twentieth century, it seems unlikely that farm
buildings in Italy have altered much in form and finish since the days of the
Roman Empire. Italian Romanesque architecture had been much closer to
classical design than any other examples of the style in Europe, and we have
seen in the previous section how closely buildings like the Cathedral and the
Baptistry at Pisa followed the classical tradition, both in the proportions and
general character of their design. From this orderly and stable architecture
the transition to Italian Gothic did not mark any severe break: there were
some minor concessions to the new vertical conception of design, but they were
inclined to be superficial, as in Milan Cathedral, where tall narrow windows,
flying buttresses, and a multiplicity of pinnacles give the impression, not so
much of upward striving, as of prickliness—all those spiky pinnacles and lonely
isolated figures, and the dimness and narrowness of the interior, suggest an
imperfect understanding of the spirit that elsewhere gave such forcible emotional
properties to Gothic churches. Milan Cathedral is a late example, begun towards
the end of the fourteenth century and finished one hundred years later; it
was erected by the first Duke of Milan. It is said that some fifty architects
were employed on it, and some of them came from Central Europe, so the cathedral has certain Germanic characteristics. It is unlike any other Italian excursion
into the Gothic style.

St. Antonio, Padua (1232–1307), with its seven domes, exhibiting
traces of Byzantine influence, and recalling the form of St. Mark's
at Venice. The west front has an upper arcaded gallery of pointed
arches.

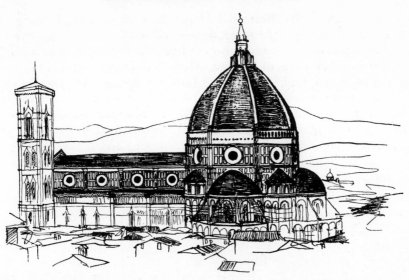

The cathedral of St. Maria del Fiore, Florence (1296–1462), designed by Arnolfo di Cambio. The campanile (1334–1387), was designed by Giotto. (See frontispiece.) The Renaissance dome of the cathedral (1420–1434) was added by Brunelleschi (see page 193). Both examples on this page show how Italian Gothic architecture differed in spirit and character from French, English, and German interpretations of the style.

Generally there is an harmonious balance between the horizontal and vertical features of Italian Gothic buildings. Venice represents quite a separate development, moulded by a commercial aristocracy, and brightened by Byzantine influence. Apart from concessions to such typical Gothic features as the pointed arch, Italian buildings of the thirteenth, fourteenth and fifteenth centuries have a closer relationship to the preceding Romanesque phase of design than to Gothic architecture in the rest of Europe. For example the window never expanded to the same extent in Italian churches as in French and English churches; walls remained walls, and façades were treated with decorative marble facing, and within, mosaics and frescoes occupied a large amount of space, and the coloured translucent glass window, that great pictorial feature of French and English churches, was never developed: it never transcended its function as a window, and the glaring light of a hot sky limited its size. The moulded details of many churches, particularly those in north Italy, were almost identical with those used in the classic orders—another instance of the continuity with Roman tradition. Italy was well prepared for the revival of classical architecture; it was of all places in Europe more richly endowed with knowledge of the form and character of classical design. In the previous section it was suggested that the Italian Romanesque style was in the nature of architectural training for the Renaissance: Italian Gothic, as exemplified by such buildings as St. Maria del Fiore, the cathedral at Florence (1296–1462), and St. Antonio of the seven domes at Padua (1232–1307), was wholly different in form and spirit and meaning from the Gothic style as it had been interpreted in other parts of Europe. Many buildings of that time, by their design and character, make it clear that Italy was the obvious place for classical architecture to be re-born. The event occurred in Florence in the fifteenth century, and in that century two other events of lasting importance for European art and life took place: the conquest of Constantinople by the Turks in 1453, which extinguished the East Roman Empire; and the weakening of the Church's authority through the rise of humanism. Mediaeval civilisation was dying, and as it sank, the vitality of Gothic architecture diminished.

The mediaeval city of Canterbury is shown in the background of this illustration, which appears in a manuscript of *The Story of Thebes* (MS. Reg. 18 Dii.) by John Lydgate (*circa* 1370–1451). Drawn by F. W. Fairholt from the original manuscript, and included in Thomas Wright's books, *The Homes of Other Days*, and *A History of Domestic Manners and Sentiments in England*.

VII

THE MEDIAEVAL ACHIEVEMENT

MEDIAEVAL civilisation is recorded by an architecture more richly and emotionally diversified than any other in the previous history of Europe. The Greeks had created the three classic orders; the Romans had adopted them as a system of design, and their conventional reiteration throughout the Empire deprived architects of opportunities for innovation and Roman citizens of the occasional refreshment of unfamiliar and striking forms. Early Christian, Byzantine, and Romanesque buildings foreshadowed the advent of an architecture with an emotional content comparable to the intellectual content of the Greek temple, as moving in its appeal to the human heart as the Parthenon is to the reasoning mind. We have seen how Gothic architecture emerged, how it transcended Romanesque, and the incipient nationalism that differentiated its forms in France, England, Germany, Spain, and Italy. That restless and boldly experimental architecture which spread over Europe, and was interpreted with such striking local variations, was indicative of a new, turbulent spirit. It gave voice to the aspirations and desires and the sturdy practical ability of a robust society, where conflict was in progress, for that old battle between the country and the town was once again being fought.

In the towns burghers and citizens were quietly, consistently and legally defying feudalism; making money through trade, organising the industrial arts and crafts; acutely aware of the conflicting interests of kings and nobles. They were as conscious of the significance of *divide et impera* as any Roman proconsul, with untamed barbarian tribesmen on the borders of the province he governed. They could always drive a golden wedge between a monarch and his nobles; buying privileges and charters and trading rights, and having them confirmed by Royal authority, increasing their powers of collective bargaining, and keeping their city walls in good repair.

175

In the country-side, the stark, military strongholds of the feudal aristocracy intimidated the more docile rural population; and there the great landlords reigned unchallenged, exercising a savage paternalism over their serfs, and living themselves in conditions of squalor that would have disgusted a Roman citizen. It was long before mediaeval towns approached the efficient material standards of the Roman towns which they had succeeded. Their importance as social units, and their significance as wealth-creating communities were long unrecognised; partly because a largely illiterate aristocracy despised trade, partly because the Church, with its official condemnation of usury, hampered the operations of commerce. "Wealth might be created by their citizens; kings might condescend to recognise their trading and to grant protective charters; but they were of small account in the pattern of political life, for it was the land and the shifts and schemes for the possession of land that absorbed the energy of the rulers. The landlord was the symbol of power, and the mainten-ance of his rights and the enlargement of his possessions, carried even to the length of private warfare, were activities proper to his caste, however disastrous they may have been for the prosperity of the country. Trade became a furtive and fearful business in such a wilderness of insecurity, and towns were mere bolt-holes for traders in this clamorous age of chivalry and easy-going bloodshed."[123]

Yet upon these bloodstained foundations a great civilisation arose that created an architecture of such power and beauty that it can still exalt and comfort men and women of the present day. The recurrent appeal of Gothic forms and ornament suggests that this style, perfected in the Middle Ages, acts as an anodyne in periods when people are painfully aware that something is missing, that something has been drained out of life, when unfamiliar ideas and ugly things are all about them, and mediaeval society and architecture, although remote in time, seem reassuring, friendly, and warmly romantic. It was a society of practical Christians, whose members imparted their spiritual convictions and victories to the things they built and adorned. Lisle March Phillipps has described the dual character of this mediaeval age, which generated a potent period in art and architecture. "The curious and so far unique charac-ter of the age," he said, "consists in the intermingling, with the mundane temper which so conspicuously belongs to it, of an equally clearly marked spirit of devout contemplation and emotional ecstasy. The age is not only that in which material aims are pursued with the greatest vigour and the keenest realisation of their practical value; it is also that in which spiritual aims are pursued with an equally intense concentration. If mediaeval society derived a quite unusual satisfaction from the prosecution of all kinds of human endeavour, so did it also derive more felicity than ever before or since from the inward contemplation of the truths revealed by spiritual consciousness. Mediaeval society appears like a cord composed of two strands, one white the other red, twisted together, yet still distinguishable the one from the other."[124]

Inside the mediaeval city: Westminster Hall and its surroundings, which still perpetuated the character of the Middle Ages when this view was engraved by Wenceslaus Hollar in the seventeenth century.

It is the unacknowledged and perhaps unconscious awareness of the spiritual content of mediaeval architecture that has struck a responsive chord in the hearts of people during the last hundred and fifty years; for the appeal of Gothic forms and ornament is largely emotional, however much we may admire the dexterity and inventiveness of the craftsmen who fashioned them. It is because those forms have such vital spontaneity, and because the mediaeval masons and joiners, carvers and glaziers, had a common and inspiring faith

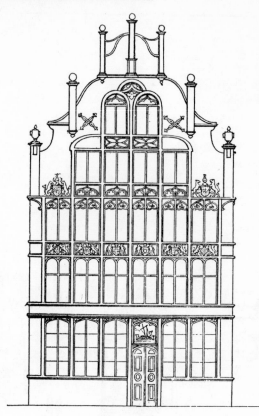

House at Ghent, from Thomas Hope's *Essay on Architecture*. Hope's drawing is a simplified version of The Skipper's House, in that city, built about 1531, and showing how traceried windows dominated the façade and reflected the contemporary Gothic forms. It was one of the Guild houses of Ghent, and shows how secular architecture commanded a magnificence comparable with and often exceeding ecclesiastical building.

which they could honour by their work, that any attempt to reproduce any phase of the Gothic style results in buildings as empty of life as a wax image. Gothic architecture could not be revived as classic architecture was revived in the fifteenth century. The classic orders represented a system of design: its rules could be recalled, its proportions re-established, and its Greek origin was intellectual. Gothic architecture was no part of a system of design; it could not supply a body of rules for the guidance of architects of later ages; and its origins were not intellectual. Its practical achievements demanded good brains for the direction and practice of skill; but brain power was used for that only: unless reason was underwritten by Faith it was heresy.

The mediaeval city with its towers and spires and tall houses, ringed by walls with guarded gates, has been idealised by romantic writers and painters since the eighteenth century; and some of the reconstructions made by architects who were also superb draughtsmen, like Pugin, were not unduly fanciful, if we compare them with walled cities that still survive and with illustrations in contemporary manuscripts. Over a hundred years ago, Augustus Welby

Northmore Pugin (1812–1852) published a book which he called *Contrasts: or a Parallel between the noble edifices of the Middle Ages and corresponding buildings of the present day, showing the present decay of taste,* and the first plate showed a town of 1840 compared with an idealised view of it in 1440. These views appear on pages 180 and 181, and they are included in this section as an example of the tendentious propaganda of the nineteenth century Gothic revivalists. "Those contrasting views were inspired less by a desire for objective criticism than by a passionate sense of loss—loss of beauty and serenity and spiritual significance. To restore such properties to life was, Pugin obviously felt, the mission of the Gothic revival—which was only part of the greater mission of reuniting Christendom. Who could deny, after examining his drawing of an industrialised town in 1840, that the buildings themselves reflected the inhumanity of an age that created, and found good, such harsh, fantastic chaos? Today, in many industrialised parts of England, mediaeval church towers and spires stand in mute reproof of our unlovely materialism, emphasising the comparison between an age of faith and an age of greed, which Pugin found intolerable—the more so because many of his contemporaries were incapable of appreciating what was missing from life. In plate after plate of his book of *Contrasts*, he attacked the shams and stupidities that had invaded civic life, and had produced an architecture which reflected only a bleak utilitarianism."[125]

The Gothic revival is discussed and examined in Section X; but its influence must be taken into account in any assessment of the architectural character of mediaeval towns, for it still colours the views of the English-speaking peoples, and has given them a perverted impression of the Gothic style by reproducing its superficial characteristics in churches and chapels and other buildings in Britain, the British Commonwealth, and the United States. Externally, the walls of cities changed very little from Roman times to the end of the Middle Ages. Compare Fairholt's drawings of towns, in Section V, page 112, which are copied from a ninth century manuscript, with the view of Canterbury from a manuscript of John Lydgate's poem, *The Story of Thebes*, on page 174: externally they differ only in the design of the towers. Walk round the walls of Chester, which still completely encircle the mediaeval area of the city, or those of York, which are nearly complete; or visit Carcassonne, the capital of the department of Aude in south-western France, one of the best preserved of the fortified towns of Europe, or Avila in central Spain, and you may then believe that Pugin's idea of a mediaeval city was more than a nostalgic exercise.

Behind their walls many European cities grew rich, and patronage for architecture passed into the hands of the business community. Some of the results of this patronage have been described in the previous section; and after the middle of the thirteenth century commercial patronage expanded, and cities throughout Western Europe recovered the importance they had formerly enjoyed under the Roman Empire, for about that time the commercial association originated which became the Hanseatic League. This fluid federation of

A Gothic revivalist's vision of a mediaeval city. This idealised reconstruction of a "Catholic town in 1440" was drawn by Pugin and included in his book of *Contrasts*, and this is reproduced from the second edition, published in 1841. (See pages 181 and 312.) Some European cities present a comparable array of spires and towers. The contrast between the mediaeval city and its early nineteenth century counterpart shown opposite is not exaggerated.

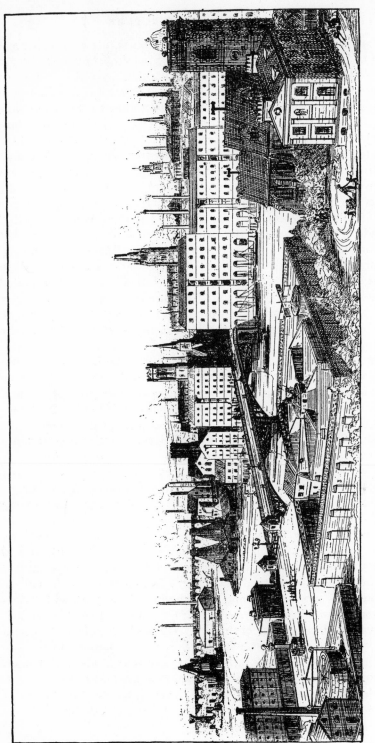

The early nineteenth century town, separated by four hundred years from the mediaeval city shown opposite. The visual amenities of the town of 1840 are few: a gas works and a prison in the foreground, and industrial plant and warehouses set down in a planless muddle. Pugin's book of *Contrasts*, from which both these drawings are reproduced, was a work of passionate propaganda for the revival of the Gothic style. That revival, essentially artificial, tends to obscure or distort or misinform our appreciation of mediaeval architecture. (See pages 112, 174, and 183.)

cities, situated on important water-ways and trade routes, grew to be a great financial power in Europe, which could pass the sentence of commercial death on a city or a nation by its boycott; its merchant rulers were the back-room boys whose interests shaped the policy of kings and emperors; it was dedicated to money-making and nothing else, and was opposed alike to the democratic pretensions of citizens and the privileges of noblemen. Nearly all the important towns in Germany and the Low Countries belonged at some time to the League during the thirteenth, fourteenth and fifteenth centuries; and in England, London, and King's Lynn, in Norfolk, were members; but the most important member cities were Lübeck, Bremen and Hamburg, which remained in the League from its beginning to its end. The number of cities in the League fluctuated; in Germany they adjoined the rivers Oder, Elbe, Weser, Ems and Rhine; in Flanders, the Rhine and the Maas; but at different periods other places were included: Bergen in Norway, Novgorod in Russia, and Danzig, Elbing, Königsberg, Stralsund, Frankfurt, Cologne and Hamlin, and in Flanders, Ghent, Bruges, Antwerp and Dordrecht. Other cities were affiliated with the League, like Augsburg, Ulm and Nuremberg, which were in direct communication with Venice; and there were cities in France, Spain, Portugal, and England which had dealings with the League but were never Hanseatic cities.[126]

In Europe the growing power of commerce enriched the life of cities; but civic authorities were aware of the precarious tenure of their prosperity; they kept their walls intact, and within those boundaries encouraged builders and craftsmen to create and embellish splendid civic structures and noble dwellings. European cities enjoyed their powers and privileges quietly; there were some hideous warnings of what could happen if they paraded their independence too openly or were too insistent on exacting liberal concessions from their episcopal and royal overlords, and one of these occurred in 1468 when Charles the Bold, Duke of Burgundy, destroyed the wealthy industrial city of Liége, giving it over to his soldiers for three days to sack and pillage, and then razing it to the ground.

In England, protected by the sea, and threatened only in the north by marauding Scots, cities like London expanded far beyond their walls, and as early as the fourteenth century the castle which William the Conqueror had erected at Cambridge was being used as a quarry for materials by the college builders. London grew westwards along the Thames, linking up with Westminster, and after the twelfth century, although the walls and gates remained, they no longer restricted the growth of the city. William Fitzstephen, the friend and biographer of Thomas à Becket, whose descriptions of London in the late twelfth century are quoted by Stow in his *Survey*, had said: "The wall is high and great, well towered on the north side, with due distance between the towers. On the south side also the city was walled and towered, but the fishful river of Thames, with its ebbing and flowing, hath long since subverted them."

Above: Part of the walls of Carcassonne, a fortified mediaeval town. The inner and outer walls, with their towers, date from the thirteenth century. *Below:* Part of the walls of Avila, a city in central Spain, once included in the kingdom of Old Castile, and built on the level summit of a rocky hill. The walls are built of brown granite, with a breastwork above, and eighty-six towers and nine gateways.

Of London's gracious expansion, Fitzstephen said: "On all sides, without the houses of the suburbs, are the citizens' gardens and orchards, planted with trees, both large, sightly and adjoining together. On the north side, are pastures and plain meadows, with brooks running through them, turning water-mills with a pleasant noise. Not far off is a great forest, a well wooded chase, having good covert for harts, bucks, does, boars, and wild bulls. The corn fields are not of a hungry sandy mould, but as the fruitful fields of Asia, yielding plentiful increase, and filling the barns with corn. There are near London, on the north side, especial wells in the suburbs, sweet, wholesome, and clear. Amongst which, Holywell, Clarkenwell, and St. Clement's well, are most famous, and most frequented by scholars and youths of the city in summer evenings, when they walk forth to take the air."

Stow's *Survey*, published in 1603, records the growth of London beyond the walls, east and west, following the course of the Thames. The river was a highway, busy with craft, providing the most rapid route from the suburbs to the city, and remained so for centuries. In his *Description of England* (1577–1587), William Harrison gives details of the river traffic and mentions "two thousand wherries and small boats, wherby three thousand poore watermen are maintained," also "huge tide-boats, tiltbotes, and barges, which either carrie passengers, or bring necessarie provision from all quarters of Oxfordshire, Barkeshire, Buckinghamshire, Bedfordshire, Herfordshire, Midlesex, Essex, Surrie, and Kent, vnto the citie of London." This is a vivid picture of teeming waterways serving a great city.

In Europe the idea of home became identified with a house, or part of a house, in a city, which could be sumptuous or simple, according to the means of the owners or tenants. In England there was, and still is, a different conception of what constitutes a home. The English home has a long history, beginning with the Saxon forerunner of the great hall, the thatched single-chamber house of timber, described in Section V, and resuming its interrupted development within two centuries of the Norman Conquest, when the two civilisations, Norman and Saxon, were welded into something that was recognisably English. Thereafter the country enjoyed strong government; houses in the country-side were gradually freed from the limitations of fortification, and an English style of architecture arose, regionally diversified by the use of characteristic local building materials. The owners of fortified manor-houses and the larger farm-houses were, by the middle of the fourteenth century, beginning to enlarge the area of their windows, filling their moats and turning them into gardens, so their homes were no longer separated from the woods and fields by a treeless belt, the width of a bow shot. Orchards and plantations and gardens could be close to the dwelling, and house and garden could enjoy the artistic partner-ship that had ended long before when Britain ceased to be a Roman province. Only in the monastic establishments had that partnership been preserved through the troubled centuries of Saxon and early Norman England.

Wood, plaster and stone were the principal materials used for English town and country houses before the thirteenth century, for brick-making was not reintroduced until then. At that time country houses were stoutly built, whether they were small fortified manor-houses or the living quarters of a castle; the need for protection conditioned their character; a grim, defensive look was impressed upon them. Within, the country house was a great hall, from which other chambers and the kitchens budded off, as it were; and for some centuries this great hall remained the core of the house, determining its general form, and reflecting the communal, though far from democratic, way of life that was lived by the household.

Penshurst Place, in Kent, is a typical example of a mediaeval house, with a great hall and adjacent chambers. It was built during the first half of the

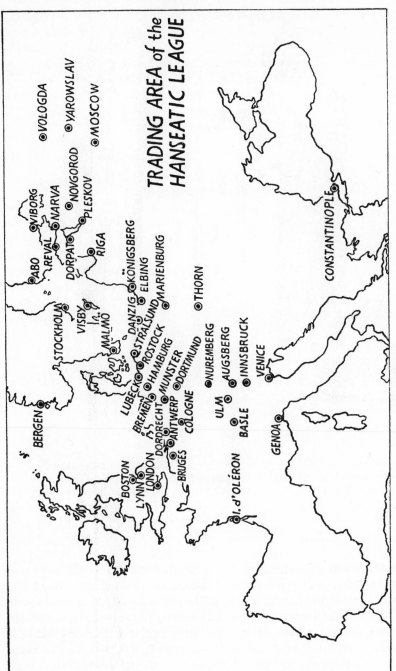

TRADING AREA of the
HANSEATIC LEAGUE

VOLOGDA
YAROWSLAV
MOSCOW
VIBORG
NARVA
NOVGOROD
PLESKOV
ABO
REVAL
DORPAT
RIGA
KÖNIGSBERG
DANZIG
ELBING
MARIENBURG
STOCKHOLM
VISBY
MALMÖ
THORN
STRALSUND
ROSTOCK
HAMBURG
MÜNSTER
DORTMUND
LÜBECK
BREMEN
NUREMBERG
AUGSBERG
INNSBRUCK
VENICE
ANTWERP
COLOGNE
ULM
BASLE
DORDRECHT
GENOA
BERGEN
BOSTON
LYNN
LONDON
BRUGES
I. d'OLÉRON
CONSTANTINOPLE

The Hanseatic League increased the power and prestige of commerce in Europe. Nearly all the important towns in Germany and the Low Countries belonged at some time during the thirteenth, fourteenth and fifteenth centuries to the League, which extended its influence and affiliations from England to Turkey, from Genoa to Russia. Protected by their walls, many cities grew wealthy, and patronage for architecture passed into the hands of the business community. *Drawn by Marcelle Burton.*

The keep of Rochester Castle, Kent. *Circa* 1130. This is essentially military architecture, one of the early stone castles built by the Normans after the Conquest of 1066. For many years they built castles of wood, perched on high mounds, surrounded by a deep ditch: the first stone castle they built was the Tower of London, and the keep, which was the White Tower, was finished within the lifetime of William the Conqueror.

fourteenth century, and the large hall had a central hearth; at the west end was a dais, or raised platform for the high table, and behind and above the dais was the solar, or retiring room. New habits of privacy were being established in the country house, and the tendency of the lord and the lady of the household to retire to the solar was deplored by William Langland, the English poet who was born in 1332, a few years before Penshurst Place was built. The great hall was deserted by masters and mistresses who were more fastidious than their ancestors. "There the lorde ne the lady liketh noute to sytte," Langland com-

Stokesay Castle, Shropshire (1240–1290), is an early English castle with
a gatehouse and a moat. The gatehouse has been re-built, and the half-
timbered projecting storey shown above is a late sixteenth century addition.
The date of the great hall is 1249.

plained.[127] In appearance, Penshurst Place associates the characteristics of
a castle and a church: embattled walls, towers, turrets and buttresses, and tall
windows, their pointed heads filled with tracery, give the house an air of strength
and of welcome.

"An earlier building that shares some of the characteristics of Penshurst
Place and is also a typical mediaeval house is Stokesay Castle in Shropshire.
Here, too, a great hall forms the core of the building, and the solar, high above
the floor level of that hall, has small windows on either side of its fireplace,
which open on to the hall. Stokesay was built during the first half of the
thirteenth century, but the form is not unlike that of Penshurst; though in

common with many English country houses, it has continued to grow, acquiring
additions and out-buildings and new internal furnishings century by century.
By the end of the fifteenth century, the English house began to acquire the
same structural characteristics as the church; but, instead of being a stone
lantern for coloured glass, it was a strong wooden cage, with the spaces between
the wooden framework filled with glass, brickwork or plaster—a great articulated frame of timber, infinitely flexible in form, admitting light generously,
and using windows, not merely as apertures, but as integral parts of the structure.
Ockwells Manor at Bray in Berkshire, built in the second half of the fifteenth
century, is an early example of such a half-timbered house, and the wooden
cage remained a standard structural form for nearly two centuries. This same
form was followed even when stone was used, as it was in the West Country,
and in Yorkshire; the same generous use of windows and their incorporation
into the structure of the house is apparent, particularly in such small examples
as Tribunal House and the George Inn at Glastonbury in Somerset, and in
large early sixteenth century country houses, such as Cowdray House at
Midhurst in Sussex, and Compton Wynyates in Warwickshire. When Henry VII
came to the throne and the long Tudor period began, a rich and beautiful
native domestic architecture had become established. Its kinship with the
Perpendicular phase of Gothic architecture was marked, and that likeness was
impressed upon all the products of the ancillary building crafts, woodwork
and metalwork, providing a formal unity with the interior treatment and
furnishing of the churches and religious houses."[128]

Builders in England continued the development of their native style long
after their fellow-craftsmen in Europe had deserted Gothic forms and had
placed their copious inventive powers under the regulating discipline of the
revived classical orders. Even in Europe, which was effectively influenced by
the Renaissance over a century before England, there were indecisions and
compromises and some spirited editing of the five orders. In England the
introduction of the orders during the sixteenth century was resented as a
tyrannical imposition of foreign ideas. That inarticulate resentment is often
disclosed by the clumsy parodies of the orders by English craftsmen, and a
complete lack of comprehension of their significance as a flexible system of
architectural design.

In England the record of the mediaeval achievement in architecture has
been injured on three occasions: by the dissolution of the monasteries in the
first half of the sixteenth century, by the iconoclasm of the Puritans during the
Commonwealth, and lastly by the so-called "restorations" of mid-Victorian
architects. When Elizabeth I began her reign, the land was mournful with
the ruins of abbeys and priories and chantries. They were the casualties of the
spiritual and social revolution that had occurred, of the transition from a
theoretically co-operative to an openly acquisitive, adventurous and enterprising
society. Far more was preserved in Europe, where the wrecking of mediaeval

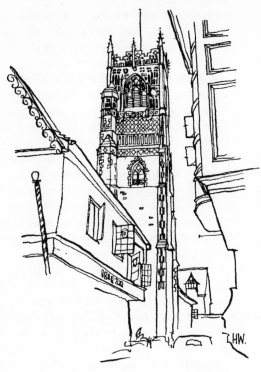

In England, the parish churches record the skill of masons in the use of local materials. *Left:* Flint and stone used in the mediaeval church tower at Ipswich, Suffolk, is in contrast with the less permanent (though still surviving) houses of timber and plaster. *Below:* the interior of the parish church at Cuckfield, Sussex: an Early English example, typical of the structures that gave serene and lovely architecture to villages throughout the country.

buildings was usually an incident of warfare, and seldom the consequence of religious conviction, though there were some disastrous exceptions. Enough survives in Europe and England for the scale and significance of mediaeval architecture to be appreciated.

During the period that, for the last three hundred years, we have labelled the Middle Ages,[129] architecture recorded a partnership between artists and highly skilled craftsmen, who exercised their gifts with greater freedom of imagination than builders had ever before enjoyed. These men invented and experimented; they also assimilated ideas from the East—not only the ideas that strayed into Christian Europe from Moslem Spain, but those brought back by the Crusaders and commercial adventurers. The influence of their work spread all over Europe, north to Scandinavia, overseas to Iceland, and even to the settlements in Greenland, those mediaeval outposts in the New World, which lost touch with Europe in the early years of the fifteenth century.[130] In such remote places architectural achievement was limited, but there are ruins of stone-built churches in Greenland, twelve in the eastern and four in the western settlement, and the first bishop, Arnold, was consecrated in 1124, and resided at the farm of Gardar in Einarsfjördr in the eastern settlement, where a cathedral was erected.[131] That cathedral, which was built of red sandstone, measured externally 86 feet in length, the breadth of the nave being 36 feet and that of the original chancel 24 feet. From the ruins it has been deduced that in design "it resembled the first stone churches, built from the Irish-Anglo Saxon models immediately after the introduction of Christianity by King Olaf Trygvesson in Norway."[132] Some of the churches were constructed of large, undressed granite stones, laid in turf, upon heavy and broad foundations. The walls were carefully built, but their greatly varying thickness disclosed a lack of technical skill.[133]

From the Greenland settlements to the cities of Germany, from Ireland to Italy, the mediaeval builders have left enough evidence to refute the belief, first popularised three centuries ago when the phrase "the Middle Ages" was coined by a German scholar named Keller or Cellarius, that the period "was simply a long halting-place, an interlude between the fall of the Roman empire in the West in 476 and the sack of Constantinople in 1453, a time of deterioration when, instead of progress, there was decline, instead of civilisation, barbarism, instead of enlightenment, ignorance and bigotry."[134] The empty shells of English abbeys, like the roofless remains of Greek temples, are records of artistic altitudes that could be reached only in a great civilisation. The Gothic cathedrals of Europe and England attest the vitality and power of the age of faith, which made as remarkable a contribution to Western architecture as the former age of reason.

VIII

THE RENAISSANCE IN EUROPE

NTIL the early fifteenth century, the evolution of Western architecture had been continuous. That progressive development began with the early Christian churches of the fourth century, was temporarily arrested after the fall of Rome, but was resumed during the eighth century and quickened by a new vigour which generated the Romanesque style. The period of relative inactivity in the West during the fifth, sixth and seventh centuries coincided with the perfection of Byzantine architecture in the East; but, as recorded in earlier sections, Byzantine architecture stagnated, while Romanesque was followed by Gothic, with its daring structural ambitions and matchless splendour of decoration, until Europe was richer and more diversified with fine buildings than it had been since the Graeco-Roman civilisation. Then came the break in evolution at the beginning of the fifteenth century, when a new concept of architectural design arose in Italy, at Florence. This concept was new only by contrast with the prevailing Gothic style; it interrupted, distorted, and finally stopped the growth of the characteristic national variations of that style, and replaced them with the classic orders of architecture. The Renaissance came as a revival; a conscious and ardent revival of the ideas, the learning and the arts of the ancient world; and it was natural that such a movement should begin in Italy, "because there men's minds had ever been predisposed to the reception of antique culture. The Italian spirit had never lost touch with classic harmony and simplicity. It could expand freely and naturally in the restored forms of classic expression."(135)

It was easy and obvious for Italian architects to become leaders in the restoration of the system of architectural design which the Greeks had originated and the Romans had amplified and finally ossified. In Florence, Rome, and Venice, men of exceptional genius were able to reinstate classic architecture,

191

Left: The Pazzi Chapel, Florence (1420), by Brunelleschi.

Below: Alberti's Renaissance façade to the Gothic church of St. Maria Novella, Florence.

but with many things added, for all that had been learned during a thousand years was incorporated in building technique. The use of the Tuscan, Doric, Ionic, Corinthian, and Composite orders did not imply a return to the limitations of trabeated architecture or to Roman inhibitions about the use of the arch as an integral and dominant element in composition; the dependence of Gothic architecture upon the arch and the vault had changed the viewpoint about design, and the architects of the Early Renaissance had a lighter touch than their Roman predecessors. This is apparent in such buildings as the Pazzi Chapel at Florence (1420), a church in miniature, set in the cloisters of St. Croce, designed like a Roman temple with an open portico, with six Corinthian columns supporting an entablature that is broken by a semicircular arch. This portico is an elaborate vault, the vestibule to the interior of the church, which is covered by a dome on pendentives. The Pazzi Chapel is the work of Filippo Brunelleschi (1379–1446), the most gifted of all the pioneers of the Italian Renaissance. He was responsible for adding the dome to the cathedral at Florence, which blends in perfect harmony a Renaissance form with a Gothic structure. (See frontispiece and illustrations on page 173 and opposite.) Another example of a Renaissance addition to an existing Gothic church is the principal façade of St. Maria Novella, Florence, one of the first examples of the use of flanking scrolls for uniting in one composition the nave and the aisles. (See page 192.) This addition was designed by Leone Battista Alberti (1404–1472), a painter, poet, philosopher, musician and architect, who wrote books on painting and sculpture, and, most famous of all, *De Re Aedificatoria*, his treatise on architecture which was translated into French, Spanish and English.

Men of this creative stature could use the classic orders with a deep and rich understanding of the system that supplied rules for composing buildings with all the vertical and horizontal elements harmoniously and symmetrically disposed. They were often masters of many arts and highly skilled executant craftsmen. For example, Brunelleschi had a talent for mechanism, and began his career in the guild of goldsmiths; he was a skilled draughtsman and a sculptor. These men lived and worked in an age of intellectual speculation, for Europe in the fifteenth century was seething with fresh ideas, which found an outlet through the revival of classical literature and learning. In the preceding century there had been a new movement in literature; Petrarch and Boccaccio had familiarised an attentive public with the richness of the heritage from Greece and Rome, and earlier still Dante (1265–1321) in his *Commedia* had, with a boldness that is astonishing in view of the immense authority of the Church at the time he wrote, brought into association with Christian saints and heroes and the Christian image of Hell, characters from the pagan past. His guide through Hell was the spirit of Virgil, and when he encountered the shades of Homer, Horace, Ovid and Lucan, their presence in an agreeable oasis was explained by Virgil, into whose mouth Dante put these tolerant words:

> " . . . The renown of their great names,
> That echoes through your world above, acquires
> Favour in heaven, which holds them thus advanced."[136]

A thousand years earlier the Delphic oracle's last utterance seemed to have proclaimed for all time the death of the gods, but in the fourteenth and fifteenth centuries, those old, jocund, irresponsible deities, with their animistic affiliations and deplorable morals, turned in their sleep; and a tentative flirtation with the pagan cults was an alarming but short-lived by-product of the spreading interest in classical culture. In an atmosphere of curiosity and conjecture about the significance of forgotten sciences, lit by increasingly vivid glimpses of the Greek and Roman past, the re-introduction of the orders of architecture was welcomed by wealthy, educated patrons, and by the Church. In the Italian city states of the fourteenth and fifteenth centuries, patronage for the arts came from the great nobles and merchants, who adorned their own palaces and town houses with an unrestrained appetite for luxury, building for pleasure without any troublesome stirrings of conscience, glorifying themselves and their riches, and encouraging the arts. The age of faith, and all the dank shadows it had created, appeared withered and repressive in the light of the new learning and of humanism, and even if no literature from that time had survived, the proud buildings of the Renaissance would have shown how the reasoning, agile, curious and imaginative human mind had once again been released for new intellectual triumphs.

The character of early Renaissance architecture in Italy reflects the rapturous pleasure of the Italians after that release, which introduced the age of human- ism. Architecture once again became an intellectual exercise, as it had been two thousand years earlier in Greece. One of the greatest writers on Renaissance architecture, Geoffrey Scott, defined humanism as "the effort of men to think, to feel, and to act for themselves, and to abide by the logic of results. This attitude of spirit," he said, "is common to all the varied energies of Renaissance life. Brunelleschi, Macchiavelli, Michaelangelo, Cesare Borgia, Galileo are here essentially at one. In each case a new method is suddenly apprehended, tested, and carried firmly to its conclusion. Authority, habit, orthodoxy are disregarded or defied. The argument is pragmatical, realistic, human. The question, 'Has this new thing a value?' is decided by the individual in the court of his experience; and there is no appeal. That is good which is seen to satisfy the human test, and to have brought an enlargement of human power."[137]

In architecture the authority of the classic orders was never absolute or regarded as such; all kinds of un-Roman liberties were taken with them; their proportions were respected, but in the arrangement of colonnades and the grouping of columns, in composition and ornamentation, a lively, gay inventive- ness refutes the belief that Renaissance architecture is purely mimetic. That belief was popular in the nineteenth century, and has long persisted, for it was part of the faith of the Gothic revivalists, and the influence of that revival was potent and prolonged. As great a man as Flinders Petrie dismissed the Renaissance as "the resort of copying an earlier period, owing to the decay and loss of the true style of the VIIIth, or Mediaeval, age of Art." In his *Revolutions of Civilisation* he had described eight periods of Mediterranean civilisation, of which the last was mediaeval. He amplified his view by vilifying copying as "an artificial system, which has no natural development or root in the mind, and which browses indifferently on anything that may be the fashion of the day."[138]

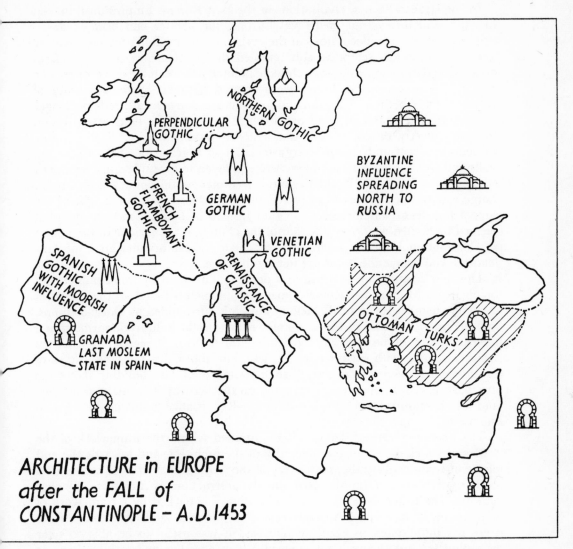

PERPENDICULAR GOTHIC

NORTHERN GOTHIC

BYZANTINE INFLUENCE SPREADING NORTH TO RUSSIA

FRENCH FLAMBOYANT GOTHIC

GERMAN GOTHIC

VENETIAN GOTHIC

SPANISH GOTHIC WITH MOORISH INFLUENCE

RENAISSANCE OF CLASSIC

OTTOMAN TURKS

GRANADA LAST MOSLEM STATE IN SPAIN

ARCHITECTURE in EUROPE after the FALL of CONSTANTINOPLE – A.D. 1453

The last phase of Gothic architecture was demonstrating the undiminished vigour of the style, and the creative fertility of the master masons and craftsmen who still followed the mediaeval traditions; but in Italy, at Florence, Rome, and Venice, a new concept of architectural design arose in the first half of the fifteenth century. The classic orders were revived, and the re-conquest of Europe by Rome, in terms of architecture, began. The political life of the Roman Empire, prolonged by the strength of the walls of the last Roman city, ended when Constantinople was conquered by the Ottoman Turks in 1453. Before that event, the influence of Byzantine architecture had spread northwards to Russia, as, in earlier times, it had spread over the Balkans, to its meeting-place with Gothic at Venice. *Drawn by Marcelle Barton.*

In the Graeco-Roman civilisation, in the East Roman Empire until its end in 1453, and throughout mediaeval Europe, the painter had been regarded primarily as a mural decorator; in the early days of the Renaissance, painting and to some extent sculpture still retained that dependence on the surfaces of walls and ceilings; and as architect, painter and sculptor were often one and the same person, buildings were created with an impressive unity of purpose. They became three-dimensional pictures: structural needs no longer controlled their character: and architecture enjoyed a freedom of expression that was utterly different from that enjoyed by the makers of the Gothic cathedrals. Form and colour were associated in a grand design, and all the skills and techniques of earlier ages were employed to give substance to superb compositions. For example, the Byzantine treatment of the dome was improved. Large square open spaces were roofed by great domes, but the height of the supporting drum was increased, so that instead of being a modest cylinder, pierced by arched windows, like that of the church of St. Saviour in the Chora at Constantinople or St. Luke of Stiris (plate 12), it became an important feature, which gave the dome greater significance.

This new relationship of drum and dome is illustrated by the Tempietto in St. Pietro in Montorio at Rome (1502–1510), which is based on the design of a Roman temple. It is a small, elegant building, surrounded by Doric columns, and the interior is only 15 feet in diameter. Behind the balustrade surmounting the entablature of the peristyle, the drum of the dome rises, pierced by windows which alternate with shell-headed niches; and above this the bold curves of the dome are crowned by a cross. (See opposite page.) This building shows the new part played by the drum in carrying on the vertical elements of a façade; and also demonstrates the fresh inspiration Renaissance architects brought to the use of the classic orders.

The unending variety that could be attained within the framework of the orders was a challenge to the ingenuity of the architect, and towards the end of the fifteenth century the rediscovery of the writings of Vitruvius brought an authoritative voice from the past for the instruction of architects all over Europe. Thereafter the great system of design was backed by a framework of regulations, though European architects of the fifteenth and sixteenth centuries were not intimidated by those regulations; it was useful to be able to refer to authority; but they seldom allowed Vitruvian rules to frustrate them or to limit their imaginative prowess. The first edition of Vitruvius was issued in Latin in Rome in 1486, another appeared ten years later, and a further edition in 1497. Nine editions were published in Latin during the sixteenth century, two in French, two in German, and seven in Italian. Marcus Vitruvius Pollio was a Roman architect and engineer, and his treatise, *De Architectura Libri Decem*, consists of ten books, which cover every branch of architectural design, the use and governing rules for the orders, the appropriate area and character for different types of buildings, the various structural techniques to

The Tempietto in St. Pietro in Montorio, Rome (1502–1510). This small, elegant
building, shows the new relationship between drum and dome, which was characteristic of Renaissance architecture. Compare this with the illustrations of St. Peter's
on page 211, with the later French examples, the Church of Val de Grâce and the
Hôtel des Invalides on pages 221 and 223, and with St. Paul's Cathedral on page
260, where the significance of the drum has increased.

Group of houses, eighteenth and early nineteenth centuries, near the cathedral at Angoulême, in south-western France; typical of the houses that line the streets and squares of many European towns and cities. There is a family likeness between such houses, depending largely upon the symmetrical disposition of door and window openings, and, in Central and Southern Europe, on the use of balconies and window shutters. In Northern Europe, roofs were visible and steep, there were fewer balconies, but the windows were still arranged in an orderly way, as exemplified by the seventeenth and eighteenth century waterfront houses in Copenhagen, shown below.

employ and the nature and quality of the materials available. The opening chapter of the first book defines the scope of architecture and the extent of the education an architect should receive. "In architecture, as in other arts," he wrote, "two considerations must be constantly kept in view; namely the intention, and the matter used to express that intention; but the intention is founded on a conviction that the matter wrought will fully suit the pur-

pose. . . . "(139) In the following chapter he said that "architecture depends
on fitness (*ordinatio*) and arrangement (*dispositio*)" and that "it also depends
on proportion, uniformity, consistency, and economy. . . . "(140) Bramante,
Michelangelo, Vignola and Palladio were diligent students of the work of
Vitruvius. Giacomo Barozzi da Vignola (1507–1573) interpreted Vitruvian
rules in his book, *The Five Orders of Architecture*; Andrea Palladio (1518–1580)
published *I quattro libri dell' Architettura*, which recorded his study and measurements of ancient Roman buildings: both works had a profound and lasting
effect upon architectural design.

The Renaissance placed the architect in a new position in society. For over
three hundred years, from the end of the fifteenth to the beginning of the
nineteenth century, he was acknowledged as the master designer, whose trained
imagination could direct taste, initiate and guide fashions, and keep all those
who practised the arts and crafts that served architecture mindful of the proportions and proprieties of the universal system of design represented by the classic
orders. He was a professional man who employed teams of craftsmen to carry
out his designs; and although the leaders of the early Italian Renaissance had,
as mentioned earlier, often been executant artists and craftsmen, painters and
sculptors as well as architects, such skills and abilities were seldom at the
command of one man after the sixteenth century, though Bernini, who designed
the great colonnade of St. Peter's at Rome, was also a sculptor of genius.
Professor Wittkower has described him rightly as "the last of that great line
of humanist artists of all-round performance and many talents, which included
men like Piero della Francesca, Leonardo and Michelangelo."(141)

As a result of the new concept of architecture, and the allegiance of architects
to the classic orders, nearly every city in Europe began to change slightly in
appearance. The spires and tall towers reared by mediaeval builders were now
rivalled by domes and cupolas of every size and shape. Side by side with the
Gothic façades of cathedrals, new churches and palaces and civic buildings
exhibited an almost pagan gaiety of embellishment, a disciplined luxuriousness
of ornament—disciplined, because the placing and massing of such decoration
was determined by the proportions and moulded details of one or other of the
orders. Another result of the work of Renaissance architects was the re-discovery
of the architectural significance of the street. "The mediaeval town had grown
up within its walls, its houses surging about the few big buildings it could
boast—the cathedral, the palace, the guildhall. A market would secure an open
space, but other open spaces were rare. The main streets were processional
ways, and as such, curved and wound towards the cathedral. The life of the
place flowed along dark and narrow lanes between houses that were built with
the intensive individualism that made every street-side a hotch-potch of dis-
connected units. Under the beneficent rule of commercial individualism (every
man for himself and the devil take the street) we have reverted to this pre-
Renaissance disorder, but with an aesthetic debasement wholly unknown in

the towns of the Middle Ages. The Renaissance architects brought coherence to the street, and ended the discord that arose from regarding each site as a space isolated for the self-expression of its owner. The old haphazard method of building had made the adoption of Gothic verticality easy and obvious; and the results would certainly have satiated our modern hunger for the picturesque. Cities of crooked streets, with towers and spires rising into the sunlight above the shouldering roofs of the cramped houses, girt by thick walls which granted protection but forbade expansion, were to be found all over Europe; and the rebuilding of those cities so that the streets became articulate and were drained of their shadows and stagnant air was the work of men whose taste inclined to horizontal instead of vertical forms. The street was conceived as a series of horizontally related units, and the nobility of its character thus revealed was enduringly impressed upon the minds of architects."[142]

It was this linking up of the sides of the street, the tendency to compose them in related units, and to create splendid vistas, that left a permanent mark upon the cities of Europe. The great avenues and boulevards of Paris, the majestic open spaces of Rome, the lay-out of cities like Berlin, were all affected by the Renaissance architect's assumption of responsibility for large-scale planning, so that he could design not only individual buildings, but could bring whole areas of a city into one grand plan.

These changes led to the ruthless destruction of many buildings, and in the fifteenth, sixteenth, seventeenth and eighteenth centuries almost as much demolition took place in the interests of improvement and rebuilding as that brutally caused by war. The wrecking of cities or large parts of them by soldiers still continued, and the sacking of Rome in 1527 by the Lutheran *Landsknechts* and the imperial forces under the Constable of Bourbon did far more damage than any of the barbarian invasions.[143] The rebuilding and extension of European cities led to the development of a type of domestic architecture that has since spread over the Continent. Whether you are in cities as far apart as Copenhagen or Belgrade, Paris or Milan, Munich or Malaga, there is a perceptible family likeness between town houses, large or small. You know without question that you are in a European street. This common character was established during the seventeenth and eighteenth centuries, and it depends superficially upon the symmetrical disposition of door and window openings, the use of window shutters and balconies, with moulded detail, sparingly but appositely emphasising horizontal and vertical features. With a few variations continental streets have a loose horizontal unity; façades are of painted plaster or stone, and, save in Holland and certain parts of Germany, brick is seldom exposed and treated as a finished surface material. This characteristic European domestic style was consistently used until the late years of the nineteenth century.

The classic orders, interpreted by Spanish and Portuguese architects, travelled overseas to the New World, and in Central and South America developed an

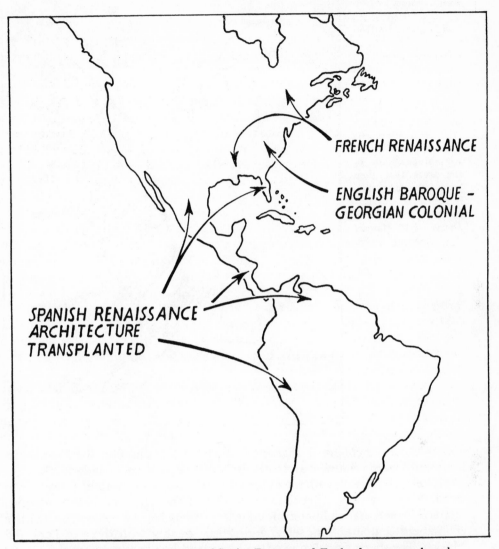

The Renaissance architecture of Spain, France, and England was transplanted to the colonies of those countries in the New World. In Central and South America the classic orders, interpreted by Spanish and Portuguese architects, acquired a new, almost tropical richness of character, particularly in the cathedrals and churches of Mexico, Peru, Ecuador, Colombia, Venezuela, and Brazil. (See map on the following page.) *Drawn by Marcelle Barton.*

During the seventeenth century France, Spain, England, Sweden, and Holland all had flourishing colonies on the eastern seaboard of North America. Sweden and Holland lost their American possessions, but France and England left a permanent mark on the architectural character of the areas that they governed, and Spanish influence is still apparent in Florida. *Drawn by Marcelle Barton.*

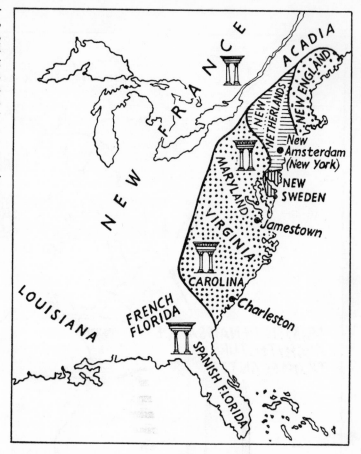

almost tropical richness of character. Some cross-fertilisation with native art is suggested by the churches and cathedrals of Mexico, Peru, Ecuador, Colombia, Venezuela, and Brazil, with their copious, intricate ornamentation, flowing over façades and interiors. French and English architecture in North America retained its national characteristics, for the settlers had no contact with native civilisations comparable in social and artistic quality with those of Peru and Mexico. The sparse population of the hinterland had barely emerged from the neolithic stage of culture. "Apart from innumerable place names that have a rich, musical quality, the Indians contributed little to the new nation that grew up in North America. To the frontiersman, the explorers and adventurous traders, they imparted a knowledge of woodcraft and hunting and fighting that was invaluable; but although they had arts and crafts, and practised them with great skill, they were not a creative people."[144] They had no architecture; no plastic or decorative arts which could have influenced, even remotely, the ornamental conventions and moulded details associated with the classic orders. Although Dutch and Swedish settlements had been made in North America, separating New England and Maryland, they did not survive; the character of architecture, as it developed in the towns of the eastern seaboard, between Spanish Florida in the south, and French territory in the north, was determined by English prototypes, and with regional variations was an agreeable version of Carolean, Queen Anne, and Georgian architecture. In Canada, French Florida, and Louisiana, the contemporary architecture of France exerted a comparable influence.

In Europe, national interpretations of classical architecture were as distinctive as the national variations of the Romanesque and Gothic styles had been. Renaissance architecture passed through three easily recognisable periods in the course of its development in Italy, France, Spain, Germany, and the Netherlands. In each of those countries there were early, classical and late periods, though in Italy the second is more appropriately described as the middle period, for there the transition from Gothic to classic had been made without any compromises between the styles. In Florence, the new concept of architectural design signified an unequivocal supplantation of Gothic forms by the orders: in Rome the classical tradition had always remained. In his admirable study of some aspects of the architectural history of the city, Mr. James Lees-Milne has said that "The secret of Rome's survival up to date has been abundantly clear. It is quite simply a faithful adherence to her classical tradition. Once that tradition is abandoned, Rome is finished. Had she lost signs of it in the Middle Ages and adopted the Gothic style, she would have forfeited continuity with her great architectural past which she might never have recaptured."[145] Those links with the Roman past had never been broken in northern and central Italy. "The Italian spirit," as Professor Huizinga has pointed out, "had never lost touch with classic harmony and simplicity. It could expand freely and naturally in the restored forms of classic expression."[146]

The three periods of the Italian Renaissance are as follows: Early (fifteenth century), Middle (sixteenth century) and Late (seventeenth and eighteenth centuries). Comparable phases occurred at different times in the countries of Europe: Italy was the first to develop the classical style, England the last, and in England there were only two periods, Early and Late. In France the Early period began with the reign of Louis XI in 1461 and lasted until the end of the sixteenth century. The Classical period occupied the whole of the seventeenth century, ending at the death of Louis XIV in 1715. The Late period, which included the reigns of Louis XV and Louis XVI, was checked and changed but not ended in 1793, for classical architecture survived the French Revolution, though Louis XVI did not, and during the brief period of the French Empire, Napoleon's grandiose taste was gratified by sumptuous variations of Greek and Roman motifs. Throughout the nineteenth century, French architects continued to use the classic orders, and the École des Beaux-Arts perpetuated an exacting respect for their conventions, which tended to exclude imagination and hampered experiment.

The Early period of the Spanish Renaissance began in 1492, after the conquest of Granada, the last Moslem state in Spain, and ended in the middle years of the sixteenth century. The Classical period which followed lasted for one hundred years, and the Late period from 1650 to 1800. In Germany, Renaissance architecture, like the Gothic style which preceded it, was introduced from France about fifty years after it had been established in that country; the Early period concluded with the sixteenth century; the Middle period lasted throughout the seventeenth, and the Late ended with the eighteenth century. Obviously all these periods in different parts of Europe overlapped, and in no country were there rigid divisions, though in England, as we shall see in the next section, the work of one architect, Inigo Jones, clearly marked the end of the Early period.

Russia was the exception, and was not affected by the Renaissance until the eighteenth century, after the founding of St. Petersburg in 1703. Classical architecture was introduced by Peter the Great, who employed English and Dutch workmen to build his new city, and invited foreign architects to Russia as part of his policy of Westernising his country. During the eighteenth century French and Italian architects were constantly employed on palaces and public buildings, and the Scottish architect, Charles Cameron (1740–1812), carried out many works for the Empress Catherine (see page 388).

By the middle of the seventeenth century the initial inspiration of the Renaissance had become exhausted: architectural design was no longer lit by the innovating, experimental spirit of the pioneers: many architects had become sobered by observing Vitruvian rules too strictly, though men of genius were never mastered by them. Fortunately for European architecture there was no shortage of men of genius, and their work and example saved architectural design from the paralysis that had restrained its development in Roman times. In the seventeenth century there was a reaction against the timid formality which had inclined even imaginative men to do everything according to the book, instead of indulging their creative gifts, a reaction that generated the Baroque, an entirely new phase of architectural design—fantastic, ornate, occasionally voluptuous and vulgar, but richly satisfying the ancient human need for and love of ornament. The framework provided by the classic orders was frequently over-burdened with a gay profusion of carved decoration, and hitherto unheard-of liberties were taken with columns and entablatures—shafts were twisted, pediments were loaded with sculptured figures, swags and festoons of flowers and fruit, trophies of arms and armour, scrolls smothered in coiling acanthus leaves, gave to the façades of churches, palaces and public buildings a ponderous intricacy that sometimes threatened though it could never destroy the good, basic proportions of a design that was composed in accordance with the rules of one of the five orders; for the reaction had not been against the rules, but against their stultifying influence and their repression of spontaneity.

The Baroque phase began in Rome, and gradually affected the whole of Europe, and everywhere it liberated architects from the nervous discouragement of mere scholars, and allowed them to interpret classic forms in a new, dynamic way. In France, the Rococo movement arose, almost as a by-product of Baroque: it became, to quote the perfect phrase used by Mr. Lees-Milne, a "symphony of hilarity,"[147] characteristic of the early years of Louis XV's reign, and developing its asymmetrical intricacies with fantastic extravagance throughout the eighteenth century. Rococo was a style of decoration rather than an architectural style, and was initiated by the work of Pierre le Pautre, a designer and engraver, who was the eldest child of Jean le Pautre (1618–1682), also a designer and engraver who had worked in the Baroque style. The word is derived from *rocaille*, which means "rock-work," a term originally used to describe the artificial grottos and fountains in the gardens of Versailles, designed by le Nôtre, and executed between 1662 and 1688, perhaps the most impressive example of Baroque in Europe. The characteristic forms of Rococo included foliage, slender and complex exaggerations of the acanthus leaf, shells, scrolls and trophies.[148]

The Rococo style reveals a further change in the artistic and social status of the architect: in addition to being a recognised professional man, he was a man of fashion too, concerned primarily with planning and building and the correct interpretation of the classic orders, but also with designing innumerable inutilities, the charming trifles and frills which adorned the surface of life as it was lived by the European aristocracy. Architecture had become detached from the people, for the popular element in European art, like the spiritual element, had been forsaken. The art and architecture of the Renaissance was fundamentally undemocratic: it was, to quote Dr. Dearmer's indictment, "the conscious, artificial work of a small class of grammarians, princes, and rich merchants. It had nothing to do with the people: it robbed the people of their art, till artists had to be the parasites of the rich, and the people relapsed into barbarism. The art of succeeding ages, beautiful as it has often been, has been the art of the drawing-room, not of the street. . . . "[149] Lisle March Phillipps believed that the popular element had been renounced "in order to promote the idea of art as a matter of culture and the perquisite of an exclusive and privileged minority. Henceforth the national life lost the pleasure which it can derive from art, while art lost the robustness and sincerity which it derives from life."[150]

These views, by a churchman who was a professor of ecclesiastical art, and by a critic with a vigorously original mind, are concerned with the rift between art and everyday life that occurred in Europe in the fifteenth century and in England after the dissolution of the monasteries: they take no account of the broadening of patronage, the improvement in the civilised quality of the patrons, or the passion for beauty for its own sake that exalted the taste of princes, nobles and merchants, and gave to Europe a superlative splendour in architecture, in painting and the decorative arts and crafts. As Chesterton once wrote: "It was not, as in popular Gothic craftsmanship, the almost unconscious touch of art upon all necessary things: rather it was the pouring of the whole soul of passionately conscious art especially into unnecessary things. Luxury was made alive with a soul."[151] The results were remarkable for their capricious variety and consistent excellence of taste.

The sobriety that had threatened to impose universal dullness in the mid-seventeenth century was dissolved by the advent of Baroque, and after Europe was captivated by the Rococo style a wave of Oriental taste rippled over the surface of fashionable life. In the Middle Ages such waves of taste had come from the Middle East and from Moslem Spain; but after the middle of the seventeenth century they emanated from the Far East, and there was a succession of them. In France these Oriental ideas became so commingled with the Rococo style, that Chinese and classical forms of ornamentation were inextricably associated, to the point where they became almost identical. There was an affinity between the Rococo style and Chinese art, which has been analysed by Adolf Reichwein in his study, *China and Europe*. The boldness of form and clarity of colour, characteristic of the Baroque, was replaced by the subtle lines and delicate gradations of colour of Rococo art. It was Reichwein's belief that in this subtlety of feeling lay the secret of the affinity in style of Rococo and ancient Chinese culture. "It was not so much the written word which gave Rococo its conception of China," he wrote. "Sublimated in the delicate tints of fragile porcelain, in the vaporous hues of shimmering Chinese silks, there revealed itself to the minds of that gracious eighteenth century society in Europe a vision of happy living such as their own optimism had already dreamed of."[152]

The borrowing of Chinese motifs became a common practice in France, Germany, and England. In Germany, Rococo was known as "French Grotesque"—in England it was acknowledged, by cabinet-makers and upholsterers rather than by architects, as the "French style." The Chinese elements in Rococo encouraged designers to discard symmetry, and to indulge their fancy in the form of taste that in England was called *sharawadgi*. This term, which Mr. Hubert de Cronin Hastings has defined as "the art of not doing regularly," was first used by Sir William Temple in his *Essay on Gardening*, written about 1685, when he compared the charms of regularity and irregularity in the laying out and planting of gardens, cautiously commending the manner in which the Chinese created asymmetrical effects.

Although French and German architects were attracted by the effervescence of Rococo and Chinese forms, they indulged their taste for them within the framework of the classic orders, which allowed large licence for extravagant fancies, but never permitted anarchy. The only structural form that was borrowed from China was the concave roof, and its use was generally confined to such small, decorative buildings as garden houses and pavilions. Reichwein records that "the builders of the European pleasure-house of the Rococo took from their Chinese models the habit of bringing the rooms into as close touch as possible with nature outside by means of high window-like openings reaching to the ground. Moreover they disliked sharp angles and corners in their rooms. Even to these smallest details the spirit of the times penetrated and made its influence felt. Smooth-mannered men, flexible and supple, were the men of the Rococo, and their character expressed itself in every trifling production of their art. Thus the affinity they felt for Chinese art led them to welcome the latest refinement of Chinese interior-architecture, the 'round corner,' if the expression is allowed."(153) In time this smoothing of angles and the general softening of outlines led to a preoccupation with ornamental effects which degenerated into complexity. Form ceased to have significance : in the interests of elegance, ornaments, furniture and all the articles that went into buildings became so attenuated, so flimsy as a result of exaggerated delicacy, that they disclosed far more than the taste of "smooth-mannered men"—they showed the corruption and frivolity of a society that had become divorced from reality. The last phases of architectural design, interior decoration and furnishing in France before the Revolution, faithfully record the character of that exquisite but feckless civilisation. The transition from the studied magnificence of the Baroque to the irresponsible gaiety of the Rococo was almost the last great creative phase of the Renaissance in Europe. Throughout the whole period, the classic orders were used for the regulation of proportions ; the most ornate excesses of Rococo ornament were never permitted to disrupt the excellence of those proportions ; and the art and architecture of the eighteenth century aristocracy in Europe never lost the coherence that is derived from educated patronage.

The three periods of the Renaissance in Europe may be followed in detail in each country, where architecture records each change of style, and the buildings speak better than words. Italy and France are richer in examples than other countries, though nearly every city and town in Europe can supply evidence of the impact made by the Renaissance upon taste and design. Throughout Italy, there are hundreds of buildings which attest the ability of architects, and show how triumphantly and with what sensitive perception the Roman classic orders were reinstated in the home of their origin. From Italy our first examples are to be found in Florence, and some of the earliest Renaissance work in that city has been mentioned at the beginning of this section, namely the Pazzi Chapel, the façade of St. Maria Novella, and the dome of the Cathedral. The fifteenth century was the greatest period of Florentine achievement in architecture, when Brunelleschi, Alberti, Michelozzo and Il Cronaca were all at work.

Of the secular buildings by Brunelleschi the most famous is the Pitti Palace (1434–1440), designed for Luca Pitti ; a superb composition, designed on a

The Riccardi Palace at Florence (1430), designed by Michelozzo (1391–1472?). The architect was a Florentine by birth, a sculptor who had been a pupil of Donatello, and who worked in marble, bronze and silver. The Riccardi Palace is an example of the use of contrasting building techniques, for the ground storey is heavily rusticated masonry, broken by semicircular arches which act as frames for windows, with pediments; the first floor has drafted stone walling, and the upper storey plain ashlar masonry. The first and second storeys have windows with arched hoods, divided into two smaller arched openings, with a little tracery.

A massive projecting cornice terminates the façade. (See plate 18.)

The Pitti Palace, Florence (1435), designed by Brunelleschi. It is, with the exception of the Vatican, the largest palace in Italy. Some additions were made in 1640, and the projecting wings were added in 1763. (See plate 18.)

symmetrical plan, and, apart from the Vatican, the largest palace in Italy. The façade is astylar—that is, without columns or pilasters—and its stately simplicity is derived from the boldness with which great blocks of masonry are used, and the harmonious disposition of the three tiers of arches. The projecting wings which face the piazza were not added until 1763. (See illustration above.) Another magnificent architectural gesture by one of the great Florentine families is the Riccardi Palace (1430), built by Michelozzo. No orders are used, though extremely slender columns appear in the windows of the first and second storeys. The masonry of the building, the use of heavy, rusticated blocks on the ground storey, and the significance given to the windows of that storey by enclosing them within semicircular arches, make the whole design rely for much of its effect upon the use of contrasting building techniques. (See illustrations on page 208 and plate 18.)

After Florence, Rome provides the greatest abundance of buildings for study, and two groups in particular illustrate the Italian genius for conceiving architecture on a stupendous scale. These are the Capitol, by Michelangelo, and St. Peter's and the Vatican, fronted by Bernini's Piazza. The Capitol (1540–1644) was the noblest of Michelangelo's civic projects, for he remodelled the

approaches to the Piazza, and designed the façades of the palaces which flank
it. (See plate 7.) Michelangelo, like Leonardo da Vinci, was a universal genius
of incredible versatility, an accomplished specialist in several arts. Giorgio
Vasari, who published *The Lives of Painters, Sculptors and Architects* at Florence
in 1550, mentions some thirty-two men who practised architecture. Of these,
only eleven were purely architects; eleven were both sculptors and architects;
six practised architecture and painting; three were masters of all three arts;
and one was an architect and engineer.

St. Peter's at Rome, built between 1506 and 1626, was the work of many
architects during that period of a hundred and twenty years. For the original
design a competition was organised, and Bramante was the winner. In 1506
the foundation-stone of his church was laid, but in 1513 Bramante was superseded by Giuliano da Sangallo, Fra Giocondo and Raphael. Two years after
their appointment, da Sangallo and Giocondo died, and Raphael died five
years later, when Baldassare Peruzzi was appointed to succeed him. All these
architects made changes in the plan, and when Peruzzi died in 1536, Antonio
da Sangallo (the younger) again altered the plan, and on his death in 1546
Michelangelo, who was then 72, succeeded him and created the church
that is familiar to us to-day. After Michelangelo's death in 1564, various other
architects took a hand in the design, including Vignola, and Carlo Maderna
added the vast façade that dominates the Piazza. The building was completed
in the 1620's and finally, after the middle of the seventeenth century, Bernini
designed the entrance piazza with its Tuscan columns. (Plate 25.) The Cathedral, Piazza and Vatican are gigantic in scale; they form one of the most
famous groups of buildings in the world, and refute the suggestion, quoted
earlier, that the Renaissance was the mere resort of copying the architecture
of ancient Rome, for here the classic orders have acquired a new and impressive
flexibility, and the great dome of St. Peter's, formed by two shells of masonry,
triumphantly asserts the splendour of this new development of an ancient
feature. Unlike the shallow domes of Byzantine churches, which were comparatively inconspicuous externally, the dome had now become in architecture the
most striking and dominant feature.

One of the smaller churches of Rome, the Gesù church, designed by Vignola,
shows how, on a reduced scale, a majestic effect could be created by this new
dominance of the dome. This church has a nave with side chapels instead of
aisles, only slightly projecting transepts, with the dome rising above the crossing.
It was built between 1568 and 1575, and is perhaps better known than any
other works by Vignola. (See page 212.)

Palladio, who exercised such a powerful influence upon the architecture of his
time and later generations, carried out his chief work in his native city of
Vicenza, and there the Villa Capra, which was also called the Rotunda,
provoked the imitation of many architects in Europe and England. It is a
square building with a portico of the Ionic order on each face. These four

St. Peter's, Rome (1506–1626). The view above shows the Cathedral from the Janiculum. Below is a view of the Piazza. The building was the work of many architects during a period of over a century. (See plate 25.)

porticoes lead to a circular central hall, which is roofed with a shallow dome, of which a glimpse is caught above the tiled roof. The best-known imitation was Lord Burlington's villa at Chiswick, built in 1725, which only superficially resembles Palladio's Rotunda. The Corinthian order is used instead of the Ionic, and the dome rises on a drum. (See illustrations on pages 213 and 276.) One of Palladio's great churches was St. Giorgio Maggiore at Venice (1556–1579), where the classic orders were used with a basilican plan, and the most impressive

The Gesù Church, Rome (1568–1575), is one of the smaller churches of the city, which shows how, on a reduced scale, a majestic effect may be created by the dome used as a dominant feature. It was designed by Vignola, and is perhaps the best known of his works.

effect is created by the tall Corinthian columns of the façade. This façade was completed by Scamozzi in 1575. (See page 214.)

The mediaeval part of the Doge's Palace at Venice has been described in Section VI, and it was one of those buildings that grew continuously. The Grand Cortile (1486) by Antonio Rizzi, was continued by Pietro Lombardo (1499–1511) carried on by Bergamasco (1520), and completed by Scarpagnino in 1550. The Cortile, with its arcaded façades, is a light and airy design, richly decorative without being over-elaborate, and achieving dignity and grandeur. The Bridge of Sighs, that most photographed of all examples of Venetian architecture, connects the palace and the prison, and its graceful elliptical arch is familiar the world over. Its romantic and sinister associations incline many people to ignore, or at least to regard perfunctorily, its grace of design. (See plate 18.)

The magnificence of Baroque architecture is exemplified by St. Maria della Salute, the octagonal church facing the Grand Canal, designed by Baldassari Longhena (1600–1682), with a vast dome above the central space, rising from an exceptionally high drum, and, like a diminished shadow behind it, a smaller dome over the chancel, flanked by turrets with cupolas. Large scrolled buttresses flow down from the drum of the principal dome, their graceful spirals connecting it with the outer walls. For the columns of the portico, the pilasters on the facets, and the columns at the angles within the church, the Corinthian order is used. The foundation-stone was laid in 1631, but the building was still unfinished thirty years later. Longhena was a pupil of Vicenzo Scamozzi of Vicenza (1552–1616), and was one of the most accomplished masters of Baroque. In 1630 he was appointed official architect to the Venetian Republic, a position he held for fifty years. His greatest work was St. Maria della Salute,

The Villa Capra, Vicenza, by Andrea Palladio (1518–1580), a square building with a portico on each face, opening into a central circular hall, which is covered by a shallow dome. This building has inspired a good many imitations, of which the best known was Lord Burlington's villa at Chiswick. (See illustration on page 276.)

and, like his master Scamozzi, he designed palaces, of which the Pesaro and the Rezzonico adorn the Grand Canal.

At Venice Italian Baroque escaped the complexities that elsewhere burdened buildings with broken pediments, an excessive use of scrolls and sculpture, and such involved features as façades following serpentine curves. Architects who practised there seldom attempted to "Load some vain church with old theatric state." Their designs were gay and sparkling; an Oriental air still brightened the city, although its trade had declined, and it was becoming a pleasure resort for Europe instead of a commercial centre. Already the tourist era was fore-shadowed. Venice could still attract architects and artists who gave to this period of political and military twilight an unforgettable splendour. One by one the Republic lost her overseas possessions—Cyprus, Crete and finally her foothold in Greece. The fragments of Venetian watch-towers are visible, most uninteresting of ruins, as you pass from Attica into Boetia on the road from Eleusis to Thebes; gaunt, grim structures, built to intimidate a passive peasantry as well as strong-points against attack by the Turks; and in eastern Peloponnese, Larissa of Argos is still crowned by a large Venetian ruin. The artistic achieve-ments of Venice were not for export to such military outposts. There was no eastward flow of Renaissance influence. Venice lost all her Greek possessions after a short campaign in 1715–1716, and by the Treaty of Passarovitch, signed in 1717, all that was left of her Eastern empire were a few fortresses in Dalmatia, Albania and Herzegovina. That treaty bore her last signature as a European power.[154]

In Rome the Baroque churches displayed many of the florid characteristics of the style; but even Borromini, its leading practitioner in the seventeenth century, knew how to resist the temptation to become ornate at the expense of structural sense. His works include St. Agnese in Piazza Navona, which he

St. Giorgio Maggiore, Venice (1560–1575). The façade has a pediment supported
by tall Corinthian columns rising from a plinth.

designed on a Greek cross plan with a curved façade; also the church of the
Collegio di Propaganda, and the churches of La Sapienza and St. Carlo alle
Quattro Fontane. He was responsible for restoring the church of St. John Lateran,
though the principal façade, with its open loggia, was built in 1734 to the
design of Alessandro Galilei (1691–1737).

In Florence, the Baroque never flourished. The great buildings, the architectural glories of the city, belong to the fifteenth and sixteenth centuries, when
the Renaissance was young, and its inspiration fresh and buoyant, and the

gifts, skill and wisdom of the painter, sculptor, musician, engineer, architect
and natural philosopher could be combined in the mind of a genius like
Leonardo da Vinci. Clarity of mind, and an objective approach to any problem
are basic characteristics of humanism, and Leonardo's definition of an arch
illustrates the lucidity of the new way of thought that originated the scientific
attitude. "An arch," he said, "is nothing other than a strength caused by two
weaknesses; for the arch in buildings is made up of two segments of a circle,
and each of these segments being in itself very weak desires to fall, and as the
one withstands the downfall of the other the two weakness are converted into
a single strength."(155) Dr. Waddington has described science as "the organised
attempt of mankind to discover how things work as casual systems,"(156) and
this four-hundred-year-old process of research and deduction began with men
like Leonardo, whose desire for knowledge for its own sake was comparable
with, though more far-reaching than, the speculations and diverse curiosities
of the ancient Greek philosophers. Leonardo has been well named The Forerunner: it is the title of Dmitri Merejkowski's novel, which is based on the life
of the greatest Florentine of the Renaissance.

No other European country produced men of the intellectual or artistic
quality of those Italians who gave such resounding fame to their city states in

Villa d'Este at Tivoli. Originally a Benedictine convent, it was rebuilt as a villa
about 1550, under the direction of Pirro Ligorio, an architect and antiquary,
born in Naples. The work was done by order of Cardinal Ippolito II d'Este.

The Renaissance façade of St. Croce in Jerusalem, one of the seven churches of Rome visited by pilgrims. Tradition ascribes its foundation in the early fourth century to St. Helena, and an alternative name for it is the Basilica Sessoriana, derived from the Sessorium, Helena's Palace. It has been restored and rebuilt and additions made to it in the eighth, tenth, and twelfth centuries. In 1743–1744, by order of Pope Benedict XIV (1740–1758), it was almost entirely rebuilt by Domenico Gregorini and Pietro Passalacque.

the fifteenth and sixteenth centuries. France was nearly three-quarters of a century behind Italy in practising with any real comprehension the principles of classical design, or the new methods of building. French master-masons continued in the ways of their mediaeval predecessors, reluctantly accommodating the demands of a few rich or noble patrons who had seen highly ornamented buildings in Italy, or had heard of them, and wanted something after the same fashion. With no guidance apart from the wishes of wealthy amateurs who "knew what they liked," such men as the court financiers, Thomas Bohier who built Chenonceaux and Gilles Berthelot who built Azay-le-Rideau, the French master-masons erected great houses in their own tradition. (See page 220.) These were coated externally with arabesques and medallions and the inevitable acanthus leaves, such decoration being applied by Italians—not always of great ability—but more often by French craftsmen who were imitating forms they neither liked nor understood. The results of this purely superficial use of Italian ideas were muddles, though picturesque muddles, for picturesque effect is often a by-product when decoration is mistaken for design.

The association of Gothic features and classical ornament marked this early, / transitional period of the French Renaissance. It was an uneasy partnership, in which the vertical characteristics of Gothic predominated, while the scraps of ornament, borrowed from Italian sources, often appeared as trivial after-thoughts, stuck on as trimmings to the frames of windows and doors. Such ornamental details might be graceful, but they contributed little to the design of a building as a whole, and were often used without point or any understanding of architectural composition. Typical of this period is the Château de Chambord, a fantastic building with conical roofs and angle towers, which would have a distraught air unless the façade had been unified, tied together as it were by the horizontal lines below the windows. (See plates 20–21.) Even so it lacks the tranquillity and easy harmonies of contemporary Italian buildings, though it is indubitably picturesque. Externally the château retains the military quality of a fortified building, with an inner block corresponding to the keep of an English castle. Within, is the famous double spiral staircase, which is a development of the mediaeval newel staircase.[157] It is enclosed in a cage of stone, and the double spirals are so arranged that people ascending are invisible to those descending. A simpler and much smaller English example

St. Maria in Montesanto and St. Maria dei Miracoli, two Baroque churches with symmetrical façades, in the Piazza del Popolo, Rome. Designed by Carlo Rainaldi in 1662, they were built by Bernini and Fontana in 1675–1678.

The crossing of St. Maria del Popolo, a church that originated from a chapel
built by Pope Paschal II (1099–1118) above the tombs of the Domita family.
It was enlarged and rebuilt at different times, and became one of the richest
churches in Rome. The architect for the second chapel was Fontana; the
apse was by Bramante; and the Chigi Chapel was designed by Raphael.
The interior was renovated by Bernini.

is the staircase in the south-west turret of the tower of the Collegiate Church of Tamworth in Staffordshire, where "two flights of steps wind one above the other round the same newel, so that the floor of the one forms the roof of the other, all enclosed within a cylinder six feet in diameter and lighted from without by loopholes."[158] Although it has been suggested that Chambord was built after a small scale model, made by Domenico da Cortona, an Italian architect, that model did not include the central staircase, which is apparently the work of the master-mason.[159]

French builders were severely handicapped in the early days of their contact with the architectural ideas that were flowing from Italy. The professional architect, the master designer who could have inspired and directed their work, was usually an Italian and was resented as such. Generally, builders worked from scale models made of wood. It is known that some famous Italian architects visited France and worked there, but it is difficult to identify their work. For example, Fra Giocondo (1453–1515) has been credited with many buildings, but we only know for certain that he designed the Pont Notre Dame in Paris. Sebastian Serlio (1475–1554) may have designed the château of St. Germain, and possibly the château of Nancy-le-France, but little is known of his work in France, apart from his lucrative appointment at Fontainebleau. Although he could not influence them by example, he ultimately gave authoritative guidance to French masons by publishing a work on the classic orders, I cinque libri d'Architettura. Despite the efforts of Francis I and his courtiers to introduce Italian architecture, they were unsuccessful in attracting the best talent, although they spent large sums of money in the hope of coaxing Italian artists and architects to visit France and work there. Men like Serlio were frustrated by the implacable opposition of the master-masons who were resolved to maintain their monopoly of building, and there was a national antipathy between Italians and Frenchmen at this period, caused perhaps by the conscious superiority of Italians who with some reason regarded themselves as the artistic and intellectual leaders of European civilisation. Serlio disliked France and had some sharp things to say about the standards of life that satisfied his patrons.

Working under royal patronage had its disadvantages, for the ordering and prosecution of any major building operation was characterised by lack of practical system and general incoherence of procedure. The rebuilding and enlargement of the Palace at Fontainebleau illustrates the haphazard manner of setting about such work. A "devis" or specification was drawn up by the King's "varlet de chambre," which was not the sort of specification that gave any details about materials or structural methods, but merely described the work that had to be done. There was no reference to drawings; only approximate prices were fixed for the building, and no supervising architect watched costs or checked payments. The royal patrons were fleeced handsomely, and the work was often so badly executed that the royal houses collapsed. Francis I, a volatile egomaniac, started off a good many schemes but allowed them to

The Château de Chenonceaux (1515–1523), like the Château de Chambord shown on plates 20 and 21, records the conflict between mediaeval traditions of building, championed by the French master-masons, and the new ideas of architectural composition which were being practised in Italy. The result was often a picturesque compromise: buildings remained traditional in mass and outline, the Renaissance was ignored in the matter of composition, and acknowledged only by the use of classical detail for ornamental trimmings.

Right: The Château d'Azay-le-Rideau (1520), in which the traditional mediaeval French style predominates.

lapse when his enthusiasm ebbed away; he was bored with them long before they were completed. Vast and enormously expensive buildings were commissioned at Blois, Fontainebleau, St. Germain, Villers-Cotterets, la Muette and the Château de Madrid, which all engaged the transitory interest of the King and drained the royal purse. Some of them became ruinous because the King ignored them and made no effort to keep them up.

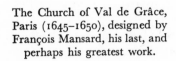

The Church of Val de Grâce,
Paris (1645–1650), designed by
François Mansard, his last, and
perhaps his greatest work.

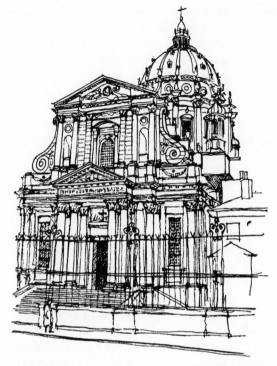

Until the middle of the sixteenth century Italian architecture was an exotic
plant which failed to flourish in a country whose people and craftsmen were
still mediaeval in outlook. Although there were both French and Italian architects in the country, their status was uncertain, though their national taste
was not. Mr. Martin Briggs, in *The Architect in History*, has observed that the
Frenchmen "were survivors of the mediaeval system, and the Italians heralds
of a new dawn, when the light of the Orders came to illumine the dark world
of Gothic ignorance."[160] He records a French example of the sort of versatility
that was usually associated with Italy, in the person of Hugues Sambin (1520–
1602), "who began as a joiner like his father, later became borough-surveyor
of Dijon, built a slaughter-house, a drinking-place, and windmills there,
diverted the river, improved the fortifications, carved a 'Last Judgment' and
many other subjects, arranged a triumphal progress, designed the Hôtel de
Ville at Besançon, and published a book of *Termes*, containing eighteen astonishing plates of terminal figures."[161]

This uncertainty of status did not last. By the middle of the century the
architect, as a professional designer, had attained the position of control that
he was to exercise in France for the next four hundred years. He was not a master
builder; he was an artist and an organiser; a designer and director of architectural projects who had studied antique prototypes at first hand in Italy. With

the rise of this new professionalism in France, men like Philibert de l'Orme introduced a new orderliness and an air of gracious stability into building. His first work was for Cardinal Jean du Bellay, at St. Maur-les-Fossés, on the banks of the Marne near Charenton, a large house grouped about an internal court. De l'Orme's Italian studies imparted a Roman air to its logias and arcades. The house no longer exists for it was destroyed before the French Revolution. De l'Orme was ultimately employed on several of the royal palaces, notably Fontainebleau, Villers-Cotterets and St. Germain-en-Laye. His last and perhaps most important work was the Tuileries, an enormous building, the largest palace that had been designed by one architect since Roman times. It was burnt down in 1871 by the Commune. A fragment of the façade remains in the Tuileries gardens.

Unfortunately de l'Orme and his contemporaries had introduced with the new orderliness a stiff, over-precise respect for classical models. The Doric, Ionic, and Corinthian orders were used with wearisome repetition, and pilasters and columns, introduced with conscientious frequency, were often as devoid of significance as Italianate ornament had been in the first half of the sixteenth century. The flexibility of the classic orders was not appreciated; instead of using their established proportions as a system of design, architects seemed for a time to be content merely with displacing traditional forms by painstaking reproductions of the antique. The conflict between mediaeval and classical forms persisted, and the steep roofs and dormer windows of the Middle Ages survived. Throughout the sixteenth century, French architecture illustrated the line from Kipling's poem on France:

"First to follow Truth and last to leave old truths behind . . . "

The influence of Gothic architecture and the social outlook of the Middle Ages remained for generations. "France had been the mother-land of all that was strongest and most beautiful in the products of the mediaeval spirit," as Professor Huizinga has said. "All mediaeval forms—feudalism, the ideas of chivalry and courtesy, scholasticism, Gothic architecture—were rooted here much more firmly than ever they had been in Italy."[162] It was not until the beginning of the seventeenth century that the conflict between Gothic survivals and the classic orders was determined, and French architects evolved a domestic style, based on the use of brick and stone, and free from the ornamental superfluities that had been draped over the façades of buildings during the reign of Francis I. That pleasant vernacular style was identified with Henry IV (1553–1610), a conscientious and discerning patron of architecture, the best king France ever had, who encouraged the arts as a matter of state policy.

Until the middle years of the seventeenth century, French architecture was unpretentious, distinguished by bold, firm lines, regulated, but not slavishly so, by classical proportions. Among the best examples of this style are the buildings of St. Germain-en-Laye, where de l'Orme's structures were enclosed by a new

The Hôtel des Invalides, Paris, was begun by Bruant in
1670, and the scheme was completed and the dome
designed by Jules Hardouin Mansard in 1706.

façade fronting the river, with a series of terraces and stairs on a grand scale
descending to the water level. In Paris some extensive town planning schemes
were put in hand. The Place Royale, now the Place des Vosges, was planned
and built. Those bland façades, rising above continuous arcades, exhibit the
harmonious adjustment of horizontal and vertical elements which characterises
good composition. Steep roofs have been incorporated in the design; the dormers
are linked with the general pattern of fenestration; only the chimneys, those
regrettable afterthoughts in so many buildings, strike a discordant note. (See
plate 26.) The Place Royale was part of a great scheme that was drawn up
but never finished. In the course of carrying out this grand plan the Pont
Neuf was completed, the Place du Pont Neuf begun and the Place Dauphine
laid out, and although work ceased after Henry IV was assassinated (May 14th,
1610), it had inaugurated a new era of town planning. Thereafter the rulers
of France thought in terms of spacious ways, broad avenues and fine vistas,
of gardens, parks and squares, and did indeed confer upon their capital a
magnificence that in the course of three hundred years transformed Paris from
a congested mediaeval city into one of the finest examples of town planning
in the world.

There were a few departures from the agreeable vernacular style which matured during the first half of the seventeenth century; a revival of interest in the exact interpretation of the classic orders led to a phase of pomposity, when inspiration was dulled and pedants came into their own. It did not last; the French mind, too irrepressibly gay to submit to the restrictions imposed by unadventurous scholars, ultimately found release through the Baroque style. The period between the death of Henry IV and the beginning of Louis XIV's reign was distinguished by the work of many able architects who were employed by imaginative and lavish patrons. Of those patrons the most imaginative and lavish was Cardinal Richelieu. It is said that his town house in Paris, the Palais Richelieu—afterwards known as the Palais Royal—cost 10,000,000 livres. In 1628 he commissioned his architect, Jacques Lemercier (1583–1654) to build a magnificent château in Touraine, with a little town, symmetrically laid out on a rectangular plan, to house his suite and attendants. This town, which is named Richelieu, still exists, though the great château is largely destroyed. Lemercier was the designer of the Sorbonne; Richelieu laid the foundation of the new building in 1635, and it has a classical perfection that reflects the knowledge of ancient architecture which the architect acquired at first hand, for he is believed to have spent some years in Rome, between 1607 and 1620.[163] Lemercier was the official Court Architect, correct rather than brilliant, with more skill than inspiration in his handling of the classic idiom, though not a pedantic scholarly type, and pre-eminently a professional man who enjoyed the consistent confidence of his patrons.

Very different from Lemercier was that unpredictable genius, François Mansart (1598–1666), the greatest French architect of the seventeenth century, very different too in character from his grand-nephew, Jules Hardouin Mansart, Louis XIV's architect. François Mansart was born in Paris, the son of a carpenter; nothing is known about his early life and training, but at some period he must have acquired a profound knowledge of classical architecture, which he used with such mastery and perfect judgment in his buildings. He could wear the eccentricities of genius lightly, though his clients had to pay for them; he never bothered about the cost of a building, was indifferent to economic conditions of any kind, concerning himself only with the pursuit of perfection in design, and using the most extravagant means to attain that end. When he built Maisons, on the banks of the Seine, at a cost of about 12,000,000 livres, he had one of the wings of the house pulled down because, although he had designed it himself, he disliked its appearance when it was erected. He had previously taken the precaution of insisting that his client, René de Longueil, should allow him to alter his work as he saw fit. Before he built Maisons, he had rebuilt Blois for Gaston, duc d'Orléans, which is a masterpiece of domestic architecture in the classic manner.

His last, perhaps his greatest work, was the design for the church of Val de Grâce (1645–1650), which was intended to form the central part of a great monastery that was to be rebuilt to Mansart's designs. A year after the laying of the foundation-stone, when the building had been carried some 9 feet above ground, he was superseded by Lemercier; Anne of Austria, the Queen Mother, who had commissioned the work, had become alarmed by Mansart's recklessness about costs; he was also the victim of political intrigue. His career coincided with the period when the Renaissance in France passed from the urbane simplicities of the Henry IV style, through a classical revival with its obstinate loyalties to Vitruvian rules, to the new freedoms of the Baroque.

The second half of the seventeenth century was the most expansive period of French architectural design. Buildings were outwardly stately and correct in classical detail, their architects employing the orders with dignity and imagination; while behind those majestic façades the convolutions of the Rococo style were foreshadowed by the decorative scrollwork and frivolous sculptured figures of nymphs and cupids and the fauna of classical mythology that adorned the interiors of royal palaces and great houses. The greatest activity in building took place between 1661 and 1690, when Louis XIV, sunning himself in the light of his own magnificence and showing off to the whole of Europe, employed architects and artists to create some of the greatest monuments to human vanity that had been built since the royal Pyramids of ancient Egypt. Deeply concerned with his personal splendour, intent on having magnificent surroundings that would do justice to his royal presence, "Le Roi Soleil" had a passion for building and prided himself on his taste. In Jean Baptiste Colbert (1619–1683) he had a minister whose ambition was to make France the leader of the arts, crafts and industries of Europe. His policy succeeded; and the effects of it continued for over two and a half centuries: France still has an unrivalled reputation for her sense of style.

Two outstanding names are associated with architecture during those first thirty years of Louis XIV's reign: André le Nôtre, who laid out the grounds and gardens of Versailles, and Jules Hardouin Mansart, the designer of the Palace. The site at Versailles was a bad one; the gardens, planned on geometrical lines, were not completed for twenty years; the expense of the work was colossal, but the results were more impressive than anything else in France. They recall another line from Kipling's poem, quoted earlier:

"Furious in luxury, merciless in toil . . . "

The furious luxury was the prerogative of the King and the aristocracy; the merciless toiling was done by the peasantry. By 1680 over 25,000,000 francs had been spent on Versailles. The Palace was largely the work of Mansart, who was not only an accomplished architect but had many of the attributes of a public relations specialist, whose powers of persuasion were exerted not only upon the King, but upon a lot of far more difficult, obstructive and jealous people. It was not too exacting a task to sustain the King's belief in the infallibility of the royal judgment about architecture: it was a matter of well-timed

The façade of the Cathedral at Montauban, in south-western France, dating from the eighteenth century. A correct exercise in the use of the Tuscan and Ionic orders, though somewhat deficient in inspiration.

suggestion, so that the architect's ideas could be assimilated by Louis, who would later believe that he had thought of them himself—a technique that has been practised by architects and artists for centuries.

When Bernini came to Paris to discuss the restoration of the Louvre he was far too much of an individualist to play that sycophantic game either with the King or his ministers. When he first arrived in June, 1665, he was revered and consulted as the highest authority on all matters of art and architecture, but he soon fell out with Colbert, and afterwards with Colbert's *premier commis*, Charles Perrault. The servants of an absolute monarchy were not to the taste of "the old reserv'd Italian," as he was called by Christopher Wren who met him during his stay in Paris and was permitted a brief, tantalising glimpse of the designs for the Louvre. Those plans were abandoned, and the commission for the façade of the Louvre was finally given to Perrault's brother, Claude, three years after Bernini had left Paris in disgust. All he had done in his five months' stay was to complete a superb marble bust of the King. But for those who were prepared to be obsequious, the rewards were alluring. Mansart pursued those rewards throughout his life. His real name was Hardouin; he was born in 1645, and on his mother's side was a grand-nephew of François

Mansart. When his great-uncle died in 1666, Jules Hardouin adopted the name of Mansart. As an architect he was highly successful. Apart from Versailles he undertook a huge volume of work and was engaged on most of the official architecture executed between 1680 and 1688. He designed the Place Vendôme in Paris in 1690–1691 (plate 27); he was engaged on the Invalides, and designed the Church of the Dome, below which the tomb of Napoleon I now lies, and when he died in 1708 he had to his credit not only a great number of buildings, but was the director of the Academies of painting, sculpture and architecture. The Academy of Architecture had been founded in 1671.

Mansart's style varied: it could display a bold simplicity of conception, as illustrated by the Place Vendôme, with its arcades and Corinthian pilasters and columns above, rising through two storeys, with dormers in the steep roof, terminating the vertical elements of the façade; it could be monumental, and show his capacity for handling the orders to build up a base, as it were, for some Baroque flourish, like the dome of the second church of the Invalides; or he could create a composition in the grand manner, like the Palace of Versailles, of which the Orangery is the most distinguished part, though some authorities credit le Nôtre and Desgodetz with the design of the Orangery.[164] (See plates 28 and 29 and page 223.) His work was always impressive, though with all his appointments and activities it is unlikely that he could have designed all the buildings attributed to him. He probably had more opportunities than any architect in the long history of architecture. That great ebullition of building activity in the latter part of the seventeenth century was never surpassed in France, and the cost of it reduced the state to the most desperate financial plight, while the condition of the people sank to lower and lower levels.

While the King was engaged in reducing his country to bankruptcy with expensive building projects and even more disastrously expensive wars, the country houses of the nobility were largely neglected, in some cases falling into ruin. It had been Richelieu's policy to deprive the nobility of all their powers and responsibilities so that they had nothing left but the life of the court, and there they fluttered round the King, performing all kinds of trivial and indeed menial services, which were graciously allotted by the monarch and eagerly sought by men who bore the greatest names in France. This separation of the aristocracy from the life of the country was ultimately fatal, and the preoccupation of what should have been a ruling class with the puerilities of court etiquette, frivolous gossip and adroit intrigue, encouraged a flight from realities which was accelerated in the reign of Louis XV (1715–1774). The waste, the folly and the charm of that society have been described in contemporary letters and memoirs, and its character is given away completely by the architecture that supplied its environment: outwardly staid, as apparently society was outwardly stable, inwardly empty of purpose and dedicated to luxury. What better background could there be for the posturings of this hedonistic aristocracy than the gilded froth of the Rococo style? The origin

The Petit Trianon at Versailles, designed for Madame du Barry by Ange Jacques
Gabriel, and built between 1762 and 1768. Such sedate, well-proportioned
buildings often sheltered the most outrageously extravagant furnishing and
interior decoration, for the Rococo style was passing into its final and most
unrealistic phase in the second half of the eighteenth century. Externally, society
appeared to be well ordered, placid, and secure: but the state was in a turmoil
and modish life was as wildly divorced from practical realities as the Rococo style.

and nature of that style have been described earlier: its manifestations were
confined largely to the decoration and furnishing of the drawing-rooms of Paris,
to pavilions and such small structures, and the ornamental features of gardens.

Externally, French architecture of the middle and late eighteenth century
had an elegant formality; even buildings intended wholly for pleasure were
placid and sedate. Of these one of the best examples is the Petit Trianon at
Versailles, designed for Madame du Barry by Ange Jacques Gabriel (1710–
1782) and erected between 1762 and 1768. On the entrance façade the
Corinthian order is used, four fluted pilasters rising from the base formed by
the rusticated ground storey, and ascending through the first and second storeys
to support an entablature with a balustrade above. The Gabriels, Jacques Jules
the father (1667–1742) and Ange Jacques the son, were the two outstanding
architects of the century. The former was a great designer of bridges, the fine
one over the Loire at Blois, and seven others, including those at Poissy and
Pontoise; he was responsible too for some notable work in the provinces, the
Place Royale (now the Place de la Bourse) on the quay at Bordeaux, and the
cathedral at La Rochelle. The original lay-out of the Place de la Concorde in

Paris was the work of Gabriel the younger, and some of his buildings on the north side remain. The École Militaire (1751–1773) is considered to be his best work, and was perhaps the last inspired example of classical architecture in France.

France in the eighteenth century led the fashion in everything: clothes, furniture, decorative trifles of every kind; and French architecture was admired, though not in England. Horace Walpole claimed that the researches of English travellers and their published studies of antique designs "have established the throne of architecture in Britain, while itself languishes at Rome, wantons in tawdry imitations of the French in other parts of Europe, and struggles in vain at Paris to surmount their prepossession in favour of their own errors— for fickle as we call that nation, their music and architecture prove how long their ears and eyes can be constant to discord and disproportion."[165] In expressing such aggressively insular views, Walpole may have had in mind the palace of Sans Souci, which had been built for Frederick the Great in 1745–1747, and the other royal palaces, parks and pleasure grounds at Potsdam, which has been called the German Versailles, though it was not a tawdry imitation of the original. Germany, in common with other European countries, might have been superficially influenced by French modes, but in architectural design, Germany and Austria had interpreted the Renaissance in their own characteristic manner, and had given to the Baroque a richness which depended partly upon a superabundant use of ornament, partly upon a free and unusual employment of the orders.

The Renaissance in Germany passed through its early and middle phases, compromising at first with traditional Gothic, and by the seventeenth century acquiring a respect for the formal modulations of the orders. For a time Baroque was resisted; as a style it was associated with the Jesuits, and Protestant Germany would have none of it, until the incandescence of religious fanaticism was dimmed and eventually quenched by the tolerance and scepticism of the eighteenth century. It was resisted too in Holland for the same reasons, although there are some Baroque towers at Amsterdam and Haarlem, but the style flourished in Belgium.

Greatest of all the Central European architects of the late seventeenth and early eighteenth centuries was Johann Bernhard Fischer von Erlach (1656–1723), who was born at Graz, the capital of the old Austrian duchy and crown-land of Styria, south-west of Vienna. From 1680 to 1685 he studied in Rome and north Italy, and although he was in practice before he went to Italy, nothing can be definitely attributed to him before 1687, and his first major work was the University Church at Salzburg, where he also designed the Holy Trinity Church. Most of his work was done in Vienna, and the Hofburg, in particular the Imperial Library, shows his masterly handling of great decorative themes. The façade of the Chancellery, like that of the summer Palace of Schönbrunn, has a tranquil dignity, very different from the urgently decorative quality of the Palace of the Hungarian Bodyguard with its groups of sculpture over the coupled Doric columns of the entrance, the carved keystones of the arched windows on the first floor and the figures above their curved pediments: Corinthian pilasters ascend through the first and second storeys, and above the entablature is the pediment with its tympanum filled with carved figures. Dr. Lanchester has said that "Fischer von Erlach possessed, in common with the leading men of his time, the capacity for fusing the arts into a consistent design which is characteristic of some, though not all, of the culminating periods in the art of architecture. In the finest work of the Baroque no dividing line can be found between architecture and sculpture as the one flows insensibly into the other."[166] This capacity is illustrated by the Palace of the Hungarian Bodyguard and many other examples, in particular the doorway of the Liechtenstein Palace, the façades of the Schönborn Palace and the Ministry of Finance in Vienna, and the interior of the Karlskirche, where the architect displays such easy control over decorative features. German and Austrian Baroque has a solid magnificence that does not always avoid corpulence; but the work of Fischer von Erlach was never touched by any suggestion of grossness.

The Baroque phase of the Renaissance assumed variously fantastic forms in Central Europe, and an example of the tawdry complexities the style occasionally engendered is provided by the church that forms the central part of the great Benedictine Abbey at Einsiedeln in Switzerland. A staid, dull classic façade dates from the eighteenth century, and includes monastery, college and church in its impressive length. Within, the church is well proportioned, but its blanched white walls are smothered with gilded scrollwork, and the whole interior is overcrowded with Rococo ornamental extravagances. The paintings on the ceiling carry their aggressive realism to the point of detaching clouds, which float away from the gilded frames to impinge on the curves of the tall arches. In the Sanctuary there are pilasters of Sienna marble, enriched with panels of purple marble, the hue of bruised flesh, enclosed in writhing gilded frames; and the most famous spectacle of the church, the Chapel of the Black Virgin, resembles an enlarged black marble clock case. Most of the ornamental indiscretions have been committed by devout hands; the same tributes of the faithful may be seen in many Italian churches where there is a careless if vulgar gaiety about such extraneous adornments, but at Einsiedeln they are merely dull and the beauty of the church has been defaced. The intrusion of Renaissance ornamental features to the detriment of architectural character is exemplified by the interior of the Storkykran, or Great Church, dedicated to St. Nicholas, at Stockholm, where Baroque carving emphasises the individual richness of pulpit and canopy, screen and stalls, which disrupt the austere lines of the piers and pointed arches. (See illustration on page 159.)

We have said that although Baroque was acceptable in Catholic Belgium, it was rejected in Protestant Holland on religious rather than aesthetic grounds,

The University Church at Salzburg, by Fischer von Erlach (1656–1723). This example of Austrian Baroque illustrates the command architects of the middle period of the Renaissance exercised over the decorative features with which their buildings were lavishly embellished. Within, the church is disappointing, over-powered by ornate decoration, which detracts from the dignity its loftiness and tall Corinthian columns and pilasters could have conferred.

though there are a few isolated examples of the style; but before the advent of Baroque, the Renaissance was luxuriantly interpreted in the Low Countries, with results similar to the early developments in France, but free from the torpid simulation of Italian ornamentation of the French transitional period, for classical motifs were adopted and used with a picturesque prodigality unknown in France. Dutch civic and domestic architecture of the sixteenth and seventeenth centuries is characterised by a robust inventiveness, sometimes

The Town Hall, Haarlem, originally a Gothic Palace, was largely rebuilt in 1620.
The classical features that have been grafted on to the mediaeval building are
in detail, and finer and far more restrained than the exuberant façade of the Town
Hall at Leyden, built some forty years earlier. (See opposite page.)

boisterous, and occasionally coarse in detail. It was the architecture of an
industrious, independent, commercial people; creating wealth by trade, fond
of display, and impatient of control or interference. Control and interference
came from Spain, and the Spanish Netherlands rebelled, fought and defeated
the greatest military power in the world, and in 1609, after a long war in
which the Dutch won and kept command of the sea, a twelve years' truce
was concluded—a face-saving device for Spain—which recognised the independence of the Netherlands and acknowledged their right to trade in Spanish
waters. Stubborn, resourceful and impatient of restraint, the Dutch were averse
to abiding by any rules or laws that were not of their own making, and their
valiant disrespect for regulation is apparent in the way their architects handled
the classic orders. The Spanish occupation left its mark lightly, not indelibly,
as might have been expected from those savagely intent champions of Catholic
orthodoxy, and, paradoxically, it was an Oriental and not a Christian influence
that Spain disseminated. Moorish ornamental flourishes adorn many spires
and towers in Holland. Late in the seventeenth century, Dutch trade with the
Far East introduced other Oriental features, such as the bulbous dome.

There are various examples of the vivacious interpretation of the orders,
and one of the liveliest is the Town Hall at Leyden (1579), where the Ionic
order is treated with a levity that must have been as shocking to orthodox

The Town Hall, Leyden, built in 1579. The scrolls which extend the face of the gable laterally, form a pyramid, which is linked to a base by the external stairway. The façade is an animated medley of scrolls and strapwork, sculptured figures, masks and Ionic pilasters, and, rising from all this vivacious froth of ornamental features, are seven obelisks, which mark the ascent of the gable and provide it with a finial.

Vitruvians as the reformed beliefs were to heresy-hunting Spanish Inquisitors. The façade presents an animated medley of scrolls, strapwork, Ionic pilasters, sculptured figures and masks, and a richly ornamented gable, with seven obelisks marking its ascending steps. A slender octagonal wooden spire has Moorish characteristics. (See page 233.) Another, though more restrained example, is the Town Hall at Haarlem, where classical features have been grafted on to a Gothic palace. (See page 232.)

In Belgium as in Holland there was great versatility in design and an irrepressible exuberance, which was recorded not only by the buildings with their characteristic regional variations, but in the published works of Jan Vredeman de Vries of Antwerp, whose *Architectura* first appeared in 1563 and was followed by his *Compartimenta* in 1566, both full of subversive ideas about the proportions of the orders and their association with the geometrical intricacies of strapwork. In the tall, comely, brick-built houses of Dutch and Belgian towns the high-pitched roof had a special function, for it not only suited the climate, but was used for storage, as many dwellings were also offices and warehouses. Inside the stepped or scrolled gable a crane was fixed for hoisting goods from the street. Windows were generous in size, and reduced the wall surface to a minimum, and this dominance of the window is well illustrated in the florid façades of the Guild Houses in the Grande Place at Brussels. (See plate 23.) Five of them date from the last decade of the seventeenth century; the Butchers was built in 1720 and the Brewers in 1752. Their aggressive individualism shows a complete disregard for the horizontal unity of the Grande Place. They are squeezed together, their four or five storeys marked by vertical elements which give them a Gothic air of urgent ascent, of upward-striving lines. The prosperity of the fraternities that commissioned them is perhaps a little too obviously proclaimed by the plethora of ornamental features, and the overloaded gables with their pediments, scrolls, finials and obelisks.

The marks of prosperity are conveyed with greater moderation and far more impressively by the Town Hall at Antwerp, where the Gothic verticality of the central portion is contrasted with the bland horizontal lines of the rest of the 300-foot façade. The rusticated ground storey is arcuated, and forms a base for superimposed orders, Doric on the first and Ionic on the second storey, with an open gallery above, and a steep-pitched roof. The central feature, Gothic in feeling, classical in detail and pyramidal in treatment, rises above the roof line to form a tower, flanked by obelisks. The building was designed by de Vriendt, erected in 1565, and shows how traditional forms and the classic orders could be associated without conflict. (See plate 22.) Baroque was introduced from Italy during the seventeenth century, and many of the churches of the Jesuits exhibit the ornate convolutions of the style. The church of St. Michael at Louvain, built for the Jesuits between 1650 and 1666, bears an unmistakable resemblance to the Gesù church at Rome and the church of the Val de Grâce at Paris, but unlike the Italian and French examples, it is ostentatiously overloaded with carved ornament, and the large framed panel below the pediment on the façade gives the design a top-heavy look. Baroque, and later Rococo, led Belgian designers into so many complexities of form that their respect for good proportions was often defeated by their love of opulent decoration.

In Spain the early period of the Renaissance was an admixture of Gothic forms, classical details, and the glittering fantasies of Moorish ornament. There was a jewel-like quality about this early sixteenth century Spanish architecture, which as a style had such decorative richness that it was known as Plateresque, a term derived from the Spanish word *platero*, a silversmith. Many Moorish structures were incorporated in Christian churches, like the Giralda which stands at the north-east corner of Seville Cathedral, and was originally a minaret. The cathedral at Jaen, in southern Spain, is an example of early Renaissance architecture, built from plans made by Pedro de Valdelvira and founded in 1532, though not completed until the eighteenth century. The twin towers and the ornamentation of the façade bear the impress of Moorish influence. In southern Spain especially the exotic inflections of Oriental taste affect the character of classical details, and give them a warmth and richness which were preserved throughout the classical period which followed the Plateresque, when a less flexible approach to design gave buildings greater formality, though they never became austere, for austerity was always rejected by that nation of passionate individualists in the arts.

The comparative simplicity of a great group of buildings like the Escurial is relieved by the picturesque vertical elements, the dome with its flanking towers, and the subordinate towers marking the angles of the frontage. The Escurial, which is some thirty miles north-west of Madrid, was built between 1559 and 1584 on the slopes of the Sierra de Guadarrama, over 3,400 feet above sea-level. The group of buildings on this isolated site consists of a monastery, church, college and a palace. (Plates 24 and 25.) Spanish architects had a fondness for towers, and one of the distinctive features of the larger Renaissance churches is the steeple or attached bell tower, preserving perhaps the memory of the minaret, but certainly endowing such buildings with monumental character.

During the classical period, which began in the middle of the sixteenth century and lasted for about a hundred years, some of the liveliness of the early Renaissance was lost, and this loss of spontaneity is apparent in the grave façades of the Escurial. The discipline of the Roman orders was enforced, and had a slightly numbing effect on design. The vigour that is apparent in the Palace of Charles V at Granada (1527), and other buildings dating from the first half of the sixteenth century, was subdued, and not revived until the Baroque was initiated in Spain by José Churriguera, the architect and sculptor. Baroque released the national genius for decoration, temporarily stifled by the academic classical period, and gave to the churches of Spain and Spanish

The Giralda, which stands at the northeast angle of Seville Cathedral. (See plate 16.) This was originally the minaret of the mosque that stood on the site of the cathedral, and was built in 1196 by Jebir, architect to Yusuf I. The lower part of the tower, to a height of 185 feet, retains its Moorish character, and originally rose to 230 feet, terminating in a platform which supported four huge balls of brass. In 1568 an open bell chamber was added, with diminishing stages above, to the design of Fernando Ruiz, this Renaissance addition making an abrupt break with the delicate Moorish details of the lower part of this graceful tower. The bronze figure which crowns the belfry represents the Faith, and is by Bartolomé Morel. The Giralda is unique, the finest example of its kind in Spain, affording conclusive evidence of the architectural competence and the genius of Moslem Spain.

The cathedral at Jaen, the capital city of an inland province of southern Spain. This example of Spanish Renaissance architecture was founded in 1532, but was not completed until the eighteenth century. The twin towers and the exuberant decoration of the façade bear the mark of Moorish influence.

America their ornate façades and sumptuous interiors. The Baroque period continued until the middle of the eighteenth century, and is sometimes known as the Churrigueresque. Among the best examples of the style are the western façades of the cathedrals at Granada (1667) and Santiago de Compostela (1738).

A few examples only have been selected from Europe to show the national interpretations of the Renaissance, and the characteristics of its three main periods. The architectural achievements of the Renaissance went far beyond the re-establishment of the classic orders and the system of design for which they supplied the rules and proportions. Architects recovered powers that had been lost in the Dark Ages, and imperfectly apprehended during the mediaeval civilisation; imbued with the scientific spirit, they sought broader responsibilities, and often found encouragement through the intelligent patronage of kings, nobles and civic authorities. The urban traditions of Europe were rehabilitated: cities were replanned, occasionally in a piecemeal way, but with a generosity of conception that often resulted in moving beauty; the country-side, no longer overcast by military architecture, was adorned with graceful buildings; and although villages and small towns could still be squalid, the visual environment of Europeans was free from ugliness.

Architecture in the Western world had become identified with the classic orders, as it had been in the Graeco-Roman world. This serene and gracious period was disturbed by the Romantic Movement at the end of the eighteenth century; during the fifty years that followed, informed appraisal of architectural design was decried by artistic demagogues, and amid the emotional incoherencies that followed, the inspiration of the Renaissance expired.

IX

THE RENAISSANCE IN ENGLAND

ENGLISH architecture was not conspicuously influenced by the European Renaissance until the middle years of the sixteenth century. That final phase of the Gothic style, the Perpendicular, still exhibited its rich harmonies of stone and glass and brick in sacred and secular buildings, and this characteristic native style was interrupted by the Renaissance fashions which were adopted with enthusiasm by the nobility. Fashions they were, and fashions they remained for generations, regarded by masons and other craftsmen brought up in the Gothic tradition as an ephemeral eccentricity of aristocratic taste; but before they were Anglicised, they begot some odd, hybrid buildings.

During the first half of the sixteenth century the native style persisted, and some fine examples of its placid, comfortable beauty have survived. The decorative possibilities of wall texture were explored: brickwork was diversified with geometric patterns, and the diaper work of the Tudor builders, often used to enrich the texture, did not invariably follow a regular pattern. Burnt or vitrified bricks were used, laid so that the ends, known as headers, marked the pattern. Windows still followed Perpendicular forms, with slender stone mullions and transomes framing the glass. Among the best examples of early Tudor brick buildings are Cardinal Wolsey's great house at Hampton Court, built between 1515 and 1530, with the north and south wings added later (1532–1536) by Henry VIII, when it had become a royal palace; St. John's College, Cambridge (1511); Sutton Place, Guildford (1523–1525); and many smaller structures, such as Denver Hall, near Downham in Norfolk (1530). These buildings are unmistakably English in character, affected only superficially by foreign ideas; for instance, the terra-cotta medallions of Roman Emperors by Giovanni da Majano at Hampton Court are applied ornaments, without architectural significance, representing Wolsey's tribute to the current

239

The entrance gateway of St. John's College, Cambridge (1511). An outstanding
example of the native English style which preceded the Italianate fashions of the
Early English Renaissance. The use of patterned brickwork gives richness to
the texture of the wall surfaces, and the gateway with its four angle turrets is a
dominating feature.

fashion for employing Italian craftsmen; and the extent of Italian influence
at that time was, with a few exceptions, confined to the use of such embellishments. The most notable exception is the tomb of Henry VII (1512–1518) in
Westminster Abbey, by Pietro Torregiano, the Florentine, who in 1512
contracted to make "well, surely, cleanly, workmanly, curiously, and substan-
tially," for £1,500, a marble tomb with "images, figures, beasts, and other
things, of copper gilt."(167) Although this is an example of Renaissance design
in England, it is not an English interpretation of classical architecture; those
delicate Corinthian angle pilasters and the whole composition of the table tomb
in black marble were conceived by a master craftsman whose native city was
the cradle of the Italian Renaissance. A hundred years passed before anything

Sutton Place, Guildford, Surrey (1523–1525), built for Sir Richard Weston. This shows the entrance to the great hall, in the centre of the south side of the courtyard. Another example of the native English style, which illustrates the increasing attention given to the texture of wall surfaces and the generous amount of space alloted to windows. The influence of the Italian Renaissance is apparent in the terra-cotta which appears in the panel above the doorway.

comparable in purity of design and comprehension of classical proportions and detail could be seen in England. This tentative interest in Italian ideas was not pursued; the taste for antique architecture was as yet unformed, and nearly half a century elapsed before *The First and Chief Groundes of Architecture*, by John Shute, was published, with plates of the classic orders and explanatory letterpress.[168]

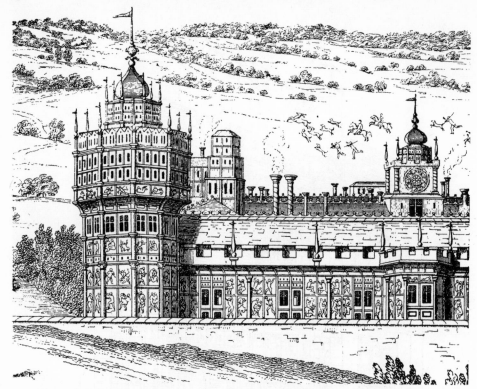

Nonsuch Palace, which Henry VIII began to build in 1538, at Cheam in Surrey, is shown above and on the opposite page. The illustration is a simplified version of the drawing made by Joris Hoefnagel in 1568 and is reproduced from Lysons' *Environs of London* (Vol. I, second edition, 1811). This immense, fantastic building was both unusual and un-English in character. It may have been modelled on the Château de Chambord (see plates 20 and 21), though there is an emphatic clarity in the skyline and octagonal towers of Nonsuch which is absent from the French château, with its agglomeration of conical roofs and angle towers.

Meanwhile it was from contemporary France, from the grandiose court of Francis I, that English ideas of design and composition were derived; and it was not the Italianate whimsies of the French monarch that Henry VIII and his courtiers imitated—it was the work of the largely anonymous French master-masons which inspired their respectful emulation. That large, unusual and un-English palace of Nonsuch, which Henry VIII built at Cheam in Surrey, was probably modelled on the Château de Chambord, which was still being built when Nonsuch was begun. In some ways, Nonsuch with its huge angle towers and pinnacles and cupolas was an architectural freak: Joris Hoefnagel's drawing of its fantastic façade shows how dissimilar it was from the traditional English style, how extravagantly different from its French prototype. It is

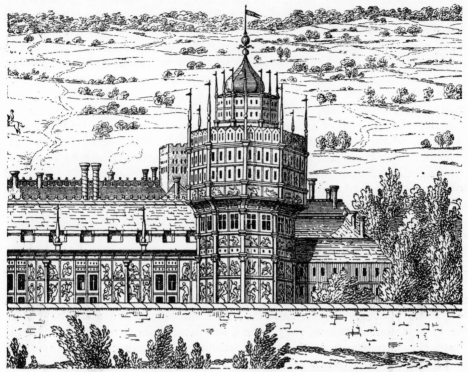

Continuation of the view of Nonsuch Palace. The octagonal towers that flanked the façade splayed outwards as they rose above the roof line of the main building, and the broad upper part contained many pavilions, and these terminated in pointed roofs, from which several pinnacles rose. Nonsuch was an essay in grandeur, unrelated to the native English style of the late fifteenth and early sixteenth centuries, and only acknowledging the infiltration of classic architecture by the character of the external and internal ornament. The palace was demolished about 1670.

known that Toto del Nunziata, an Italian artist, was employed, and it is likely that other foreign craftsmen contributed to its ornamental character. There was nothing like it anywhere else in the country, and its shape was so decorative that it was used as an inlaid ornamental motif on the fronts of chests, which were known as Nonsuch chests. "The Palace consists of two courts," wrote John Evelyn, who visited it in 1666, "of which the first is of stone, castle-like, by the Lord Lumleys (of whom it was purchased), the other of timber, a Gothic fabric, but these walls incomparably beautiful." (*Diary*, January 3rd, 1665–1666.) Pepys, who saw it a few months earlier, noted that "all the house on the outside [was] filled with figures of stories, and good painting of Rubens' or Holben's doing. And one great thing is, that most of the house is covered, I mean the post, and quarters in the walls, with lead, and gilded." (*Diary*, September 21st, 1665.) Nonsuch ultimately passed into the hands of one of Charles II's rapacious mistresses, Barbara Palmer, Duchess of Cleveland, and was pulled down.

An earlier example of French influence on Tudor architecture was the Royal Palace at Shene, as Richmond in Surrey was formerly called, which occupied an area of ten acres between the Green and the Thames. The palace was largely destroyed during the Commonwealth, but several pictorial records exist, and they show a tall structure, with twelve towers, raising their crowns and vanes above the battlements of a large, irregular, three-storeyed brick building. Like Nonsuch, which was begun thirty-seven years later, Richmond Palace is an exceptional building, though its marked Gothic features relate its design to the English traditional style; only those gay, slender rounded and octagonal towers, with the lead crowns flaring up from their summits, assert their foreign origin. (See opposite page.)

The first half of the sixteenth century was the prelude to the English Renaissance, which has two main divisions: the Early Renaissance, covering the Elizabethan and Jacobean periods, and the Late, extending from 1625 to 1830, and including the Stuart and Georgian periods, and the Baroque, Palladian and Neo-Classic schools of design. At first England, like France, passed through a phase of resistance to the new notions about architecture that came from Italy, and although English builders began their resistance much later than the French master-masons, they were if anything more persistently stubborn. Many people, particularly those with serious minds, deprecated the new and fanciful ideas that were being introduced by young noblemen who had travelled in Italy. From that country they imported, according to William Harrison (1534–1593), many highly undesirable things, such as "meere atheisme, infidelitie, vicious conversation, & ambitious and proud behaviour, whereby it commeth to passe that they return fare worsse men than they went out."[169] The manners, morals and fashionable quirks and foibles of those well-travelled aristocrats were condemned in that popular and much-quoted couplet:

"The Englishman Italianate
Is the Devil incarnate."

The preliminary flirtations of the English ruling class with the new Italianate architecture followed the spiritual, social and economic revolution that began after the old, supposedly chivalrous aristocracy had committed class suicide in the Wars of the Roses, when a new business-like king reigned, and England entered upon a period of prosperity, arbitrarily and inequitably allotted, so that the mediaeval pattern of society was destroyed. The new, rich mercantile class which came into power ended the social traditions and usages of the Middle Ages, and finally abandoned the native style of domestic architecture which had achieved such matchless perfection by the opening of the sixteenth century. The new architecture to which they turned was thought of as Italian:

The Palace built at Sheen on the south bank of the Thames, for Henry VII, completed in 1501, and called Richmond Palace. It was built on the site of the Royal manor, known as the Palace at "Kynge's Shene," which had been destroyed by fire in 1497; Sheen or Shene was the old name of Richmond in Surrey, and it was changed by Henry VII, the former Earl of Richmond, a title taken from the town in Yorkshire of that name. The engraving reproduced above is based on the drawing made by Anthonis van den Wyngaerde in 1562, though it varies in detail. The Palace was built of brick about a courtyard, and was distinguished by its tall, narrow towers: it retained some of the features of the mediaeval castle, the three storeys rising to a line of battlements. Although, like Nonsuch, it is an exceptional building, its kinship with the traditional English style is obvious: it was not a piece of individual, ornate extravagance.

it was regarded primarily as a fashion, not as a revival of Roman rules and methods of building, for England, unlike most of the European countries, had no visible links with the Roman Empire: there were no majestic ruins, no striding aqueducts or great amphitheatres, triumphal arches or forsaken temples. Apart from the walls of Silchester, a few massive pieces of Roman masonry at Leicester and Wroxeter, nothing survived above ground to indicate that Britain, like France and Spain, had once been a Roman province. The antiquary John Leyland (1506–1552) recorded a visit to the site of Silchester; but such fragmentary remains gave no hint of the form or significance of classical architecture. The Roman orders returned to England after an interval of some eleven hundred years: the last great building erected in the province of Britain had been the temple to Nodens at Lydney in A.D. 365: so the orders came back as foreign and unfamiliar shapes, and as such were likely to be condemned by a proudly insular people whose aversion to foreigners was proverbial. Since the fourteenth century England had stood outside the main stream of European civilisation; with the rise of the Tudor monarchy, the influence of the Continent was greatly diminished, and when that influence was partly reinstated in terms of architecture, it provoked resentment, misunderstanding and active resistance. Perhaps English builders were more consistently resolute individualists than the French master-masons; but it is certain that although great houses were built, and architects were responsible for their design, the architect as a professional man did not come to effective maturity until the seventeenth century, and then he was very often a gifted amateur.

Throughout the sixteenth century houses were built and decorated and furnished on a lavish scale, though traditional methods of building with timber framing persisted, as Harrison recorded. "The ancient manours and houses of our gentlemen," he wrote, "are yet, and for the most part, of strong timber, (in framing whereof our carpenters have beene and are worthilie preferred before those of like science among all other nations). Howbeit such as be latelie builded, are comonlie either of bricke or hard stone, (or both;) their roomes large and comelie, and houses of office further distant from their lodgings. Those of the nobilitie are likewise wrought with bricke and hard stone, as provision may best be made; but so magnificent and statelie, as the basest house of a baron dooth often match (in our daies) with some honours of princes in old time. So that if ever curious building did flourish in England, it is in these our years, wherein our workmen excell, and are in a manner comparable with skill with old *Vitruvius*, (*Leo Baptisa*), and *Serlo*."[170]

Curious building certainly did flourish in England during the reigns of Elizabeth I and James I, though a reaction set in against the almost oppressive magnificence of the late Elizabethan period, and the opening sentence of Francis Bacon's essay "On Building" is a sober plea for utility. "Houses," he wrote, "are built to live in and not to look on; therefore let use be preferred before uniformity except when both may be had." This was an attack on extravagance and the symmetrical composition of buildings, a plea for the comfortable, haphazard agglomerations that satisfied the basic needs of indoor life; perhaps it was also a suggestion that the lessons of the Renaissance, as yet ill-digested and expressed in a faltering, tentative manner, were best forgotten. English builders were certainly not comparable with Vitruvius and the Italian masters, as Harrison suggested; for the classic orders were not used with understanding and ease, and although *The First and Chief Groundes of Architecture*, by John Shute, published in 1563 with later editions in 1579, 1584 and 1587, was an admirably clear exposition of the character and proportions of the orders, it was from the Low Countries that the Elizabethan architects derived their ideas of design, and a complex and often coarse Flemish style was impressed upon much of their work. An intricate system of surface ornamentation was introduced, known as strapwork, which consisted of interlacing bands and scrolls, enriched with diamond and lozenge-shaped patches, shields,

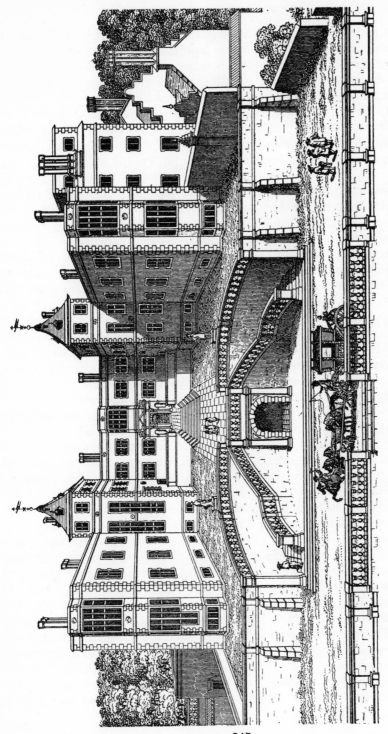

Wimbledon House, Surrey, begun in 1588 for Thomas Cecil. The drawing is reproduced from Lysons' *Environs of London* (Vol. I, second edition, 1811), and is copied from an engraving by Henry Winstanley, made in 1678, when the house was owned by the Earl of Danby. Wimbledon was probably the first large house to be built on an H-plan, and it became the prototype of many of the great houses of the late sixteenth and early seventeenth centuries. It was demolished early in the eighteenth century.

cartouches and shells. This was used with little restraint, almost as though it was cut from paper and pasted over the façades of buildings; and in rooms and galleries it sprawled along the plaster friezes above the wooden panelling, and covered the ceilings. Mingled with this riot of decoration, were snippets of classical ornament, applied as decorative features, unrelated to the composition of the building, and occasionally disrupting its elevation. An example of the disruptive influence of such features is the porch at Kirby Hall, Northamptonshire (1572), which was probably the work of Thomas Thorpe, the Northamptonshire mason, and father of John Thorpe. Many houses are attributed to this John Thorpe (*c.* 1563–1655), largely because a book of his drawings has survived, of which many were records of well-known houses, built in his lifetime or earlier. He was employed in the Office of Works, which he entered about 1583, and remained there for some eighteen years, but it is doubtful whether he was a practising architect.

Robert Smythson (? 1536–1614), the most accomplished English architect of the Elizabethan period, was concerned with the building of such great houses as Hardwick Hall, Wollaton, Worksop Manor and Longleat. Hardwick Hall, in Derbyshire, built between 1590 and 1597, is rectangular in plan, with projecting bays, rising through four storeys, and terminating in pierced scroll-work, with the initials E.S., for Elizabeth, Countess of Shrewsbury. These bays form towers which break the skyline above the third storey: they have large, generous windows, which are repeated in the façade, and the popular rhyme, "Hardwick Hall, more glass than wall," is justly descriptive. This gaunt building of grey stone has broken away from the native English style without much outward dependence upon classic architecture, for it is markedly different from Longleat, where superimposed orders are used for the pilasters on the bays—Tuscan, Ionic, and Corinthian—and a Tuscan porch supports a broken pediment; it is different too from Wollaton Hall, where a profusion of classical detail is used, like the strapwork on the top of the flanking towers, purely as surface decoration.

Montacute House in Somerset, completed in 1599, recaptures some of the comfortable good looks of the early Tudor houses; it is free from the bleakness of Hardwick and the fussy frills of Kirby, and its concession to the classic idiom is the delicate balustrade, broken by curved Flemish gables, which terminates its upper storey. Built for a prosperous lawyer, Edward Phelips, it basks in the sunlight of the West Country, a home designed for comfort and pleasure and not for grandeur.

The spacious houses of the sixteenth century had lost all traces of mediaeval lay-out; buildings were no longer grouped round a courtyard: the shape of the house, its mass as a building, could be seen and its proportions appraised: the great hall had ceased to be the core of the house, with smaller apartments adjoining it: instead, each floor was divided into rooms of various sizes and shapes, lit by large windows, each with its fireplace, which led to a

Hardwick Hall, Derbyshire, built between 1590 and 1597 to the design of Robert Smythson. This shows a marked departure from the native English style that distinguished the early years of the sixteenth century, though it exhibits little outward dependence upon classic architecture. The windows of the projecting bays ascend through four storeys and are virtually glazed towers: great expanses of glass dominate the façade, justifying the popular rhyme: "Hardwick Hall, more glass that wall." (From *Building for Daylight*, by Richard Sheppard and Hilton Wright.)

proliferation of chimneys. Harrison has described how astonishing this seemed to the older generation of men in the middle years of the century. "There are old men yet dwelling in the village where I remaine," he wrote, "which have noted three things to be marvellouslie altered in England within their sound remembrance. . . . One is, the multitude of chiminies latelie erected, wheras in their yoong daies there were not above two or three, if so manie, in most uplandith townes of the realme (the religious houses, & manour places of their lords alwaies excepted, and peradventure some great personages) but ech one made his fire against a reredosse in the hall, where he dined and dressed his meat."[171]

Montacute House, Somerset, completed in 1599, has the same air of deep, settled comfort that characterised early sixteenth century houses. Apart from the delicate balustrade that terminates the upper storey, it makes no external concessions to classic architecture: Flemish influence is apparent in the gables which break the balustrade. It is pre-eminently a home, not a show place built to proclaim magnificence: it caters modestly for the comfort and pleasure of its owner, who was a prosperous Elizabethan lawyer, Edward Phelips. Compare this accomplished design with Hardwick Hall on page 249 and Wimbledon House on page 247.

The open fireplace, and the love of the fireside, have been formative influences on the design and character of English houses since the fifteenth century, and Sir Henry Wotton in his paraphrase of Vitruvius, which he published in 1624 under the title of *The Elements of Architecture*, quotes a note from Palladio "who observeth that the *Ancients* did warm their Rooms with certain secret *Pipes* that came through the Walls, transporting heat (as I conceive it) to sundry parts of the House from one common *Furnace*; I am ready to baptize them *Cali-ducts*, as well as they are termed *Venti-ducts*, and *Aquae-ducts*, that convey Wind and Water; which whether it were a custom or a delicacy, was surely both for thrift, and for use, far beyond the German *Stoves*; and I should prefer it likewise before our own fashion, if the very sight of a fire did not adde to the *Room* a kind of *Reputation*. . . . "(172)

Sir Henry Wotton begins his essay with a statement that has been repeated ever since. "In architecture," he wrote, "as in all other operative arts, the *End* must direct the *Operation*. The *End* is to build well. *Well-building* hath three Conditions, *Commodity, Firmness*, and *Delight*." The second part of his essay opens with these words: "Every Man's proper Mansion House and Home, being the Theater of his Hospitality, the Seat of Self-fruition, the Comfortablest part of his own Life, the noblest of his Sons Inheritance, a kind of private Prince-dome; Nay, to the Possessors thereof, an Epitomie of the whole World; may well deserve by these Attributes, according to the degree of the Master, to be decently and delightfully adorned."

The English loved their homes: they preferred orderliness to extravagance, never permitting fashion to interfere with basic comforts or to become too fantastical; and in architecture, and its ancillary arts and crafts, they absorbed foreign ideas, anglicised them, and at length evolved a domestic and civic architecture that employed the classic orders with felicitous grace.

The first architect in England who recognised the classic orders as a system of design, who comprehended their rules and employed them with a thorough knowledge of their proportions, was Inigo Jones (1573–1652). The son of a Smithfield cloth-worker, he was born in London; but where and how he was educated is not known, though it seems certain that he had visited Italy before the first reference to him was recorded in 1603, when his name appeared in the household accounts of the Earl of Rutland, where he is described as a picture-maker. He was a superb and creative draughtsman, and in learning to draw had liberated his ideas from the correct but rather stilted draughtsmanship of his contemporaries. He visited Italy again in 1613–1614, in the suite of Lord and Lady Arundel, where the work of Palladio provided an inspiring subject for study, in particular the buildings at Vicenza. A copy of Palladio's *I quattro libri dell' Architettura* annotated by Inigo Jones is one of the important sources of information about him, and may have fostered the popular belief that it was from Palladio that he drew all his ideas as an architect. Undoubtedly the great Italian's work helped to enlarge his understanding of the possibilities of the orders, but Inigo Jones sought out the antique originals, and from first-hand knowledge of Roman buildings and monuments he attained the consummate mastery of classic architectural design which is apparent in all his surviving work.

His genius first found expression in designing settings for the magnificent masques which were staged for the entertainment of the Court of James I, and he impressed many potential patrons with his fertility of invention and

The Sessions Hall at Woodbridge, Suffolk, with the Corn Market below, erected in the centre of Market Hill. It was built in 1587, and is of brick. As in Montacute House, shown opposite, the gable shows Flemish influence.

Left: The Banqueting House, Whitehall, London (1619–1621), designed by
Inigo Jones: the earliest and perhaps
the most accomplished piece of classic
building in England which reveals not
only the genius of the architect but
the re-birth of a national style. "For
this architect's buildings," as Stanley
C. Ramsey has said, "were not merely
Italian transcripts, but were as
English as the stone of which they
were built."

Lindsey House, Lincoln's Inn Fields, London, the only part built of a large scheme
designed by Inigo Jones, and erected in 1640–1642. This first, lucid phase of the
English Renaissance, which followed the indecisive experiments of the sixteenth
century, when the work of Inigo Jones revealed the significance of the classic
orders, was curtailed by the Civil War, which curbed and finally destroyed
Royal patronage, the only form of patronage at that time which could have
encouraged town planning and building on a large scale.

The piazza in Covent Garden, designed by Inigo Jones, with St. Paul's Church flanked by new classical buildings, in contrast with the huddle of mediaeval houses in the background. Reproduced from part of an engraving made by Wenceslaus Hollar.

architectural knowledge. He transformed the character of the English theatre; for the stage, as he saw it, should not remain as an arena or an elevated platform, but should become a moving picture; and for that picture he contrived an ample frame, thus following an Italian prototype—the Teatro Olimpico, at Vicenza, designed by Palladio and completed by Scamozzi.

After his return from Italy in 1614, Inigo Jones was appointed Surveyor of Works to the King. He was now launched upon his architectural career. Three years later he designed the Queen's House at Greenwich, which was not completed until 1635. Early in 1619 the Banqueting House in Whitehall had been burnt down, and as the rest of the palace was in a deplorable state of disrepair, the Surveyor of Works was ordered to prepare plans for a new palace. He submitted two designs, and of these the second was of stupendous dimensions and overwhelming grandeur. Had it been built, it would have outshone every other royal palace in Europe, not only by its scale, but by the nobility of its lines. Of this ambitious plan a section only was built, the Banqueting House, which was apparently one of four similar sections, which were to form one of the subsidiary buildings of a great court, 800 feet by 400 feet, double the size of the Louvre. One of the principal façades of the Palace would have faced the Thames, with St. James's Park for its western boundary. He worked on plans for Lincoln's Inn Fields, for he was appointed as one of the Commissioners in 1618, but only a small part of his scheme was carried out, and Lindsey House, which is all that now survives to illustrate the faultless beauty of the project, was not built until 1640–1642. (See page 252.) The confident vitality of everything he designed swept away the indecisions and hesitant fumbling of the Early period of the English Renaissance, and established instead a new architecture, formal but flexible, expressed through the Roman orders. He was the progenitor of the urbane beauty that for two centuries distinguished English architecture and all the arts and crafts that served it. His buildings asserted their national character in contrast with the attempts to anglicise Italianate fashions, made by his contemporaries and immediate forerunners. There is a world of difference between reciting the alphabet and spelling words with it; and Inigo Jones learned not only how to spell, but had much to say, a lesson to impart, a doctrine of unity and order to proclaim.

He did not lack patrons, and his work and example conferred new dignities upon English domestic building, but they were not alien dignities. A profound sense of civic responsibility is apparent in all his designs for houses; he respected the character of the street and the compact relationships between buildings that preserve horizontal unity and bring spaciousness to thoroughfares; and some of his country houses appear to be components of some gracious city. Inigo Jones could see the potential nobility of the town: like Wren, he saw the urbane orderliness that awaited it; like Wren, he was tantalised by opportunities of splendid promise, which were only partly fulfilled. Those two great men had to deal with Stuart minds and weaknesses: those scholarly but unstable minds always supplied discerning encouragement; but the encouragement generally lacked financial backing.

Although Inigo Jones was actively engaged in creative work until his death in 1651, his last years were darkened by a sense of shrinking opportunities for public work, and by the hostility of the Puritans to art. The brilliant Court had vanished, the King had been executed, the institution of regicide had been condoned by a militant moral earnestness, and it was a sad time for people with creative gifts. If the Puritan Commonwealth had survived Cromwell, the English Renaissance might have been arrested in its development; all the enlightenment brought to architecture by Inigo Jones eclipsed by the glum godliness of art-proof fanatics; and that gifted young man, Christopher Wren, who was already distinguishing himself at Oxford, might have remained throughout his life a professor of astronomy.

John Evelyn, when visiting Oxford in the summer of 1654, met Wren, "That miracle of a youth." He described a dinner party with "That most obliging and universally-curious" Dr. Wilkins at Wadham College, and recorded that "He had above in his lodgings and gallery variety of shadows, dyals, perspectives, and many other artificial, mathematical, and magical curiosities, a way-wiser,

The south porch of St. Mary the Virgin, Oxford, 1637. Flemish influence is apparent, for many of the mannerisms of the Low Countries were adopted by English masons in the late sixteenth and early seventeenth centuries. The work was executed, and probably designed, by John Jackson, a master craftsman. The design has some affinities with the Baroque style, though the English rendering of Baroque did not appear until the late seventeenth century.

a thermometer, a monstrous magnet, conic and other sections, a ballance on a demi-circle, most of them his owne and that prodigious young scholar Mr Chr. Wren, who presented me with a piece of white marble, which he had stain'd with a lively red very deepe, as beautiful as if it had ben natural." (*Diary*, July 13th, 1654.)

"Universally-curious" was a description that fitted many learned and cultivated people in the middle years of the seventeenth century: it was certainly applicable to Wren, whose range of intellectual and scientific interests was as wide as that of Leonardo da Vinci, though, unlike the Florentine, Wren was not an executant craftsman. To Evelyn he was "that incomparable genius my worthy friend Dr Christopher Wren" (*Diary*, October 24th, 1664); and incomparable genius he certainly was, with a mind that ranged over all learning, and, happily for England, a taste for architecture. His aptitude for applying scientific facts to the mechanical amplification of life anticipated, in theory, many modern inventions. That casual record, published by his grandson in 1750, and entitled *Parentalia*, includes a "Catalogue of New Theories, Inventions, Experiments, and Mechanick Improvements, exhibited by Mr Wren at the First Assemblies at Wadham College in Oxford for Advancement of Natural and Experimental Knowledge." The following items indicate not only the agility of Wren's intelligence, but his practical character: "To build in the Sea, Forts, Moles, etc." "Ways of Submarine Navigation," "A Speaking Organ, articulating Sounds," "A Scenographical Instrument, to survey at one Station," "Several new Ways of Graving and Etching." There are fifty-three items, including "New Designs tending to Strength, Convenience, and Beauty in Building." Robert Hooke (1635–1703), that accomplished scientist, said of Wren: "Since the time of Archimedes there scarce ever met in one man in so great perfection such a mechanical hand and so philosophical a mind."

In 1657, at the age of 24, he was appointed Professor of Astronomy at Gresham College. On November 28th, 1660, the Royal Society was founded after one of Wren's lectures at Gresham College. In 1661 Wren became Savilian Professor of Astronomy at Oxford, and in that year the King sent for him to act as Assistant to the Surveyor-General. A pleasant gentleman, a very minor poet named Sir John Denham, held the office of Surveyor-General, and he had already one assistant, John Webb, who had served Inigo Jones in that capacity and had hoped to succeed him; but Denham had been an active Royalist in the Civil War, had helped the young Duke of York to escape from England, lived with the exiled Court in Holland, and, with Lord Crofts, had raised £10,000 in Poland for Charles II. At the Restoration in 1660 he was rewarded for those services by a knighthood and the office which should have gone to Webb, who was technically qualified to hold it, for Denham's knowledge of architecture hardly exceeded a polite interest: as Webb observed in a tactless memorial to the King about the appointment, Denham might, in common with most gentlemen, have some acquaintance with the theory of architecture, but was without practical experience and would have to depend upon and employ an assistant. Wren's knowledge was also largely theoretical, and to the end of his long life he exercised his talents with the untrammelled taste of an amateur. Until he was over thirty he devoted nearly all his creative powers to scientific studies and pursuits. Inigo Jones had spiritual affinities with mediaeval England; he was a Catholic, and had been persecuted as such by the Puritans; Wren belonged intellectually to the new age of scientific curiosity and commercial enterprise, which seemed to hold such abundant promise for mankind three hundred years ago.

Mid-seventeenth century England was in an experimental mood, not only in politics, which led to such startling innovations as regicide, but in architecture, industrial methods, and mechanics. There was widespread interest in the invention of spring- and weight-driven devices, and machines operated by

Monmouth House, on the south side of Soho Square, built for the Duke of Monmouth and demolished in 1773. The clumsy upper storey suggests the influence of some Flemish copybook. The view of Soho Square on pages 280 and 281 is taken from the courtyard of Monmouth House. (From *Antiquities of London*, by John Thomas Smith, 1791.)

The Customs House, formerly the Exchange, at King's Lynn, Norfolk, designed by Henry Bell, and built in 1683 at the expense of Sir John Turner. Henry Bell was an alderman and an architect, probably the son of Henry Bell who was twice Mayor of Lynn, and he was elected to that office himself in 1692 and 1703. He was an amateur of architecture, not a professional man; he was also an engraver; and his architectural work owes much to the influence of Wren. (See examples of civic buildings by local architects on pages 278 and 292.)

gravity. It was the unrecognised prelude to the machine age. In 1631 the Clockmakers Company of London was granted its charter by Charles I, and the great period of English clock-making began in the second half of the century, distinguished by the works of such masters as Thomas Tompion (1639–1713), Daniel Quare (? 1632–1724) and the famous clock-making families—the Easts, Ellicotts, Fromanteels, and Knibbs. Evelyn records several examples of the mechanical gifts of English craftsmen, and in particular describes a door lock that he examined in the gate-house of Broad-Hinton, the seat of Sir John Glanvill, "that for its filing and rare contrivances was a master-piece, yet made by a country blacksmith. But we have seene watches made by another with as much curiositie as the best of that profession can brag of; and not many yeares after, there was nothing more frequent than all sorts of Iron-work more exquisitely wrought and polish'd than in any part of Europ, so as a dore-lock of a tolerable price was esteem'd a curiositie even among forraine princes." (*Diary*, July 16th, 1654.)

Many scientific instruments were developed and improved, and there were advances in the technique of glass-making and ironfounding. Dud Dudley, that vocal and unfortunate iron-master, published his famous though rather misleading work *Metallum Martis* in 1665, though, as Professor Ashton has observed, "there is no valid reason why this Balliol undergraduate, rather than any one of a dozen other projectors of the seventeenth century, should have been singled out for fame."[173] Already the industrial revolution was foreshadowed.

Curiosity was encouraged; natural science was honoured, and men with a philosophic turn of mind no longer sought authority in a library—instead they proved or disproved their theories by devising practical experiments, and in the devising of experiments Dr. Christopher Wren excelled. Some seven pages of Bishop Sprat's *History of the Royal Society* record Wren's intellectual fecundity: the substance of his papers and experiments are included, as the author said, "on the meer consideration of Justice: For in turning over the Registers of the *Society*, I perceiv'd that many excellent things, whose first *Invention* ought to be ascrib'd to him, were casually omitted. . . . [174] Among those excellent things were astronomical and optical instruments. "He has fitted and hung *Quadrants*, *Sextants*, and *Radii*, more commodiously than formerly: *He* has made two *Telescopes*, to open with a joynt like a Sector, by which Observers may infallibly take a distance to half minutes, and find no difference in the same Observation reiterated several times; nor can any warping or luxation of the Instrument hinder the truth of it. *He* has added many sorts of *Retes*, *Screws*, and other devices to *Telescopes*, for taking small distances and apparent Diameters to Seconds. He has made apertures to take in more or less light, as the Observer pleases, by opening and shutting like the Pupil of the Eye, the better to fit Glasses to *Crepusculine Observations*: *He* has added much to the Theory of *Dioptrics*; much to the Manufacture it self of grinding good Glasses. *He* has attempted, and not without success, the making of Glasses of other forms than Spherical: *He* has exactly measur'd and delineated the Spheres of the *Humours* in the Eye, whose proportions one to another were only ghess'd at before. This accurate discussion produc'd the Reason, why we see things erected, and that *Reflection* conduces as much to *Vision* as Refraction."[175]

Some of Wren's discoveries anticipated contemporary industrial and medical techniques. "He has found out perpetual, at least long liv'd lamps, and Registers of Furnaces, and the like, for keeping a perpetual temper, in order to various

St. Paul's Cathedral, London, viewed from the east. Erected
between 1675 and 1710, it is Sir Christopher Wren's greatest
building, and one of the finest Renaissance cathedrals in
Europe. The height from pavement level to the cross above the
lantern is 366 feet. It has a triple dome, and the lantern is
carried by the intermediate conical dome of brick. This is
shown in the section on the right, taken from Pugin's *Principles
of Pointed or Christian Architecture* (1841), who used the diagram
to reinforce his criticism that "the upper part of St. Paul's is
mere imposing show, constructed at a vast expense without any
legitimate reason." The triple dome is carried on eight piers,
and the outer dome rises from a high drum. See interior view
on page 263.

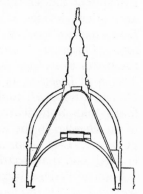

uses; as hatching of Eggs, Insects, production of Plants. . . . ''[176] He also initiated anatomical experiments for injecting liquids into the veins of animals. "Hence arose many new *Experiments*, and chiefly that of *Transfusing Blood*, which the *Society* has prosecuted in sundry instances, that will probably end in extraordinary success."[177] Thousands of lives have been saved by blood transfusion, though few people know that the originator of the technique was the designer of St. Paul's Cathedral.

A mind enriched with such diverse scientific knowledge, habituated to experimental methods of work, and regulated by familiarity with the laws of light and vision, could recruit fresh inspiration for the use of the classic orders. His architectural career did not really begin until he became Denham's assistant, and during the first two years of that association he had no commissions for public works. In 1662 he was appointed to survey old St. Paul's, and the following year work began on his designs for Pembroke Chapel, Cambridge, and the Sheldonian Theatre at Oxford. Before he was 35 he had a large and growing architectural practice, for London was burnt down in 1666, and that disaster gave Wren his greatest opportunity.

In the spring of that year he had returned from an eight months' visit to Paris. There he met and conversed with Bernini, and was given that quick peep at the designs for the Louvre, of which he wrote "I would have given my skin for, but the old reserv'd Italian gave me but a few minutes view . . . I had only time to copy it in my fancy and memory." His visit to France refreshed his ideas and enlarged his stock of knowledge, though he deplored the effect of fashion on contemporary French architecture. This subordination of design to the whims of the modish world he attributed to feminine influence, remarking as women "make here the Language and Fashions, and meddle with Politicks and Philosophy, so they sway also in Architecture; Works of Filgrand, and little Knacks are in great Vogue; but Building certainly ought to have the Attribute of Eternal, and therefore the only Thing uncapable of new Fashions."

The Great Fire of London began on September 2nd, 1666; Wren was ordered by the King to survey the ruined area; and he made and submitted a plan for rebuilding the city. Had it been carried out, London would have had streets capable of graceful expansion, a solvable traffic problem, and an embankment extending from the Temple to the Tower. The opportunity was lost; the difficulties of adjusting the claims of various property owners were insuperable, and the problem was finally put into the hands of the Royal Commissioners and the City Surveyors, of whom Wren was one. Wren built fifty towers and spires which gave London a superb skyline, but spaciousness was denied to the city streets, and his greatest building, St. Paul's, had a mean and muddled environment. The dome of the cathedral still dominates the city; throughout the world it is recognised as a symbol of London, for St. Paul's is one of those great buildings that become imprinted upon the visual memory of mankind.

Within the cathedral, space is shaped and controlled with proficient command of the proportions and details of the Corinthian order. Below the dome, daylight appears to have been fabricated into gracious forms. The atmosphere acquires sombre substance.(178) This may be some trick of optical fancy; possibly the impress of a mind acquainted with optical laws and applying scientific knowledge with the inspiration of an artist. The arches piled upon the piers are calmly powerful: curve melts into curve in a majestic ascent to the lantern. The Gothic cathedral-builders made a stone framework for light working pictorially through coloured glass: Wren designed a temple, far greater in conception than anything Roman, and made daylight work in relation to form instead of through colour; for everywhere in St. Paul's daylight is used to cast shadows for the greater glory of noble shapes, and to touch with brightness the beauty of masses, harmoniously assembled. Only when daylight fails, and the high spaces are dim, does the interior acquire all the solemn mystery of a great church. By day every line interprets the intellectual and classical interests of an age when the character of Heaven had become discreetly indefinite and the minds of many able men were directed towards the improvement of the material world. St. Paul's may be regarded as the great exemplar of the English Baroque style, which was to arise from Wren's work. The decoration of the interior is florid, but is disposed with such taste and judgment that it escapes any suggestion of the bloated profusion that occasionally deformed the interiors of Baroque churches in Europe; and in that accomplished sculptor, Grinling Gibbons, Wren discovered a brilliant collaborator.

Ever since he had been appointed to survey old St. Paul's in 1662, Wren had been considering the rebuilding of the cathedral. At first he advocated a reconstruction of the interior "after a good Roman manner" to harmonise with the western portico added by Inigo Jones and that architect's scheme of exterior refacing, which had been partly completed. After the destruction of the old church by the Great Fire, the need for complete rebuilding was obvious; but even so a committee was formed to attempt some impossible patchwork to the roofless, tottering fabric, and more than a year was wasted before everybody was convinced that clearance of the ruins and a new design for the cathedral were the only solutions.

In his preliminary and final designs for St. Paul's Wren showed his mastery of the "good Roman manner." Classic architecture was his medium; and as his wonderfully varied spires and steeples witness, he was boldly unconventional in associating architectural elements. A few of his city churches were Gothic in manner; and there must have been some compelling reason for his use of a dead architectural language, for although he understood it, he spoke it indifferently. The nobly proportioned Tom Tower (1681–1682) above Wolsey's gateway at Christ Church, Oxford, is a rare example of his sympathetic treatment of Gothic forms, which he used in harmony with the existing Tudor work, though he may have been interpreting some earlier record of the original designs by Wolsey's architects. In rebuilding Hampton Court Palace for

Interior view of St. Paul's Cathedral, showing the piers which support the dome. (See page 260.)

263

William III, he showed no tenderness for Tudor building. The death of William III prevented the new plan for Hampton Court from being carried through completely; had the work been finished, Wolsey's palace would have disappeared.

Wren's activity was stupendous, comparable with that of Mansart in France. St. Paul's was begun in 1675 and finished in 1710. After his appointment as Surveyor-General on Denham's death in 1669 he built fifty-three parish churches, fifty in the city of London, and such secular buildings as Chelsea Hospital, Greenwich Hospital and Kensington Palace. His architecture was conspicuously national; even his palaces, especially Hampton Court, were endowed with an air of hospitable comfort, a note of settled domesticity, unmistakably English. He designed libraries at Trinity College, Cambridge, and at Queen's College, Oxford; and up and down England his work and the example of it consolidated and extended the use of classical architecture as a universally applicable system of design. Inigo Jones, who had first apprehended the immense significance of that system and had elevated the orders from their debased status of mere ornamental trimmings, was the great English preceptor of architectural design; but Wren was the great national architect. When he began his career, England was still in an age of architectural confusion. When he died in 1723, in his ninety-first year, the new architecture that Inigo Jones had first made articulate was alive and fluent and established in town and country.

From the restoration of Charles II to the death of William IV, England enjoyed a golden age of good design, when the architect was the master designer who influenced the form and decoration of everything that went into buildings, nearly everything, indeed, in common use, and jewellers, goldsmiths, silversmiths, coach-builders, carpenters, joiners, cabinet-makers and ironfounders were all familiar with the rules and proportions and ornamental conventions of the classic orders. In that period, the patrons of architecture were animated by a lively and informed interest in the subject—an interest that was never withered by specialisation. It was natural and obvious that an educated gentleman should be an amateur of architecture.

During the opening decades of the eighteenth century architectural design was inclined to be florid. English Baroque, never unduly extravagant, was followed by a period when architectural taste was refreshed and refined by a revival of interest in classical sources. Many architects turned their attention to the works of Palladio, and occasionally chilled and contracted their powers of expression as a result. Before the rise of Palladianism, English Baroque had flowered, and the work of its two great masters, Vanbrugh and Hawksmore, had brought a majestic opulence to the style.

Nicholas Hawksmore (1661–1736) had entered Wren's service when he was 18, and three years later he was a responsible assistant. Before the end of the seventeenth century he was also associated with Vanbrugh, and by 1707 had started his own practice. Within a few years he had built a number of

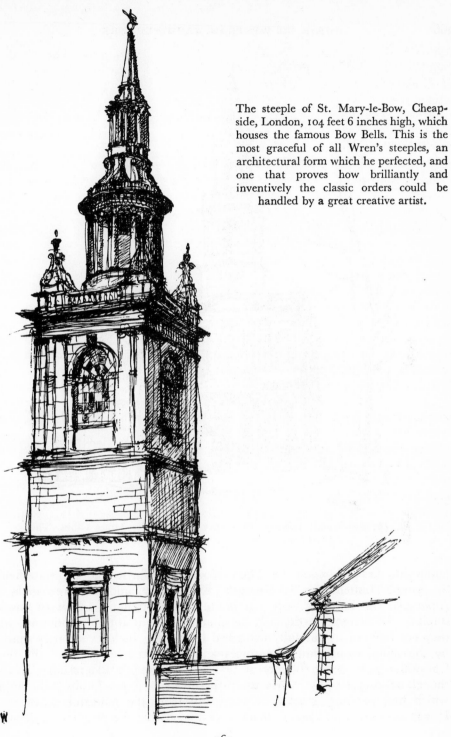

The steeple of St. Mary-le-Bow, Cheapside, London, 104 feet 6 inches high, which houses the famous Bow Bells. This is the most graceful of all Wren's steeples, an architectural form which he perfected, and one that proves how brilliantly and inventively the classic orders could be handled by a great creative artist.

St. Mary-le-Strand, London, 1714–1717, designed by James Gibbs. This shows the semicircular porch on the west front.

noble churches in London: St. Mary Woolnoth; Christ Church, Spitalfields; St. Anne's, Limehouse; St. George's, Bloomsbury, and, at Greenwich, St. Alphege's. Hawksmore's work has boldness and strength, an air of massive stability; his designs, particularly his churches, might appear ponderous, were they not relieved by carefully contrived horizontal shadows, strongly marked by the skilful disposition of cornices and string courses. One of the finest Corinthian porticoes in London is that of St. George's, Bloomsbury, rivalled though not surpassed by St. Martin-in-the-Fields, by James Gibbs (1682–1754), which has, perhaps, greater delicacy, but lacks the powerful character of Hawksmore's design. "It is difficult to define of what the peculiar merit of the

Bloomsbury portico consists," Mr. Goodhart-Rendel has said in his monograph on Hawksmore, "but that merit will not be doubted by any competent critic. It surprises by its Roman air: here surely is one of the temples of Londinium preserved and adapted for Christian use."(179) This Roman affinity, and its pagan implications, were to awaken doubts in the minds of earnest Christians before the end of the eighteenth century about the suitability of classic architecture for sacred edifices. William Woty, in his poem on Church-Langton, published in 1780, voiced those doubts when he complained of St. Paul's,

> " . . . beneath whose ample dome
> No thought arises of the life to come.
> For, tho' superb, not solemn is the place,
> The mind but wanders o'er the distant space,
> Where 'stead of thinking on the GOD, most men
> Forget his presence to remember *Wren*."(180)

No such doubts troubled the patrons, the designers or the congregations of the superb churches built during the reigns of Queen Anne and George I. The English Baroque school was short-lived, but it was unforgettably enriched by the work of Hawksmore, Archer and Vanbrugh. Thomas Archer (*c.*1668–1743) designed the north front at Chatsworth, the seat of the Duke of Devonshire in Derbyshire, and, more expressive of the character of Baroque, St. Philip's at Birmingham (1709–1715), which is now the cathedral of that city.

Of the three exponents of the style, the most distinguished and versatile architect was Sir John Vanbrugh (1664–1726). Like Wren he was an amateur; like Inigo Jones he was concerned with the theatre, although only incidentally as a designer, for he was a successful dramatist, remarkable for his exuberance. His flamboyant personal character is disclosed by his plays and his buildings: he was a master of the grand manner: he enjoyed extravagant flourishes in conduct and magnificence in architecture, and was impelled to take liberties with every art he practised. He was of Flemish descent, born in London, and educated at King's School, Chester, for his family had moved to that city to avoid the plague. At 19 he went to France to complete his education, remaining there for two years. Upon his return he became an ensign in the Army. During another visit to France in 1690 he was arrested at Calais on a charge of espionage, and after being detained at Vincennes was transferred by *lettre de cachet* to the Bastille. During his imprisonment he drafted his play, *The Provoked Wife*, and after his release in 1692 he remained in Paris until he was exchanged, and returned to England. The first of his plays to be staged was *The Relapse, or Virtue in Danger*, which was produced at Drury Lane on Boxing Day, 1696. Its vigorous unseemliness diverted London audiences as much as it outraged the pious Jeremy Collier, who attacked it in his *Short View of the Immorality and Profaneness of the English Stage*. This attack by a sour Puritan was to have an important effect upon the history of English architecture, as it turned public

The south side of Seaton Delaval, Northumberland, designed for Francis Delaval in 1720 by Sir John Vanbrugh. A small country house in the grand manner of which Vanbrugh was a master, and a robust example of English Baroque. A part of the north front is shown opposite.

opinion against Vanbrugh's plays, and diminished his interest in the theatre. Christian Barman, in his study of Vanbrugh, suggests another cause for the transition from dramatist to architect: "It is possible that the designing of the Queen's Theatre, Haymarket (the site for which he acquired in 1703 at a cost of £2,000), may have launched him on his architectural career. . . . "(181)

In 1702 he had been appointed Comptroller of the Royal Works, under Wren. In the following year he wrote to his friend, Jacob Tonson, the bookseller, for a copy of Palladio. The witty playwright, the man of fashion, now nearly 40, was studying the rules of another profession. Not that rules ever restrained the opulent boldness of his imagination. He built with the same disregard for conventional trimming and polishing that characterised his boisterous plays. Unencumbered by excessive technical knowledge, he jotted down fine conceptions of country houses, which grew into masterpieces of radiant stateliness. Without apparent effort, without profound scholarship, but with the eye of an artist, he arranged his stone masses so that from every point of approach some fresh beauty of associated forms was disclosed.

In Castle Howard, which he built for the Earl of Carlisle, the power and freedom of his imagination are fully revealed. The majestic stabilities of that mansion have been called ponderous; but in the garden elevation, where the alleged ponderousness should surely be apparent, the massive effect is relieved by tall arched windows, while fluted Corinthian pilasters are disposed to secure a most harmonious adjustment of horizontal and vertical lines; and everywhere upon the face of the building shadows are trapped so that sunlight underlines and daylight always discloses the perfections of grouping which illustrate Vanbrugh's genius for composition. Blenheim Palace and Castle Howard are the works of a man who invented beautiful shapes and made them accord so exactly with their surroundings that it seems as though he had designed a whole tract of country as well. The character of his work suggests his detach-

The north front of Seaton Delaval, by Sir John Vanbrugh. The use of rusticated Doric columns is a sharp contrast with the portico in the Ionic order on the south front. (See opposite page.) (Reproduced from *Vitruvius Britannicus*, by Colen Campbell. Volume III. London: 1721.)

The temple in the garden of Eastbury in Dorset, designed by Sir John Vanbrugh
for George ("Bubb") Doddington. Eastbury was one of the last great houses
built to Vanbrugh's designs, and this temple, in the form of a Corinthian portico,
was placed at the end of the garden—which was laid out by Charles Bridgeman—
and faced the house. The house, and the buildings in the garden, the temple and
bagnio, were built in 1718. (From *Vitruvius Britannicus*. Vol. III.)

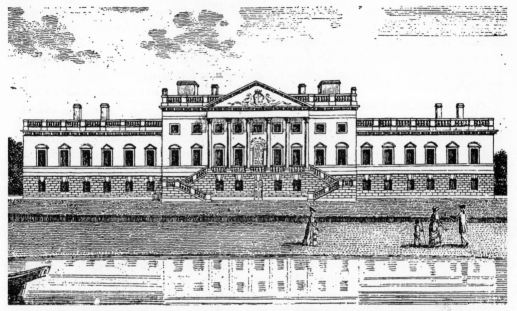

Wanstead House, in Essex, designed by Colen Campbell for Sir Richard Child, and built between 1715 and 1720. (It was demolished in 1822.) This was an impressive block of building, treated in the Palladian manner, with a great portico of six Corinthian columns, rising from above the ground storey, and ascending through the first and second storeys of the central block. (Reproduced from a contemporary print in the author's possession.)

ment from architectural convention; intent upon personal expression, he used the classic orders as media through which coherent form was given to sublime visions of beauty. Castle Howard and Blenheim, and such smaller houses as Seaton Delaval, enabled him to develop his dreaming with a grandeur of manner that was not always appreciated by his contemporaries or by the critics and amateurs of succeeding generations. Nearly half a century after Vanbrugh's death, Horace Walpole subscribed to the popular misconception of his work by saying, " . . . as Vanbrugh dealt in quarries, and Kent in lumber, Adam, our most admired, is all gingerbread, filigraine, and fan-painting." (Letter to Sir Horace Mann, April 22nd, 1775.)

Vanbrugh was an emphatic and independent nationalist in his work. In architecture he spoke Latin with fluent ease, but continued to think in English. Some of his contemporaries and successors imagined that an ability to speak Latin in terms of design absolved them from the fatiguing necessity of thinking at all. This was apparent when the brief flowering of English Baroque was followed by the renewal of interest in the works of Palladio. That earlier admirer of the Italian master, Inigo Jones, had been inspired by his studies to exercise his own imaginative powers with an enlightened confidence; unfortunately many of the architects who practised in the early eighteenth century conspicuously lacked the genius of Inigo Jones, and bartered their imaginative liberty as designers for the unexciting comfort of dependence upon classical precedent, thereby achieving a correct and slightly vacuous formality.

The phase of the English Renaissance which followed this return to the purity of Palladio's interpretation of the orders, became known as Palladian: it began with the second decade of the eighteenth century, and lasted into the 1760's, appealing alike to architects and fashionable leaders of taste, and encouraged by two intellectual noblemen with a passionate interest in architectural design who financed and encouraged the study of classical prototypes. They were Henry Herbert, ninth Earl of Pembroke (1693–1751), known as "the architect earl," and Richard Boyle, third Earl of Burlington (1695–1754), described by Colen Campbell, the sycophantic author of *Vitruvius Britannicus* as "not only a great Patron of all Arts, but the first Architect."[182] These noblemen sought and discovered talent, sent promising young men to Italy, and when they had completed their studies, gave them opportunities to exercise their gifts. William Kent (*c.* 1685–1748) was one of Burlington's protégés. Kent was a Yorkshireman who had been apprenticed to a coach-painter, but he broke his articles and went to London, where he met his first patrons, some Yorkshire gentlemen, who sent him to Rome. There he remained until he was brought back to England in 1719 by Burlington, who lodged him in his own house for several years, and became not only his principal patron but his friend.

A translation of Palladio's *I quattro libri dell' Architettura* was issued in 1715 in two folio volumes, with plates redrawn by Giacomo Leoni, another architect who enjoyed Lord Burlington's patronage. Those plates were severely criticised by Isaac Ware, whose own translation of Palladio appeared in 1737, because Leoni had "thought fit not only to vary from the scale of the originals, but also in many places to alter even the graceful proportions prescribed by this great master, by diminishing some of his measures, enlarging others, and putting in fanciful decorations of his own. . . . "[183]

In 1730 Burlington published his own book of fine engravings made from Palladio's drawings, and Pope expressed his fears that the examples illustrated would be sadly misused.

> "You show us Rome was glorious, not profuse,
> And pompous buildings once were things of use.
> Yet shall, my lord, your just, your noble rules
> Fill half the land with imitating fools;
> Who random drawings from your sheets shall take,
> And of one beauty many blunders make,
> Load some vain church with old theatric state,
> Turn arcs of triumph to a garden gate. . . . "

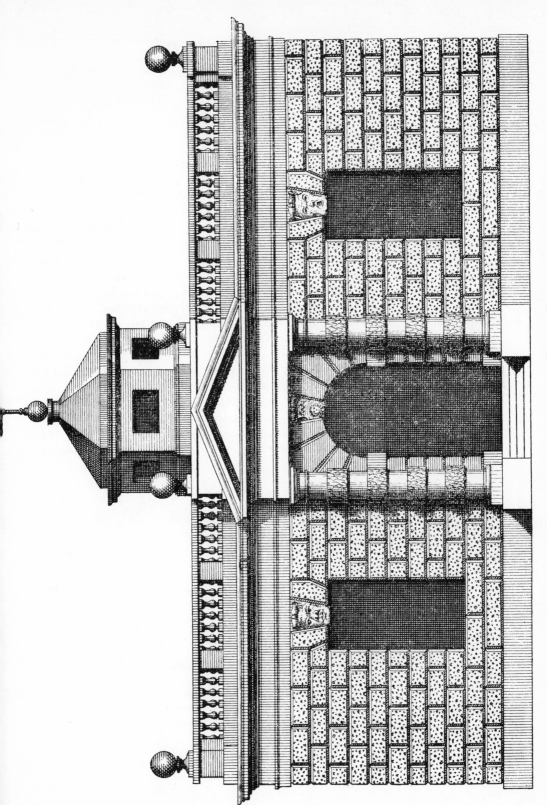

Ebberston Lodge, near Scarborough in Yorkshire, designed for William Thompson in 1718 by Colen Campbell. (From *Vitruvius Britannicus*, Vol. III.)

Those lines have been quoted so often, by nearly every author who has written about Palladian architecture, that they have become almost hackneyed. They are quoted yet again because they show the alert criticism to which architecture was subjected by men whose influence on taste was lively and consistently well-informed. Pope was always ready to castigate folly in building as well as in a good many other activities; so were other men of letters. Long before Pope wrote the moral essay in which those lines occur, Anthony Ashley Cooper, the third Earl of Shaftesbury, had described the enlightened character of the society which architects served in the great century of good design. "The ordinary Man may build his Cottage, or the plain Gentleman his Country-house according as he fancys," he wrote; "but when a great Man builds, he will find little Quarter from the Publick, if instead of a beautiful Pile, he raises, at a vast expence, such a false and counterfeit Piece of Magnificence, as can be justly arraign'd for its Deformity by so many knowing Men in Art, and by the whole *People*, who, in such a Conjuncture, readily follow their Opinion."[184]

There were enough "knowing men in art" to counterbalance the "imitating fools," and the latter, when they did commission buildings, were at least well-mannered, thanks to the universal respect paid to the classic orders. Builders throughout the country followed a familiar system for determining correct proportions, and carried out in local materials a standardised range of designs. Gothic initiative had gradually faded from the building craft, and except in a few districts—notably the Cotswolds—the assimilation of classic forms during three generations had by the beginning of the Georgian period made them commonplace among country craftsmen. They could use those forms with national, and, to some extent, regional variations; for the established

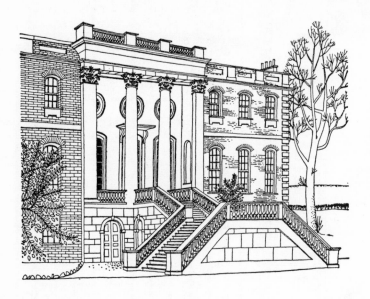

Sudbrooke Lodge, at Petersham, near Richmond, Surrey, built by James Gibbs for the second Duke of Argyll, 1726–1728. *Drawn by David Owen.*

Four early eighteenth century houses on Richmond Green, Surrey, known as Maids of Honour Row. They were built in 1724 to house the Maids of Honour attending the Princess of Wales. *Drawn by A. S. Cook.*

and accepted system of design determined not only the proportions but indicated the appropriate mouldings and ornamentation for nearly everything that was made. Books with plates setting forth details of the orders were part of the equipment of innumerable workshops, and when books on specialised subjects were published, like *The Gentleman and Cabinet-Maker's Director*, by Thomas Chippendale (1754), and *The Chair-Maker's Guide*, by Robert Manwaring (1766), they included (to quote Manwaring's preface), "a Geometrical View of the Five Orders of Columns in Architecture, with a full Explanation. . . . " Chippendale began the preface to the *Director* with these words: "Of all the Arts which are either improved or ornamented by Architecture, that of CABINET-MAKING is not only the most useful and ornamental, but capable of receiving as a great assistance from it as any whatever. I have therefore prefixed to the following designs a short explanation of the five orders. Without an acquaintance with this science, and some knowledge of the rules of Perspective, the Cabinet-Maker cannot make the designs of his work intelligible, nor shew, in a little compass, the whole conduct and effect of the piece. These, therefore, ought to be carefully studied by every one who would excel in this branch, since they are the very soul and basis of his art."

So many vastly different things shared a characteristic elegance; and because of the common origin of their proportions and embellishment, they had a family likeness, no matter how greatly they differed in form and function. Sedan chairs, cream jugs, door knockers, sideboards, gates, railings, fan-lights, cabins on pleasure barges, stern galleries on ships, clock faces and tea-chests were all obviously related. Those regulating proportions, derived from the classic orders, made it possible for designers to borrow extensively from foreign

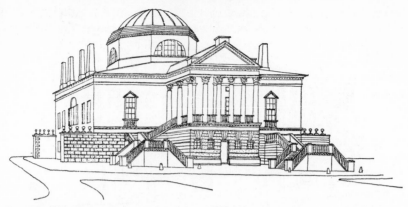

Lord Burlington's ornamental villa at Chiswick, built in 1725 in imitation of
the Villa Capra, Vicenza, by Palladio. The original is illustrated on page 213.
Drawn by David Owen.

fashions, and to incorporate without incongruity the variegated ornamental
eccentricities washed up by those waves of taste—Oriental, Rococo or Gothic—
that periodically engaged the interest of the modish world.

Nothing disturbed the tranquil urbanity of the Georgian scene. "Whether
you drove up to a mansion like Chatsworth, to an ornate palace by Vanbrugh
or a quiet and stately house like Sudbrooke Lodge at Petersham, near Richmond
in Surrey (which James Gibbs built for the Duke of Argyll, 1726–1728), you
were impressed not only by the perfection of the appointments, the refinement
and appropriate placing of ornamental details, but by the admirable proportions
of the house itself. Two lines from one of Lady Winchilsea's poems are generally
applicable to the Georgian home, for nothing

> 'But graceful symmetry without is seen,
> And use with beauty are improv'd within.'

No matter what rank or station in society your host enjoyed, you were always
conscious of approaching and entering a home when you accepted hospitality.
Although the magnificence might be almost overpowering, it was never flashy.
Pope's gibe that Blenheim was 'a house but not a dwelling' was directed not
at the scale or elaboration of the architecture, but at the difficulty of feeling
at home in a place that seemed pre-eminently intended for display and not
for the well-ordered, comfortable life sought by all ranks."[185] Well-educated
public opinion, and the knowledge that "knowing men in art" were watchful,
ready to pounce upon architectural indiscretions, prevented designers and their
employers from committing the vulgarities of form that were to become commonplace, and to pass unnoticed in the mid-nineteenth century. "What you were
supposed to see when you visited your friends could only gratify the sense of

sight. From the moment the great gates had been opened to admit your coach, and you passed the neat lodges of brick or stone, whose classical details often reflected in miniature the design of the great house beyond, you were aware only of ordered beauty, of formal harmonies which suggested that nature had obligingly collaborated with a landscape architect, and that the trees themselves were acquainted with some arboreal equivalent of the classic orders, for their proportions were noble."[186]

To these felicities the Palladian school brought new refinements, and the delicate transformation of English architecture that followed owed more to the influence of Lord Burlington's patronage than to his own work as an architect. Although he was the chief exponent of Palladianism, the character of

General Wade's house in Great Burlington Street, designed by the Earl of Burlington in 1723: a beautiful façade, but so ill-planned and inconvenient that Lord Chesterfield said "as the General could not live in it to his ease, he had better take a house over against it and look at it." (Reproduced from *Vitruvius Britannicus*, Vol. III.)

his buildings hardly confirmed Colen Campbell's fawning description of his ability as a designer. The ornamental villa he erected on his estate at Chiswick in Middlesex was a superficial imitation of Palladio's Rotunda (see page 276), and his contemporaries were frank about its defects. It was, said Horace Walpole, "a model of taste, though not without faults, some of which are occasioned by too strict adherence to rules and symmetry. Such are too many correspondent doors in spaces so contracted; chimneys between windows, and which is worse windows between chimneys; and vestibules, however beautiful, yet too little secured from the damps of this climate. The trusses that support the ceiling of the corner drawing-room are beyond measure massive, and the ground apartment is rather a diminutive catacomb, than a library in a northern latitude. Yet these blemishes, and Lord Hervey's wit, who said *the house was too small to inhabit, and too large to hang to one's watch*, cannot depreciate the taste that reigns in the whole. The larger court, dignified by picturesque cedars, and the classic scenery of the small court that unites the old and new house, are more worth seeing than many fragments of ancient grandeur, which our travellers visit under the dangers attendant on long voyages."(187)

Burlington's designs for the Duke of Richmond's house in Whitehall and General Wade's in Great Burlington Street were described by Walpole as "ill-contrived and inconvenient, but the latter has so beautiful a front that Lord Chesterfield said, *as the General could not live in it to his ease, he had better take a house over against it and look at it.*"(188)

Great town houses were emphatically individual in design; standing amid gardens or separated from the street by an ample courtyard, they were occasionally the dominating feature of a square. Sometimes a square would be planned with some large existing house occupying a commanding position, and this occurred when Gregory King built Soho Square as a speculation, when the

The Town Hall at Blandford, Dorset, a classic edifice of Portland stone, built in 1734 to the designs of John Bastard (1688–1770) and his brother William (1689–1766), local joiners and architects and members of a family of builders. They also designed the church of St. Peter and St. Paul (1735–1739), which is shown beyond the Town Hall.

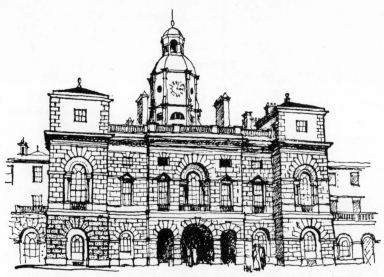

The Horse Guards, Whitehall, London, built to the designs of William Kent after his death, by John Vardy and William Robinson, 1750–1758.

West End of London was developed. It was begun in the reign of Charles II— for many years a statue of that monarch stood in the gardens—and the Duke of Monmouth's house occupied the centre of the south side, so it was first named Monmouth Square,[189] being changed, probably after the Duke's execution, to King Square after the speculator, changing again to Sohoe or Soho Square in the middle of the eighteenth century. According to a contemporary guide-book, there was "not much taste or regularity in the Buildings . . . but the place, if it has nothing to excite our praise does not appear to have anything to provoke censure. My Lord Bateman's house on the south side is the most remarkable. It has the appearance of grandeur and magnificence, and though it may have some defects, it has elegance sufficient to make us excuse them."[190] Monmouth House had been bought by Lord Bateman, and was demolished in 1773. (See page 257.) Soho Square in the mid-eighteenth century, despite the views of the anonymous writer in the guide-book, enjoyed a comparatively rare horizontal unity, though, as shown by the illustrations on pages 280 and 281, the houses on either side of Sutton Street on the east side of the square have a higher cornice line than those in the north-east corner. The engraving, from which sections are reproduced on those pages, was made about 1754, before No. 32, in the south-western corner of the square, was built by Robert Adam. That house, gay and elegant in design, was the largest in the square after Monmouth House had been pulled down, and it was occupied by Sir Joseph Banks, President of the Royal Society, from 1777 until his death in 1820. (It was demolished in 1937.)

Above and opposite are sections from a contemporary engraving (*c.* 1754) of Soho Square, which was part of the development of the west end of London in the late seventeenth century. It was originally named King Square, after the speculator, Gregory King, an engraver and political writer who invested money in building schemes. Tiborn Road, which is seen running parallel with the north side of the square, is the modern Oxford Street and Rawbone Place is Rathbone Place. The windmill gave the name to Windmill Street, which now connects Charlotte Street with Tottenham Court Road.

This completes the view of the north side, and shows part of the east side of Soho Square. Development schemes did not always exhibit such comparative horizontal unity, and even here the houses in the centre of the east side have a higher cornice line than those in the north-east corner. As this print shows, London was still in partnership with its rural environment, roads soon became country lanes. The area north of the windmill was developed late in the eighteenth century, and included Fitzroy Square. (See page 257 and opposite.) (From a print in the author's possession.)

Soho Square was typical of the piecemeal development of London and other cities, which gained a few well-planned areas adorned with fine houses, because speculators could and did command for the execution of their schemes the services of the most accomplished architects. Town planning on the grand scale could be carried out only when the speculation was on a comparable scale, large enough to embrace a whole city, or at least large parts of it. This happened at Bath, where John Wood (1704–1754) undertook a vast rebuilding scheme for the Duke of Chandos, and, with his son who succeeded him, made Bath famous for the excellence of its architectural manners, and the august, classical perfection of those splendid examples of Georgian architecture, Queen Square, the Circus and the Royal Crescent. London, unfortunately, became a patchwork of architectural ambitions and indecisions: the capital acquired a few gracious squares and crescents, and such isolated pieces of town planning as the Adelphi, Portland Place and, at the beginning of the nineteenth century, in the last phase of the English Renaissance, Carlton House Terrace, Regent Street and Regent's Park.

Even the uniform respect for the principles of architectural composition, based on the use of the classic orders, could not give to the streets of London or other cities more than a fragmentary and intermittent horizontal unity: but the general effect was orderly, despite the irregularity of the buildings, and this arose largely from the use of the double-hung sash window. In large or small houses, the vertical form and admirable proportions of the sash window, very often based on a double square, became and remained the most characteristic feature of English domestic architecture. In the late seventeenth and early eighteenth centuries the double square was generally divided by glazing bars into four vertical and six horizontal sections, making twenty-four panes; in the middle and late eighteenth century, sashes were divided into three vertical and four horizontal sections, making twelve panes—a form that persisted in the nineteenth century and is still used, both in England and the United States. Such external features as porches followed classical patterns, and the details of mouldings—cornices and door and window architraves— were related to Roman prototypes; but it was the enlargement of windows that made rooms airy and light and spacious, and their regularity of arrangement in a façade that gave streets a smiling aspect. To avoid the window tax, existing windows were often blocked up, and new houses were designed with framed blank recesses, to preserve the air of well-balanced fenestration. Such unglazed spaces were not always used to mark the place of a window to be pierced if and when the tax was one day repealed: recessed panels in brickwork sometimes completed the vertical lines established by the fenestration, as for example in Maids of Honour Row, at Richmond Green in Surrey. This row of four red-brick houses was built in 1724 for the Prince of Wales (who became George II), to accommodate the Maids of Honour attending his Princess. The windows of these houses mark a departure from the use of six panes for each

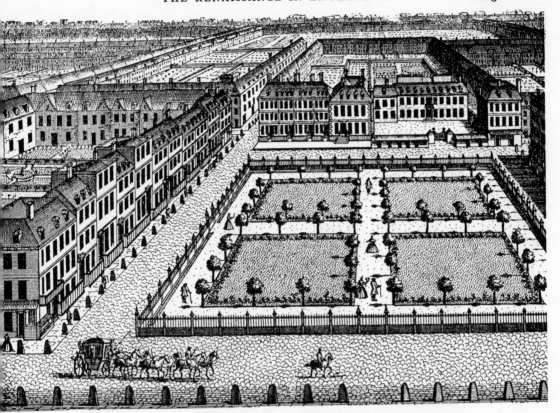

Leicester Fields, about 1750, described in a contemporary guide-book as "a very handsome square, the inner part of which is enclosed with iron rails, and adorned with glass plats and gravel walks, in the center of which is an equestrian statue of his present majesty gilt." (The engraving, from which this illustration is reproduced, was made before this statue adorned the square.) The guide-book approved of the neat but irregular architecture of the square, describing the buildings as "very good, especially the north side, where is Leicester house, once the seat of the Earl of Leicester, and now inhabited by her Royal Highness the Princess Dowager of Wales. This is a large brick building, neat and commodious, though not magnificent. It has a spacious court before, and a fine garden behind. . . ." (From *London and its Environs Described*, London, 1761, Vol. III, pages 302–303.) The view above is taken from the south, and Leicester House is shown breaking the north side with its courtyard.

sash: in those on the ground and first floors, four panes only are used, while the square windows of the second storey have twelve panes. The storeys are divided by white string courses, and the top storey has a series of recessed brick panels, which continue the lines of the windows, so the vertical elements of the façade are not terminated by the cornice. (See page 275.)

A section through a Georgian terrace-house, showing the steps rising from the street to the front door over the "area," and the arrangement of the floors from the basement to the attic. Windows in the principal rooms were carried from the cornice line to the skirting, and the area of glazing was adjusted to give the quality of daylight best suited to the character of Georgian interior decoration. (From *Building for Daylight*, by Sheppard and Wright.)

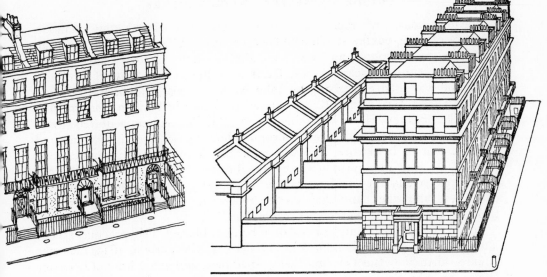

The terrace house with its basement, and three or four storeys above, and an attic storey lit by dormer windows, imposed a vertical pattern of living. It implied endless journeys up and down flights of stairs for the domestic staff. As Sheppard and Wright point out in *Building for Daylight* (from which the illustrations on this page are reproduced): "This arrangement of terraces, which faced on to wide access roads with small gardens behind, and beyond them the mews with its own service road, formed the social unit. The provision of an adequate angle of light was considered in the spacing of the blocks, and the alternation of the high terraces with the lower mews buildings gave added interest. This type of layout was developed further during the latter half of the eighteenth century and continued during the Regency period and the early Victorian era."

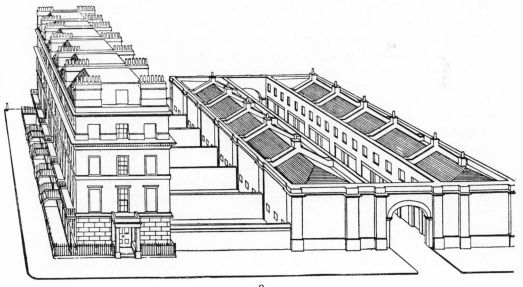

For town houses, whether large or small, brick was used: the grand mansion might be of stone, but few streets could boast continuous façades of that material. Bath was the exception, and was built almost wholly of stone. Early in the nineteenth century brickwork was faced with stucco and painted, and this technique was used extensively by John Nash and his contemporaries when Carlton House Terrace and Regent Street were built in London, and growing towns like Brighton, Hove, Worthing, Tenby and Cheltenham acquired streets and crescents, squares and terraces of commodious houses. Stucco was plastered on as a coat to brickwork, and was impressed with lines to simulate stone jointing. It was first introduced by the brothers Adam, who came from Edinburgh, a city they had re-planned and partly rebuilt, where stone was cheap and abundant, and they wanted to create an effect of stonework for their speculative building schemes in London.

Long before Robert and James Adam had established their practice, speculators had been busy in London and in other cities. As early as 1635, Leicester Square—then known as Leicester Fields—had been laid out in front of Leicester House, as Soho Square, in 1681, was laid out in front of Monmouth House, and Bloomsbury Square, in 1661, in front of the great town house of the Earl of Southampton. (See page 283.) The most famous and enduringly fashionable of the London Squares, St. James's, dates from about the same time, for a lease of the site was granted to the first Earl of St. Albans in 1660. Grosvenor Square, that spacious American enclave in Mayfair, dates from the 1720's, when the east side was developed by a speculator, John Simmonds, who built seven houses, designed to look like one impressive mansion, with the central house larger than the others and surmounted by a pediment. The north side was the work of Edward Shepherd, the proprietor of Shepherd's Market and other buildings in Mayfair, an active but mediocre architect, whose enterprise exceeded his capacity as a designer. His conception for the architectural treatment of a complete block for the north side was marred in its execution, because other builders refused to conform with the elevation he designed; but he was able to group a few houses behind a façade like that of a Palladian mansion—an innovation which inspired other architects, including John Wood the elder, who developed the idea with exceptional success in Bath. Thereafter street design was occasionally dignified by the interpolation of some large block of buildings, horizontally unified by a classical elevation, which would often include some central feature, with attached columns rising through two or more storeys supporting an entablature with a pediment above.

Another practice which encouraged horizontal continuity in the street was the grouping of houses of identical design in a row, and these terrace-houses, as they were called, imposed verticality as a living condition, though the attendant inconveniences of household life, narrowly distributed over three or four floors, were unremarked in an age when domestic servants were plentiful and ideas of labour-saving rudimentary. The development of the terrace

Houses on the front at Littlehampton, Sussex, early nineteenth century, similar in character to the Clifton Park houses on page 288.

Early nineteenth century terrace houses in Clifton Park, Clifton, Bristol. Georgian graces are still preserved, and the verandahs on the first floor are light and elegant, with their cast iron balustrades and vertical members. The proportions of the windows have remained unchanged for over a hundred years, though the glazing bars that frame the panes have been fined down until they are slender, delicate mouldings. By the middle years of the nineteenth century, classic details were used with a heavy hand: compare the Clifton Park houses above with those on the opposite page in mid-Victorian Kensington.

followed improvements in house design made in the late seventeenth century, when more compact plans became possible, largely as a result of the invention of the dog-legged stairway, or "pair of stairs," which had a half-landing between floors. This space-saving device solved the problem of stairs in the relatively small house. Before its introduction, houses of two or more storeys had stairs rising from an entrance hall to a gallery at first floor level which overlooked the hall, an arrangement that conferred dignity upon the stairway of a mansion, but was wastefully inconvenient in a small or moderately sized house. The individual house in a terrace usually had a narrow frontage, a basement, with the front door approached by steps, arched over the "area," the space below pavement level which allowed some daylight to penetrate the windows of the front basement rooms. (See page 284.) The larger and more spaciously planned terraces faced broad access roads, with small gardens behind, and mews beyond. Occasionally the desire to make the street frontage showy was satisfied at the expense of the backs. "Queen Anne fronts, and Mary Ann backs," was the phrase minted by Sir Edwin Lutyens to describe this sort of architectural duplicity.

The house of modest size rather than the town mansion or country villa provides a faithful record of the constancy of good taste throughout the Golden Age of English design: the larger houses, more susceptible to the idiosyncrasies of fashion, record the three well-marked phases of English architecture between the late seventeenth and early nineteenth centuries—Baroque, Palladian, and Neo-Classic, the last beginning with the work of the brothers Adam and their contemporaries and ending with the Greek Revival. In small provincial cities and market towns and throughout the country-side, those phases were reflected, at first indistinctly, but with increasing clarity after the middle years of the eighteenth century, largely as a result of the multiplication of books on architecture.

A fresh and unmistakable English style of domestic and civic architecture emerged in the late seventeenth century, comparable in character with the earlier native style which had been interrupted and abandoned one hundred

Houses in Campden Hill Road, Kensington, London: respectable Victorian classic, orderly, a little dull in effect; correct in detail, though uninspired in conception. The spirit had departed from the Renaissance in England: it began to flicker in the 1820's and 30's: by the 50's it was out.

Timber-built houses were common in some districts of Essex, Kent, Middlesex, Surrey, and Sussex. The exteriors were faced with wooden boards, overlapping each other like courses of tiles, and these houses with weatherboards or clapboards were easy to build. Above, is a large-scale example, Romney's House at Hampstead, which has a large section of it built in wood. To the right, is the mill at Barcombe, Sussex. Both buildings date from the eighteenth century, and both illustrate a technique of building which became common in the American Colonies, and still survives in the United States.

and fifty years earlier. From Scotland to the English Channel, in Wales and Ireland, architects and builders used the classic orders and their moulded and ornamental details gracefully and discreetly, and elegance was by no means confined to the structures that adorned the streets of London, Edinburgh, Dublin and such fashionable resorts as Bath. At King's Lynn in Norfolk, a port with a long history of prosperous trade, a local architect, Henry Bell (1653–1717), designed the Exchange, now the Customs House (1683), and the Duke's Head Inn (1685). His work shows traces of Dutch influence, for King's Lynn traded with Holland, and even closer contacts with that country had been established earlier in the seventeenth century, when the Norfolk Fens were drained under the direction of Cornelius Vermuyden, the Dutch engineer. The Lynn Customs House is a square structure, with superimposed pilaster

In the rural domestic architecture of England, the native style survived, and there was little difference in the small farm houses and cottages built between the early sixteenth century and the middle of the Georgian period. The windows were improved, but local materials, brick, tiles, stone or flint, and the technique of using them, gave continuity to the English tradition. The two houses shown above, facing the churchyard at Cuckfield, in Sussex, illustrate the local technique of using tiles, hung on a wooden framework in the upper storey, with brick below and brick chimney stacks. Weatherboarding was sometimes used for upper storeys, or for the entire exterior. (See opposite page.)

The Customs House at St. George's Quay, Lancaster, built in 1764 from the designs of Richard Gillow, the architect son of Robert Gillow, founder of the great firm of Lancaster cabinet-makers. This design was clearly influenced by the work of the brothers Adam. *Drawn by Marcelle Barton.*

orders, Tuscan on the ground storey, Ionic on the first. (See page 258.) Another example of civic architecture, built over eighty years later in 1764, is the Customs House on St. George's Quay, Lancaster, also designed by a local architect, Richard Gillow, son of Robert Gillow who founded the famous Lancaster firm of cabinet-makers. This building has four Ionic columns, formed from single stones, each being 15 feet high, crowned by angular capitals that owe their refinement of design to the influence of Robert Adam, while the window architraves and their pediments may well have been taken from the illustrations of such features in *A Complete Body of Architecture*, Isaac Ware's monumental guide-book, which was issued about 1735 and reprinted many times.

Plenty of talent was everywhere available for those who wished to build; patronage was enlightened, even the patronage of speculators, who, embarking on their schemes in order to make money, knew that their potential tenants or purchasers would be people with high standards of taste. Beginning with Wren and ending with Soane and Nash, a galaxy of talent illuminated the practice of architectural design during those three phases, Baroque, Palladian and Neo-Classic. Some of the characteristics of English Baroque were perpetuated in the work of James Gibbs and William Kent, and although Horace Walpole's gibe, quoted earlier, that "Vanbrugh dealt in quarries, and Kent in Lumber" was unjust, it was a natural enough comment to expect from that fastidious leader of taste at a time when the refining influence of the Palladian movement had made the bold vigour of Vanbrugh's work appear to be rather heavy, and the florid decoration of Kent almost corpulent.

Periodically, architectural taste was refreshed by the investigation of classical sources, and at the beginning of the second half of the eighteenth century the buried Roman cities of Pompeii and Herculaneum were re-discovered and partly excavated, an event that gave fresh impetus to the study of antique remains. Robert Adam, for example, lived in Italy from 1754 to 1757, where he made an intensive study of Roman monumental planning, and crossed the Adriatic to Spalato, situated in the old Roman Province of Illyricum, where he made a detailed record of the palace of Diocletian. Assisted by two draughts-men whom he had engaged in Rome, he made innumerable drawings of those remains and their ornamental details, which enabled him to use Roman forms and ornament not only with authority, but supplied him with authentic models upon which to base a new and delicate style of architecture and interior decoration, which became associated with his name. Robert and James Adam revived "the good Roman manner" with a refinement that never degenerated into flimsy or attenuated forms. An important event which gave fresh direction to architectural design was the publication in 1762 of the first volume of *The Antiquities of Athens*, by James Stuart and Nicholas Revett. In all, four volumes were published, and the appearance of the first was perhaps the starting-point of the Greek Revival which gained momentum in the 1790's and continued during the first third of the nineteenth century. The authors sailed from Italy to Greece in 1751, and spent five years in that country, where they made measured drawings of great numbers of ruins, and the beautifully engraved plates in their four volumes attest the thoroughness of their work. (See plate 2.)

We have mentioned the waves of taste that rippled over fashionable society, and fresh enthusiasms were generated for the Chinese taste by the treatise published by Sir William Chambers in 1757 on *Designs of Chinese Buildings, Furniture, Dresses, Machines and Utensils*, which that gifted architect wrote and illustrated from first-hand information culled during his extensive travels in the East. The Chinese elements in the Rococo style, and the *sharawadgi* form of taste, which encouraged asymmetrical design, have been referred to in the previous section. The *sharawadgi* taste was reinforced by an increasing interest in picturesque effects, and the incorporation of ruins, actual or artificially contrived, in landscape architecture. The study of ruins was conducted not only in the interests of purifying classical taste; it had a powerfully romantic appeal, and could be conducted at home in England, for the country was rich in ruins of religious houses, abandoned since the early sixteenth century, and far gone in decay. This taste for mediaeval ruins was encouraged by the work of artists and engravers, and in the late 1720's a series of popular engravings of ruined abbeys, churches and castles was made by Samuel and Nathaniel Buck. The series was a great success; thousands of engravings were sold; and

The Pagoda at Kew Gardens, Surrey, a well-proportioned example of the Chinese taste, as interpreted in England. The Pagoda was one of several ornamental buildings designed by Sir William Chambers when he planned the gardens for the Dowager Princess of Wales. These little ornamental structures, pavilions, temples, and the Pagoda, were built between 1757 and 1762. *Drawn by David Owen.*

they promoted widespread interest in Gothic remains and helped to create a receptive atmosphere for the Gothic taste, which was well established several years before Horace Walpole made his characteristic contribution to its development as a fashion. Professor Isaacs has identified three distinct phases in the growth and development of the Gothic taste, which he has aptly named Baroque, Rococo, and Romantic.[191]

Horace Walpole's famous villa at Strawberry Hill, Twickenham, belongs to the second—the Rococo—phase, but before he acquired that villa in 1747, the fashion for studying, delineating and imitating Gothic ruins was popular. Some attempt had been made to regularise the use of Gothic forms, and Batty Langley (1696–1751) had invented five Gothic "orders." Langley's attempt "to adapt Gothic architecture to Roman measures" was contemptuously condemned by Horace Walpole, who said "All that his books achieved, has been to teach carpenters to massacre that venerable species, and to give occasion to those who know nothing of the matter, and who mistake his clumsy efforts for real imitations, to censure the productions of our ancestors, whose bold and beautiful fabrics Sir Christopher Wren viewed and reviewed with astonishment, and never mentioned without esteem."[192]

Although Horace Walpole cultivated a fondness for Gothic forms, and indulged a collector's pleasure in acquiring odds and ends of Gothic ornament, he had an educated gentleman's dislike of the hybrid though indubitably picturesque buildings of the transitional period between the native English Gothic and the work of Inigo Jones. In a letter to George Montagu, he described Gosfield House as "all modernised but in patches, and in the bad taste that came between the charming venerable Gothic, and pure architecture." (July 25th, 1748.) His use of those words "charming" and "venerable" reveal the romantic character of his affection for Gothic; though as a discerning Georgian gentleman he admitted that "pure architecture" was unconnected with the antiquarian foibles he was indulging at Strawberry Hill, his "little plaything-house." Over the years, he altered and enlarged the villa, softening the strenuousness of Gothic lines, and incorporating Gothic motifs merely as components of a modish pattern. For example, the upper panes of the sash windows were diminished by glazing bars curved to fit within a pointed arch. (The same arched form was used by Thomas Chippendale and his contemporaries for the glazed doors of bookcases and for chair-backs.)

Sometimes the master of Strawberry rebelled against his own antiquarian adventure, when, for instance, he wrote to Richard Bentley (from Tonbridge,

Strawberry Hill, Twickenham, which was acquired by Horace Walpole in 1747, and became the vehicle for his experiments in the Gothic taste. (From a contemporary print in the author's possession.)

An example of English Rococo, with antique ruins as the principal motif. This girandole, designed by Thomas Chippendale, and published in the third edition of *The Gentleman and Cabinet-Maker's Director* (1762) shows the influence of Piranesi, whose views on antique ruins had a great effect on English taste. (See plates 6 and 7.)

August 7th, 1752) of Mereworth: " . . . which is so perfect in a Palladian taste, that I must own it has recovered me a little from Gothic. . . . " Within a year he was writing eagerly of the "satisfaction in imprinting the gloomth of abbeys and cathedrals on one's house. . . . " He was undecided whether he wanted it to be a castle or a pseudo-abbey; but as it expanded and housed a collection of rare and beautiful things, it satisfied his carefully controlled appetite for romantic surroundings. Horace Walpole never pretended that Strawberry Hill was anything but an amusing and admittedly eccentric expression of his personal taste. He had no mission, no intention of starting a great movement, and was far too great an aristocrat to experience such a plebeian emotion as enthusiasm about anything, though he was delighted when his friends fell in with his Gothic whims. Occasionally, he recorded the names of his converts, and once, in a letter written from Strawberry Hill to the Earl of Strafford, he mentioned a macaroni named Storer as a fresh convert to the Gothic taste. "I am as proud of such a disciple," he said, "as of having converted Dickie Bateman from a Chinese to a Goth. Though he was the founder of the sharawadgi taste in England, I preached so effectually that his every pagoda took the veil." (June 13th, 1781.) Although he attributes the founding of the *sharawadgi* taste to the Honourable Richard Bateman, it probably originated earlier, after it was first mentioned in the late seventeenth century by Sir William Temple in his *Essay on Gardening*. (See page 206.)

Gothic ruins, ruins of any kind for that matter, were considered desirable in the creation of picturesque effects, and a preoccupation with the creation of such effects led to a revival of the *sharawadgi* taste in the late eighteenth century, and the asymmetrical forms of design which it engendered. Sir Uvedale Price's famous essay, *On the Picturesque*, was written in 1795, and the fashionable world eagerly pursued the variegated eccentricities which he described. Towards the close of the eighteenth century, the religious aspects of the Gothic style began to appeal, not only to churchmen, but to a good many earnest-minded people. This did not prevent mediaeval churches, which were sometimes in good condition, from being pulled down and replaced by classical structures. The parish churches of Banbury in Oxfordshire and the Thames-side village of Battersea were both demolished in the second half of the eighteenth century. The destruction of the former in 1792 to make way for a classic design by Samuel Pepys Cockerell (1754–1827) aroused the most strenuous local opposition. There were many instances of classic additions being grafted on to a Gothic structure, but although a few churchmen might harbour the sort of doubts about the seemliness of classic architecture for Christian worship that William Woty expressed in the poem on Church-Langton, quoted earlier, there were no serious attempts to revive the Gothic style. The tentative flirtations with its outward forms and characteristic ornament were nothing more than a fashionable indulgence, and although such wealthy amateurs of architecture as William Beckford might amuse themselves with Gothic extrava-

No. 7 Adam Street, Adelphi, London, designed by Robert Adam, *circa* 1770. The Greek anthemion ornament has been used as a motif for the pilasters and the balcony railing on the first floor.

ganzas like Fonthill Abbey, the Greek Revival was a far more potent influence on taste in the late eighteenth and early nineteenth centuries than the charming and gentlemanly fashion for Gothic.

Although the Greek orders were used, and their proportions and ornament reproduced, architects were not then aware of the delicate and elaborately calculated inflections that in buildings like the Parthenon rectified the imperfections of human eyesight; nor were they discovered until F. C. Penrose undertook his detailed measurements of the Parthenon in the last quarter of the nineteenth century. The churches and civic buildings and mansions in the Greek style, though not distinguished by such subtle refinements, had a distinction of their own; massive or delicate, they had impressive dignity. The fourth Earl of Aberdeen, in his *Inquiry into the Principles of Beauty in Grecian Architecture*, published in 1822, had said that the remains of Greek buildings "should form the chief

Ironmongers' Hall, Fenchurch Street, London, rebuilt in 1748–1750 to the design of Thomas Holden. The hall was demolished in 1917. Reproduced from a contemporary engraving.

299

St. Peter's Chapel, Regent Square, London, designed by William Inwood
(1771–1843), in collaboration with his eldest son, Henry William (1794–1843).
This church, built in 1824–1826, shows the restraint and dignity of the Greek
Revival in architectural design. Henry William Inwood had travelled extensively
in Greece; his knowledge of the Grecian style which he practised was drawn from
authentic sources; and in 1827 he published his studies and records of *The
Erechtheion at Athens*, and in 1834 a work on *The Resources of Design in the Architecture
of Greece, Egypt, and other Countries.*

study of the architect who aspires to permanent reputation; other modes are
transitory and uncertain, but the essential qualities of Grecian excellence, as
they are founded on reason, and are consistent with fitness and propriety, will
ever continue to deserve his first care. These models should be imitated however,
not with the timid and servile hand of a copyist; but their beauties should be
transferred to our soil, preserving, at the same time, a due regard to the changes

of customs and manners, to the difference of our climate, and to the condition of modern society. In this case it would not be so much the details of the edifice itself, however perfect, which ought to engross the attention of the artist, but he should strive rather to possess himself of the spirit and genius by which it was originally planned and directed; and to acquire those just principles of taste, which are capable of general application."[193] The "timid and servile hand of a copyist" was not apparent in such buildings as the High School at Edinburgh, by Thomas Hamilton; the Master's House at Downing College, Cambridge, by William Wilkins, or the churches designed by William Inwood in collaboration with his eldest son, Henry William, particularly St. Pancras Church (1819–1822) and St. Peter's Chapel, Regent Square (1824–1826).

The revival of Greek forms made a far greater impact upon interior decoration and furnishing than upon architecture, and the chairs depicted on Greek vases and the curves of the stone seats in ancient Greek theatres inspired an elegance of shape that is associated with the furniture of the Regency period. The use of Greek motifs was popularised by such scholarly and well-travelled amateurs of design as Thomas Hope (c. 1770–1831), whose folio volume of drawings, published in 1807 under the title of *Household Furniture and Interior Decoration,* contained not only Greek but Egyptian examples of furnishing, which supplied cabinet-makers, chair-makers and decorators with ideas. Hope was not a professional architect, but he was an ardent propagandist for everything Greek. He was a very wealthy man, a collector and an enthusiast, who actively and consistently influenced the ideas of his contemporaries. The Greek Revival was the final expression of coherent taste in the history of the English Renaissance: thereafter the classic orders were seldom used discerningly as a system of design.

Comparable developments in taste and architectural design occurred in the American colonies until after the War of Independence, when the American nation became culturally as well as politically separated from Britain, though the new nation remained faithful to the classic orders. The Colonies had already established their own regional variations of Georgian architecture, and on the eastern seaboard the tide-water aristocracy built sumptuous mansions, rivalling in elegance their English prototypes. Early in the eighteenth century churches had been built in New England which followed the designs of Wren, Hawksmore, and James Gibbs. The material in which the designs were executed was wood, painted white; stone was rarely used. These classical churches and civic buildings adorned many of the towns of New York, Connecticut and Massachusetts, and, farther south, Pennsylvania, Maryland, Delaware, Virginia, the Carolinas, and Georgia.

The cities of the United States grew up from small settlements; only one was planned from the start—the "new federal town" of Washington. Wisdom and foresight were displayed in laying out that capital city, named after the first

President of the Republic, and the plan was made by Pierre Charles L'Enfant, an American engineer of French birth, who came to the country in 1777 with La Fayette. He had been made chief of the corps of military engineers, and was a practising architect whose ability had been proved by his work in remodelling the City Hall of New York and the Federal House of Philadelphia. Thomas Jefferson, who was a distinguished amateur of architecture, had favoured a grid plan for Washington, but L'Enfant designed the city with radiating avenues, which permitted it to grow gracefully in any direction. It became a city of white marble, like those sparkling white cities of the Graeco-Roman civilisation, though on an immensely larger scale, veined by green avenues, refreshed by large parks and fine gardens; and the two focal points from which the avenues radiated were the Executive Mansion—the White House—and the Capitol.

New York, originally the Dutch settlement of New Amsterdam, had a totally different history. Until the end of the eighteenth century it had grown in the haphazard, traditional English way, occupying the south-western tip of Manhattan Island, a small, congested city, clustering about the port and docks. (A map published in 1778 is shown opposite.) In 1800, with a population of 60,000, it resembled in appearance any English maritime city of comparable size. Its architecture was classical, its most visible and distinguished buildings were churches, but it was a prosperous and busy city, and its wealthy merchants began to separate their residences from their offices, and to move northwards, away from the business localities. To regulate this northward movement, a city plan was made in 1811, that set out the future development of the island, up to 145th Street—an ambitious, far-sighted plan that could have been made only by people confident of their future prosperity. It was articulated by ten broad avenues, crossed at right angles by streets, thus dividing the city into convenient building plots. Across this grid of avenues and streets, Broadway traced a wavering diagonal line, preserving the old trail from the Battery to Yonkers.

In the 1770's the built-up area of New York was bounded on the east by the shipyards opposite Brooklyn (or Brookland as it was sometimes called), by Canal Street on the north, while the fort, better known as the Battery, was on the present site of the Ferry buildings. There were docks and wharves on the East River and the Hudson. The Bowery district was undeveloped; but after 1800 New York began to spill out northwards, and after 1811 it expanded on predictable lines. By 1840, the southern ends of the ten avenues were fringed with buildings, and isolated patches of development sprang up on the plots determined by the grid plan. New York still retained the appearance of a Georgian city; its skyline broken only by church towers and spires; its buildings seldom exceeding four storeys. Its subsequent growth was unparalleled in the history of architecture.

During the first fifty years of its national history, many of the cities and

New York City in the late eighteenth century, before the grid plan of 1811 was made, when the city was still confined to the tip of Manhattan Island. The line of Broadway, running from New York to Bloomingdale, is clearly marked, and it was then called Bowry Lane at its lower end, and Bloomingdale Road farther on. (Reproduced from a map published in the *London Magazine*, 1778.)

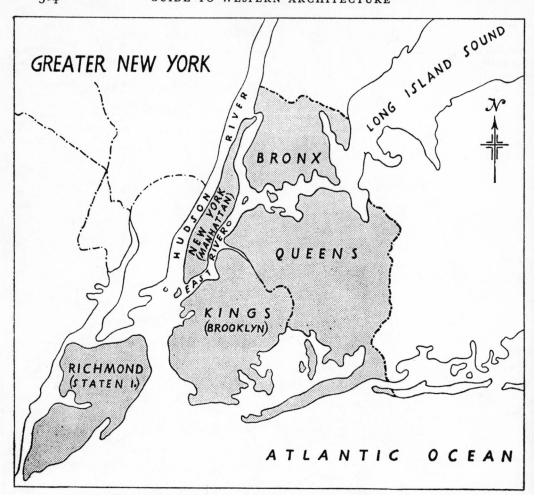

New York in under two centuries has grown far beyond the tip of Manhattan Island: it has absorbed the whole island, and spread south across the harbour to Staten Island, north to the Bronx, and eastwards to a vast extent. New York City itself grew on Manhattan Island according to a wise, far-sighted plan, which was made in 1811, and set out the lines of future street development for the whole island, right up to 145th Street. The horizontal future of New York was thus predictable: in 1811 neither town planners nor architects anticipated the vertical growth of the city, but a plan had been made, a fine conception, articulated by ten broad avenues, crossed at right angles by narrower streets, thus dividing the city into convenient town plots. Broadway, still preserving the old trail from the Battery to Yonkers, ambled across this grid plan. The street plan of mid-twentieth century New York is shown opposite: only the main lines of the plan are indicated, but from this the resemblance to the street plan of ancient Alexandria becomes apparent. (See page 50.) *Drawn by Marcelle Barton.*

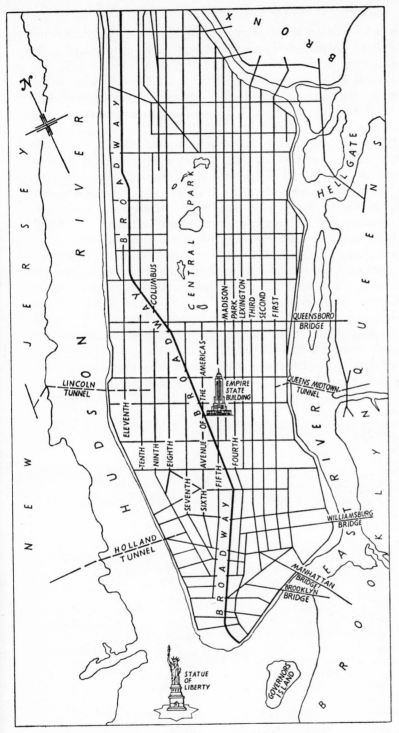

New York to-day, showing the grid plan that was made in 1811, and has now been built up for the whole length of Manhattan Island. Compare this with the map of the city in 1778 on page 303, and the map of ancient Alexandria on page 50. *Drawn by Marcelle Barton.*

towns of the United States were recognisably of English origin. They inherited the graces of the Georgian period: houses were admirably proportioned, the sash window was almost universally used, and the ornamental details and conventions of classical architecture distinguished both domestic and public buildings. An indigenous domestic architecture of wood found expression in two forms: one, as simple as the wooden halls of Saxon England, was the log cabin, the other was the timber-framed house with an external skin of white-painted overlapping boards laid horizontally, and called clap boards (in England, they were called weather boards). This type of timber-built house had been common in some localities in England during the eighteenth century.

After the War of Independence, when the United States became a nation in its own right, no visible break was made with architectural traditions. Classical design persisted, and although some superficial attempts were made to establish a national fashion, it seldom went beyond a rather unimaginative use of the American eagle as a decorative motif. During the early nineteenth century, French taste had some influence on American architectural design. Though England was at war with France almost continuously from 1798 to 1815, America had no such break of contact with French fashions, though it was on furniture and interior decoration rather than architecture that French taste left a mark in America. Until the middle years of the nineteenth century the loyalty of American architects to the classic orders was scarcely disturbed. The last phase of English Renaissance architecture was prolonged in the United States: in both countries it ended with the Greek Revival.

X

THE NEW WESTERN ARCHITECTURE
AND ITS ORIGINS

WESTERN architecture throughout its history has been identified with the character of Western civilisation, and has reflected the rise and decline of the Age of Reason, the rise and decline of the Age of Faith, the humanism of the Renaissance, and the scientific and industrial rationalism of the nineteenth and twentieth centuries. Its varying forms are part of our cultural heritage, our way of thought, our way of life. As Henry John Randall has said in *The Creative Centuries*: "We may wonder at Egyptian pyramids, Sumerian temples and Assyrian reliefs, but they are far off and exotic things. They are eastern and we are western; we feel that they do not belong to us; that the spirit that inspired them is not ours, that they may stimulate our interest and rouse our curiosity, but do not appeal as models for imitation or ideals for homage."[194]

The inspiration of the Renaissance had run down before the first third of the nineteenth century was completed; architectural design was unhappily separated from essential contemporary needs and confused by the emotional revival of Gothic forms, while architects engaged in controversies about the disposition of ornamental details, rather in the way that the Gallo-Roman nobles of the fifth and sixth centuries had squandered their leisure on puerile literary pursuits, unmindful of the changing world that was challenging their established ideas. Although the classic idiom persisted throughout the nineteenth century, the use of the orders tended to become a mechanical and superficial operation, related to the decoration of a façade, with results far inferior to the work executed in the previous century when Europe enjoyed its most gracious period of architectural and artistic unity. During the eighteenth century the Romantic movement had become associated, as already described, with the taste for picturesque ruins and Gothic remains; an engaging fashion, and at first nothing more than a fashion, appealing only to fastidious and well-mannered people who abhorred the emotional vulgarities of enthusiasm in any form. So long as the movement was directed by people of good breeding, it was safe from extravagance. Intermittent interest in Oriental decoration and ornament might encourage a taste for asymmetrical compositions, but that taste would be under control; it would never become untidy. Only when a movement was lubricated by emotion did it run away with its prophets and practitioners, and before that happened to the Gothic Revival, through which the Romantic movement found architectural incoherence, there were, as we have seen, deliberate attempts to revive classical styles like the Greek, and even to derive inspiration from such remote antique sources as ancient Egypt. So the Gothic taste long retained its modish status as a charming style, and, like the Greek, was fitted, though with less ease, into the framework of classical design. It only became a revival charged with spiritual emotion as the nineteenth century advanced toward middle age, and moral earnestness infected architecture.

Meanwhile a new force in the economic and social life of Europe had, by the end of the eighteenth century, inspired a potent but anonymous revolution that was destined within a hundred and fifty years to change the whole nature of architectural design and to alter the technique of building in every country touched by Western civilisation. This new force was organised industry, which first found its greatest and most expansive outlet in the mills and foundries of Britain; and among its products were new materials that could be used in building, and were used at first with imagination and ability. Of these, cast iron was soon recognised as a promising structural material, and it was used for a bridge, the first of its kind in the world, over the River Severn in Shropshire in 1777–1779. The designer, a Shrewsbury architect and builder named Thomas Farnolls Pritchard, created a light and elegant structure. (See opposite page.) Unfortunately cast iron was soon misused; even John Nash employed it as a cheap substitute for stone in casting columns for Carlton House Terrace, the North Lodge of Buckingham Palace, and the colonnades of Regent Street; while many other architects, following his example, neglected its intrinsic virtues as a building material. Its properties, and the contribution it could make to new architectural forms, were not appreciated—and then not fully—until Joseph Paxton designed the Crystal Palace, one of the first buildings in Europe that openly employed the resources of industrial production. Constructed of prefabricated units of cast and wrought iron and glass, it gave expression to the industrial revolution in terms of architectural design. In 1851 when it was erected in Hyde Park, the new form that Western architecture would take within a century had its earliest and most publicised demonstration; but even its designer was unaware that a new architecture had been born. To the end of his life, Paxton remained an unconscious parent, and when his success with the Crystal Palace brought him commissions for other work, he reverted to a

When new industrial materials were first introduced, they were used with boldness and confidence by architects in the Western world. In the eighteenth century they were regarded not as a challenge but as another convenient way of expressing the infinite versatility of the system of design represented by classical architecture. When the first cast iron bridge in the world was designed by Thomas Farnolls Pritchard, an English architect and builder of Shrewsbury, he used the material to create a light and elegant structure in the classical tradition of architectural design. The bridge spanned the River Severn between Madeley and Broseley in Shropshire, was erected in 1777–1779, and constructed by Abraham Darby, the ironfounder of Coalbrookdale. Above is a side elevation of the bridge, and below a drawing of it made from a steel engraving, *circa* 1782, in the possession of the Coalbrookdale Company.

limp and pallid classic convention, with indifferent results. Only when his imagination was roused could he produce original ideas, like his project for the Great Victorian Way: an immense iron and glass arcade, eleven and a half miles long, to girdle London. This proposal, and others like it, intended to improve metropolitan communications, was examined by a Committee set up by the House of Commons, but never got beyond the stage of discussion. (Paxton's drawings for the project have not survived.)

By the middle of the century, when the Crystal Palace had been admired by many and execrated by some, English architecture had become the subject of a controversy, conducted with such passion that it was generally known as "The Battle of the Styles." The protagonists were engaged so intently, fighting for Gothic or Classic, that the characteristic architecture of their own age was seldom recognised, though it was arising everywhere, serving the new railways, carrying their permanent ways across superb viaducts, covering with majestic roofs of steel and iron stations like Paddington and St. Pancras in

Detail of one of the bays of the Crystal Palace. Each bay was 8 feet in width, and the iron units had an elegance and lightness of character, comparable with that earlier example of the use of cast iron, the bridge over the Severn, erected in 1777–1779. (See page 309.) This illustration is reproduced from the *Official Catalogue of the Great Exhibition.*

Interior of the Crystal Palace, viewed from the south entrance. Built to house the Great Exhibition of 1851, this structure, with its iron and glass units and its "airy lightness," gave a pre-view of the New Western Architecture that was to develop during the next hundred years. It was conceived by Sir Joseph Paxton (1801–1865), who never suspected that he had created a new technique that was to have a profound influence on architectural design. In the *Official Catalogue of the Great Exhibition*, from which this illustration is reproduced, it was stated that "the lightness of the proportions will at once assure the spectator of the nature of the material which forms the main supports of the building. While the vertical supports consist entirely of cast-iron, the horizontal connections and girders are constructed of both wrought and cast iron." (Volume I, page 53.) The frank acknowledgment of the logical use of contemporary industrial materials had no immediate effect on the ideas of architects, who were too intent on exhuming the Gothic style or fighting a rearguard action in defence of the classic orders, to recognise the advent of a new architecture.

London, or such smaller provincial stations as Lime Street, Liverpool, and Woodside, Birkenhead; again, with super-Roman engineering efficiency, taking canals across valleys on vast aqueducts, like those of Chirk and Pont-Cysylltau, designed by Thomas Telford. Such achievements, though not ignored, seemed irrelevant to the subject of architecture, which had become a game played on a drawing-board, with columns and capitals or pointed arches, according to personal taste or moral conviction.

Unfortunately the Gothic Revival acquired a religious significance; it became identified with Christian architecture, and corresponded with the rise of the Evangelical movement and a fairly widespread belief among devout people that the classic orders supplied an unsuitable environment for Christian worship. Pugin's book of *Contrasts* has been mentioned in Section VII, and his illustrations of a town in 1440 and 1840 reproduced on pages 180 and 181: he was the most fervid advocate of the Gothic style, which to him represented a way of thought and belief, rather than a style, and this gave ferocious emphasis to his attacks on classical architecture, particularly on the Greek Revival, which he stigmatised as "the revived pagan style." He lampooned the classic school, and was savagely severe on his contemporaries who used the orders, not because he despised the architectural achievements of the Graeco-Roman world, but because he believed that "the adapters of pagan architecture" were "violating every principle, that regulated the men whose works they profess to imitate," and such "uncompromising advocates of classic styles would be utterly repudiated by the humblest architect of pagan antiquity, were he now to return to earth." He added: "Vitruvius would spew if he beheld the works of those who glory in calling him master."[195]

Vitality had ebbed from the Renaissance, but Pugin and his contemporaries were unable to perceive that their resurrected Gothic forms were as devoid of living significance as the classic orders had become. Their works proved that moral earnestness lacks the artistic potency of burning faith. Henry John Randall has pointed out that "The Gothic revival, especially in the nineteenth century, was one in which the perfection of the mechanism failed to conceal the departure of the spirit."[196] Pugin was a genius, and his own work had the distinction that genius can alone confer; but there were many lesser men who built churches and parish halls, mansions and monuments in what they sincerely believed to be true Christian Gothic, though such edifices merely showed the feebleness of an architectural movement based on copyism. The Gothic Revival did not restore any system of design comparable to that represented by the classic orders; instead it popularised an emotional taste for mediaeval forms, without comprehension of the lively sense of adventure or the experimental boldness of the builders who originated them.

As in the eighteenth century, architectural copy-books abounded, but instead of spreading a sense of orderliness, they gave licence to anarchy in design. Some were best-sellers, and by far the most influential was Loudon's *Encyclopaedia*

Pugin's attack on the Greek Revival was bitter and continuous. Describing it as "the revived Pagan style," he was outraged by its use for churches and considered it equally inappropriate for domestic structures. It was absurd, he said, "to see two or three tiers of windows introduced in the shell of a Greek temple, the roof of which is broken by numerous stacks of vainly disguised chimneys." (From *The True Principles of Pointed or Christian Architecture.*)

Cut-price Gothic, and all the shams and absurdities that it encouraged, were attacked by Pugin as vigorously as he attacked classic architecture. In 1841 he published *The True Principles of Pointed or Christian Architecture*, from which the illustrations above are reproduced, that on the left showing the street elevation of a cheaply built church, with the side view on the right. "How often," he wrote, "do we see a front gable carried up to a respectable pitch, and we might naturally infer that this is the termination, both as regards height and form, of the actual roof; but on turning the corner we soon perceive that it conceals a very meeting-house, with a flat roof and low thin walls, perforated by mean apertures, and without a single feature or detail to carry out the appearance it assumed towards the street."

of Cottage, Farm and Villa Architecture and Furniture, first published in 1833, which went through many editions. The compiler, John Claudius Loudon (1783–1843), was a successful landscape gardener who had cultivated a corresponding interest in architecture. He made some original contributions to the structure of conservatories and hot-houses; between 1816 and 1818 he developed a form of curvilinear roof construction, and perfected the "ridge and furrow" glazing that was subsequently adopted by Joseph Paxton for the great glasshouse at Chatsworth and later for the Crystal Palace.[197] Loudon designed a few buildings himself, but he was primarily a writer and compiler of reference books, and although he is remembered chiefly for his monumental *Arboretum,* the effect of the illustrations and specifications in his *Encyclopaedia of Cottage, Farm and Villa Architecture and Furniture,* was profound: his pages provide a pre-view of the Victorian period, and the drawings that thronged them were given substance in brick and stone all over the country, occasionally with deplorable variations. The lodges and gate-houses, the small farm buildings, the stables and outhouses of the stately homes of Victorian England and Scotland acquired new and occasionally incongruous forms; and so widespread was the popularity of Loudon's models among architects and builders that it is difficult to go very far along any road in the English countryside without coming across some reminder of his influence. In the pages of the *Encyclopaedia* he collected so many ideas, so many hints and suggestions, that it became the ideal source for what used to be called, rather vulgarly and very unprofessionally by architects and their assistants, "crib stuff." In the United States, Andrew Jackson Downing (1815–1852) had a comparable influence. Like Loudon, he was a landscape gardener, a horticulturist, and an architect. His work was well known: he was commissioned to lay out the grounds of the Capitol, the Executive Mansion, and the Smithsonian Institute at Washington, though he died before the work was completed. In 1841 he published *A Treatise on the Theory and Practice of Landscape Gardening Adapted to North America;* the following year his first book on building appeared, *Country Residences, or a Series of Designs for Rural Cottages and Cottage Villas and their Gardens and Grounds, adapted to North America,* which became very popular. His most ambitious work was *The Architecture of Country Houses,* published in 1850, and lavishly illustrated with examples that ranged from imitation Gothic cottages to Swiss chalets. He was an advocate of what may be called the Creeper School of design, for he believed that the charm and character of rural buildings depended largely on the flowering vines and creepers which clung to their walls. "Cottage architecture, especially," he said, "borrows the most winning and captivating expression from foliage." He recommended "the most hardy, valuable, and beautiful species" for such natural adornments. Some of the illustrations in the furniture section of this book were reproduced, with acknowledgment, from Loudon's *Encyclopaedia;* and this work of Downing's certainly helped to transplant Victorian taste in architecture and furnishing to North America, where it flourished with the

The Britannia Bridge, completed in 1849, carries trains over the Menai Strait, through a double series of iron box girders. Designed by Robert Stephenson, it showed an imperfect grasp of the possibilities of industrial materials, and lacked boldness of conception. "The design of the masonry," wrote Samuel Smiles, "is such as to accord with the form of the tubes, being somewhat of an Egyptian-character, massive and gigantic rather than beautiful, but bearing the unmis-takable impress of power." (Drawn from an engraving formerly in the possession of the L.M.S. Railway, and reproduced by permission.)

same undisciplined comfort and clumsiness that characterised its growth in Britain. The examples illustrated in both Downing's books on architecture, though less extravagant than many of Loudon's suggestions, had an equally unfortunate effect upon the American rural and urban scene.

Loudon made it clear in the text of his *Encyclopaedia* that he did not always approve of what he described and illustrated; but in it went all the same, and made the task of the speculative builder who wanted to do a bit of Gothic or something Italian very much simpler. Robert Louis Stevenson, in *The Wrecker*, significantly named one of the characters, a working mason who rose to be a speculative builder, Alexander Loudon. There is a passage in Chapter

The Albert Memorial, in Kensington Gardens, 1863–1872, designed by Sir
George Gilbert Scott. Dr. Pevsner has described it as "the epitome in many
ways of High Victorian ideals and High Victorian style, rich, solid, a little
pompous, a little vulgar, but full of faith and self-confidence." (*The Buildings
of England*, volume on London, except the cities of London and Westminster. Kensington, page 254.) It has come in for more critical abuse than
nearly any other monument, and that outspoken Victorian, John T. Emmet,
observed that "the unenlightened public has been left to wonder why a
work so perseveringly and highly praised should seem so unimpressive and
ungainly." That was written in 1880, and was at that time an unusual and
unpopular opinion. The illustration above is reproduced from Emmet's
book on architecture, issued in 1891 under the title of *Six Essays*. (See page
322.)

One which describes how this old man took his artistic young nephew, Loudon
Dodd, round the suburban developments in Glasgow for which he had been
responsible, and in the nephew's words: "The purpose of our excursions was
not to seek antiquities or to enjoy famous prospects, but to visit one after another
a series of doleful suburbs, for which it was the old gentleman's chief claim
to renown that he had been the sole contractor, and too often the architect
besides. I have rarely seen a more shocking exhibition: the brick seemed to
be blushing in the walls, and the slates on the roof to have turned pale with
shame; but I was careful not to communicate these impressions to the aged
artificer at my side; and when he would direct my attention to some fresh
monstrosity—perhaps with the comment, 'There's an idee of mine's; it's cheap
and tasty, and had a graand run; the idee was soon stole, and there's whole

deestricts near Glesgie with the goathic adeetion and that plunth,' I would civilly make haste to admire and (what I found particularly delighted him) to inquire into the cost of each adornment."

The adoption of some "goathic adeetion" was fatally easy after a study of Loudon's pages, and the examples he supplied of buildings in what he called the "castellated style" were despised and consistently attacked by discerning critics like Pugin.

Occasionally a classic sense of order and symmetry distinguished some Gothic composition, and this is apparent in the Houses of Parliament, the Palace of Westminster, designed by Sir Charles Barry (1795–1860), with the assistance of Pugin, who worked on the interior decoration and equipment of the building. It has been suggested that Pugin was the master mind behind the whole design, though this conjecture is dubious, for the building is too sedate and orderly and lacking in emotional content to reflect the passion and turmoil of Pugin's vision of Gothic architecture. The Gothic Revival coincided with a series of great architectural competitions: the first was for Westminster Palace, launched in 1835, a year after the original building had been burnt down, and in the conditions the style required was to be "Gothic or Elizabethan."[198] Among the chief exponents of the Gothic style were Sir George Gilbert Scott (1810–1877), George Edmund Street (1824–1881) and William Butterfield (1814–1900). Scott had an enormous architectural practice, and his buildings included many churches—St. Mary's Cathedral, Edinburgh, St. Mary Abbotts, Kensington, St. Matthias, Richmond, Surrey, to name only a few. He was also a great restorer of old churches, generally to their detriment. Perhaps his most familiar work is the Albert Memorial, which was greatly admired when it was built, but has since become the target of more abusive criticism than almost any other monument. (See opposite page.) Street was the architect of the Law Courts in London, which was the subject of the third big government competition of the mid-nineteenth century: Butterfield designed Keble College, Oxford.

Pugin was the great pioneer and by far the most outstanding figure of the Gothic Revival; and the doctrines he preached and practised were expounded and amplified by many writers, of whom the greatest was John Ruskin (1819–1900). As a youth of 19 his genius was first perceived by Loudon, who in 1838 wrote to Ruskin's father and said that his son was "the greatest natural genius that ever it has been my fortune to become acquainted with." John Ruskin had written a series of papers on "The Poetry of Architecture," under the pseudonym of Kata Phusin, which Loudon published in *The Architectural Magazine*, which he had started in 1834; earlier, when Ruskin was 15, Loudon had printed an essay by him in the *Magazine of Natural History*, on the strata of mountains and the colour of the Rhine.

Ruskin's influence as a writer and lecturer was vast. He believed with immoderate passion in the revival of Gothic architecture, and as he identified

St. Paul's, the parish church of Hammersmith, built in 1882 to the designs of Hugh Roumieu Gough (1843–1904) and John Pollard Seddon (1827–1906). It replaced a small, unpretentious and well-proportioned edifice which was opened in 1631. Mock-Gothic churches like this were built all over Britain, the British Dominions, and the United States during the nineteenth century, establishing in the minds of people a wholly false idea of the character of Gothic architecture. William Morris was angry with Seddon "for replacing old Hammersmith Church, a harmless silly old thing, with such an excrescence." (*Life of William Morris*, by J. W. Mackail. 1899. Vol. II, page 97.)

the idiosyncrasies of his personal taste with eternal principles, and could express himself in beautiful English, he was able to confuse many issues and to turn the minds of his audiences away from the world they were living in to a dream world of mediaeval romance. He set forth his beliefs under six headings in an appendix to his *Lectures on Architecture and Painting*, when they appeared in book form, and revealed his preoccupation with the purely superficial aspects of architectural design. "1. That Gothic or Romanesque construction is nobler than Greek construction. 2. That ornamentation is the principal part of architecture. 3. That ornamentation should be visible. 4. That ornamentation should be natural. 5. That ornamentation should be thoughtful. 6. And that therefore Gothic ornamentation is nobler than Greek ornamentation, and Gothic architecture the only architecture which should now be built." The expounding of these propositions led him to assert (in support of the second) that "the highest nobility of a building does not consist in its being well built, but in its being nobly sculptured or painted." He had said much the same thing in the preface to the second edition of *The Seven Lamps of Architecture*. "The fact is, there are only two fine arts possible to the human race, sculpture and painting. What we call architecture is only the association of these in noble masses, or the placing of them in fit places. All architecture other than this is, in fact, mere *building*; and though it may sometimes be graceful, as in the groinings of an abbey roof; or sublime, as in the battlements of a border tower; there is, in such examples of it, no more exertion of the powers of high art, than in the gracefulness of a well-ordered chamber, or the nobleness of a well-built ship of war."

He rejected uncompromisingly the classic orders of architecture, and in *The Stones of Venice* denounced them in these words: "Whatever has any connection with the five orders, or with any one of the orders; whatever is Doric or Ionic or Corinthian or Composite, or in any way Grecised or Romanised; whatever betrays the smallest respect for Vitruvian laws or conformity with Palladian work—that we are to endure no more." He regarded the Renaissance as "a foul torrent," an arrogant and impious attempt by man to set himself above Nature, by seeking to impose unity and symmetry. He urged people not to fear incongruities, not to think of unities of effect, and in one of his more confused lectures, in which moral earnestness raised its dreary head, he said, "Introduce your Gothic line by line and stone by stone; never mind mixing it with your present architecture; your existing houses will be none the worse

House in Campden Hill Road, Kensington, London, built when enthusiasm for the Gothic Revival was at its height.

for having little bits of better work fitted to them; build a porch, or point a window, if you can do nothing else; and remember that it is the glory of Gothic architecture that it can do *anything*. Whatever you really seriously want, Gothic will do it for you; but it must be an *earnest* want."

The result of all this teaching and preaching was to make architects more intent upon disguise than design. The works of novelists like Sir Walter Scott had endowed the Middle Ages with a spurious charm, and mediaeval building terms had, according to Ruskin, a "strange and thrilling interest." He instanced "Vault, Arch, Spire, Pinnacle, Battlement, Barbican, Porch, and myriads of such others, words everlastingly poetical and powerful whenever they occur. . . . " What happened, he asked, if you removed from Scott's romances "the word and the idea *turret*?. . . Suppose, for instance, when young Osbaldistone is leaving Osbaldistone Hall, instead of saying 'The old clock struck two from a *turret* adjoining my bedchamber,' he had said, 'The old clock struck two from the landing at the top of the stairs,' what would become of the passage? And can you really suppose that what has no power over you in words has no power over you in reality? Do you think there is any group of words which would thus interest you, when the things expressed by them are uninteresting?"

Intoxicated by melodious words and bemused by the romantic appeal of such features as turrets, battlements, pinnacles, crockets and buttresses, architects crowded their sketch books with picturesque bits and pieces of ornament when they travelled in England or Europe. These studies they hoarded, applying selections from their hoard to whatever they happened to be building, a practice that led to many incongruous mixtures of Gothic motifs and industrial materials. The architect ceased to be the master-designer; he became separated from contemporary life, and lost that comprehensive sense of social and civic responsibility that, in England, he had formerly shared with the educated aristocracy of the Georgian period. From the 1820's he was working increasingly for a new rich class that had acquired wealth from the Industrial Revolution, and its members were very different in taste and judgment from the urbane Georgian aristocrats. This class, grimly impatient of the arts of life, was infected with the Puritanism of the Evangelical Movement and the Nonconformist sects, but it was also purse-proud, two characteristics which made it susceptible to the Christian respectability of the Gothic Revival, and to an ostentatious style of furnishing and interior decoration that originated in Germany after the end of the Napoleonic wars, and was known as Biedermeir. This debased variation of the French Empire style, named after a Philistine character who figured in the journal *Fliegende Blätter*, depended upon the luscious use of elaborate carving and embossed metal, so that every surface suffered from an indisciplined lavishness of ornament. The classic system of design had been challenged, and without its regulating framework—which had controlled though it had never subdued the Rococo style—the proportions of buildings and their contents were governed only by romantic whim or vulgar appetite.

The Forth Bridge, begun in 1882 and completed in 1889, was designed by Sir Benjamin Baker (1840–1907). It is an example of industrial architecture that makes no concessions to tradition, and is not a pretentious and uneasy partnership between metal and masonry, like the Britannia tubular bridge. (See page 315.)

In Britain and America and large parts of Europe, creative vitality in architecture was dormant. The Crystal Palace gave evidence of latent powers, but it was not until 1889 that an authentic adventure in design began in the United States, when the eleven-storey Tower Building broke the Georgian skyline of New York City. That year 1889 was an important one in the history of architectural design, for at the Paris Exhibition two buildings openly proclaimed their steel construction. One became famous as the tallest building in the world, and retained its title until 1931, when the Empire State Building was completed in New York. It rose to a height of 984 feet from its 2½-acre base in the Champs de Mars, and was designed by Alexandre Gustave Eiffel, an engineer who had built many large-scale bridges. The other, which has been demolished, was the Halle des Machines, designed by the engineer Contamin and the architect Dutert. This combination of steel and glass enclosed a space 1,377 feet 6 inches long, 377 feet wide, and 147 feet 6 inches high; its steel members, curving gracefully, gave an impression of airy lightness. In 1889 the

Forth Bridge was completed in Scotland; another structure that made no concessions to tradition, for Sir Benjamin Baker, the designer, rejected the type of partnership between metal and masonry that Robert Stephenson had favoured forty years earlier, when he built the Britannia Bridge over the Menai Strait. (See pages 315 and 321.)

For the majority of European, British and American architects, the frank acknowledgment of steel construction, exemplified by such structures as the Halle des Machines and the Forth Bridge, had little significance: they were works by engineers, and from the early seventeenth century until the beginning of the nineteenth, the architect had tended to abdicate his over-all responsibility for certain types of constructional work. One of the first instances of the separation of engineering work and architecture occurred in 1620, when Lemercier was sent with an engineer to make a report on a bridge near Rouen.[199] Baker's Forth Bridge might, as Flinders Petrie suggested, "be the typical example of freedom from needless restriction, in meeting one of the oldest needs of man with methods and material already well known, apart from fresh discovery."[200] No architect in Britain appeared to be aware of its significance; but by then architecture had become "a light, genteel employment, giving the position, social and financial, due to gentlemen and scholars."[201] That blunt description of the architectural profession was written by John T. Emmet, a critic who derided Victorian taste and the architecture that satisfied it. Some of his views had a prophetic flavour, for he said that aspiring architects did not see "the social revolution now in progress, less demonstrative but far more general than that of France. There the few thousands of the aristocracy were the chief sufferers; with us the millions of the middle class will feel the change. In but a few years' time the children of the labouring man will be as well conditioned in the world, as well prepared to assert their personal and mental claims before society, as the sole heir of any manufacturer or wealthy merchant."[202]

Not only were architects unaware of the social movements that were to lead ultimately to the British welfare state of the mid-twentieth century; they were too preoccupied with spurious "revivals" to be aware of any genuine movement in architectural design, although revolutionary ideas were shining through the work of engineers. Unfortunately, engineers were generally as purblind as architects about the potency of their contribution to architectural design: architecture, they felt, was something that was *applied* to their work, as scraps of Gothic ornament were *applied* by architects to their buildings. Some engineers were prepared to recommend the architectural styles appropriate, in their view, for clothing various types of industrial structures. Early in the 1860's, Sir Robert Rawlinson, a civil engineer, published "a noble folio volume of lithographs, all of them examples of tall chimneys which, without being decorated, are thoroughly decorative. Their ornamentation is a part of themselves; and this is an ornamentation which shows how readily the most unsightly

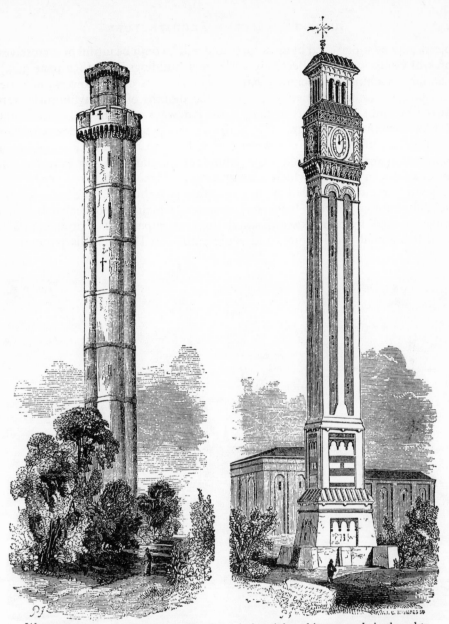

When Victorian engineers thought about industrial architecture, their thoughts turned to methods of disguising it. In Sir Robert Rawlinson's *Designs for Factory, Furnace, and other Tall Chimneys*, published about 1862, he said: "It will be no new thing to add beauty to a tall chimney, as some of our best architects have designed and erected ornamental tall chimneys in England." The illustrations on this page are reproduced from his work, which was apparently privately printed for the author, as no publisher's name appears on the title-page. (See page 322.)

objects may be superseded by structures that will be both beautiful in themselves, and will group well and effectively with other buildings."[203] (See page 323.)

So factory chimneys became gigantic watch-towers or bell-towers; factories were built to imitate Venetian palaces; the mouths of railway tunnels were flanked by embattled towers to suggest the gateways of mediaeval castles; and such forms of disguise became so inextricably confused with the idea of design, that the very meaning of the word design became doubtful. Fine pieces of engineering were often masked by redundant masonry, as, for example, the Tower Bridge in London, which is a suspension bridge with a secondary bascule bridge in the centre span that opens to let ships pass through. The main towers, and the abutment towers, have steel skeletons, which are concealed by stone facing, backed with brickwork, simulating the superficial characteristics of Scottish baronial architecture, and representing, as H. G. Wells pointed out

The Tower Bridge, completed in 1895, is, with the mock-Gothic Houses of Parliament and the clock tower, Big Ben, accepted all over the world as a structure symbolic of London. Seven years after it was built, H. G. Wells wrote in his *Anticipations* of "that feeble-minded contemporary shirking of the truth of things that has given the world such stockbroker in armour affairs as the Tower Bridge and historical romance. . . ."

in *Anticipations*,"that feeble-minded contemporary shirking of the truth of things that has given the world such stockbroker in armour affairs. . . . "[204]

The Tower Bridge was a regrettable result of the taste for mediaeval forms that, established by the Gothic Revival, had disseminated throughout Britain, the British Dominions and the United States of America, a wholly false idea of the architecture and art of the Middle Ages. Even the mellowing effect of a century of weathering has not made the churches and other buildings of that imitative period comparable in character or beauty with their mediaeval prototypes; so many of them were designed by mediocre copyists, and even architects of genuine ability, like Sir George Gilbert Scott, were hampered by loyalty to a dead style. Only one man of outstanding genius, after Pugin, understood that the spirit which had inspired the art of the Middle Ages should be revived, and that, imbued with this spirit, artists and craftsmen might resume the English tradition from the point where it had been interrupted in the sixteenth century, re-establish the native English style, and restore creative validity to architecture and the arts and crafts. His name was William Morris (1834–1896), and although his influence was limited at first in his own country, it persisted, and spread to Europe, where it was taken far more seriously, particularly in the Scandinavian countries. He was a poet, a writer of majestic prose, an artist and an executant craftsman. He originated two revivals: the domestic revival in architecture, and the handicraft revival, which attempted to rejuvenate the declining arts and crafts.

The domestic revival was not consciously sponsored by Morris, though it was generated by his friendship with Philip Webb the architect, who built a house for him at Bexley Heath in Kent, called the Red House, which became a model for many others built during the last four decades of the nineteenth century and the opening years of our own. Webb used an L-shaped plan, and, rather oddly, the sitting-rooms, the dining- and drawing-rooms, and the hall all faced north; the house had two storeys with a high-pitched roof of red tiles, and walls of warm red brick. It had a careless and comfortable independence of character; its romantic features, the gables and oriel windows, were not self-conscious additions, advertising allegiance to the Gothic style, and Webb and Morris came nearer to picking up the threads of the old English native style and weaving them into something fresh than any other architects and designers in the nineteenth century. That native English style had survived, with various modifications, from the sixteenth to the early eighteenth century; even in the lifetime of Morris, country masons, particularly in stone-using districts like the Cotswolds, would build such internal features as fireplaces in exactly the same way as a Tudor mason, not consciously, not from carefully made drawings, but by rule-of-thumb methods handed down for generations. (Such craftsmen survived in Worcestershire and Gloucestershire as late as the 1920's.)

Morris had been trained as an architect and a painter, but he soon became

The entrance to Shugborough Park tunnel, illustrated in *Our Iron Roads*, a book written by Frederick S. Williams, and first published in 1852. The author stated that tunnel entrances "should be various in style, yet consistent with the style of work. They should be massive, to be suitable as approaches to works presenting the appearance of gloom, solidity, and strength. Mr. Simms, the engineer, has well remarked, that a light and highly decorative structure, however elegant and well-adapted for other purposes, would be very unsuitable in such a situation: it is plainness combined with boldness, and massiveness without heaviness, that in a tunnel-entrance constitute elegance; and it is at the same time most economical. These conditions may be answered without cramping the taste of the engineer, as far as taste enters into the composition of such designs; for architectural display in such works would be as much misplaced as the massiveness of engineering works would be, if applied to the elegant and tastefully designed structures of the architect." This quotation discloses the rich confusion of Victorian writers about the relationship of architecture and engineering.

aware of that rift between art and life that began with the Renaissance, when the practice of any art tended to become a professional operation, detached from and unrelated to the common arts and crafts of the people in any country. He was the first artist, as Dr. Pevsner points out, "to realise how precarious and decayed the social foundations of art had become during the centuries since the Renaissance, and especially during the years since the Industrial Revolution."[205] Morris and the artists and architects who endorsed his beliefs felt that architecture should arise naturally and with a new, robust vigour from a revival of the crafts. The task of building and furnishing the Red House had proved to him and his friends that the decorative arts and crafts of England were moribund, for it was impossible to buy well-designed furniture or good patterns of textiles or wallpapers; and it was to supply this deficiency, and to elevate standards of design, that in 1861 the firm of Morris and Company was founded, which was prepared to undertake carving, metalwork, stained glass, and also to produce wallpaper, chintzes, carpets and furniture. Philip Webb, Burne-Jones, Rossetti, Ford Maddox Brown, Faulkner and Marshall were associated with Morris in this venture. The attempt to revive handicrafts was expensive in practice. Making things by hand was now a costly business, compared with mechanical production, which Morris abhorred, so he and his associates found themselves catering only for that relatively tiny section of the community that had both wealth and artistic sensibility. The lives and homes of the common people and the prosperous middle classes were untouched, and common art, apart from sporadic manifestations at country fairs and in some of the crafts of the country-side, remained in a state of suspended animation.

In Sweden and Denmark the work and example of Morris helped to ease the transition from handicrafts to machine production; and one of the fine architectural results of the application of his teaching is Ragnar Östberg's Town Hall at Stockholm, perhaps the last great romantic building in Europe, certainly the last to be built before the influence of Morris was displaced by the Modern Movement in architecture, with its initial austerities, arising from a puritanical regard for structural frankness and an avowed dislike of ornament. (See plate 30.) The modern movement, which fostered the new Western architecture, was consciously conceived in the last decade of the nineteenth century; its pioneers identified it with the industrial age in which they lived, and openly proclaimed that the engineer was the real architect of that age. Suspicion and dislike of mechanised industry were commonplace then among people with any pretensions to artistic taste; and it was difficult for many educated people to believe that, apart from such comfortable conveniences as railways and steamships, the machine was an unmixed blessing.

In their books and lectures, both Ruskin and Morris had denounced the devastation caused by the Industrial Revolution, through the debasement of the visual environment of Britain and large areas of Europe. London and other

London, in the mid-nineteenth century was still a city of spires and towers, and the streets still exhibited some traces of Georgian grace. In 1851, *A Balloon View of London* was published by Banks & Co., giving a bird's-eye picture of the city. Above is the view west of the Tower and east of St. Paul's. These views are continued on the opposite page and the two that follow.

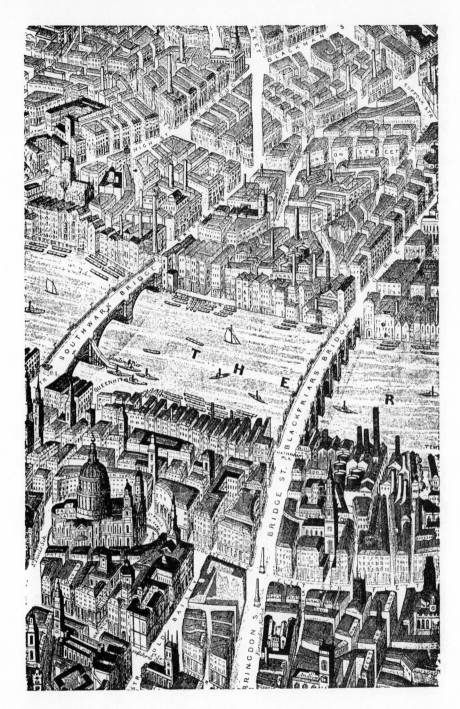

From St. Paul's along Fleet Street, the balloon view continues. In 1851, Ludgate Hill had not been crossed by a railway bridge, so St. Paul's could be seen from Ludgate Circus. The destruction of that view is shown on page 333, where Doré's impression of Fleet Street, Ludgate Circus and St. Paul's, is reproduced.

329

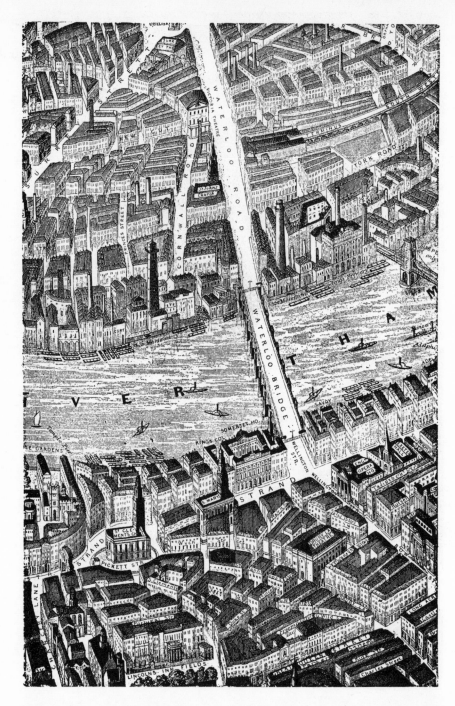

From Temple Bar, westwards along the Strand, the balloon view continues. The south bank is already showing a promising crop of factory chimneys, and a couple of shot towers. Part of the Hungerford Suspending Bridge is shown above, and it is continued on the opposite page. When this was removed, it was replaced by an iron railway bridge, outstanding in its brutality of design.

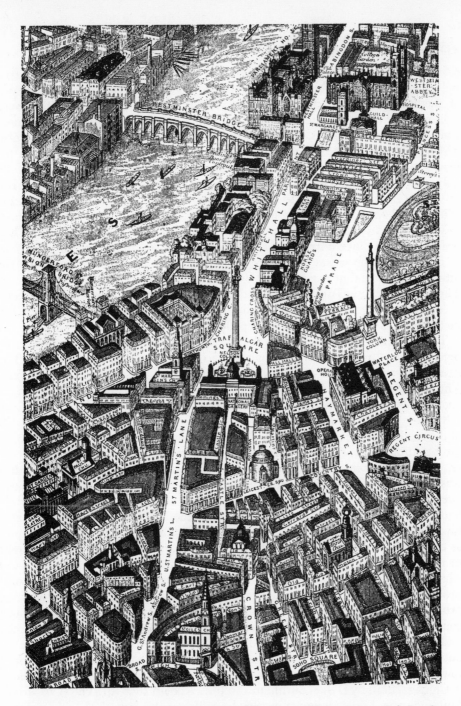

From mid-Strand to Regent Circus, as Piccadilly Circus was formerly called, London was as yet uninvaded by industrial buildings; though many residential areas had become offices and a few of them had become converted to workshops. (See opposite page, and pages 328, 329, and 333.)

331

cities in England and Scotland were disfigured by the intrusion of industrial buildings, with tall, reeking chimneys that competed with the spires and steeples of mediaeval and Georgian churches. "Enlightened self-interest," that slick Victorian phrase for efficient selfishness, was boorishly unenlightened about civic and rural amenities. The fine tradition of humanised landscape, diversified by villages and towns with architectural character, was broken; and the new additions to towns which followed the expansion of industry were brutally ugly and morally indefensible, for they were badly built, insanitary, and run up at the minimum of cost to accommodate the new and growing population of industrial operatives. Everywhere the activities of organised industry appeared to justify the strictures of Ruskin and Morris, and their followers. Morris had written of "the black horror and reckless squalor of our manufacturing districts, so dreadful to the senses which are unused to them that it is ominous for the future of the race that any man can live among it in tolerable cheerfulness. . . . " The immense, casual untidiness of industrial development, alienated architects: even the young generation, though they might have become bored by the pallid piety of the Gothic Revival, were repelled by the machine.

The first men to understand that architecture could be inspired by the machine and by industrial materials like iron and steel were not English. The revelation came to five men: two Americans, two Austrians and a Belgian. The Americans were Louis Sullivan (1850–1924) and Frank Lloyd Wright (born 1869); the Austrians, Otto Wagner (1841–1918) and Adolph Loos (1870–1933), and the Belgian, Henry van de Velde (born 1863). These pioneers of the modern movement saw very clearly the absurdity of ornamental disguises for buildings. Their views were often extreme. Adolph Loos, in an article entitled "Ornament and Crime," suggested that love of ornament in an adult was indicative of arrested mental development, that the greatness of the early twentieth century was proved by inability to invent new ornament, that men had vanquished ornament, learned to do without it, that the streets of new towns would be resplendent with great white walls, and the city of the future as bare and dazzling as Zion. Van de Velde declared that beauty was inherent in machines, that "the engineers stand at the entrance of a new style," and what was needed in architecture was "a logical structure of products, uncompromising logic in the use of materials, proud and frank exhibition of working processes."[206] Meanwhile architects were ignoring the significance of steel construction, as the Romans had formerly ignored the significance of the arch; and with few exceptions the new, tall buildings in American cities made no outward acknowledgment of the structural revolution. Some were huge masonry towers, without a steel skeleton, like the twenty-two storey Monadock Block in Chicago, built by Daniel Burnham and John Root in 1890–91. The Wainwright Building in St. Louis, designed in 1890 by Sullivan, did tentatively acknowledge the fact of its steel construction, thus achieving, as Dr. Pevsner has put it, "the splendid simplicity of rhythm and the unfaltering directness of effect."[207]

Ludgate Hill, which could have become a grand approach to the classical magnificence of St. Paul's Cathedral, was obliterated by muddled commercial buildings, and barred across by a railway bridge. No other capital in Europe exhibited such disregard for order and beauty as mid-nineteenth century London, when Doré drew this scene of squalid congestion.

Nearly all the skyscrapers erected during the first half of the present century hid their steel construction behind walls which still gave the impression that they were thick enough and strong enough to support the building, though actually they were mere skins, hanging from and concealing the internal skeleton of steel: curtain walls, as they are now called. Sullivan had said that "the architects of Chicago welcomed the steel frame and did something with it. The architects of the East were appalled by it and could make no contribution to it. In fact, the tall office buildings fronting the narrow streets and lanes of lower New York were provincialisms, gross departures from the law of common sense. For the tall office building loses its validity when the surroundings are uncongenial to its nature; and when such buildings are crowded together upon narrow streets or lanes they become mutually destructive."[208] While architects like Sullivan and Frank Lloyd Wright were fortifying their independence of traditional forms by courageous experiments, and finding patrons to back their ideas, many American architects were engaged on immense building projects, Roman in appearance, though far exceeding in scale anything attempted in the Roman Empire. The famous partnership between McKim, Mead and White was responsible for adorning New York and other cities with buildings that reproduced the elegant proportions and classical details of the Italian Renaissance; the life of the classic orders was thus renewed and prolonged. As buildings they were not, apart from their size, characteristically American. In his monograph on the partnership, written in 1924, Sir Charles Reilly said "These noble, reticent buildings of McKim, Mead and White's express a universal spirit such as our present-day civilisation should do, even if it does not. They would be equally at home in London as in New York."[209]

Some of those buildings were gigantic in scale, like the Pennsylvania Railway Station in New York, built in 1906, with its enormous waiting hall modelled on the Tepidarium of the Baths of Caracalla at Rome. The growth of New York, and other American cities, during the nineteenth century, had stimulated such architectural assertions of commercial and civic prosperity. The pace of growth, the rapid replacement of buildings which had outlived their economic usefulness, and the speedy development of new sites, had no precedent in the history of cities in Europe or Britain.

Hitherto cities had expanded slowly; sometimes in accordance with a pre-conceived plan; but in the United States they changed within a lifetime from a group of shacks to a roaring business community, thronged with traffic, and diversified with buildings in every suitable or unsuitable style that builders and architects had resurrected, for American architectural fashions closely followed those of nineteenth century England, particularly in New York. "The flood of bad taste in design that had inundated Europe and England in the middle years of the century also reached America, though the regional variations of bad taste in American building were less distinctive than the regional variations that had given to colonial Georgian architecture and to American

The Turbo factory, designed by Peter Behrens, and erected in 1909 in the Hutten-strasse, Berlin. The first large building in Europe that disclosed the character of the modern movement, and a forerunner of the new Western architecture.

design generally such agreeable character during the eighteenth century. New York continued to grow at a speed that far outstripped contemporary English cities; and it had this considerable advantage over most English cities—it was confined to an island, and a street plan had been made and followed. Horizontal development was therefore under some kind of control. That control was orderly rather than imaginative, but at least it saved the city on Manhattan Island from becoming an untidy cat's cradle of streets. Some open spaces were preserved and, as in London, a few were adorned with inferior statuary, for despite their independence of spirit, the American nation cherished many English ceremonial habits and ideas, and, throughout the nineteenth century, displayed a comparable incapacity for artistic perception."[210] The largest open space in New York was Central Park, that was purchased for the city in 1856, after ten years of public-spirited agitation by leading citizens, and planned by Frederick Law Olmsted and Calvert Vaux. Work on the Park began in 1857 as a relief project during a period of depression.[211]

Despite set-backs caused by transient financial panics, New York expanded until the limits of the island were reached. After the elevator had been invented in the early 1850's the engineer and the architect could defy horizontal limitations, and when the electric elevator was introduced the upward growth of New York and Chicago began, and was widely imitated. The vertical development of Chicago rivalled that of New York, and its expansion was even more spectacular and rapid than that of the older city. In 1804 the Federal Govern-

Bush House, Aldwych, London, designed by Helmle and Corbett, and built during the nineteen-twenties on the island site between Aldwych and the Strand. The northern façade, shown here, closes the long vista down Kingsway. An example of the monumental classic style that was still popular in Britain and the United States between the two world wars.

ment established a post on the site of Chicago, called Fort Dearborn. Shortly after it was founded, the post attained the dignity of a settlement with fourteen houses, and even in 1830 its population was still below 100; but within ten years it rose to 4,500, and by 1870 it was a great railway junction and a city where 306,000 people lived and worked. In 1871 a disastrous fire swept away the original city, and it was rebuilt on a grid plan, with some magnificent boulevards. To-day the buildings of the lakeside area give Chicago a skyline of fantastic beauty, rivalling that of New York.

The growth of towns in the United States followed the extension of the railway, which was the new road, and often the only road, which linked up the huge territory of the Republic. (It was called the rail*road*, not the railway.) Often it became the backbone, the main street, of a village; and when villages grew into towns, their growth and plan were determined by the railroad that bisected them. Generally, the grid plan was adopted in the laying out of new towns, and in the early phases of their growth nearly all the buildings in them followed the traditional wood-framed, prefabricated type of structure. To support the dignity of civic and educational buildings and great commercial establishments, classic architecture was usually deemed essential, and when such work was entrusted to architects of the capacity of McKim, Mead and White, the results were distinguished. This classic revival produced some fine monumental architecture. Few modern buildings in America or Europe attain the calm, dignified beauty of the Lincoln Memorial at Washington, D.C., a Doric structure designed by Henry Bacon and completed in 1922. An earlier building, the New York Public Library, finished in 1911, is an example of diligent scholarship: correct, competent, but spiritless. Designed by Carrère and Hastings, it has an impressive façade of white Vermont marble, with a tall, triple-arched portico fronting Fifth Avenue. The Corinthian order is used skilfully. Surrounded and dwarfed by high buildings, it seems far more incongruous as an architectural survival than such buildings as the Temple of the Scottish Rite at Washington, which is not overshadowed by examples of contemporary design. That Masonic Temple, by John Russell Pope, completed in 1915, derives its character from the Mausoleum of Halicarnassos.

There was no widespread classical revival in England comparable in purity and vigour with the American revival of the late nineteenth and early twentieth centuries. Only a few men interpreted the classic orders with the fertility of invention that had given such robust warmth to the work of the great architects of the English Renaissance, to Wren, Hawksmore, Vanbrugh and Gibbs—and of these the greatest was Sir Edwin Lutyens (1869–1944). In his early, romantic period he built large country houses for wealthy and discerning people, displaying a mastery of the traditional English domestic style, and his richness of invention is exhibited in such works as Orchards, Godalming, in Surrey (1898–1899), Marsh Court, Stockbridge, in Hampshire (1901), and Little Thakeham, Sussex (1902). There were many others; but as he matured, he became convinced that by using the classic orders he would be able to exert to the full his gifts as an artist and an architect. Mr. Christopher Hussey, in his masterly biography of Lutyens, has described this moment of recognition and deliberate choice. "As he became more conscious of his powers he discovered delightedly the logic, force, and subtlety of the Orders, and impatience began to consume him for opportunities wider than the largest of country houses could afford for exercising his and their capacities."[212] One of the early examples of his new vision of architectural design is the classic villa of Heathcote at Ilkley, which he undertook in 1906, where he used the Doric order with a freshness and vitality unknown in England for over a hundred and fifty years.

He left a great body of work to mark the last inspired interpretation of classic architecture by an English architect, great houses, banks and city offices, the Cenotaph in Whitehall, and the majestic buildings at New Delhi.

This revival of pure classic was the last flicker of the Renaissance spirit, momentarily rekindled in the United States and England, and wholly different from the debased "free classic," popular at the turn of the century, which was partly a reaction from the Gothic Revival, and led to many unhappy mutilations of the orders. One of the most accomplished practitioners of "free classic" was Norman Shaw (1831–1912), who, with an inventiveness that recalled the early work of the Flemish Renaissance architects, used classic motifs and often distorted them. His best-known building is New Scotland Yard in London; and his Piccadilly Hotel, ungainly in form and dull in detail, was one of the first buildings to destroy the scale of Nash's Regent Street. Neither the classic revival nor "free classic" had any relationship with the modern movement in architectural design, which was developing concurrently; but the romantic domestic style, originated by Philip Webb and William Morris, and the decorative motifs of the *Art Nouveau* school, had some formative influence. Louis Sullivan in America used the undisciplined naturalistic motifs of *Art Nouveau* to embellish some of his buildings, until he repudiated ornament. The movement was certainly a conscious attempt to create a non-historical style; as revolutionary as the attempt by the makers of the modern movement to derive their architectural inspiration from the machine and industrial materials. It had a passing effect only on interior architecture in Europe, Britain and America, not because it was rootless, but because it was a fashion, ornamental in character and out of tune with the real revolution in architectural thought. In his first published essays, Adolf Loos attacked the *Art Nouveau* style.[213]

During the 1890's and until 1914, the romantic domestic style flourished in England, and was practised by such architects as Charles Annesley Voysey (1857–1941), whose houses, revolutionary in their day, have since established a form that has been accepted, imitated, and grossly parodied by speculative builders. This domestic style was adopted for the new garden cities and suburbs that were built in England between the 1870's and 1914. The term "garden city" was popularised by Ebenezer Howard, who used it in his book, *To-morrow: a Peaceful Path to Real Reform*, published in 1898, though it was first employed by Alexander T. Stewart, who founded a model estate on Long Island, New York, in 1869. Stewart, who was the head of the largest retail stores in New York which subsequently became the establishment known as John Wanamakers, had bought 8,000 acres on Long Island, where he built a model town for his own and other city workers.[214] In England two garden estates were planned for the employees of Lever Brothers and Cadbury's. For the former, Port Sunlight was begun in 1888, on a site near Lower Bebington, in the Wirral peninsula of Cheshire: Bournville in Worcestershire, a few miles south-west of Birmingham, dates from 1895. W. R. Lethaby defined the garden city as "a town which exists in proper relation to the country round about it—a relation as between heart and lungs, between a centre of community life and distributed country labour by which each reacts beneficially on the other."[215] The idea of the independent garden city, advocated by Ebenezer Howard, was taken up in 1904 when Letchworth, in Hertfordshire, was planned and begun, and three years later the Hampstead Garden Suburb was laid out. (Raymond Unwin and Richard Barry Parker were the architects responsible for planning these two garden cities.) The earliest of the garden estates was Bedford Park, near Chiswick in the west of London, begun in 1875, and consisting of semi-detached houses built to the design of Norman Shaw.

The influence of exceptional architects like Voysey and a few of his contemporaries spread slowly; while the work of another outstanding architect, Charles Rennie Mackintosh (1868–1928), though admired in Europe, was largely ignored in his own country. His principal building, the Glasgow School of Art (1898–1899), was in advance of its time, and, like the early work of Frank Lloyd Wright in America, has, after the passage of half a century, a contemporary air.

In Europe, the first large building that disclosed the character of the modern movement, perhaps the first example of the new Western architecture, was the Turbo factory, erected in 1909 in the Huttenstrasse, Berlin, designed by Peter Behrens (1868–1940). The outline of that building was determined by the steel roof; the exposed steel stanchions of the flank wall formed the vertical members, which, like gigantic mullions, framed vast windows. That factory did not represent the dictatorship of materials, of steel and glass and concrete, any more than the Parthenon represents the dictatorship of Pentelic marble. Materials and techniques condition design; only unimaginative designers permit

The modern movement in England was being fought for by many young and enterprising architects in the nineteen-thirties. This example at Redhill, Surrey, of the work of Connell, Ward and Lucas was completed in 1935: it was an addition to an existing house, and was designed as a home for old people, who had separate flats. The box-like projections on the façade are larger cupboards, serving four separate kitchens.

The department store of Peter Jones, Sloane Square, London, designed by William Crabtree (in association with Slater and Moberley and Professor Sir Charles Reilly). Lightness, grace, and the harmonious adjustment of horizontal and vertical elements, characterise this English example of the modern movement in the late nineteen-thirties.

them to control it; and they stimulate the ideas of inventive architects, leading them on to fresh adventures in structure and composition. (See page 335.)

Steel and concrete and glass, used openly, and without traditional inhibitions, have allowed architects to solve with greater ease and economy an ancient problem. Secular architecture has always been influenced by the need to modify or annul some climatic condition. At all times and in most countries, buildings have been designed to give protection against extremes of temperature; and in the long struggle to conquer climate, architects and engineers have, in this century, been able to create artificial conditions that are acceptable, for domestic, civic, commercial and industrial architecture. This has led to the use of large areas of transparent wall, to the enlargement of windows. At first this characteristic of the new Western architecture was apparent chiefly in industrial buildings, like the Turbo factory by Peter Behrens, or the Fagus Boot-Last Factory at Alfeld-an-der-Leine, designed in 1911 by Walter Gropius in collabora-

Above: Highpoint Flats, Highgate, London, designed by Tecton, and built in 1935.
The shape of the plan is a double cross, with lifts and stairways at the two intersections.
On each floor, one flat occupies each arm of the cross, with two flats on the central
part that joins the crosses. This is a reinforced concrete building, and the structural
method and the material liberated the architects from any obligations to traditional
forms.

Left: House at Witham, Essex, designed by
Thomas Tait, F.R.I.B.A. The horizontal
features are deliberately emphasised.

Right: The Sun House, Frognal Way,
Hampstead, London, by E. Maxwell
Fry, F.R.I.B.A. The horizontal character is marked, but the windows and
balconies are light and graceful.
Compare the illustrations on this page
with the early house by Frank Lloyd
Wright and the Italian apartment
blocks on plate 31.

Traditional methods of building, with local materials, still account for the vast majority of houses put up in different European countries and the United States. The new Western architecture is spreading slowly, but despite the logic, convenience, and economy it represents, its form is unfamiliar; particularly for domestic buildings. The Swiss house shown above is comfortably familiar, and suits the landscape, of which it appears to be as much a part as the trees and fields.

tion with Adolf Meyer, those forerunners of such light, soaring crystalline towers as the Lever Building in Park Avenue, New York. (See plate 32.)

In American domestic design, Frank Lloyd Wright, far ahead of his time, was at the turn of the century beginning to stress horizontal lines, to use long balconies, to widen windows, to make all those innovations in the character and form of houses and the disposition of their apartments which would lead to intimate partnerships between rooms and gardens and landscapes, made possible by the picture window. Those bland, comprehensive relationships between the interior and the environment of a dwelling had not been attempted with such subtlety since the Renaissance, when houses and landscapes, palaces, parks and gardens, were regarded as elements of one great exercise in architectural design. Frank Lloyd Wright's early houses have had as marked an effect upon the modern domestic architecture of Europe and America as The Red House had upon the romantic domestic style in England. (See plate 31.)

Before 1914, the prophets and practitioners of the modern movement in architecture were still regarded either as courageous revolutionaries, inspired leaders, or impossible cranks. Their rejection of traditional ideas, their refusal to disguise their materials or structural techniques, ultimately allowed Walter

Gropius to announce that "the morphology of dead styles has been destroyed; and we are returning to honesty of thought and feeling."[216] In that atmosphere the new Western architecture was generated; between the world wars it commanded the talents of a young, enterprising generation of architects in Europe, America and Britain; and it had its educationalists and master-propagandists: Walter Gropius, who founded the great design school for technical and architectural education, the Bauhaus, which moved to Dessau in 1925; and Le Corbusier (Charles Eduard Jeanneret), whose books, *Vers une Architecture* and *Urbanisme*, published during the 1920's, made an impact upon European thought that helped to change not only the ideas of architects, but of those who controlled patronage.[217]

The modern movement was occasionally misinterpreted, as the classic orders were occasionally misinterpreted during the early Renaissance in Europe and England; as an architectural movement it is still young; but it has created a distinctive type of Western architecture which is to-day arising in every continent. Its form, though still experimental, is unmistakable: wherever it appears it expresses a way of thought, an approach to architectural design as recognisable and lucid as the system of design once disseminated by the classic orders, though far more pliant; and, as the classic orders once regulated the architecture of the Graeco-Roman world, the new Western architecture is now travelling round the modern world, everywhere challenging, replacing, absorbing or giving fresh life to national traditions of building. Although its early practitioners thought they were evolving an international style, each nation gives its own characteristic interpretation to the free and adventurous use of contemporary techniques and materials, as the European nations interpreted the classic orders when they re-emerged at the Renaissance, five hundred years ago. The characteristics of the new Western architecture are distasteful to some, inspiring to many; they are present in buildings and groups of buildings as widely different in function and locality as the Hilton Hotel at Istanbul, the housing estates of the London County Council in Wandsworth, the "Bastei" office building in Zürich, the buildings of London Airport, the Rhine Birsfelden hydro-electric power station, the new Concert Hall in the Hardenberg Strasse in Western Berlin, the schools in new English towns like Harlow in Essex, the tall office blocks of glass and aluminium in Pittsburg, Pennsylvania, or that spacious Technical Centre of General Motors, twelve miles south of Detroit, with its green areas, its central lake, its clusters of elegant buildings, which has been aptly called the industrial Versailles.

Attempts to interpret the significance of contemporary architecture can only be tentative. Much less of it is likely to survive than the architecture of former ages, not because of some inevitable and inescapable catastrophe, but because so many buildings now have a calculated economic life, like an ocean liner— after their earnings have covered the initial outlay for their construction and shown a return on the investment, they are replaced. Modern cities, particularly

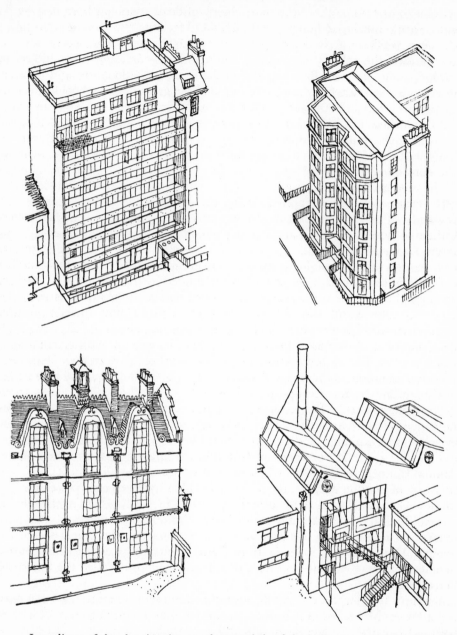

Ingredients of the chaotic mixture, characteristic of the built-up areas of English cities and their suburbs in the second half of the twentieth century. (From *Building for Daylight,* by Richard Sheppard and Hilton Wright.)

in the United States, have a comparatively rapid rate of replacement in commercial, industrial and residential areas. Of one thing we may be sure: what does survive for the scrutiny of posterity will reveal, as architecture always reveals, the truth about the people who created it, used it, and found it satisfying.

The extent, nature and accuracy of such revelations have been suggested by the ten sections of this book. The changes in the character of architecture caused by structural inventions and the introduction of new materials have been described and illustrated. The effect of the three basic structural inventions may be summarised as follows:

I. In post-and-lintel construction, horizontal and vertical members carry the building, and walls (which act as vertical members) have holes left in them for doors and windows.

II. The use of the arch led to the vault and the dome, and when buildings were carried by an internal frame, both post-and-lintel and arcuated construction were employed, for the internal frame carried a vaulted roof, and the outside parts of the frame were buried in the outside walls. The Gothic cathedrals had an internal frame of stone, linked with and penetrating the external walls.

III. Steel construction and reinforced concrete have made it possible for an internal frame to be set back within a building, so that the whole external wall becomes a light curtain, touching but not supporting the floors, which are carried by the inner steel frame and project from it like shelves. Buildings which used to be like crustaceans with a hard external supporting shell now resemble vertebrates, with an internal skeleton. Walls have become thin, protective skins.

Those three structural discoveries have liberated the gifts of architects from the fifth century B.C. to the present day. The Greeks brought post-and-lintel construction to its highest level in their temples, and in the Byzantine churches of the Eastern Roman Empire they employed arcuated construction with comparable genius. The mediaeval builders of the Gothic cathedrals used the arch with an experimental verve that created a new, adventurous architecture, unmatched by the achievements of the Graeco-Roman world. Irrespective of national characteristics, individual taste, and ultimate purpose, architectural design has been conditioned, and sometimes inspired, by the three basic constructional inventions. Periods of experimental development and great achievement have often been followed by static periods, when the latent possibilities of a structural technique have been ignored, and its true nature masked or minimised. We have just emerged from such a static period, and, with the rise of the new Western architecture, are at the beginning of what may well be mankind's greatest adventure in building.

SOURCES OF REFERENCES IN THE TEXT

(1) *The History of the Decline and Fall of the Roman Empire*, by Edward Gibbon. (London: 1807.) Volume XII, Chapter LXXI, pages 411–412.

(2) Gibbon. Volume XII, Chapter LXXI, pages 414–416.

(3) *In the Desert*, by Lisle March Phillipps. (London: Edward Arnold, 1905.) Chapter XVII, pages 240–241.

(4) Ibid., page 241.

(5) *The Caliph's Last Heritage*, by Sir Mark Sykes. (London: Macmillan & Co., 1915.) Part I, Chapter XVII, pages 186–187.

(6) *The Revolutions of Civilisation*, by Sir William Flinders Petrie. (London: Harper & Brothers. Third edition, 1922.) Chapter VI, page 112.

(7) *Londinium: Architecture and the Crafts*, by W. R. Lethaby. (London: Duckworth & Co., 1923.) Chapter III, page 83.

(8) Lethaby, *op. cit.*, Chapter I, page 13.

(9) *Building in England down to* 1540, by L. F. Salzman, F.S.A. (Oxford: the Clarendon Press, 1952.) Chapter IX, page 154.

(10) *Theory and Elements of Architecture*, by Robert Atkinson, F.R.I.B.A., and Hope Bagenal, A.R.I.B.A. (London: Ernest Benn Ltd., 1926.) Volume I, Part I, Chapter V, page 162.

(11) Translation by W. G. Newton, F.R.I.B.A., and included in his paper: "Imperial Building: What we may learn from Rome." *Journal of the Royal Institute of British Architects*, Volume XXVIII, No. 9, March 5th, 1921.

(12) *Theory and Elements of Architecture.* Chapter IX, page 319.

(13) *Glass in Architecture and Decoration*, by Raymond McGrath, B.Arch., F.R.I.B.A., and A. C. Frost. (London: The Architectural Press, 1937.) Section I, page 6.

(14) *The Land of the Great Image*, by Maurice Collis. (London: Faber & Faber Ltd., 1943.) Chapter III, page 31.

(15) *Glass in Architecture and Decoration.* Section I, page 7.

(16) *Londinium, op. cit.* Chapter I, page 32.

(17) *Architecture, an Introduction to the History and Theory of the Art of Building*, by W. R. Lethaby. (Home University Library.) Chapter XIII, page 227.

(18) *Glass in Architecture and Decoration, op. cit.* Section II, page 97.

(19) *Theory and Elements of Architecture, op. cit.* Chapter IX, footnote on page 333.

(20) "Machinery and Methods of Manufacture of Sheet Glass," by Professor W. E. Turner. A paper given to the Institution of Mechanical Engineers on December 5th, 1930.

(21) The historical survey of window design in England, which occupies pages 17 to 30, is condensed from the author's introduction to *Building for Daylight*, by Richard Sheppard, F.R.I.B.A., and Hilton Wright, A.R.I.B.A. (London: George Allen & Unwin Ltd., 1948.)

(22) *A History of Egypt*, by J. H. Breasted. (London: Hodder & Stoughton. Reprint of 1909 edition, January 1939.) Book I, Chapter VII, page 144.

(23) Genesis xi. 4.
(24) *A History of Egypt, op. cit.* Book II, Chapter V, page 101 and Fig. 47.
(25) *Discoveries in the Ruins of Nineveh and Babylon,* by A. H. Layard. (London: John Murray, 1853.) Chapter VII, pages 163–165.
(26) *Theory and Elements of Architecture.* Chapter VI, pages 196–197.
(27) *The Past in the Present,* by Arthur Mitchell, M.D., LL.D. (Edinburgh: David Douglas, 1880.) Lecture III (dated April 25th, 1876.) Pages 63–65.
(28) *The Diffusion of Culture,* by G. Elliott Smith. (London: Watts & Co., 1933.) Chapter V, page 215.
(29) *The Works of Man,* by Lisle March Phillipps. (London: Duckworth & Co. Second edition, 1914.) Chapter I, page 41.
(30) *A History of Egypt, op. cit.* Book V, Chapter XVIII, page 378.
(31) *A Study of History,* by Arnold J. Toynbee. (Oxford University Press, 1934.) Vol. I: "The Comparative Study of Civilisations," page 92.
(32) *Pausanias' Description of Greece,* translated by Arthur Richard Shilleto. (Bohn's Classical Library. London: George Bell & Sons, 1900). Book II, Chapter XVI, page 121.
(33) *Op. cit.,* page 121.
(34) *Ancient Hunters,* by W. J. Sollas. (London: Macmillan & Co. Third edition, 1924.) Chapter VIII, pages 398–399.
(35) *The Works of Man,* by Lisle March Phillipps. Chapter IV, pages 109–110. *A History of Architecture on the Comparative Method,* by Sir Banister Fletcher. (London: B. T. Batsford Ltd. Tenth edition, 1938.) Page 75.
(36) *The Architecture of Marcus Vitruvius Pollio,* translated by Joseph Gwilt. (London: Priestley & Weale, 1826.) Book IV, Chapter I, pages 101–102.
(37) *Ancient Town-Planning,* by F. Haverfield. (Oxford University Press, 1913.) Chapters II and III, pages 29–30.
(38) Suyuti (*Husn al Muhâdarah*), quoted by Dr. Alfred J. Butler, in *The Arab Conquest of Egypt.* (Oxford University Press, 1902.) Chapter XXIV, pages 369–370 and 390–391.
(39) *The Arab Conquest of Egypt.* Chapter XXIV, page 369.
(40) *How the Greeks Built Cities,* by R. E. Wycherley. (Macmillan & Co. Ltd., 1949.) Page 39.
(41) *Ancient Town-Planning,* by F. Haverfield. Chapter IX, page 129.
(42) *Ibid.,* Chapter IX, pages 127–128.
(43) *Londinium: Architecture and the Crafts,* by W. R. Lethaby. (London: Duckworth & Co., 1923.) Chapter XI, pages 217–218.
(44) *Ancient Town-Planning,* by F. Haverfield. Chapter XI, pages 143–144.
(45) *The Mythology of the British Islands,* by Charles Squire. (London: Blackie & Son Ltd., 1905.) Chapter XVI, page 275.
(46) *Mithraism,* by W. J. Phythian-Adams. (London: Constable & Co., Ltd., 1915.) Chapter VII, page 94.
(47) *Op. cit.,* pages 43–47.
(48) *The Mythology of the British Islands,* by Charles Squire. Chapter XVI, pages 253, 254.
(49) *The History of Count Zosimus.* (London: printed for J. Davis, 1814.) Book II, pages 52–53.

(50) *Gibbon*. Volume VII, Chapter XL, page 116.
(51) *The Church of Sancta Sophia, Constantinople*, by W. R. Lethaby and Harold Swainson. (London: Macmillan & Co., 1894.) Chapter XI, page 247.
(52) *Ibid.*, pages 247–248.
(53) *Gibbon*. Vol. VII, Chapter XL, page 121.
(54) *Theory and Elements of Architecture*, by Atkinson and Bagenal. Volume I, Chapter III, page 89.
(55) *Vitruvius*, Gwilt's translation. (London: 1826.) Book VI, Chapter XI, page 187.
(56) *The Caliph's Last Heritage*, by Sir Mark Sykes. (Macmillan & Co. Ltd., 1915.) Part I, Chapter VI: "Romans and Persians," pages 38 and 39.
(57) *Op. cit.*, Part I, Chapter V, "Romans and Parthians," pages 26–27.
(58) *A Diversity of Creatures*, by Rudyard Kipling. (London: Macmillan & Co., 1917.) "Regulus," page 245.
(59) Sir Mark Sykes, *op. cit.*, page 27.
(60) *Gibbon*, Volume IX, Chapter XLVIII, pages 2–3.
(61) *Op. cit.*, Volume IX, Chapter XLVIII, page 3.
(62) *Good Behaviour*, by Harold Nicolson. (London: Constable & Co., 1955.) Chapter V, page 94.
(63) *Roman Society in the Last Century of the Western Empire*, by Sir Samuel Dill (Macmillan & Co., 1898.) Book II, Chapter IV, pages 169–170.
(64) *Ibid.*, page 177.
(65) *Sidonius, Poems and Letters*, translated by W. B. Anderson. (The Loeb Classical Library. London: William Heinemann Ltd., 1936.) Volume I, Letters. Book II, Letter II to Domitius.
(66) *Sidonius*, Volume I, Book II, Letter X to Hesperius.
(67) *Roman Society in Gaul in the Merovingian Age*, by Sir Samuel Dill. (Macmillan & Co. Ltd., 1926.) Book II, Chapter IV, pages 317–318.
(68) *Op. cit.*, Book III, Chapter III, page 447.
(69) *Op. cit.*, Book II, Chapter IV, page 325.
(70) *Sidonius*, Volume I, Book II, Letter IX to Donidius.
(71) *Glass in Architecture and Decoration*, by Raymond McGrath and B. A. Frost. (The Architectural Press, 1937.) Section I, page 8.
(72) *English Glass*, by W. A. Thorpe. (A. & C. Black Ltd. "The Library of English Art." Second edition, 1949). Chapter II, page 77.
(73) *Roman Society in Gaul in the Merovingian Age*, by Sir Samuel Dill. Book II, Chapter II, pages 245–247. Book III, Chapter III, pages 469–472.
(74) *A Study of History*, by Arnold J. Toynbee. (Oxford University Press, 1954.) Volume VIII, Section IX, A, ii, sub-section 5, "The Modern West and the Jews," pages 278–279, and note 3.
(75) *English Glass*, by W. A. Thorpe. Chapter II, page 77.
(76) *Sidonius, Poems and Letters*. Volume I, Letters. Book I, Letter II to Agricola.
(77) *Verulamium: a Belgic and two Roman Cities*, by Sir Mortimer Wheeler and T. V. Wheeler. (Oxford University Press, for the Society of Antiquaries, 1936.) Page 2.
(78) *Ibid.*, pages 2–3.
(79) *Roman Britain and the English Settlements*, by R. G. Collingwood and J. N. L. Myres. (Oxford University Press, 1936.) Section XII, page 202.

(80) *The Ecclesiastical History of the English Nation*, by the Venerable Bede. (Everyman Library edition.) Book I, Chapters VII and VIII.

(81) *Christianity in Early Britain*, by Hugh Williams, M.A., D.D. (Oxford: the Clarendon Press, 1912.) Chapter IX, page 142. *Chapters of Early English Church History*, by William Bright, D.D. (Oxford: The Clarendon Press. Third edition, 1897.) Chapter I, page 10.

(82) *Byways in British Archaeology*, by Walter Johnson. (Cambridge University Press, 1912.) Chapter I, page 4.

(83) *Chapters of Early English Church History*, by William Bright, D.D. Chapter I, page 11.

(84) *Byways in British Archaeology*, by Walter Johnson. Chapter I, page 23.

(85) *Ibid.*, Chapter I, page 5.

(86) *Ecclesiastical History*. Book III, Chapter IV.

(87) *Celtic Scotland: a History of Ancient Alban*, by William Skene, D.C.L., LL.D. (Edinburgh: David Douglas. Second edition, 1887.) Volume II, Book II, Chapter I, page 2. Chapter II, page 46.

(88) Skene, *op. cit.*, Chapter II, page 46.

(89) *Ecclesiastical History*. Book III, Chapter IV.

(90) *Roman Britain and the English Settlements*, by R. G. Collingwood and J. N. L. Myres. Section XIX, page 310.

(91) *The Works of Gildas and Nennius*, translated by J. A. Giles, LL.D. (London: James Bohn, 1841.) Section II, "The History," page 8.

(92) *Ecclesiastical History*. Book I, Chapter XXVI.

(93) *Religion and the Rise of Western Culture*, by Christopher Dawson. The Gifford Lectures delivered in the University of Edinburgh, 1948–1949. (London: Sheed & Ward, 1950.) Chapter III, page 66.

(94) *Gildas, op. cit.* Section II, "The History," pages 7 and 22.

(95) *Ecclesiastical History*, Book II, Chapter VI.

(96) *The Transition from Roman Britain to Christian England*, by Gilbert Sheldon. (Macmillan & Co., 1932.) Chapter V, page 86.

(97) *London Before the Conquest*, by W. R. Lethaby. (London: Macmillan & Co., 1911.) Chapter VII, pages 157–158.

(98) *Heimskringla*: the Olaf Sagas, by Snorre Sturlason. (Everyman Library edition.) King Olaf Trygvesson's Saga, Chapter LXIX.

(99) *The Illiterate Anglo-Saxon*, by John William Adamson. (Cambridge University Press, 1946.) Chapter I, page 15.

(100) *Anglo-Saxon Art*, by T. D. Kendrick, F.S.A. (London: Methuen & Co. Ltd., 1938.) Section VI, page 119.

(101) *Religion and the Rise of Western Culture*, by Christopher Dawson. Chapter III, page 71.

(102) *Ibid.*, page 71.

(103) *Anglo-Saxon Art*, by T. D. Kendrick. Section VI, page 120.

(104) *The Illiterate Anglo-Saxon*, by John William Adamson. Chapter I, page 15.

(105) *The Holy Roman Empire*, by James Bryce. (London: Macmillan & Co. Third edition, 1871.) Chapter VI, page 80.

(106) *A History of Europe*, by H. A. L. Fisher. (London: Edward Arnold & Co. 1936 edition in one volume.) Chapter VIII, page 95.

(107) *Diary of John Evelyn*, November 6th, 1644.

(108) *An Historical Essay on Architecture*, by Thomas Hope. (London: John Murray, 1835.) Introduction, page vi. The essay was published posthumously: the author died in 1831.

(109) *Architecture*, by Christian Barman, R.D.I., F.R.I.B.A. (Benn, 1928.) Section IV, pages 39–40.

(110) *Ibid.*, page 40.

(111) *Three of Them*, by Norman Douglas. (London: Chatto & Windus, 1930.) "One Day," pages 47–48.

(112) *Mont-Saint-Michel and Chartres*, by Henry Adams. (London: Constable & Co. Ltd. New edition, 1936.) Section I, page 9.

(113) *Building in England*, by L. F. Salzman, F.S.A. (Oxford: at the Clarendon Press, 1952.) Section I, page 26.

(114) *Men and Buildings*, by John Gloag. (London: Chantry Publications Ltd. Second revised and illustrated edition, 1950.) Chapter IV, pages 40–42.

(115) *Architecture*, by Christian Barman, R.D.I., F.R.I.B.A. Section IV, pages 47–48.

(116) *Heaven and Hell*, by Aldous Huxley. (London: Chatto & Windus, 1956.) Pages 28–29.

(117) *Men and Buildings*, by John Gloag. Chapter IV, pages 50–51.

(118) *Byways in British Archaeology*, by Walter Johnson. Chapter V, page 230.

(119) *Ibid.*, Chapter V, page 233.

(120) *Ibid.*, Chapter V, page 233.

(121) *Ibid.*, Chapter V, page 238.

(122) *A Glossary of Terms, used in Grecian, Roman, Italian, and Gothic Architecture*, by J. H. Parker. (Oxford. Fourth edition, 1845.)

(123) *Men and Buildings*, by John Gloag. Chapter IV, pages 34–37.

(124) *Form and Colour*, by Lisle March Phillipps. (London: Duckworth & Co., 1915.) Part III, Chapter XI, page 192.

(125) *2,000 Years of England*, by John Gloag. (London: Cassell & Co. Ltd., 1952.) Chapter XIX, page 263.

(126) *The Hansa; its History and Romance*, by E. Gee Nash. (London: John Lane, 1929.) Part I, Chapter II, pages 15–16.

(127) *Social Life in the Days of Piers Plowman*, by D. Chadwick. (Cambridge University Press, 1922.) Page 55.

(128) *2,000 Years of England*, by John Gloag. (Cassell & Co., London, 1952.) Chapter XIV, pages 156–157.

(129) *History in a Changing World*, by Geoffrey Barraclough. (Oxford: Basil Blackwell, 1955.) Section IV, page 54.

(130) *Greenland*. Published by the Commission for the Direction of the Geological and Geographical Investigations in Greenland. (London: Humphrey Milford, 1929.) Volume III: "History of the Trade and Colonization until 1870," by Louis Bobé. Pages 80–81.

(131) *Greenland. Op. cit.*, Volume II: "On the Icelandic Colonization of Greenland," by Finnur Jonsson. Pages 343–345.

(132) *Greenland. Op. cit.*, Volume II: "Old Norse Farms in the Eastern and Western Settlements," by Captain Daniel Bruun. Pages 396–397.

(133) *Greenland. Op. cit.*, Volume II: "The finds from Herjolfsnes," by Poul Nörlund. Page 406.

(134) *History in a Changing World*, by Geoffrey Barraclough. Section IV, page 54.

(135) *The Waning of the Middle Ages*, by J. Huizinga. (London: Edward Arnold & Co., 1924.) Chapter XXIII, page 297.

(136) *The Vision of Hell*, by Dante Alighieri. Translated by the Rev. Henry Francis Cary. (Cassell & Co., 1913.) Canto IV, lines 72–74.

(137) *The Architecture of Humanism*, by Geoffrey Scott. (London: Constable & Co., 1924.) Chapter VII, page 191.

(138) *The Revolutions of Civilisation*, by Sir William Flinders Petrie. (London: Harper & Brothers. Third edition, 1922.) Chapter V, page 74.

(139) *The Architecture of Marcus Vitruvius Pollio*, translated by Joseph Gwilt. (London: Priestley & Weale, 1826.) Book I, Chapter I, page 3.

(140) *Op. cit.*, Book I, Chapter II, page 11.

(141) *Bernini's Bust of Louis XIV*, Charlton Lecture on Art, delivered at King's College, Durham University, by Rudolf Wittkower. (Printed by Geoffrey Cumberlege, Oxford University Press, 1951.) Page 5.

(142) *Men and Buildings*, by John Gloag. (London: Chantry Publications Ltd. Second edition, 1950.) Chapter V, pages 68–69.

(143) *A History of Europe*, by H. A. L. Fisher. (London: Edward Arnold & Co., 1936.) Book II, Chapter V, pages 536–537.

(144) *The American Nation*, by John and Julian Gloag. (London: Cassell & Co., Ltd. Revised and enlarged edition, 1955.) Section I, Chapter IV, pages 36–37.

(145) *Roman Mornings*, by James Lees-Milne. (London: Alan Wingate, 1956.) Renaissance I, pages 63–64.

(146) *The Waning of the Middle Ages*, by J. Huizinga. (London: Edward Arnold & Co., 1924.) Chapter XXIII, page 297.

(147) *Roman Mornings*, by James Lees-Milne. "Rococo," page 147.

(148) *Georgian Grace*, by John Gloag. (London: A. & C. Black Ltd. New York: The Macmillan Co., 1956.) Part I, Chapter IV, page 101.

(149) *Mediaeval Contributions to Modern Civilisation*, edited by F. J. C. Hearnshaw. (London: George G. Harrap & Co., Ltd., 1921.) Chapter V, "Art," by the Rev. Percy Dearmer, D.D., pages 164–165.

(150) *Form and Colour*, by Lisle March Phillipps. (London: Duckworth & Co., 1915.) Chapter XI, page 213.

(151) *A Short History of England*, by G. K. Chesterton. (London: Chatto & Windus. Phoenix Library edition, 1930 reprint.) Chapter XI, page 137.

(152) *China and Europe*, by Adolf Reichwein. (London: Kegan Paul, 1925.) "Rococo," pages 25–26.

(153) *Op. cit.*, "Rococo," page 64.

(154) *The Story of Venice*, by Thomas Okey. (Mediaeval Towns Series. London: J. M. Dent & Sons Ltd. 1924 reprint of original 1905 edition.) Chapter XI, page 211.

(155) *The Notebooks of Leonardo da Vinci*, arranged and rendered into English and introduced by Edward MacCurdy. (London: Jonathan Cape, 1938.) Volume II, Section XXXVIII, page 422.

(156) *The Scientific Attitude*, by C. H. Waddington, Sc.D. (Pelican Books, 1941.) Foreword, page 9.

(157) *Three Hundred Years of French Architecture*, by Sir Reginald Blomfield. (London: Alexander Maclehose & Co., 1936.) Chapter I, page 12.

(158) *The History and Antiquities of the Collegiate Church of Tamworth*, by Charles Ferrers R. Palmer. (Tamworth: J. Thompson. London: Simpkin, Marshall & Co., 1871.) Chapter VI, page 65.

(159) *The Architect in History*, by Martin S. Briggs, F.R.I.B.A. (Oxford: The Clarendon Press, 1927.) Section VI, page 193.

(160) *Op. cit.*, Section VI, page 203.

(161) *Op. cit.*, Section VI, page 203.

(162) *The Waning of the Middle Ages*, by J. Huizinga. (London: Edward Arnold & Co., 1924.) Chapter XXIII, page 297.

(163) *Three Hundred Years of French Architecture*, by Sir Reginald Blomfield. (London: Alexander Maclehose & Co., 1936.) Chapter III, pages 45–46. *The Architect in History*, by Martin S. Briggs. Section VI, pages 210, 216.

(164) *Three Hundred Years of French Architecture*, by Sir Reginald Blomfield. Chapter V, page 85.

(165) *Anecdotes of Painting in England*, collected by the late Mr. George Vertue and now digested and published from his original MSS. by Mr. Horace Walpole. (London: J. Dodsley. Third edition, 1786.) Volume IV, Chapter VI, page 122.

(166) *Fischer Von Erlach*, by H. V. Lanchester, F.R.I.B.A. (London: Ernest Benn Ltd., 1924.) Pages 9–10.

(167) *Westminster Abbey and the Kings' Craftsmen*, by W. R. Lethaby. (London: Duckworth & Co., 1906.) Chapter XI, pages 236–237.

(168) *The First and Chief Groundes of Architecture* used in all the auncient and famous monymentes: with a farther and more ample discourse upon the same, than hitherto hath been set out by any other. Published by Jhon Shute, Paynter and Archytecte. Imprinted at London in Fletestrete near to Sainct Dunstans churche by Thomas Marshe, 1563.

(169) *Harrison's Description of England in Shakespere's Youth*, edited by Frederick J. Furnival. (Published for the New Shakespere Society, by N. Trübner & Co., London, 1877.) Volume I, Book II, Chapter V, page 129.

(170) *Op. cit.*, Volume I, Book II, Chapter XII, page 238.

(171) *Op. cit.*, Volume I, Book II, Chapter XII, pages 239–240.

(172) *The Elements of Architecture*, by Sir Henry Wotton. The First Part. (Included in *Reliquiae Wottonianae*. London: third edition, 1672.)

(173) *Iron and Steel in the Industrial Revolution*, by T. S. Ashton. (Manchester, the University Press, and Longmans, Green & Co., London, 1924.) Page 12.

(174) *The History of the Royal Society*, by Thomas Sprat. (London: 1722. The third edition, corrected.) Section XL, page 311.

(175) *Op. cit.*, Section XL, page 314.

(176) *Op. cit.*, Section XL, pages 316–317.

(177) *Op. cit.*, Section XL, page 317.

(178) *Men and Buildings*, by John Gloag. (London: Chantry Publications Ltd. Second edition, revised and illustrated, 1950.) A few passages between pages 261 and 264 and 267 and 271 are condensed from Chapters VI and VII of

that book, which describe the development and decline of English Renaissance architecture.

(179) *Nicholas Hawksmore*, by H. S. Goodhart-Rendel. (London: Ernest Benn Ltd., 1924.) Page 25.

(180) *Poems on Several Occasions*, by W. Woty. (Derby: printed for the author by J. Drewry. M,DCC,LXXX.)

(181) *Sir John Vanbrugh*, by Christian Barman. (London: Ernest Benn Ltd., 1924.) Page 8.

(182) *Vitruvius Britannicus, or the British Architect*, by Colen Campbell. (London: 1731.) Volume III, page 1.

(183) *The Four Books of Architecture*, by Andrea Palladio, literally translated from the Italian by Isaac Ware. (London: printed for R. Ware, at the *Bible* and *Sun*, on *Ludgate-Hill*.) The quotation is from the "Advertisement" which follows the dedication page, and is dated 1737. No date appears on the title-page.

(184) *Characteristicks of Men, Manners, Opinions, Times*, by the Right Honourable Anthony, Earl of Shaftesbury. (Originally published anonymously in 1711. The quotation is from the sixth edition, 1737.) Volume III, page 402.

(185) *Georgian Grace*, by John Gloag. (London: A. & C. Black Ltd. New York: The Macmillan Co., 1956.) Part I, Section 3, pages 58–59.

(186) *Op. cit.*, Part I, Section 3, pages 61–63.

(187) *Anecdotes of Painting in England*. (London: J. Dodsley. Third edition, 1786.) Volume IV, Chapter VI, pages 232–233.

(188) *Op. cit.*, page 234.

(189) *Some Account of London*, by Thomas Pennant. (London: the fifth edition, 1813.) Page 171.

(190) *London and its Environs Described*. (London: printed for R. and J. Dodsley, 1761.) Volume VI, page 41.

(191) "The Gothick Taste," by J. Isaacs, M.A.(Oxon.), Professor of English Language and Literature in the University of London, Queen Mary College. A lecture given at a General Meeting of the Royal Institute of British Architects, June 17th, 1952. *Journal of the R.I.B.A.*, Volume 59, No. 9, July 1952, page 337.

(192) *Anecdotes of Painting in England*. (London: J. Dodsley. Third edition, 1786.) Volume IV, Chapter VI, pages 8 and 9.

(193) *An Inquiry into the Principles of Beauty in Grecian Architecture; with an Historical View of the Rise and Progress of Art in Greece*, by George, Earl of Aberdeen. (London: John Murray, 1822. The substance of this essay was prefixed as an introduction to Wilkins's translation of Vitruvius, published in 1812.) Pages 215–217.

(194) *The Creative Centuries*, by Henry John Randall. (London: Longmans, Green & Co., 1944.) Chapter 9, page 61.

(195) *An Apology for the Revival of Christian Architecture in England*, by A. Welby Pugin. (London: John Weale, 1843.) Page 5.

(196) *The Creative Centuries*, by Henry John Randall. Chapter 27, page 191.

(197) *Loudon's Life and Work*, by John Gloag. *The Official Architect*, January 1951. Pages 37–40.

(198) *The Architect in History*, by Martin S. Briggs, F.R.I.B.A. (Oxford: the Clarendon Press, 1927.) Chapter VIII, page 360.

(199) *Op. cit.*, Chapter VI, page 215.

(200) *The Revolutions of Civilisation*, by Sir William Flinders Petrie. (London: Harper & Brothers. Third edition, 1922.) Chapter V, page 96.

(201) *Six Essays*, by John T. Emmet. (London: Unwin Brothers, and Hodder & Stoughton, 1891.) III. "The Profession of an 'Architect'," reprinted from *The British Quarterly Review*, April 1880. Page 46.

(202) *Op. cit.*, pages 46–47.

(203) *The Art Journal*. (London and New York. New Series, 1862.) "Tall Chimney Shafts," Volume I, page 57.

(204) *Anticipations*, by H. G. Wells. (London: Chapman & Hall Ltd. Eighth edition, 1902.) Chapter IV, page 117.

(205) *Pioneers of the Modern Movement*, by Nikolaus Pevsner. (The Museum of Modern Art, New York. Second edition, 1949.) Section I, page 9.

(206) *Die Renaissance im modernen Kunstgewerby*, by Henry van de Velde. (Leipzig, 1903.) This is one of two volumes in which van de Velde's lectures are collected. Both volumes are quoted in Dr. Nikolaus Pevsner's *Pioneers of the Modern Movement* (see previous reference), and my quotations are taken from that work, Section I, page 13.

(207) *Pioneers of the Modern Movement*, by Nikolaus Pevsner. Section V, page 82.

(208) *The Autobiography of an Idea*, by Louis H. Sullivan. (New York: W. W. Norton & Co., Inc., published by arrangement with The American Institute of Architects. Copyright, 1922.) "Retrospect," page 313.

(209) *McKim, Mead and White*, by C. H. Reilly. (London: Ernest Benn Ltd., 1924.) Page 16.

(210) *The American Nation*, by John and Julian Gloag. (London: Cassell & Co. Ltd. Revised and enlarged edition, 1955.) Chapter XI, page 111.

(211) *New York City Guide*, prepared by the Federal Writers' Project of the Work's Progress Administration in New York City. (London: Constable & Co. Ltd., 1939.) Page 351.

(212) *The Life of Sir Edwin Lutyens*, by Christopher Hussey. (London: Country Life Ltd., 1950.) Chapter V, page 77.

(213) *Pioneers of the Modern Movement*, by Nikolaus Pevsner. Section I, page 14.

(214) *Town Theory and Practice*, edited by C. B. Purdom. (London: Benn Brothers Ltd., 1921.) Introductory chapter by the editor. Page 16.

(215) *Op. cit.*, Chapter I, "The Town Itself," by W. R. Lethaby. Page 47.

(216) *The New Architecture and the Bauhaus*, by Walter Gropius. Translated by P. Morton Shand. (London: Faber & Faber Ltd., 1935.) Page 17.

(217) English translations by Frederick Etchells of Le Corbusier's two books appeared under the titles of *Towards a new Architecture* (1927), and *The City of To-Morrow* (1929). Both issued in London by John Rodker.

GENERAL REFERENCES

Joseph Gwilt's translation of Vitruvius, *De Architectura* (1826), has been used, and Isaac Ware's translation of Palladio's *I Quattro Libri dell'Architettura* (1737). General reference has been made to the following: *The Dictionary of Architecture* (issued by the Architectural Publication Society between 1852 and 1892); *A Biographical Dictionary of English Architects*, 1660–1840, by H. M. Colvin (London: John Murray, 1954); the *Journal of the Royal Institute of British Architects*, *The Architectural Review*, *The Builder*, and (for contemporary American architecture), *The Architectural Forum*.

SOME BOOKS ON ARCHITECTURE

This is not a bibliography: it is a very short annotated list of works, related to the subjects and periods covered by the ten sections of this book.

GENERAL

A History of Architecture on the Comparative Method, by Sir Banister Fletcher, PP.R.I.B.A. (London: B. T. Batsford Ltd. First issued 1896. Tenth edition, 1938.) The most comprehensive and clearly illustrated reference book: indispensable to the study of architecture, well planned and factual.

The Art of Architecture, by Sir Albert Richardson, PP.R.A., F.R.I.B.A., and Hector O. Corfiato, S.A.D.G., F.R.I.B.A. (London: The English Universities Press Ltd., 1938.) A richly illustrated study of architectural design and composition, from early Egypt to the present day.

Architecture Explained, by Sir Howard Robertson, PP.R.I.B.A. (London: Ernest Benn Ltd., 1927.) An excellent introduction to the study of architectural composition and history, and the relationship of the architect to society. *The Principles of Architectural Composition,* by the same author, is a lucid guide to the subject, using examples from traditional and contemporary building. (London: The Architectural Press, first issued in 1924.)

Architecture, by William Richard Lethaby. (Originally published in the Home University Library, and re-issued by the Oxford University Press.) A compact and most readable history.

The Architecture of Humanism, by Geoffrey Scott. (London: Constable & Co. Second revised edition, 1924.) A study of the history of taste, following the Renaissance. One of the most outstanding books ever written on architecture.

The Works of Man, by Lisle March Phillipps. (London: Duckworth & Co., first published in 1911.) A study of the revelation of national character through architecture. A later book, *Form and Colour,* by the same author, examines artistic and cultural movements that influence architecture. (Duckworth, 1915.)

The Pleasures of Architecture, by Clough and Amabel Williams-Ellis. (London: Jonathan Cape Ltd. First published 1924: new version, 1954.) An urbane, discursive, and witty book, which, throughout its twelve chapters, justifies its title.

The Architect in History, by Martin S. Briggs, F.R.I.B.A. (Oxford: The Clarendon Press, 1927.) A most readable study of the lives and works of architects, from Graeco-Roman times to the end of the Renaissance.

The Architecture of England, from Norman Times to the Present Day, by Frederick Gibberd, C.B.E., F.R.I.B.A. (London: The Architectural Press, first published 1938.) A highly condensed, well-illustrated history, which relates architecture to the arts and crafts and industrial design.

357

A Short Dictionary of Architecture, by Dora Ware and Betty Beatty, A.R.I.B.A. (London: George Allen & Unwin Ltd. Third edition, revised and enlarged, 1953.) A reliable and well-illustrated glossary, which includes building terms in common use.

GREEK AND ROMAN ARCHITECTURE

Greek and Roman architecture is fully described and illustrated with examples and reconstructions in Sir Banister Fletcher's *History of Architecture on the Comparative Method*. During the eighteenth and early nineteenth centuries, many detailed studies and records were made of antique remains, and of these the following are among the most notable:—

The Antiquities of Athens, measured and delineated by James Stuart and Nicholas Revett; a work sponsored by the Society of Dilettanti, and published in four volumes, the first appearing in 1762, the last in 1814. (*See* plate 2.) The Society also sponsored *Ionian Antiquities*, which appeared in 1769.

The Erectheion at Athens, with Marble and Terra-Cotta Fragments of Athenian Architecture, and a few remains in Attica, Megara and Eleusis, by Henry William Inwood, 1827. (*See* pages 300 and 389.)

Antiquities of Magna Graecia, by William Wilkins, containing drawings of the temples at Paestum and Syracuse. (Cambridge, 1807.) (*See* page 390.)

The Antiquities of Athens and other places of Greece, Sicily etc., by Charles Robert Cockerell, published in 1830 to supplement the work of Stuart and Revett. (*See* plate 2.) In the same year he published his study of *The Temple of Jupiter Olympius at Agrigentum*, and in 1869 his greatest work, *The Temples of Jupiter Panhellenius at Egina, and of Apollo Epicurus at Bassae*.

The Architectural Antiquities of Rome, measured and delineated by George Ledwell Taylor and Edward Cresy. (Two volumes, 1821–1822. Second edition, 1874.)

The Ruins of the Palace of the Emperor Diocletian at Spalatro, by Robert Adam, with engravings by Bartolozzi and other artists. 1764.

The Baths of the Romans Explained, with the Restorations of Palladio Corrected and Improved, by Charles Cameron. 1772. (*See* page 204.)

Etchings of Ancient Ornamental Architecture, drawn from the Originals in Rome and other Parts of Italy, by Charles Heathcote Tatham. 1799.

The engravings of Giovanni Battista Piranesi, made during the eighteenth century, and depicting the buildings and antiquities of ancient Rome, have been issued in various volumes. About 2,000 of them, collected by his son Francesco, are published in twenty-nine volumes. (Paris, 1835–1837.)

BYZANTINE, ROMANESQUE AND GOTHIC ARCHITECTURE

These periods are covered by W. R. Lethaby's *Architecture*; Dr. Nikolaus Pevsner's *An Outline of European Architecture* (London: Penguin Books, 1942; re-issued in a larger format by John Murray), an illuminating work by a great scholar; and by Sir Banister Fletcher's *History*, already cited. The Byzantine architecture of Greece is brilliantly depicted and described in *Classical Landscape with Figures*, by Osbert Lancaster (London: John Murray, 1947).

The following are more specialised works:

The Church of Sancta Sophia, Constantinople: a Study of Byzantine Building, by W. R. Lethaby and Harold Swainson. (London: Macmillan & Co., 1894.) A highly detailed technical study of Justinian's great church.

Byzantine Legacy, by Cecil Stewart, D.A.(Edin.), A.R.I.B.A. (London: George Allen & Unwin Ltd., 1947.) A superbly illustrated account of Byzantine buildings in Greece and Italy.

An Introduction to the Study of Gothic Architecture, by J. H. Parker. (Oxford: James Parker & Co. Originally issued in 1849, it reached its sixteenth edition sixty years later.) A reliable and fully illustrated work.

Mont-Saint-Michel and Chartres, by Henry Adams. (London: Constable & Co. Ltd., 1936. First issued in 1905.) A classic work that reveals the significance of Gothic architecture, and the spiritual exaltation and limitations of mediaeval builders.

An Attempt to Discriminate the Styles of Architecture in England, from the Conquest to the Reformation, by Thomas Rickman. (London: 1817. The fourth edition, 1835, was considerably enlarged.) This was the first systematic study of Gothic architecture, and Rickman (1776–1841) invented the nomenclature for the English periods: Norman, Early English, Decorated, and Perpendicular, which have since been adopted by all writers on the subject. The book is sparsely and not very well illustrated, but the text is reliable.

The Principles of Gothic Ecclesiastical Architecture, by Matthew Holbeche Bloxam. (London: David Bogue. The ninth edition, published in 1849, has more illustrations than the earlier editions.) This is a history of English architecture, from Romano-British times to the beginning of the sixteenth century. A list of technical terms is included.

Gothic England, by John Harvey. (London: B. T. Batsford Ltd., 1947.) A detailed account of the character of Gothic art and architecture in England, from 1300 to 1550.

Building in England, by L. F. Salzman, F.S.A. (Oxford: The Clarendon Press, 1952.) A documentary history of building materials and techniques down to 1540.

THE RENAISSANCE

The rise, development and decline of Renaissance Architecture in Europe are recorded in Pevsner's *Outline*, Banister Fletcher's *History*, and Richardson and Corfiato's *Art of Architecture*. *The Architect in History*, by Martin S. Briggs, deals fully with the whole period.

For the English Renaissance, a most comprehensive and reliable work is:

Architecture in Britain, 1530–1830, by John Summerson, C.B.E., F.S.A., A.R.I.B.A. (London: The Pelican History of Art, published by Penguin Books Ltd., 1933.)

MODERN ARCHITECTURE

An Introduction to Modern Architecture, by J. M. Richards. (London: Penguin Books Ltd., first published 1940.) A compact and lucid account of the rise and growth of the new Western architecture.

Pioneers of the Modern Movement, by Nikolaus Pevsner. (London: Faber & Faber Ltd., 1936. Revised and enlarged edition published by the Museum of Modern Art, New York, 1949.) The best historical study of the genesis of the modern movement, covering the period from William Morris to Walter Gropius.

In the Nature of Materials, The Buildings of Frank Lloyd Wright, 1887–1941, by Henry Russell Hitchcock. (New York: Duell, Sloan & Pearce, 1942.) A detailed record of the work of this pioneer of the modern movement in the United States.

The New Architecture and the Bauhaus, by Walter Gropius. Translated by P. Morton Shand. (London: Faber & Faber Ltd., 1935.) A well-illustrated account of the rise of the modern movement and the work of the school of design at Dessau.

Towards a New Architecture, by Le Corbusier, translated from the thirteenth French edition by Frederick Etchells. (London: John Rodker, 1927.) The author's ideas about the nature of architecture, and its proper service to twentieth century civilisation, are dramatically presented. An English translation from the eighth French edition of his *The City of To-Morrow* was published in 1929 (John Rodker), and is concerned with the logical (and slightly inhuman) planning of cities.

THE PRINCIPAL ARCHITECTS AND THEIR WORKS, FROM THE SEVENTH CENTURY B.C. TO THE END OF THE RENAISSANCE

This list, arranged in approximately chronological order, is not comprehensive, and only a selection of the works of the architects is included.

GREEK

THEODORUS OF SAMOS

Foundations of the first Temple of Artemis, Ephesus, 600 B.C.

CTESIPHON OR CHERSIPHON

Archaic Temple of Artemis, Ephesus, 550 B.C., assisted by his son, *Metagenes*.

SPINTHARUS OF CORINTH

Rebuilt Temple of Apollo, Delphi, *c.* 548 B.C.

THERON

Temple of Zeus Olympius, Agrigentum, 480 B.C.

CHIRISOPHUS OF CRETE (*c.* 500 B.C.)

Temple to Ceres and Proserpine, and Temple to Paphian Venus, at Tegea, in Arcadia, in the Peloponnese.

LIBON OF MESSENA

Temple of Zeus, Olympia, 472–450 B.C. Reputed designer of Temple to Juno, Olympia.

ICTINUS

The Parthenon, Athens, 454–438 B.C., with Callicrates. (Plates 1, 2 and 3.)
Temple of Apollo Epicurius, Bassae, 430 B.C.
Cella to Temple of Ceres and Proserpine, Eleusis, 440 B.C.

CALLICRATES

The Parthenon, Athens, 454–438 B.C., with Ictinus. Pheidias was the master sculptor. (Plates 1, 2 and 3.)
Temple of Nikè Apteros, Athens, 438 B.C. (Plate 5 and page 64.)

HERMOGENES OF ALABANDA (*c.* 453–363 B.C.)

Temple of Dionysos, Teos.
Temple to Artemis Leukophryene, Magnesia.
Temple to Bacchus, Teos.

MNESICLES

The Propylae, Athens, 437–433 B.C.
The Erechtheion, Athens, 420–393 B.C. (Plate 4 and page 67.)

HIPPODAMUS OF MILETUS

Planned Piraeus, fifth century B.C., and Thurii, 443 B.C., and Rhodes, 408 B.C.
Reputed inventor of the grid plan for street lay-out.

TARCHESIUS (400 B.C.)

Author of a treatise on the Corinthian order.

DEMETRIUS OF EPHESUS

Rebuilt Temple of Artemis, Ephesus, 380 B.C., with Paeonius of Ephesus.

PAEONIUS OF EPHESUS

Rebuilt Temple of Artemis, Ephesus, 380 B.C., with Demetrius of Ephesus.
Temple of Didymaeus, Miletus, 376–320 B.C., with *Daphnis of Miletus.*

DEINOCRATES
(DINOCRATES, DEINOCHARES, DEMOCRATES, CHEIROCRATES)

Tomb of Arsinöe.
Restored Temple of Artemis, Ephesus, 356 B.C.
Planned city of Alexandria, 331 B.C. (*see* map on page 50).

SOSTRATUS OF CNIDUS

Began building of the Pharos of Alexandria, 333–332 B.C.

PHILEUS OF IONIA
(PHYTHEOS OR PHYTHIUS)

Wrote a treatise on the Temple of Athena, Priene, 373 B.C. Some authorities identify
him with:

PHITEUS
(PHYTEUS, PYTHEUS, PYTHIOS, PYTHEOS)

Author of a work on the Mausoleum, Halicarnassos, which he built 353 B.C., with
Satyrus.

CALLIMACHUS OF ATHENS (before 396 B.C.)

Reputed inventor of the Corinthian capital (*see* pages 47–48).

ARGELIUS (lived before era of Pericles)

Temple of Aesculapius, Tralles.
Author of a work on this building, and of *De Symmetriis Corinthiis.*

ANDRONICUS CYRRHESTES

Tower of the Winds, Athens, 100 B.C. (*see* pages 63 and 69).

ROMAN

COSSUTIUS (*c.* 200 B.C.)

Reputed designer of the Temple to Jupiter Olympius, the Olympeion, Athens, 174 B.C. It was begun by Antiochus Epiphanes of Syria, only partially built, and not completed until A.D. 117, by the Emperor Hadrian. (Plate 6.)

MARCUS VITRUVIUS POLLIO (first century B.C.)

Designer of the basilica at Fanum Fortunae, the modern Fano.
Author of *De Architectura Libri Decem* (*see* pages 196–199).

BATRACHOS AND SAUROS (first century B.C.)

Temple to Jupiter, and Temple to Juno, Rome.

SEVERUS AND CELER

The *Domus* for Nero after fire of Rome, A.D. 64.
Engineers of the canal known as Lago de Licola, A.D. 67.

RABIRIUS OF ROME

Reputed designer of Domitian's palace on the Palatine, Rome, A.D. 81–96.
Many other public works in Rome.

APOLLODORUS OF DAMASCUS (died *c.* A.D. 134)

Trajan's basilica, Rome, A.D. 98.
Trajan's Forum, Rome, and many other public works for this Emperor—baths, aqueducts, roads, bridges. Temple of Venus and Rome, Rome, A.D. 123–135.

ZENO or ZENON

Worked under Marcus Aurelius, *c.* A.D. 174.
City Architect of Aspendus in Asia Minor, where he built the theatre.

ALOISIUS THE ARCHITECT (*c.* A.D. 500)

State architect at Ravenna under King Theodoric, where he completed many restorations of baths, aqueducts, and other works. Reputed designer of Theodoric's tomb at Ravenna.

JULIANUS ARGENTARIUS (*c.* A.D. 500)

Reputed designer of St. Vitale, Ravenna, A.D. 526–547 (page 90), St. Apollinare in Classe, A.D. 534–539 (page 89), and Parenzo Cathedral, A.D. 535–543.

ANTHEMIUS OF TRALLES (died about A.D. 534)

Santa Sophia, Constantinople, A.D. 532–537, with Isodorus of Miletus. (Plates 10 and 11, pages 92, 95, and 96.)

ISODORUS OF MILETUS ("The Byzantine") (died about A.D. 537)

Nephew of Anthemius, whom he assisted on Santa Sophia, Constantinople.
Baths and public porticoes, at Zenobia, with *Joannes of Byzantium*.

ROMANESQUE

Italy: eighth to twelfth century A.D.

JANUARIUS

Architect to Pope Hadrian I, A.D. 772–795.
Probably built St. Maria in Cosmedin, Rome (page 88).
Superintended restoration of buildings in Rome, notably the basilica of San Paolo.

BUSKETUS or BUSCHETTO

Pisa Cathedral, A.D. 1063 (page 141), and St. Paolo, Pistoja, A.D. 1032, are attributed to him.

DIOTI SALVI DE PETRONI

Baptistry of St. Giovanni, Pisa, A.D. 1153–1278 (page 140).
St. Sepolchro, Pisa, *c.* A.D. 1153.
St. Maria Maggiore, Florence, *c.* A.D. 1153.

BONANNO PISANO

The Campanile at Pisa (page 141), begun A.D. 1174, with a German architect, *Wilhelm von Innsbruck* (Guglielmo Tedesco).

Germany: eighth to twelfth century A.D.

EGINHARDT (died A.D. 839 or 844)

Designed a monastery at St. Gall, *c.* A.D. 820.
Court-superintendent of buildings at Aix-la-Chapelle.
Monastery at Seligenstadt, A.D. 827–830.

France: eighth to twelfth century A.D.

ROMUALDUS or RUMALDE

Worked under Bishop Ebon, on the third cathedral at Rheims, *c.* A.D. 830 onwards.

Spain: eighth to tenth century A.D.

TIODA, THIODA, or FIODA

Basilica of Salvatore, Oviedo, *c.* A.D. 839.

St. Miguel de Lino, near Oviedo.
St. Julian, near Oviedo.
St. Maria and St. Miguel, Oviedo.

GOTHIC

France: approximately 1100–1500

WILLIAM OF SENS (died 1178)

Reputedly the architect of Sens Cathedral, 1168.
Began the rebuilding of Canterbury Cathedral, 1175. (*See also* William the
  Englishman on page 366.)

ROBERT DE LUSARCHES or LUZARCHES

Amiens Cathedral, 1220.

VILLARD DE HONNECOURT, or WILANS DE HONECOURT

Author of a sketch book, containing designs and suggestions for bridges, roofs, clock
  towers, as well as drawings of figures and animals.
Attributed to him are Notre Dame de Cambrai, 1230–1250, and the churches of
  St. Elizabeth, Cassovia, and St. Yved de Braine.

PIERRE DE MONTEREAU or DE MONTREUIL (died 1266)

Improvements at the Abbey of S. Germain des Prés, Paris, 1239–1250.
Sainte Chapelle, Paris, 1242.
Sainte Chapelle, Vincennes.
The refectory in the Abbey of St. Martin des Champs, Paris, is attributed to him.

HUES or HUGUES DE LIBERGIERS (died 1263)

St. Nicaise, Rheims, 1229.

EUDES DE MONTREUIL (died 1289)

Church and hospital des Quinze Vingts, rue S. Honoré Paris, 1254.
Church de la Chartreuse de Vauvert, 1257.
Church of the Cordeliers, Paris, 1262.
Church of St. Croix de la Bretonnerie, Paris, 1268.
Began and completed parts of the church of Notre Dame, Nantes, 1280.
He was architect to the King of France, 1285.

ROBERT DE COUCY (died 1311)

Continued the building of St. Nicaise, Rheims, *c.* 1263.

RAYMOND DU TEMPLE (died after 1403)

Architect to Charles V and VI of France, for whom he worked at the Louvre.
Architect to the Cathedral of Paris, 1363–1400.
Probably designed the Collège de Beauvais, 1370–1385.
Worked on the Palais de Justice, Paris, 1387, and the Chapel of the Celestins, 1394.

JEHAN GAILDE or GAILDA
Worked at the Church of the Madeleine, Troyes, 1508–1517.

MARTIN CHAMBIGES OF CAMBRAI (died 1532)
Reputed designer of the *portail* at Troyes Cathedral.
In collaboration with Vast, he built the transepts to Beauvais Cathedral, begun
  in 1500.

England: approximately 1150–1500
WILLIAM THE ENGLISHMAN
Succeeded William of Sens in the rebuilding of Canterbury Cathedral, after 1174,
where he was responsible for the completion of the choir, the Trinity Chapel and
the Corona.

ELIAS DE DEREHAM (died 1245)
Reputed architect of Salisbury Cathedral, 1220–1258 (*see* page 154), an extension
  to Winchester Cathedral; and the hall of Winchester Palace, 1222–1235.
Advised on building at Wells, Durham (*see* plate 14), Canterbury, Lewes, and
  Westminster.

RICHARD OF FARLEIGH (died ?1363)
Steeple of Salisbury Cathedral (*see* page 154).

WILLIAM OF WYKEHAM (1324-1404)
Rebuilding at Windsor Castle, 1360–1369.
Queenborough Castle, Kent, 1361–1367.
Many other castles in Kent and Hampshire are attributed to him.
New College, Oxford, 1380–1386.
Winchester College, 1387–1393.
Rebuilding of Winchester Cathedral begun 1394.

WILLIAM DE WYNFORD (died at some time after 1404)
Chief assistant to William of Wykeham.
Worked on St. Mary's College, Winchester, 1387–1392, and at Winchester Cathedral,
  1394–1404.

ALAN OF WALSINGHAM (died 1364)
Cathedral and monastery buildings at Ely, 1316–1349.
Reputed designer of St. Michael's, Cambridge, and St. Mary the Less, Cambridge,
  1352.

WILLIAM DE WERMINGTON

Croyland Abbey: west side of cloister 1392–1417, also north and south aisles of choir, lady chapel on north, and refectory.

In 1417–1427 he built the western nave, with transepts and chapels.

Possibly much other work there, including the Abbot's Hall.

HENRY YEVELE (died 1400)

Royal master-mason to Edward III, Richard II, and Henry IV, and in that capacity responsible for much work at Westminster Hall, Westminster Abbey, Winchester, and Canterbury.

Reputed designer of many smaller churches, also bridges, towers and walls in the City of London, in Westminster and Kent, and of the Bloody Tower at the Tower of London.

WILLIAM OF COLCHESTER

Work at Westminster Abbey, 1400–1415.

Central tower of York Minster, 1419.

ROGER KEYES

Master of the Works, Eton College, 1441.

Believed to have been the surveyor in charge of All Souls College, Oxford, in the 1440's. He was still living, in 1469, at Exeter.

Scotland: fifteenth century

JOHN MURDO or MOROW (died 1485)

Master-mason at St. Andrews and Glasgow Cathedrals, the Abbey of Paisley, and ecclesiastical buildings in Nithsdale and Galloway.

Italy: approximately 1200–1450

NICOLA PISANO (1205 or 1207—*c.* 1278)

Sculptor and architect.

Church or baptistry of St. Giovanni, Siena.

St. Maria Glorioso de Frari, Venice, 1250.

Possibly St. Antonio at Padua, 1232–1307 (page 172), and the church and monastery of St. Domenico, Arezzo, 1250.

The Chiesa della Misericordia, Florence.

The pulpit of Siena Cathedral, 1265.

The Cathedral of St. Gennaro, Naples, 1260–1299.

THE COSMATI FAMILY (thirteenth century)

For four or five generations, from the thirteenth century onwards, this family produced architects, sculptors and mosaicists who worked in Rome. The first known was Lorenzo, who was followed by his son, Jacopo, and his grandson, Cosma, from whom the family name was derived. Cosma's sons, Luca and Jacopo, continued the traditional work of the family: the last recorded member was Giovanni.

ARNOLFO DI CAMBIO (c. 1232–1310)

Reputed to have restored the Ponte di Trinita, Florence, c. 1269.
Loggia of St. Michele, Florence.
Outer circle of city walls, Florence, c. 1284.
Loggia and Piazza dei Priori, Florence, c. 1285.
Alterations to the baptistry of St. Giovanni, Florence, c. 1290.
Palazzo Vecchio, Florence, 1298.
St. Croce, Florence, 1294.
Design and foundations of St. Maria del Fiore (Florence Cathedral), c. 1296 (*see* page 173).

GIOVANNI PISANO (died 1320)

Sculptor and architect, son of Nicola Pisano.
Campo Santa, Pisa, 1278–1283.
Castel Nuovo, Naples, 1283.
St. Maria de' Servi, Arezzo, c. 1286.
The monastery of St. Maria della Nuova, Naples, is attributed to him, and he worked on the Cathedral at Arezzo, and on restoration and sculpture in numerous churches, monasteries, including the pulpit of Pisa Cathedral, 1302–1311. Nunnery of St. Nicolo, Prato, 1300.

AMBROGIO BONDONE, or AMBRO GIOTTO (c. 1266–1336)

Director of all architectural works in the State of Florence, 1334.
Campanile of Florence Cathedral, 1334–1387 (*see* frontispiece).

ANDREA PISANO (c. 1270–1345)

Sculptor and architect.
Assisted Giovanni Pisano at Pisa Cathedral, with *Talenti*.
Doors of St. Giovanni, Florence, 1317–1339.
Baptistry of St. Giovanni, Pistoja, 1300–1337.
St. Martino, Pisa, 1332.
Castello di St. Barnaba, at La Scarperio in Mugello, near Florence, 1306.

TADDEO GADDI (c. 1297–c. 1352)

Worked on St. Michele, Florence, 1337.
Completed Giotto's campanile at Florence Cathedral after his death in 1336 (*see* frontispiece).

ANDREA DI CIONE or ANDREA ORCAGNA (died 1389)

Chapel and shrine at St. Michele, Florence, 1348–1359.
Piazza della Signoria, Florence, 1355.
Architect to Florence Cathedral, c. 1366–1384.

BARTOLOMMEO BUONO (or BUON)

Façades of Doge's Palace, Venice, (*see* page 163 and plate 17). The Palazzo Foscari is also attributed to him.

Germany: approximately 1250–1500

ERWIN VON or ERVINUS DE STEINBACH (died 1318)

Reputed designer and builder of a considerable part of Strassburg Cathedral, 1275–1316.

HANS VON STEINBACH (1294–1339)

The son of Erwin von Steinbach, who continued his father's work at Strassburg.

ULRICH ENSINGER

Worked on Ulm Cathedral when the building was begun in 1377, and on Milan Cathedral, 1394.
Believed to have been associated in the building of Strassburg Cathedral.
The Collegiats-kirche, Ulberlingen, 1353, and the Catherinin-kirche, Esslingen, 1370, are attributed to him.
His sons, Caspar, Matthaeus, and Matthias, were all concerned with architecture, and are believed to have worked at Ulm Cathedral, notably Matthaeus.

Spain: approximately 1000–1500

PEDRO DE DIOS, PEDRO DE DEUS TAMBER, or PEDRO DE VITANBEN (died *c.* 1066)

Rebuilt St. Isidoro at Leon, *c.* 1063.

EL MAESTRO RAYMUNDO

Cathedral of St. Maria, Lugo, 1129–1177.

EL MAESTRO MATEO

Master of Works, Santiago Cathedral, 1168–1188.

PETRUS PETRI

Architect of Toledo Cathedral, *c.* 1227–1290.

LORENZO MAITANI (*c.* 1240–1330)

Orvieto Cathedral, 1290.

JAYME FABRE or FABRA OF MALLORCA

Dominican convent, Palma, Mallorca, 1296.
Barcelona Cathedral, 1298.

JACOBUS DE FAVERIIS OF NARBONNE

Architect to Gerona Cathedral, *c.* 1320–1325.

PEDRO BALAGUER

The campanile, el Miguelete, of Valencia Cathedral, 1414. He is supposed to have removed materials and masonry from Lerida and Narbonne, where he had been giving advice on building, in order to complete his work on el Miguelete, which was begun in 1381.

RENAISSANCE

Italy: 1450–1800

FILIPPO BRUNELLESCHI or BRUNELLESCO (*c.* 1379–*c.* 1446)

(Filippo di Ser Brunellesco dei Lapi)

Chapter house and cloister, St. Croce, Florence, 1400 and 1420.
Dome of Florence Cathedral, 1420–1437 (frontispiece and page 173).
St. Lorenzo, Florence, 1425 (*see* plate 19).
Worked on Milan Cathedral, 1430.
Pitti Palace, Florence, *c.* 1434–1440 (plate 18).

MICHELOZZO DI BARTOLOMMEO (1391–1472?)

Sculptor and architect.
Built the Library of St. Giorgio Maggiore, Venice, and designed other buildings in
    the city.
Palazzo Riccardi, Florence, 1430, is his best-known building (*see* page 208 and plate 18).
Palace at Fiesole for Giovanni dei Medici.

LEONE BATTISTA ALBERTI (1404–1472)

Choir, tribune and great altar of Church of the Annunciation, Florence, 1451.
Palazzo Rucellai, Florence, *c.* 1460.
Façade, gate and loggia of St. Maria Novella, Florence, *c.* 1471 (page 192).
Chapel of the Madonna Incoronata, Mantua Cathedral, *c.* 1472.
St. Sebastiano, Mantua, *c.* 1472.
Wrote works on sculpture, *Della Statua*, on painting, *De Pictura*, and a famous treatise
    on architecture, *De Re Aedificatoria*.

LEONARDO DA VINCI (1452–1519)

Sculptor, painter, engineer and architect. In addition to canals and water works, fortifications, and frescoes, he is believed to have built, with Bramante, the church and monastery of St. Maria della Grazie, Milan. He was consulted about Milan Cathedral in 1510, though his plans for its completion were not carried out, nor were his ambitious designs for strengthening and improving the Castello.

He wrote a *Treatise on Painting*, and left a great volume of manuscript notes and drawings, which disclose the diversity of his gifts. The immense range of his interests included philosophy, medicine, optics, acoustics, astronomy, botany, geology, anatomy, the nature of the atmosphere, the flight of birds, and the construction of flying machines.

GIULIANO GIAMBERTI or GUILIANO DA SANGALLO
(1443–1517)

Military engineer and architect.

One of a family of artists, the other notable members being Antonio, his brother
(1448–1534) and Francesco, his son (1498–c. 1570).

Cloister at St. Maddalena de' Pazzi, Florence.

The Palazzo Panciatichi, Florence.

Church of the Madonna delle Carceri, Prato, 1485–1489.

Restorations at St. Maria Maggiore, Rome.

Work at Church of the Madonna, Loreto, 1500.

Façade of St. Lorenzo, Florence.

Architect of St. Peter's, Rome, 1514–1515 (see page 210).

Various engineering works and bridges.

(See Antonio Giamberti and Antonio Piccone, page 372.)

PIETRO LOMBARDO (1435–1515)

One of a family of Venetian architects.

Worked on the Cortile of the Doge's Palace, Venice, 1499.

Palazzo Vendramini, Venice, 1481.

St. Maria dei Miracoli, Venice, 1480.

DONATO LAZZARI or BRAMANTE (1444–1514)

Worked first at Milan, where the following are attributed to him:

> Church of St. Maria Incoronata, Lodi, 1476.
>
> Churches of St. Domenico, 1469, and St. Ambrogio.
>
> Church of St. Maria presso di St. Celso, 1491.
>
> Cupola of St. Maria della Grazie, 1464–1493.
>
> Church of St. Satiro.

He also carried out various engineering works and fortifications, and St. Maria di
Cane panuova, Pavia, 1492, is attributed to him.

Worked later in Rome, where he rebuilt cloister of monastery of St. Maria della
Pace; designed a palace in the Borgo Nuova, 1502; and enlarged St. Maria
del Popolo, about the same time. He designed extensive additions, and laid out
courts, to the Belvedere and Vatican, 1503–1504.

Designed and built for Ferdinand IV of Spain a chapel at the Franciscan monastery
of St. Pietro, Montono, c. 1502.

Among other works attributed to him (but with some doubt) are St. Maria del
Monte, Forli: Farenza Cathedral; St. Sepolchro, and St. Maria della
Campagna, Piacenza; church of the Madonna di Consalazione, Todi; convent
of the Madonna della Quercia, Viterbo.

BARTOLOMMEO BUONO or MASTRO BUONO OF BERGAMO
(died 1529)

Painter and architect of Venice.

Built bell chamber and spire of St. Mark's, Venice, 1510–1516. Parts of St. Rocco,
Venice, are also attributed to him.

ANTONIO GIAMBERTI (1448 or 1455-1534)
(Sangallo the Elder)

Brother of Giuliano Giamberti, whom he assisted.
Worked at the chapel of the Palazzo della Signoria, Florence.
Church of the Madonna, Montegiascone.
Palazzo at Monte Sansovino.

IL CRONACA (1454-1508)

Completed the Palazzo Strozzi, Florence, 1489.
Designed Palazzo Gaudagni, Florence, 1490.

ANTONIO RIZZI

Designed the Cortile of the Doge's Palace, Venice, 1486.

ANTONIO PICCONE (1470 or 1485-1546)
(Sangallo the Younger)

Nephew of Giuliano and Antonio Giamberti.
Palazzo Farnese, Rome, 1534.
Corridor from Vatican to castle of St. Angelo. Cathedral, Montefiascone.
Many palaces and buildings in Rome, including those of A. di Monte, d'Amelia,
and Casa Marrano St. Maria di Monserrato, Rome.
Worked at St. Peter's, Rome (*see* page 210).

SEBASTIAN or BASTIANNET SERLIO (1475-1554)

An Italian who started his career in Bologna, where he designed the Palazzo di
Malvezzi Campeggi. At Venice, he is believed to have designed the interior
of St. Sebastiano, and church of St. Francesco della Vigne. He was invited to
France, where he designed the river front of the Louvre, and worked at
Fontainebleau (*see* page 219). He was the chief pupil of Peruzzi (*see* page 373).
Published his famous work on architectural composition and the orders, *I cinque
libri d' Architettura*, in 1540.

MICHELANGELO (1475-1564)
(Michelagniolo Buonarroti)

Painter, sculptor and architect.
Architect of St. Peter's, Rome, after the death of Sangallo the Younger in 1546
(pages 210 and 211).
Reconstruction of the Porta Pia.
Church of St. Maria degli Angeli.
The Capitol, Rome, 1540-1644 (*see* plate 7).
Medici Mausoleum, Florence, 1523-1529.
Designed the Biblioteca Laurenziana, Florence, 1523-1526.

BALDASSARE PERUZZI (1481–1536)

Painter and architect.
Portal of St. Michele, Bologna.
Palazzo Albergati, Bologna.
Worked at St. Peter's, Rome, 1520–1522 (*see* page 210).
Palazzo Farnesina, Rome, 1510–1524.
Palazzo Massimi, Rome, 1532.

BERGAMASCO

Carried on work on the Cortile of the Doge's Palace, Venice, 1520.

JACOPO SANSOVINO (1477 or 1486–1570)

Sculptor and architect.
Library of St. Mark's, Venice, 1536.
Palazzo Cornaro della ca' Grande, Venice, 1532.
The Zecca or Mint, Venice, 1536.
St. Fantino, Venice.
Many other buildings and tombs in Rome, Venice, Brescia and Padua.

GIACOMO BAROZZI DA VIGNOLA (1507–1573)

Palazzo Farnese, Piacenza.
St. Agostino, Piacenza.
Palazzo di St. Giorgio dei Scotti, Piacenza.
Palazzo Farnese, Rome, 1546–1550.
Palazzo Guilio, Rome.
Villa Farnese, Viterbo, 1555–1559.
Continued Porta del Popolo, Rome.
Architect of St. Peter's, Rome, after death of Michelangelo.
Designed Gesù Church, Rome, 1568–1575 (*see* page 212).

GIORGIO VASARI (1511–1571)

Architect and painter. Author of *Lives of the Painters, Sculptors and Architects* (1550).
Work at the palace of Duke Cosimo of Florence included loggias, staircases, arches
    and decorations, 1555–1564.
Designed Palazzo degli Anziani, Pisa, 1565, and began the Palazzo Uffizi, Florence,
    1551–1560.

ANDREA PALLADIO (1518–1580)

Palazzo della Ragione, Vicenza.
Barbarano, Porti and Chieregati Palaces, Vicenza.
St. Giorgio Maggiore, Venice (page 214).
Many country houses in northern Italy, including the Villa Capra (page 213).
Teatro Olimpico, Vicenza (completed by Scamozzi).
Published *Le Antichita di Roma*, first edition in 1554, and *I Quattro Libri dell'Archi-tettura*, in 1570.

GIACOMO DELLA PORTA (died 1601)

Completed Dome of St. Peter's, Rome, 1585–1590.
Completed church of St. Maria Scala Coeli, Rome, and designed St. Paolo alle tre Fontane.
Palazzo Chigi, Rome, 1526.
Designed a number of fountains in Rome.

VICENZO SCAMOZZI (1552–1616)

Completed Palladio's Teatro Olimpico, Vicenza, 1580.
Completed façade of St. Giorgio Maggiore, Venice (*see* page 214).
Additions to the Library of St. Mark's, Venice, 1584.
Additions to the Doge's Palace, Venice.
Designed palaces near Padua and Castel Franco, 1588, and others at Venice.
The inventor of the two-foot rule.
Published *Discorsi sopra l'Antichita di Roma*, 1582, and *Dell'Idea della Architettura Universale*, 1615.

GIROLAMO RAINALDI (1570–1655)

Designed and built church at Montalto, 1585–1590.
Piazza del Gesù, Rome, 1623.
Jesuit College and church of St. Lucia, Bologna, 1623.
Also attributed to him are Palazzo Doria, Rome; Capella Spada in church of St. Maria e St. Gregorio in Vallicella; and chapel in church of St. Maria della Scala.

PIETRO DA CORTONA or PIETRO BERETINE (1596–1669)

Painter and architect.
Alterations to church of St. Maria della Pace, Rome.
Church of SS. Maria Martina and Luca Evangelista, Rome.
Chapels of the Conception at St. Lorenzo in Damaso, and St. Francisca Xaviero, Rome; also façade of St. Maria in Via Lata.

GIOVANNI LORENZO BERNINI (1596–1680)

Sculptor and architect.
Chief architect to St. Peter's, Rome, 1629, of which he built the greater part.
Designer of the colonnade in Piazza of St. Peter (plate 25).
St. Anastasia, Rome, is attributed to him.
Designer of the Palazzo Barberini, 1624–1630; Palazzo di Monte Citorio, 1651; the Scala Regia; additions to the Quirinale; restoration of the Chigi chapel; St. Andrea al Noviziato dei P. P. Gesuiti; church of the Assumption; Palazzo Chigi.
He was invited to Paris by Louis XIV, and prepared a design for the Louvre, in 1665, which was not used.

FRANCESCO BORROMINI (1599–1667)

Assisted Bernini at St. Peter's, Rome, 1629, and at Palazzo Barberini, 1624–1630.
Church and monastery of St. Carlo alle Quattro Fontane, c. 1639.
Part of the College Sapienza, and its church, c. 1639.
Oratorio di St. Felipe Neri, Vallicella.
Work at St. Agnese in Piazza Navona, c. 1652.
Restoration of façade of St. John Lateran, and of Palazzo Rufina.
Library and new building at monastery of St. Agostino.

ALESSANDRO ALGARDI (1600–1654)

Sculptor and architect.
Villa Pamfili, Rome, c. 1644.
High altar in church of St. Niccolo da Tolentino.
Façade of St. Ignazio.

BALDASSARI LONGHENA (1600–1682)

Although he came from Rome, he worked chiefly in Venice. His best-known design
    is St. Maria della Salute, 1632.
Designed the Palazzo Pesaro, Venice, 1679.

FILIPPO JUVARA (1685–1736)

Engraver and architect.
Chief architect to the King of Sicily, c. 1720.
At Turin, he built façade of the Carmelite church; church of the Blessed Virgin;
    Capella di Corte.
He completed the cupola of St. Andrea, Mantua, and of Como Cathedral, 1732.
St. Croce, Turin, and the church of St. Filipo Neri are attributed to him.

France: approximately 1460–1793

PIERRE NEPVEU (died 1538)
(Trinqueau)

It is believed that he designed the Château of Chambord, c. 1526–1544 (plates 20
    and 21), and may also have been the architect of Château de Chenonceaux
    (page 220).
He worked at the Château of Blois.

GILLES LE BRETON (died c. 1550)

The most famous of a family of master-masons, who worked on the Palace of
Fontainebleau, 1528–1534.

PIERRE DE CHAMBIGES or CHAMBICHE (died 1544)

Master-mason who assisted Cortona on the Hôtel de Ville, Paris, 1533.
Rebuilt much of Château de Chantilly, 1528–1531.
Worked at Fontainebleau and St. Germain-en-Laye, 1540.

DOMENICO DI CORTONA or BOCCADORE

An Italian architect who came to France about 1496. Worked on the Hôtel de Ville, Paris, 1533–1549.

JEAN GOUJON (*c.* 1505–*c.* 1568)

Sculptor and architect.

No buildings are definitely attributed to him, but he is believed to have worked at the Louvre, *c.* 1560–1570, and at the Château at Ecouen, with Bullant, 1545.

PIERRE LESCOT (*c.* 1510–1578)

Worked at the Louvre, *c.* 1550–1559, as superintendent of the works.

Designed the jubé at St. Germain l'Auxerrois, Paris, 1541–1544.

Superintended work of rebuilding the palace of Francis I, Paris, for which he made a design, 1546.

The design of the Hôtel Carnavalet, Paris, may be his work.

He worked closely with Jean Goujon.

PHILIBERT DE L'ORME (*c.* 1515–1570)

A military engineer in Brittany, *c.* 1546–1547. He did work at the Bois du Vincennes, 1559; the Château of Coucy: at Fontainebleau: St. Germain-en-Laye, and the Château de la Muette, Passy.

He published *Nouvelles Inventions*, 1561, and *Le Premier Tome de l'Architecture*, 1567.

JEAN BULLANT or BULLAN (*c.* 1520–1598)

Worked on the Château at Ecouen, with Goujon, 1545.

Reputed designer, with de l'Orme, of central block of the Tuileries, 1564.

Began work on the gallery of the Louvre, 1596.

Designed many royal tombs.

Author of *Reigle Generalle d'Architecture* (1563 and 1568), and *Traité de Geometrie*, 1567.

JACQUES ANDROUET CERCEAU (*c.* 1510–*c.* 1585)

Is believed to have designed various ecclesiastical buildings, including the Capucin and Feuillant monasteries in Paris, the chapel of St. Esprit for the Augustins, and the rebuilding of the churches of Notre Dame, Clery, and St. Etienne du Mont, Paris.

Completed Bullant's work on the gallery of the Louvre.

Built many hôtels in Paris, and designed and superintended works on the Pont Neuf.

JACQUES DE BROSSE or DESBROSSES (*c.* 1562–1626)

Château de Monceaux, Meaux, 1589–1610.

Château of Colomier, Brie.

Palais d'Orléans, 1615–1620.

Rebuilt great hall of Palais de Justice, Paris, 1622.

Rebuilt Protestant church at Charenton, 1623.

Second aqueduct at Arcueil, 1624.

JACQUES LEMERCIER (c. 1583–1654)

Worked on the Louvre, after 1620.
Palais Richelieu, Paris, c. 1629–1636.
College de la Sorbonne, Paris, c. 1629.
Church of Pères de l'Oratoire, Paris, 1628–1630.
Continuation of Abbaye de Val de Grâce, c. 1650.
St. Roch, Paris, 1633.

PIERRE LE MUET (1591–1669)

Published several architectural works, and began his career as an engineer, working
    on fortifications in Picardy.
Continued the Val de Grâce, 1654–1655.
Designed Church of the Petits Pères, Paris, 1656; the Hôtel Colbert, Hôtel de Torcy,
    and several others.
Chateaux de Pontz, Champagne, de Tamloy, Burgundy, and de Chavigny,
    Touraine.

FRANÇOIS MANSART (1598–1666)

Restoration of the Hôtel de Philippeaux de la Vrillière, 1620.
Church of the Filles de la Visitation de St. Marie, 1632.
Western front of Château de Blois, 1637.
Began the Church of the Val de Grâce, 1645 (page 221).
Château of Maisons-sur-Seine, 1657.
A large number of town and country houses.

CHATILLON BROTHERS

Place des Vosges, c. 1607 (plate 26).

LOUIS LE VAU (1612–1670)

Hôtel Bullion, Paris, 1630.
Château de Bercy, Paris.
Church of St. Sulpice, 1655.
Restorations at the Tuileries, 1664, and additions to the Château de Vincennes, 1660.
Director of Works at the Louvre, 1653.

CLAUDE PERRAULT (1613–1688)

Submitted successful design for the Louvre, c. 1664, and started to build this
    1665–1680.
Designed the Observatory at Paris, 1667–1672.
Worked at Versailles, on the gardens and decorations (see plate 29).
Published *Les dix livres d'Architecture de Vitruve*, 1673, among other works.

THE LE PAUTRE FAMILY

Jean, 1618–1682, and Antoine, 1621–1677, or 1691, were brothers, the former an
    engraver. Antoine was comptroller-general of buildings to the Duke of
    Orleans, 1658.

The following are attributed to him: Hôtel de Beauvais, Hôtel de Gesvres, and the Church des religieuses de Pont Royal, in Paris; two wings of the Château of St. Cloud, 1660; and the Château de St. Ouen, near Paris.

He published *Oeuvres d'Architecture*, 1652.

His nephew, Pierre, who died in 1716, was a writer on architecture, and an engraver.

LIBERAL BRUARD or BRUANT (1635–1697)

First church and buildings of Hôtel des Invalides, Paris, 1670–1679. Worked on royal buildings, and the Church of the Hôpital Général de la Salpetrière is attributed to him. His son (or nephew) Jacques, was also an architect, who died in 1732.

JULES HARDOUIN MANSART (1645–1708)

Nephew of François Mansart (see page 377).

Had the largest practice of any contemporary French architect. Apart from the Palace of Versailles, he worked on the Royal Château of Clagny, 1676–1680, and Maison-royale, St. Cyr, 1685–1686.

His work in Paris included the Place Vendôme, 1690–1691 (plate 27), the Dômes des Invalides, 1676–1706 (page 223), the Place des Victoires, 1685–1691, and the Altar of Notre Dame, 1699–1714.

THE GABRIEL FAMILY

A family of French architects. The first was Jacques, related by marriage to the Mansarts, and the builder of François Mansart's Château de Choisy-sur-Seine. He died in 1686.

His son, Jacques, 1667–1742, completed building of the Pont Royal, 1688, designed by J. H. Mansart. He also designed the Hôtel de Varangeville, 1704, and Hôtel Feuquières, 1718, both in Paris.

His son, Jacques Ange, 1710–1782, continued building many of his father's designs, including the great sewer of Paris; the *place* at Bordeaux; abbey at Grandmont, and work at the cathedrals of La Rochelle and Orleans. He built the École Militaire and Champ de Mars, Paris, in 1750. In 1753–1770 he designed the theatre at Versailles, and the Petit Trianon (*see* page 228). He built the Château of Compiégne, and worked on façades at the Louvre.

THE BLONDEL FAMILY

A family of French architects, of whom Jean François, 1683–1756, was a member of the Academy of Architecture, Paris. He built various churches, the Maison de Rouillé, Paris, and Hôtel des Gardes du Corps, Versailles. He was also an engraver.

His son, Jacques François, 1705–1774, was an engraver of architectural subjects, and professor of the Academy of Architecture, 1762. He opened the first private school of architecture in France. He carried out alterations to the Château de la Grange; improvements to the City of Metz, 1763; improvements to Cambrai, 1766, and Strassburg, 1768, and built the round church of the Royal Abbey of St. Louis.

JEAN NICHOLAS SERVANDONI (1695–1766)

Façade of St. Sulpice, Paris, 1733–1745.
Parish church of Coulanges la Vineuse, Borgogne.

JACQUES GERMAIN SOUFFLOT (1709–1781)

Dome and altar of Carthusian church, Lyon.
St. Geneviève, Paris, 1764.
Treasury and sacristy of Notre Dame, Paris, 1756.
Architect to the Louvre, 1757–1780.
He was also an engraver, and his drawings were first published in 1764.

JACQUES DENIS ANTOINE (1753–1801)

Hôtel des Monnaies, Paris, 1768–1775.
Portico of inner court, Hospice de la Charité, Paris, c. 1790.
Many other buildings, including the Mint at Berne, and works at Nancy and Madrid.

JACQUES GONDOIN or GONDOUIN (1737–1818)

Place de l'école de Médecine, Paris, 1805–1806.
Colonne de la Grande Armée, in Place de la Vendôme, Paris, with Lepère, 1806–1810
    (plate 27).
Author of *Description des écoles de Chirurgerie*, 1780.

Austria: 1670–1750
FISCHER VON ERLACH (1656–1723)

University Church, Salzburg, 1696.
Holy Trinity and St. John's Hospital, Salzburg.
Imperial Palace, Schönbrunn, 1696.
Schwarzenberg Palace, and Palace of the Hungarian Bodyguard, Vienna.
Schönborn Palace, Vienna, 1701–1710.
St. Peter's, Vienna, 1702–1707.
Karlskirche, Vienna, 1716.
Extensions and additions to the Hofburg, Vienna.
His son, Joseph Emanuel, was also an architect, and continued and completed
    many of his father's designs.

Netherlands: 1500–1790
CORNELIS DE VRIENDT or VRIEND (1518–1572)

Hôtel de Ville, Antwerp, 1565 (*see* plate 22).
House of the Oosterlings (for the Hanseatic League), Antwerp, 1564–1568.
Sculpture and carvings, notably in Tournai Cathedral, 1566.

JAN VREDEMAN DE VRIES (1527, died after 1604)

Glass painter, and author of twenty-six books of engravings on architecture,
perspective and ornament.

Spain: 1490–1800
DIEGO DE SILOE (*c.* 1480–1563)
Church and monastery of La Conception of St. Geronimo, Granada, 1519–1552.
Royal hospital of St. Juan de Dios, Granada, 1552.
Granada Cathedral, 1529–1560.
Malaga Cathedral, 1522, is attributed to him, and he advised and reported on other
buildings.

ANTONIO GUTIERREZ
Designed entrance archway to chapter house, Toledo Cathedral, 1504.

JUAN GIL DE HONTANON (died 1531)
A member of the Salamanca Cathedral junta, 1512. Was put in charge of the work
on this cathedral.
Designed and built Segovia Cathedral, 1521–1577 (*see* plate 17).

JUAN DE BADAJOZ (died before 1560)
A member of the junta who advised on the building of Salamanca Cathedral, 1512.
Work at St. Isidoro, Leon, 1513.
Monastery of St. Zoil, Castille, 1537.
Front of convent of St. Marcos, Leon, 1537.
Church and cloister of Benedictine monastery near Leon, 1545.

JUAN DE BAUTISTA DE TOLEDO (died 1563)
Architect to the Royal Works, 1559.
Began the Escurial, Madrid, 1559 (*see* plates 24 and 25).
Palace at Aranjuiz, 1566.

RODRIGO GIL DE HONTANON (died 1577)
The son of Juan de Hontanon.
Directed work on Seville Cathedral, 1538.
St. Euphemia, Becerril, *c.* 1545.
St. Esteban, Castromocho, *c.* 1545.
College of the Order of Santiago, Salamanca, *c.* 1565, where he was put in charge of
all work, as he was also at Segovia, 1568.
Church of St. Maria Magdaleno, Valladolid, 1575.
Many other churches near Valladolid are attributed to him.

JUAN DE HERRERA (*c.* 1530–1597)
Succeeded Juan Bautista de Toledo on work on the Escurial, 1567. (Plates 24 and 25.)
Directed all royal buildings from 1567.
Gave advice and was consulted on many ecclesiastical buildings, also built bridges,
published drawings, and invented a crane. Among his works are:
 South façade of Palace of Toledo, 1571.
 Valladolid Cathedral, 1585.

Exchange building, Seville, 1585–1586.
Plazuela Zocodora, Toledo, 1596.

HERMANO FRANCISCO BAUTISTA (died after 1677)

Designed St. Salvador del Mundo, Madrid, *c.* 1630.
St. Isidoro, Madrid, 1626–1651.

JOSÉ CHURRIGUERA (died 1725)

Sculptor and architect who worked in the late seventeenth and early eighteenth
   centuries.
Continued the work begun by Juan de Herrera on Valladolid Cathedral.
His robust and highly decorative work has been identified with the Spanish version
   of Baroque, which survived until the middle of the eighteenth century and
   was known as Churrigueresque.

England: 1530–1830

JOHN SHUTE (died 1563)

Author of *The First and Chief Groundes of Architecture*, 1563.

ROBERT SMYTHSON or SMITHSON (?1536–1614)

Hardwick Hall, Derbyshire, Worksop Manor, Nottinghamshire.
Longleat, Wiltshire, and Wollaton House, Nottingham, are also attributed to him,
   though without confirmation.

THOMAS THORPE (died 1596)

Father of John Thorpe (see below), and principal mason of Kirby Hall, Northants.

JOHN THORPE (*c.* 1563–1655)

Author of a book of drawings. Entered Office of Works about 1583. Was a draughtsman rather than an architect, and various great houses of the Elizabethan period
have been wrongly attributed to him.

RALPH SYMONS or SIMONS

Architect of Emmanuel and Sidney Sussex Colleges, Cambridge (1586 and
   1596–1599).
Also responsible for alterations to Trinity College, Cambridge, 1598–1604, and may
   have built Apethorpe Hall, Northants, *c.* 1580.

INIGO JONES (1573–1652)

He began his career as a designer of court masques, of which he produced a number
for James I, designing the costumes, scenery and stage effects. Appointed Surveyor
to the Prince of Wales in 1611, and Surveyor of the King's Works in 1615. Among
his works are:
   Queen's House, Greenwich, 1618–1635.

The Banqueting Hall, Whitehall, 1619 (page 252).
Lindsey House, Lincoln's Inn, c. 1620 (page 252).
Piazza and church of St. Paul's, Covent Garden, 1631 (page 253).
Began restoration of old St. Paul's, 1633.
Carried out alterations to Wilton House, Wiltshire, 1649.

SIR CHRISTOPHER WREN (1632–1723)

In his capacity as one of the Commissioners for rebuilding London after the Great
Fire of 1666, he was responsible for designing fifty City churches. Appointed
Surveyor-General of the King's Works in 1668, and the first Surveyor of Greenwich
Palace in 1696. Among his most important works are:
St. Paul's Cathedral, 1675–1710.
The Library, Trinity College, Cambridge, 1676–1684.
Tom Tower, Christ Church, Oxford, 1681–1682.
St. James's, Piccadilly, 1682–1684.
The Royal Hospital, Chelsea, 1682–1691.
Royal Hospital for Seamen, Greenwich, 1696 onwards.
Marlborough House, London, 1709–1711.
Kensington Palace.
Rebuilding of Hampton Court Palace.

NICHOLAS HAWKSMOOR or HAWKSMORE (1661–1736)

Assisted Wren and Vanbrugh.
Clerk of the Works, and later Assistant Surveyor, at Greenwich Hospital.
Clarendon Building, Oxford, 1712–1715.
All Souls College, Oxford, 1715–1740.
St. Mary Woolnoth, London, 1716–1727.
St. George's, Bloomsbury, 1720–1730.
His book, *Remarks on the Founding and Carrying on the Buildings of the Royal Hospital at
Greenwich*, was published in 1729.

SIR JOHN VANBRUGH (1664–1726)

Comptroller of His Majesty's Works, 1702.
Castle Howard, Yorkshire, 1699–1726.
Blenheim Palace, Oxon, 1705–1720.
Seaton Delaval, Northumberland, 1720–1728 (*see* pages 268 and 269).
Greenwich Hospital (Great Hall and King William Block), c. 1703 onwards.

COLEN CAMPBELL (died 1729)

Burlington House, London (with the Earl of Burlington), 1718–1719.
Wanstead House, Essex, 1715 (*see* page 271).
Houghton, Norfolk, 1721.
Mereworth Castle, Kent, 1722–1725.
Compton Place, near Eastbourne, 1726–1727.
His *Vitruvius Britannicus* was published in three volumes, in 1715, 1717, and 1725.

THOMAS ARCHER (*c*. 1668–1743)

Chatsworth House, Derbyshire (north front), 1704–1705.
Heythrop House, Oxon, *c*. 1705–1710.
Roehampton House, Wandsworth, 1710–1712.
Wrest Park, Beds (garden pavilion), 1711–1712.
Hurstbourne Priors, Hants, *c*. 1712.
Hale House, Hants, soon after 1715.
Harcourt (afterwards Bingley) House, Cavendish Square, London, 1722.
Cliveden House, Bucks.
St. Philip's, Birmingham, 1710–1715 (now the Cathedral).
St. John's, Smith Square, London, 1714–1728.
St. Paul's, Deptford, 1712–1730.

JAMES GIBBS (1682–1754)

St. Mary-le-Strand, London, 1714–1717 (*see* page 266).
Burlington House, Piccadilly (part), 1718.
St. Clement Danes, London, 1719–1720.
St. Martin-in-the-Fields, London, 1722–1726.
All Saints', Derby, 1725 (now the Cathedral).
Senate House, Cambridge, 1722–1730.
King's College New Building, Cambridge, 1724–1749.
Sudbrooke Lodge, Petersham, Surrey, 1726–1728 (*see* page 274).
Radcliffe Library, Oxford, 1737–1749.
He published *A Book of Architecture* in 1728, *Rules for Drawing the Several Parts of
    Architecture* in 1732, and *Bibliotheca Radcliviana* in 1747.

WILLIAM KENT (*c*. 1685–1748)

Architect, painter, landscape gardener, and furniture designer.
Chiswick House, Middlesex (interior decorations), *c*. 1727.
Esher Place, Surrey (additions), *c*. 1730.
Holkham Hall, Norfolk, 1734 onwards.
Treasury Buildings, Whitehall, 1734–1736.
Stowe, Bucks, *c*. 1736.
Horse Guards, Whitehall, 1750–1758 (*see* page 279).
Edited *Designs of Inigo Jones* in 1727.

GIACOMO LEONI (*c*. 1686–1746)

A Venetian architect who came to England some time before 1715, and had been
    employed by the Elector Palatine.
Wrest Park, Beds, 1715 onwards.
Argyll House, Kings Road, Chelsea, 1723.
Moulsham Hall, Essex, 1729 onwards.
Clandon Park, Surrey, 1731–1735.
He published *The Architecture of Palladio* in 1715.

HENRY HERBERT (1693-1751)
(Ninth Earl of Pembroke)

A famous amateur of the arts. In architecture, his chief collaborator was Roger
  Morris.
White Lodge, Richmond Park, c. 1727.
Marble Hill, Twickenham, 1723-1729.
Column of Victory, Blenheim Palace, 1730-1731.
Wimbledon House, Surrey, 1732-1733.
Palladian Bridge, Wilton, 1736-1737.
Water House, Houghton, Norfolk.

RICHARD BOYLE (1694-1753)
(Third Earl of Burlington and Fourth Earl of Cork)

The most significant patron of his time, largely responsible for introducing the
  Palladian style to England.
Burlington House, London (with Gibbs and Campbell).
Petersham Lodge, Surrey, c. 1721.
House for General Wade, Great Burlington Street, London, 1723 (*see* page 277).
Chiswick House, Middlesex (with Kent), c. 1725 (*see* page 276).
Holkham House, Norfolk (assisted with planning).

GEORGE DANCE, Senior (1695 or 1700-1768)

The Mansion House, London, 1739-1752.
London Bridge (alterations, with Sir Robert Taylor), 1755-1760.
Corn Exchange, Mark Lane, London, 1749-1750.
St. Leonard's, Shoreditch, 1736-1740.
St. Botolph's, Aldgate, 1741-1744.

GEORGE DANCE, Junior, F.S.A., F.R.S. (1741-1825)

The son of George Dance, senior.
All Hallows Church, London Wall, 1765-1767.
Newgate Prison, London, 1770-1778.
Additions to the Mansion House, 1755, and 1795-1796.
Rebuilding and additions at the Guildhall, London.
Theatre Royal, Beaufort Square, Bath, 1804-1805.
Coleorton House, Leics, 1804-1805.
He also carried out street planning in the district of Tottenham Court Road, and in
  the City of London.

ROGER MORRIS (1695-1749)

Whitton Park, Twickenham, Middlesex, 1724-1725.
White Lodge, Richmond Park (with Henry Herbert), 1727.
Marble Hill, Twickenham, 1728-1729.
Longford Castle, Wilts, c. 1742.
Inverary Castle, Argyllshire, 1746-1761.
Kirby Hall, Yorks.

BATTY LANGLEY (1696–1751)

Better known as an author than as an architect. He and his brother, Thomas, conducted an architectural school in Soho, London, about 1740. Best known of the great number of books he published are *The City and Country Builder's and Workman's Treasury of Designs* (1740), and *The Builder's Director, or Bench-Mate* (1746).

HENRY FLITCROFT (1697–1769)

St. Giles-in-the-Fields, London, 1731–1734.
No. 10 St. James's Square (Chatham House), London, 1734.
Woburn Abbey, Beds, 1747–1761.
Alterations and additions to Wentworth Woodhouse, Yorks, *c.* 1735 and 1770.
Houses in Bloomsbury, Dover Street, Sackville Street, and Hampstead.

MATTHEW BRETTINGHAM (1699–1769)

Norfolk House, St. James's Square, London, 1747–1755.
No. 5 St. James's Square, 1748–1751.
Benacre Hall, Suffolk, 1763–1764.
Egremont House, Piccadilly, 1756.
Assisted at Holkham Hall, Norfolk.
Published *The Plans and Elevations of the late Earl of Leicester's House at Holkham,* in 1761.

ISAAC WARE (died 1766)

Chesterfield House, London, 1748–1749.
The Lock Hospital, Hyde Park Corner (now St. George's Hospital, as rebuilt by
    Wilkins), 1733.
Wrotham Park, Middlesex, 1754.
Was the author of a number of architectural works, among them *Designs of Inigo
    Jones and Others, c.* 1735, and *The Complete Body of Architecture, c.* 1735. He issued a
    translation of Palladio in 1737.

JOHN CHUTE (1701–1776)

An amateur architect, and friend of Horace Walpole.
Designed a large part of Strawberry Hill, for Walpole, and also the Gothic chapel
    there.
Chalfont House, Bucks.
Alterations at The Vyne, Hampshire (his own house).

JOHN WOOD, Senior (1704–1754)

Bramham Park, Yorks, *c.* 1724–1725.
Prior Park, Bath (except the east wing), 1735–1748.
Bath: Gay Street, Queen Square, Royal Mineral Water Hospital, North and South
    Parades, the preliminary work on the Circus, all between 1727 and 1754.
Author of *The Origin of Building: or, The Plagiarisms of the Heathen Detected* (1741), *An
    Essay Towards a Description of Bath* (1740, 1749, 1765), and *A Dissertation Upon
    the Orders of Columns and their Appendages* (1750).

JOHN WOOD, JUNIOR (1728–1781)

The son of John Wood, senior.

Buckland House, Berks, 1755–1757.

Bath: completed the Circus begun by his father, and designed and built Royal Crescent, Brock Street, Rivers Street, Catherine Place, the New Assembly Rooms, and the Old Royal Baths, between 1767 and 1780.

Author of *A Series of Plans, for Cottages or Habitations of the Labourer* (1781, 1792, 1806).

RICHARD BENTLEY (1708–1782)

A talented amateur of architecture, who exerted considerable influence in spreading the Gothic taste. He carried out alterations to a villa in Old Windsor, in the Gothic style, designed a Gothic monument at Linton, and a Gothic stable at Chalfont House, *c.* 1760. He assisted in the extensions to Strawberry Hill for Horace Walpole.

JAMES STUART, F.R.S., F.S.A. (1713–1788)

Lichfield House, 15 St. James's Square, London, 1763–1766.

Londonderry House, Hertford Street, London, 1760–1765.

Portman House, Portman Square, London, 1775–1782.

Travelled extensively in Italy and Greece, and, with Nicholas Revett and others, planned and published *The Antiquities of Athens*, which was financed by the Society of Dilettanti.

SIR ROBERT TAYLOR (1714–1788)

Stone Buildings, Lincoln's Inn, 1774–1780.

Heveningham Hall, Suffolk, 1778–1788.

Ely House, 37 Dover Street, London, *c.* 1772.

Grafton House, Piccadilly.

Asgill House, Richmond, Surrey.

JAMES PAINE (*c.* 1716–1789)

Middlesex Hospital, London, 1755–1775.

Richmond Bridge, Surrey, 1774–1777.

Works at Chatsworth, Derbyshire.

Kedleston House, Derbyshire, 1757–1761.

LANCELOT "CAPABILITY" BROWN (1716–1783)

Began his career as a gardener, and in 1740 became gardener to Lord Cobham at Stowe, thus meeting William Kent, with whom he worked closely. In 1749 he set up on his own as a landscape gardening consultant, working with Robert Adam and Henry Holland. He had a considerable reputation as an architect, and excelled in the designing of such small buildings as gatehouses and lodges.

His principal buildings are:

Croome Court, Worcestershire (with Robert Adam), 1751–1752.

Claremont House, Surrey, 1770–1772.

JOHN CARR (1723–1807)

Built Kirby Hall, Gt. Ouseburn, designed by Lord Burlington, 1750.
The Pikeing Wellhead at York, 1752.
Grandstand at Knavesmire racecourse, York, 1754.
Armcliffe Hall, Northallerton.
Between 1759 and 1771 he built Harewood House, Yorks, rebuilt Harewood village,
    built Denton Park, Yorkshire, Constable Burton, North Riding, Basildon
    Park, Berks, Aston Hall, near Rotherham, Gledhow Hall, near Leeds, and
    houses in York.

SIR WILLIAM CHAMBERS (1723–1796)

Worked for the King and Queen, was Comptroller of the Board of Works, and
    later, Surveyor-General of H.M. Office of Works when this was formed. He
    also designed furniture, and carried out interior decoration, and was the
    designer of George III's Coronation coach. He published various works
    on gardening, design and architecture, among them *Designs of Chinese Buildings,
    Furniture, Dresses, Machines and Utensils* (1757) and *A Treatise on Civil Architecture*
    (1759). He travelled widely, and was honoured by the Royal house of Sweden
    for his achievements, and for whom he also prepared plans for a royal castle at
    Swartsjö, which were exhibited at the Royal Academy.
His chief work was Somerset House in 1775–1786, and he also built the following:
    The Pagoda at Kew Gardens, 1757–1762; Carrington House, Whitehall;
    stabling at Harewood House, Yorks; a house for Lord Melbourne in Piccadilly
    (now the Albany); Wick House, Richmond, Surrey, for Sir Joshua Reynolds;
    the Town Hall, Woodstock, Oxon; entrance gates at Blenheim and Wilton.
He produced designs for Trinity College, Dublin.

HENRY KEENE (1726–1776)

The Guildhall, High Wycombe, 1757.
Trinity College, Dublin (west front), 1752–1759.
Nos. 17–18 Cavendish Square, London, 1756–1757.
Corsham Court, Wilts (rebuilt north front), 1759–1760.
The Anatomy School at Christ Church, Oxford, 1766–1767.

ROBERT ADAM, F.R.S. (1728–1792)

Screen wall at the Admiralty, London, 1760.
Society of Arts, John Adam Street, London, 1772–1774.
No. 20 St. James's Square, London, 1722–1774.
The Adelphi Buildings, Strand, London, 1768–1772.
Osterley House, Middlesex, 1761–1780.
Kenwood House, Hampstead, 1767–1769.
Croome Court, Worcs, 1760 onwards.
Luton Hoo, Beds, *c.* 1768–1775.
Author of *Ruins of the Palace of the Emperor Diocletian at Spalatro* (1764), and *Works in
    Architecture of Robert and James Adam* (1773).

JAMES ADAM (1730-1794)

Brother of Robert Adam, with whom he worked, and some of his designs are included in *Works in Architecture* by the elder brother. The Assembly Rooms in Glasgow are attributed jointly to Robert and James Adam.

ROBERT MYLNE, F.R.S. (1734-1811)

Blackfriars Bridge, 1760-1769.
Almack's Club, London, 1764-1765.
New River Company's Offices, Clerkenwell, London, 1770.
City of London Lying-In Hospital, 1770-1773.
The Wick, Richmond, Surrey. (This is next door to Wick House by Sir William Chambers.)

CHARLES CAMERON (1740-1812)

A Scottish architect, whose book, *The Baths of the Romans Explained and Illustrated, with the Restorations of Palladio corrected and Improved*, published in 1772, brought him to the notice of Catherine of Russia, for whom he worked from the 1770's until 1805. Among his buildings in Russia are the following:

Works at the Tsarkoe Seloe, near St. Petersburg, 1783-1785.
Cathedral of St. Sophia, 1782-1787.
The Agate Pavilion, 1783-1785.
Great Palace at Pavlovsk, 1781-1796.
Batourin Palace, Ukraine, 1790-1800.
Naval hospital and barracks at Kronstadt, 1805.

THOMAS LEVERTON (1743-1824)

No. 65 Lincoln's Inn Fields, London, 1772.
Phoenix Fire Insurance Office, Charing Cross, 1787.
Watton Wood Hall, Herts, 1777-1782.
Riddlesworth Hall, Norfolk, 1792.

HENRY HOLLAND, F.S.A. (1745-1806)

Brooks's Club, 60 St. James's Street, London, 1776-1778.
Claremont House, near Esher (with Lancelot Brown), 1771-1774.
The Albany, London (additions and conversion), 1803-1804.
Southill House, Beds (rebuilding), 1795.

JAMES WYATT, F.S.A., R.A. (1746-1813)

The Pantheon, Oxford Street, 1770-1772.
No. 15 St. James's Square, London, 1791-1794.
Fonthill Abbey, Wiltshire, 1796-1807.
Henham Hall, near Southwold, Suffolk, 1793-1797.
Kew Palace, Surrey, 1802-1811.

JOHN NASH (1752-1835)

The Royal Pavilion, Brighton, 1815–1821.
Regent's Park and adjacent terraces, and Regent Street.
All Souls Church, Langham Place, London, 1822–1825.
Clarence House, London, 1825.
Carlton House Terrace, London, 1827–1833.
United Service Club, Pall Mall, London, 1827.

HUMPHRY REPTON (1752-1818)

A landscape gardener, who worked closely with John Nash, particularly on work
which involved architectural as well as landscape planning. He published a number
of books on these subjects.

SIR JOHN SOANE, R.A. (1753-1837)

Pitzhanger Place, Ealing, 1800–1803.
Bank of England (rebuilding), 1788–1833.
Nos. 12, 13 and 14 Lincoln's Inn Fields, 1792–1824.
No. 18 Park Lane, London, 1812.
Holy Trinity Church, Marylebone, London, 1824–1828.
St. John's, Bethnal Green, London, 1824–1828.
He wrote many books on architecture, including *Designs in Architecture* (1778),
    Sketches in Architecture (1793), and *Designs for Public and Private Buildings* (1828).

THOMAS HOPE (c. 1770-1831)

A wealthy connoisseur and collector of antique sculpture, pottery and so forth, who
also wrote on architecture, furniture and costume. Among his publications are
Observations on the Plans and Elevations of James Wyatt, Architect (1804), *Household
Furniture and Interior Decoration* (1809), *An Historical Essay on Architecture* (1835).

WILLIAM INWOOD (1771-1843)

Worked in close collaboration with his son. The chief buildings in which they were
jointly concerned are:
 East Grinstead Church, Sussex (completion of tower), 1813.
 St. John's, Westminster (interior), 1824–1825.
 St. Pancras Church, London, 1819–1822.
 All Saints Chapel, Camden Town, 1822–1824.
 St. Peter's, Regent Square, London, 1824–1826 (*see* page 300).
 St. Mary's, Somers Town, London, 1824–1827.

HENRY WILLIAM INWOOD, F.S.A. (1794-1843)

Son of the above, with whom he worked closely. He published *The Erectheion at
Athens* (1827), and *The Resources of Design in the Architecture of Greece, Egypt, and
other Countries* (1834).
He designed the parsonage at Radwinter, Essex, in 1812.

WILLIAM WILKINS, R.A. (1778–1839)

Was the author of many architectural works, among them *The Civil Architecture of Vitruvius* (1812).

His principal buildings were:

     Bath, The Freemasons' Hall, 1817–1819, and additions to the Lower Assembly Rooms, 1808–1809.

     The Theatre, Norwich, 1826.

     St. George's Hospital, Hyde Park Corner, London, 1828–1829.

     East India House, Leadenhall Street, London, 1828.

     The National Gallery, Trafalgar Square, London, 1834–1838.

     Downing College, Cambridge, 1807–1820.

SIR ROBERT SMIRKE, F.R.S., R.A., Hon.F.I.B.A.
(1781–1867)

British Museum, 1823–1847.

Custom House, London, 1825–1826.

Royal Mint, Tower Hill, London, 1807–1809: 1815.

Oxford and Cambridge Club, Pall Mall, London (with his brother, Sydney Smirke), 1836–1837.

General Post Office, St. Martin's-le-Grand, 1824–1829.

Royal College of Physicians, Trafalgar Square, 1824–1825.

DECIMUS BURTON (1800–1881)

Screen at Hyde Park Corner, London.

Lodges at Cumberland, Grosvenor, Chesterfield, and Prince of Wales Gates, Hyde Park, 1825–1846.

Archway on Constitution Hill, Buckingham Palace, 1828.

Buildings and gardens for Zoological Society, Regent's Park, 1826–1841.

Athenaeum Club, London, 1827–1830.

Royal Naval Club, London, 1828–1831.

Charing Cross Hospital, London, 1831–1834.

SIR EDWIN LUTYENS (1869–1944)

The last great English architect to work in the Renaissance style. Among his works are the following:

     Orchards, Godalming, Surrey, 1898.

     Tigbourne Court, Witley, Surrey, 1899.

     Grey Walls, Gullane, Scotland, 1900.

     Little Thakeham, Sussex, 1902.

     Papillon Hall, Leics, 1903.

     Country Life offices, Covent Garden, London, 1904.

     Heathcote, Ilkley, Yorks, 1906.

     Whalton Manor, Northumberland, 1908.

     Small house and cottages, Ashby St. Ledgers, 1908.

     Middlefield, Gt. Shelford, Cambs, 1908.

Houses in North Square, Hampstead Garden City, 1910.
Imperial Delhi, Viceroy's House, Saipur Column, Indian Garden, Staff
    residences and stables, 1912.
The Cenotaph, London, 1919.
Southampton War Memorial, 1919.
Britannic House, Finsbury, London, 1920.
House in New Delhi, 1921.
Midland Bank, Piccadilly, 1921.
Midland Bank Head Office, Poultry, London, 1924.
British Embassy, Washington, 1927.
Midland Bank, Leadenhall Street, 1928.
Benson Wing, Magdalene College, Cambridge, 1928.
120 Pall Mall, London, 1929.
Runnymede Memorial Lodges and Piers, 1930.
Lodges and entrance gates, Victoria Park, Leics, 1930.
Reuters and the Press Association Building, Fleet Street, 1935.
King George V Memorial, Windsor, 1936.

North America: 1727–1850
AMERICAN COLONIAL PERIOD TO 1776

DR. JOHN KEARSLEY

Christ Church, Philadelphia, 1727–1737.
Member of the building committee of St. Peter's, Philadelphia, 1758.

ANDREW HAMILTON

Carpenters Hall, Philadelphia, 1724.
Old State House, Boston, 1728.
Independence Hall, Philadelphia, 1732–1752.

EARLY UNITED STATES OF AMERICA: APPROXIMATELY 1776–1850

PIERRE CHARLES L'ENFANT

A French military engineer, who came to America in 1777.
Remodelled the City Hall of New York, and the Federal House, Philadelphia.
Appointed by Thomas Jefferson to plan the new Federal town on the Potomac,
    which was called Washington, and on which work began in 1791.

JAMES HOBAN

The Executive Mansion (the White House), Washington, 1792.
The State House, Charleston.

THOMAS JEFFERSON (1743–1826)
(Third President of the United States)

An accomplished amateur of architecture.
Monticello (his home), 1796–1809.
The Capitol, Richmond, 1785–1789, and the University of Virginia.

DR. WILLIAM THORNTON (1761–1828)

Designed the original Capitol, Washington, burned by the British in 1814.
Octagon House, Washington.
Montpellier, Va.

CHARLES BULFINCH (1763–1844)

The State House, Boston, with Upjohn.
Rebuilding of the Capitol, Washington, 1817–1830.
Maine State House, 1828.

SAMUEL McINTIRE (1757–1811)

Architect and designer of furniture.
Houses in Salem, Mass, the Court House, 1785, with Bancroft, and Old South
    Church, 1804.

ROBERT MILLS (1781–1885)

Washington Monument, Baltimore, 1815.
Washington Monument, Washington, 1836.
Treasury Buildings, Washington, 1836.

BENJAMIN LATROBE (1766–1820)

Architect of the Capitol, Washington, 1803–1817.
Bank of Pennsylvania, Philadelphia, 1799–1801.
Baltimore Cathedral, 1821.
Second Bank of the United States, Philadelphia, 1819–1824.

WILLIAM STRICKLAND (1787–1854)

Merchants Exchange, Philadelphia, 1834.
The Capitol, Nashville, Tenn.
St. Paul's, Philadelphia.

RICHARD UPJOHN (1802–1878)

Founder and first President of the American Institute of Architects.
Worked with Charles Bulfinch on the State House, Boston, Mass, c. 1830.
Rebuilt Old Trinity Church, New York, 1846.
State Capitol, Hartford, Conn., 1873.
St. Thomas, New York.

THE PLATES

The subjects on the thirty-two plates have been selected to illustrate points made in the ten sections, and, chronologically, they follow the order of those sections. With their captions, they give an outline of Western architecture from the fifth century B.C. in Greece, to the modern movement that, in our own century, has generated the new Western architecture.

PLATE I

The Parthenon at Athens, built in the time of Pericles (490–429 B.C.) by the architects, Ictinus and Callicrates, with Pheidias as the master sculptor. In no other example of Greek architecture did the Doric order attain such matchless perfection. (*Photograph by Richard C. Grierson.*)

PLATE 2

Above: A detailed restoration of t
Parthenon, drawn by Charles Rob
Cockerell (1788–1863), showing t
statue of Athena and the Erechthei
on the right, and the Propylaea in t
distance. (*Reproduced from a water-col
drawing in the Library of the Royal Instit
of British Architects.*) *Left:* The easte
portico, showing the Turkish buil
ings which occupied the Acropolis
the late eighteenth century. (*Repr
duced from Volume II of The An
quities of Athens, by Stuart and Reve
published in 1778.*) See plan of t
Acropolis on page 49.

PLATE 3

Above: The eastern portico of the Parthenon as it is to-day. *Right:* View of the angle of the eastern façade, with detail of the frieze and pediment. (*Photographs by Richard C. Grierson.*) The columns shown on plate 5, right centre, are on the north-western angle.

PLATE 4

Front and back views of the Gate of the Lions at Mycenae (*circa* 1200 B.C.). The masonry consists of hewn rectangular blocks of stone, set in regular courses. The thin triangular lime-stone slab on which the lions are carved is a rudimentary pediment. (See pages 44 and 45.)

Left: The entrance to the treasury of Atreus, Mycenae (*circa* 1185 B.C.). *Right:* The marble wall behind the Caryatid portico of the Erechtheion at Athens (430–393 B.C.), which shows the immense advance in building technique compared with the masonry of the early period, exemplified by the work at Mycenae. Pentelic marble provided the finest material, allowing joints to be ground so smoothly that they are almost invisible. *Below:* The Ionic columns and capitals of the Erechtheion. (*Photographs by the author.*)

PLATE 5

An early example of Greek Doric, the temple of Apollo at Corinth, dating from the sixth century B.C.

The flat, archaic capitals of the temple of Apollo at Corinth. The convex profile, the entasis, is omitted from the columns.

Examples of fifth century Greek Doric columns: *left*, the temple of Poseidon, at Sunium, 440 B.C., and, *right*, the Parthenon, 454–438 B.C.

Left: Ionic temple of Nikè Apteros (Athena Nikè), Athens, 438 B.C. (See drawing on page 64.) *Right:* Capital from Corinth, which resembles the palm leaf type, without volutes, in the Corinthian columns of the Tower of the Winds at Athens (see drawing on page 69). *(Photographs by the author.)*

PLATE 6

Left and right: The Olympieion, Athens, 174 B.C. A temple of the Corinthian order designed by the Roman architect Cossutius, and completed in A.D. 117 by Hadrian. (*Photographs by the author.*)

Above: The ruins of the temple of Antonius Pius at Rome, with the column of Marcus Aurelius on the extreme right, from an engraving by Piranesi. *Right:* Upper part of the wall of the temple of Augustus at Ankara, built of white marble: an example of fine Roman masonry. (*Photograph by the author.*)

Veduta del Romano Campidoglio con Scalinata che va alla Chiesa d'Aracoli

PLATE 7

The magnificent buildings of Renaissance Rome were reared amid the ruins of the ancient city. Piranesi's engraving, above, of the Capitol, Michelangelo's great conception of civic design, shows the approaches still surrounded by fragments of older buildings. Often the ruins of temples would be incorporated in buildings of a much later date. *Left:* an early nineteenth century view shows the three end columns and pilaster of the Corinthian temple of Mars Ultor in the Forum of Augustus at Rome. (*From a water-colour drawing in the author's possession.*) It was only during the nineteenth century that the remains of classical Rome were systematically uncovered and the architectural accretions of later ages removed.

PLATE 8

The Tomb of the Julii, at St. Remy in Provence, one of the relics of the ancient Roman Glanum. This is a well-preserved example of the use of the Corinthian order, and, like many Roman monuments, overcharged with ornament. (*Photograph by Richard C. Grierson.*)

PLATE 9

Arches on one of the tiers of the great amphitheatre at Arles, the Roman town of Arelate. The Corinthian columns attached to the façade have an ornamental and not a structural significance: in this, as in many other Roman buildings, the orders were used primarily for decoration. (See drawing on page 82.) (*Photograph by Richard C. Grierson.*)

PLATE 10

Santa Sophia, Constantinople, A.D. 532–537. This view, and the interior on the plate opposite, are reproduced from the drawings of Gaspard Fossati. These drawings, made in the mid-nineteenth century, were lithographed by Louis Hache, and published in book form by P. and D. Colnaghi & Co., in London, 1852. They show Santa Sophia after it had been restored by order of the Sultan, Abdul Medjid.

Interior of Santa Sophia, looking towards the apse. (See diagrams on the structural use of the arch principle on pages 92 and 95.)

PLATE 12

Above and right: The eleventh century Byzantine churches of the monastery of St. Luke of Stiris, near Delphi in Greece. (*Photographs by Richard C. Grierson.*) *Below:* Surface variation in the walls of St. Saviour in the Chora, Constantinople. (*Photograph by the author.*)

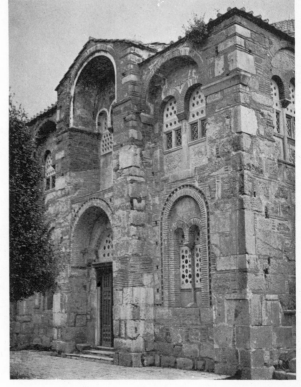

St. Miniato, Florence, A.D. 1013, a development of Italian Romanesque which showed an almost pagan levity in the use of form and colour, and a respect for the memory of the classic orders. (*Photograph by Richard C. Grierson.*)

PLATE 14

The cathedral monastery at Durham stands above the River Wear on a rocky peninsula, which is defended on the north by the castle of the bishops. South of the cathedral are the cloister and monastic buildings. The semicircular-headed windows of the nave and clear-story disclose the Norman work, which covers a period from A.D. 1096 to 1133. The central tower represents the last phase of English Gothic, the Perpendicular. Like nearly all the cathedrals of England it shows the transition from one period of Gothic to another; but it is a largely complete and magnificent example of Anglo-Norman architecture. (*Photograph by Aerofilms Ltd.*)

PLATE 15

Chartres Cathedral, the west front, 1194–1260. Famous for its thirteenth century
stained glass, and remarkable for the vitality of its sculpture. The cathedral completely
dominates the small town of Chartres, dwarfing all secular buildings, and symbolising the
immense significance of the Church and of Christendom. (*Reproduced by courtesy of the
Architectural Association.*)

Below: Arcading in the Court of Lions, at the Alhambra, Grana (1309–1354). The columns alternately single and coupl and they support wooden arcadi lavishly ornamented with stucco decoration. This type of g sparkling, complex ornament its mark on buildings in Christian kingdoms of Spa
(Photograph by the author.)

One of the doorways of Seville Cathedral (1401–1520), showing the intricate tracery, with its clear relationship to Oriental models. It is the largest mediaeval cathedral in Europe, but the interior is far more impressive than the exterior. The Giralda (see page 236) was originally the minaret of a mosque. (*Photograph by F. R. Yerbury, reproduced by courtesy of the Architectural Association.*)

PLATE 17

Segovia cathedral (1521–1577), an example of late Spanish Gothic, built on the site of an eleventh century church, and incorporating the cloisters of the earlier edifice (they were rebuilt in 1524). The pinnacles with their crockets and slender vertical lines give an air of delicacy to the building. The domes acknowledge the influence of the Renaissance.

(*Photograph by F. R. Yerbury, reproduced by courtesy of the Architectural Association.*)

In Venice, Oriental, Byzantine, classic and Gothic influences met and inspired an architecture that was unique in Europe. The Oriental affinities of the open arcades in the façade of the Doge's Palace are obvious. The upper storey is faced with white and rose-hued marble, giving an effect like patterned brickwork. (*Photographs by the author.*) See pages 163 and 165.

PLATE 18

Above: The rusticated masonry on the ground storey of the Riccardi Palace, Florence. (See page 208.) Designed by Michelozzo and built in 1430. (*Photograph by Richard C. Grierson.*) *Below:* The Bridge of Sighs, which connects the Doge's Palace at Venice with the prison. (*Photograph by the author.*)

Above: The arcade of the cortile of the Pitti Palace, Florence, looking towards the Boboli Gardens. The palace was designed by Filippo Brunelleschi and built in 1435, but the large central cortile was added in 1640, and the projecting wings, facing the Piazza, were erected in 1763. (See illustration on page 209.) Doric, Ionic, and Corinthian half-columns are used in the treatment of the cortile. (*Photograph by Richard C. Grierson.*)

PLATE 19

Interior of St. Lorenzo, Florence, a church of the basilican type, built in 1425 to the design of Brunelleschi, showing the new, rich understanding of the use of the classic orders that the early masters of the Renaissance architecture could command, The nave and aisles are separated by Corinthian columns, supporting entablature blocks from which the arches spring. (*Photograph by Richard C. Grierson.*)

PLATE 20

The Château de Chambord, built between 1526 and 1544: romantic, picturesque, and fastastic, it reveals the strenuous conflict between mediaeval traditions and the new, orderly ideas of architectural composition that were introduced from Italy. The conical roofs and angle towers, and the cluster of vertical elements in the central block above the cornice line, would give to the whole building a distraught air, if the façade had not been unified, tied together as it were by the horizontal lines below the windows. It has been suggested that Chambord was built after a small scale model, made by the Italian architect, Domenico da Cortona; but the work appears to be largely that of the French master-mason. (*Reproduced by courtesy of the French Government Tourist Office.*) See top of plate 21.

Right: The Château de Chambord, viewed from the south and showing the central block, and on the right one of the angle towers, on the north-east corner. (*Photograph by S. M. Sternfeldt, L.R.I.B.A.*) See plate opposite

The south-west façade of the Palace of Fontainebleau, seen from Cour du Cheval-Blanc. It was designed for Francis I, and built in 1528, though additions were made by Henry IV, Louis XIII, who built the horse-shoe staircase shown above, Louis XIV, Louis XV, and Napoleon I, who spent 12,000,000 francs on restorations. Louis XVIII, Louis Philippe and Napoleon III all lavished large sums on works of restoration. The architectural features of the interior provide the chief interest. (*Reproduced by courtesy of the French Government Tourist Office.*)

The Town Hall at Antwerp, designed by de Vriendt, and erected in 1565, shows how traditional mediaeval forms could be associated with the classic orders without conflict. The Gothic verticality of the central feature, classical in detail and pyramidal in treatment, is contrasted with the horizontal lines of the rest of the 300-foot façade. (*Reproduced by courtesy of the Belgian National Tourist Office.*)

PLATE 23

Two views of the Guild Houses in the Grande Place at Brussels. These were built in the late seventeenth century; the Butchers' and the Brewers' houses date from the eighteenth century (1720 and 1752); but they all reflect the prosperity of the fraternities that commissioned them. They have very obvious Gothic affinities, and their classical details are only incidental, and largely ornamental. *(Reproduced by courtesy of the Belgian National Tourist Office.)*

The Escurial, showing the façade facing the Plaza del Monasterio. The monastery entrance is on the extreme right of the picture, the college entrance is above on the left, while in the centre the grand entrance has eight Doric columns, ascending through three storeys, supporting an entablature aligned with the fourth storey: above this, four Ionic columns uphold a pediment. Below is a general view of the whole building, showing the tower and dome above the church. (*Reproduced by courtesy of the Spanish Tourist Office.*)

PLATE 25

The Escurial, built between 1559 and 1584, on a lonely site some thirty miles north-west of Madrid on the slopes of the Sierra de Guadarrama. It consists of a group of buildings which includes a monastery, a church, a college and a palace. The fondness of Spanish architects for towers is apparent, both in this view and the general view on the plate opposite. The Escurial was built at the beginning of the classical period of the Spanish Renaissance, the exuberance and florid gaiety of the earlier period have been replaced by a sober simplicity of exterior treatment, great restraint in the use of ornament, and strict attention to the correct use and proportions of the classic orders. The result, as the façades of the Escurial exemplify, was a grave and impressive dignity. (*Reproduced by courtesy of the Spanish Tourist Office.*)

Left: The north side of the Piazza of St. Peter at Rome, showing the sweep of Bernini's colonnades (1655–1667). (*Photograph by S. M. Sternfeldt, L.R.I.B.A.*)

PLATE 26

The Place des Vosges, Paris, formerly the Place Royale, designed by the brothers Châtillon, and built about 1607, is an example of the agreeable vernacular style identified with the reign of Henry IV. Like the Place Dauphine, it was part of a great town planning scheme, begun in the early years of the seventeenth century, but never completed. Compare these façades with those in the Place Vendôme on plate 27, where the arcades are surmounted by the Corinthian order, ascending through the first and second storeys. The Place des Vosges has obvious mediaeval affinities: the Place Vendôme exhibits with bold simplicity its debt to ancient Rome. (*Reproduced by courtesy of the French Government Tourist Office.*)

PLATE 27

The Place Vendôme, Paris, designed in 1690–1691 by Jules Hardouin Mansart.
The arcuated ground storey has Corinthian columns and pilasters above, rising
through the first and second storeys to support the entablature. Above the cornice
line, dormers in the steep roof terminate the vertical elements in the façade.
The firm simplicity of the design gives a placid dignity to the great square.
(Reproduced by courtesy of the French Government Tourist Office.)

PLATE 28

Part of the façade of the Orangery at the Palace of Versailles. The Palace, built for Louis XIV, was a supreme example of architecture in the grand manner, and the great park, the palace, and all the ancillary buildings were part of one great composition. The Orangery is the most distinguished part of the Palace, and although it is generally attributed to Jules Hardouin Mansart, some authorities credit le Notre and Desgodetz with the design. On the lower part of the plate opposite, a view of the park from the Palace is shown. (*Reproduced by courtesy of the French Government Tourist Office.*)

PLATE 29

A view of Hampton Court Palace from the Park, as it appeared in 1736. Wren's Palace occupies the centre; the remains of the Tudor building are on the left in the background. There is a strong resemblance to Mansart's work at Versailles—the same spacious planning, though on a more modest scale, the formal park, geometrically disposed to expand the effect of grandeur; but Hampton Court is more than a palace, it is very obviously a comfortable home, built in warm red brick, trimmed with stone.
(*Reproduced from an engraving in the author's possession.*)

The Great Park of Versailles, seen from the terrace of the Palace. (*Reproduced by courtesy of the French Government Tourist Office.*)

PLATE 30

Above: The Town Hall at Stockholm, designed by Professor Ragnar Östberg and inaugurated in 1923. The last great romantic building in Europe, it owes some of its inspiration to tradition, some to the teaching of William Morris, which was regarded far more seriously in the Scandinavian countries than in England. Like the Doge's Palace at Venice, it reflects the greatness of a maritime city, and suggests something of the opulent wealth and gaiety of the East. The wall surfaces are of warm red brick. (*Reproduced by courtesy of the Swedish Travel Bureau.*) *Below:* The new Western architecture is exemplified by such buildings as the Rhine Birsfelden hydro-electric power station, designed by Professor D. H. Hoffman (of Zürich). The long walls are glazed on both sides, and the concrete surfaces are light olive green, the Y-shaped trusses being accentuated by lines of white. (*Photograph by S. M. Sternfeldt, L.R.I.B.A.*)

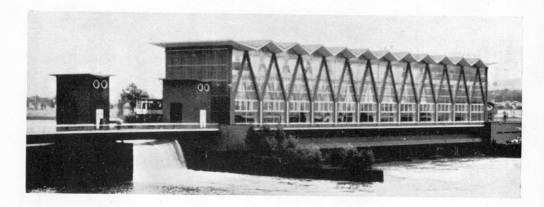

ght: House in Chicago, Illinois, de-
ned in 1906 by Frank Lloyd Wright
r Fred C. Robie. A new freedom of
rm is apparent, and the emphasis on
rizontal lines has had a marked effect
the development of Western domestic
chitecture. (*Photograph by Edward D.
Mills, F.R.I.B.A.*)

Left: The "Bastei" office building in Zürich, opened in 1955. Architect:
Werner Stucheli. Panels of black glass framed in aluminium form horizontal
bands which separate the windows on each storey. *Below:* Apartment blocks
on the Via Appia Nuova, outside Rome, showing the subsequent development of horizontal lines after the tentative experiments forty-five years
earlier. (*Photographs by S. M. Sternfeldt, L.R.I.B.A.*)

PLATE 32

The Lever Building, Park Avenue, New York. This glass tower demonstrates how contemporary architectural design has been liberated from the limitations imposed by external supporting walls. The wall is now a mere skin, transparent or translucent, with opaque glass or sheets of light alloy forming the horizontal bands between the windows. The techniques of construction perfected in the present century, the use of steel and concrete, aluminium and glass, have changed the character of Western architecture.

Left: The complete building, looking up Park Avenue. *Above* A close-up view, showing the open ground storey, and the horizontal expanse of the first storey, with the main building floating up above that level. Architects: Skidmore, Owings, and Merrill. (*Photographs by Edward D. Mills, F.R.I.B.A.*)

Figures in brackets refer to illustrations in the text or captions